D1480398

JAMES THOMSON
POETICAL WORKS

Edited, with notes by
J. LOGIE ROBERTSON

London
OXFORD UNIVERSITY PRESS
NEW YORK   TORONTO

Oxford University Press, Ely House, London W. 1

GLASGOW NEW YORK TORONTO MELBOURNE WELLINGTON
CAPE TOWN SALISBURY IBADAN NAIROBI DAR ES SALAAM LUSAKA ADDIS ABABA
BOMBAY CALCUTTA MADRAS KARACHI LAHORE DACCA
KUALA LUMPUR SINGAPORE HONG KONG TOKYO

ISBN 0 19 254151 X

JAMES THOMSON

Born, Ednam, Roxburghshire 27 September 1700
Died, Richmond, Surrey .   . 27 August 1748

*Thomson's Complete Poetical Works were first
included in the series of Oxford Standard Authors
in 1908, and reprinted in 1951, 1961, 1963, 1965
and 1971*

PRINTED IN GREAT BRITAIN
O.S.A.

PREFACE

THE chief want hitherto felt by students of the poetry of Thomson has been a variorum edition of *The Seasons*. This I have endeavoured to supply in the present edition.

The first edition of *Winter* appeared in March, 1726, and consisted of only 405 lines. The second, published in the following June, contained many variations, and increased the original text by 58 lines. I give a reprint of the first *Winter*, accompanying it with the variations of the second. Three other editions prior to 1730 were reprints of the second.

Summer was published in 1727 ; and consisted of 1,146 lines. A second edition, which appeared in the same year, was a reprint.

Spring came out in 1728, and consisted of 1,082 lines : it was followed in 1729 by a reprint.

Autumn appeared in 1730 as part of the first edition of the collected *Seasons*, and consisted of 1,269 lines. The *Hymn*, numbering 121 lines, appeared at the same time.

But in this first edition of the whole *Seasons*, which was issued in two forms, quarto and octavo, *Winter* was augmented to 787 lines (781 in the quarto), *Summer* to 1,206, *Spring* to 1,087 ; and there were numerous changes besides in the previous texts which are not indicated by mere increment in the number of lines.

Between 1730 and 1738 no change was made in

the separate or collected texts of *The Seasons.* Thomson was busy at other work.

In the edition of 1744 great changes were made— more especially in *Summer* and *Winter*—not merely by addition, but in other ways.

Thomson revised the text of *The Seasons* for the last time in 1746, making a few alterations, and increasing the length of the poem as a whole by 10 lines. The final result was a poem of 5,541 lines, made up in the following way :—

Spring	.	.	.	1,176 lines
Summer	.	.	.	1,805 ,,
Autumn	.	.	.	1,373 ,,
Winter	.	.	.	1,069 ,,
Hymn	.	.	.	118 ,,

The textual changes which *The Seasons* in their various parts underwent between 1726 and 1746 were of every conceivable kind. The author, it might almost be said, cherished a passion for correct- ing and improving. As long as he lived, and had the leisure (he never wanted the inclination), he was revising and altering. He added and he modified, withdrew and restored, condensed and expanded, substituted and inverted, distributed and trans- ferred. The final text is faithfully reproduced, word for word, in the present edition. I have modernized the punctuation, and also the spelling—retaining, however, a few characteristic forms. All changes and variations in the text from the first appearance of each part down to the last collected edition have been carefully and, it is hoped, fully and accurately noted. The labour of doing this, though mostly mechanical, has been neither short nor easy.

Some idea of the way in which *The Seasons* grew

may be gathered from a study of the history of *Winter*. On a comparison of the first draft (as I may call it) with the completed poem, not more than three-fourths of it, short though it is (405 lines), will be found in the finished work. Nearly 100 lines of it were transferred to *Autumn*, and thus it is upon an addition of some 760 lines that the reader looks who knows the poem only in its final form. Conspicuous by their absence from the first text are the now well-known passages that describe the winter visit of the redbreast, the shepherd perishing in a snowstorm on the Cheviots, the goblin story at the village hearth, the descent of the wolf-pack, skating in Holland, the surly bear 'with dangling ice all horrid', and some others ; while there is merely a suggestion, which the poet developed later, of the windstorm at sea, the calm freezing moonlight night, and the student in his snug retreat 'between the groaning forest and the shore'. It is hardly an exaggeration to say that the last edition of the text of *Winter* as put forth by its author in 1746 presents, when compared with the first text of twenty years previous, what is substantially a new poem. It excites no small degree of wonder that from such a small and unpretentious beginning Thomson's *Winter* made its way, to become the epoch-making work which we now know it to have been in the poetical literature not only of our own country but of Germany and France as well.

The many changes which Thomson made in the text of *The Seasons* were mostly improvements, but, I think, not wholly so. I wish he had retained ' a weeping thaw ', and I much prefer the single line that informs us how Cincinnatus seized

The plough, and greatly independent lived

to the two in which we are told that

> he greatly independent scorned
> All the vile stores Corruption can bestow.

The various readings show that kind of development in which refinement and repose are gained, but not without some expense of vitality and vigour. There is sound criticism in the judgement of Johnson that in the process of improvement *The Seasons* lost somewhat of their original race or flavour. The Scotticisms, too, were expressive. And the keenness of his colour-sense, which he had inherited from his country's ballads, became dulled in deference to the taste of Pope and Lyttelton. But the loss of raciness is chiefly seen in the substitution, for example, of so comparatively tame a line as—

> Then scale the mountains to their woody tops

for

> Then snatch the mountains by their woody tops,

in the description of the fox-hunt ; or in the exchange of ' Shook from the corn ' for ' Scared from the corn ', in the hare-hunt ; or by the entire omission of the robust lines—

> While, tempted vigorous o'er the marble waste,
> On sleds reclined the furry Russian sits,
> And, by his reindeer drawn, behind him throws
> A shining kingdom in a winter's day.

It is an error to suppose that when Thomson was writing *Winter* at East Barnet in the autumn and winter of 1725 he was at the same time contemplating a poem on each of the other seasons. The error has arisen from a misunderstanding of Thomson's promise to sing of autumn, a promise which undoubtedly appears in the first text of *Winter*. But the fulfilment also appears, immediately after the promise. It is contained in the 100 transferred lines to which reference has already been made. The necessity for their transference shows that the scheme of a series of poems on the seasons had not yet occurred to him when, in the autumn of 1725, he was engaged upon *Winter*. The lines have autumn, or ' departing summer ', for their theme. They were appropriately incorporated with the poem on *Autumn* when the turn of autumn came to be treated in the afterthought of *The Seasons*. His intention of describing ' the various appearances of nature' in the other seasons was first announced in the prose preface which he wrote for the second edition of *Winter* : he had done so well with the winter theme that, doubtless, friends wishing to be complimentary hoped he would favour them with poems on the other seasons too. But till he took *Autumn* in hand—and *Autumn* was taken last—he did not seek to withdraw the lines from *Winter*. They served as an approach to the main theme. Winter sullen and sad, and all his rising train of vapours, and clouds, and storms—these are his theme. At the same time he cannot choose but consecrate to 'Autumn' 'one pitying line'—for so it read when the poem was still on the anvil. But in the published text of March, 1726, it runs—

> Thee, too, inspirer of the toiling swain,
> Fair Autumn, yellow-robed, I'll sing of thee,
> Of thy last tempered days and sunny calms,
> When all the golden hours are on the wing.

And so he does, fulfilling the promise there and then, and having at the moment of so writing no separate ulterior poem in view. Commencing with the hovering hornet poised threateningly in the genial blaze of September, he sings on through falling leaves and sobbing winds and withering flowers, for nearly 100 lines, till he arrives at his ' theme in view '—

> For see where Winter comes himself, confessed,
> Striding the gloomy blast!

It was not till after March, 1726, when his first venture in the poetical arena was beginning to win popular favour, that the joy of successful authorship inspired him with the idea of ' rounding the revolving year ' in separate flights on the other seasons ; but before that, in the shadow of obscurity, bereavement, and comparative poverty, he wrote of himself as ' one whom the gay season suited not, and who shunned the summer's glare '. To him, as he was then situated, they were uncongenial both as seasons and as subjects for poetry. His personal mood when he chose winter was very much the mood of Burns when he sang, dolefully enough, more than half a century later—

> Come, Winter, with thine angry howl,
> And, raging, bend the naked tree ;
> Thy gloom will soothe my cheerless soul
> When Nature all is sad like me!

Thomson's great merit lies in his restoration of nature to the domain of poetry from which it had been banished by Pope and his school. He dared to dispute, and he disproved by his own practice and the astonishing success which at once accompanied it, the dictum of Pope that in matters poetic ' the proper study of mankind is man '. His wonderful observing power and his enthusiasm for his subject went far to make his treatment of nature a success. He was sincerely and healthily enamoured of nature. The wild romantic country was his delight. ' I know

no subject more elevating, more amusing, more
ready to awake the poetical enthusiasm, the philosophical reflection, and the moral sentiment than
the works of nature. Where can we meet with such
variety, such beauty, such magnificence—all that
enlarges and transports the soul ? . . . But there is
no thinking of these things without breaking out into
poetry.' Thus he wrote, with much more of the same
tenor, in his prose preface to the second edition of
Winter ; from which it appears that, in his view
of the question, nature was not only a fit and proper
subject for direct poetical treatment, but the greatest
and grandest of all subjects. With the whole
domain of nature before him he chose winter as the
particular subject of his ' first essay '. It is by no
means the most inviting of the seasons. The aspect
of nature in winter is in general a forbidding aspect.
Yet under his guidance we may discover the poetry
of winter. Let us look where he points, and listen
as he directs, and some share of his own enthusiasm
for nature ' in all her shows and forms ' will enter
our soul like the dawning of a new sense. His first
great scene is a rainstorm. The skies are foul with
mingled mist and rain, the plain lies a brown deluge ;
hill-tops and woods are dimly seen in the dreary
landscape ; the cattle droop in the sodden fields,
the poultry crowd motionless and dripping in corners
of the farmyard. It is a world of squalor and
wretchedness. Yet there is the bright contrast of
the ploughman rejoicing by the red fire of his cottage
hearth, talking and laughing, and reckless of the
storm that rattles on his humble roof. Meanwhile
streams swell to rivers, and rivers rise in *spate* ;
the current carries every obstacle before it—stacks
and bridges and mills : nothing can stop its

progress ; dams are burst, rocks are surmounted,
glens and gullies are choked with the mad, plunging
water.

It boils, and wheels, and foams, and thunders through !

A recent critic has limited Thomson's love of
nature to nature in her gentle and even her homely
moods. Thomson's description of the river in flood
is one of many passages in his poetry that con-
tradict the criticism. The description of the
windstorm is another. A third is the poetic
realization of the Deluge, ending with the magnificent line—

A shoreless ocean tumbles round the globe.

Applied to Cowper or Goldsmith, the criticism
would fit, but it shows a strange misconception of
the genius of Thomson.

His presentation of a snowstorm is Thomson's
highest achievement in natural description. The
approach is well led up to. As we read we recall
what we have often seen. The whole description is
a splendid specimen of Thomson's peculiar art in
the realization of a scene. It is rather a narrative
of successive events set before us with dramatic
vividness. The air grows colder, the sky saddens,
there is a preternatural hush, and then the first
flakes make their miraculous appearance, thin-
wavering at first, but by and by falling broad and
wide and fast, dimming the day. It is, as if by
magical transformation, a world of purity and peace.
It is now, by way of episode, that we have the charming vignette of the redbreast at the parlour window.
It is a perfect picture of its kind, unmatched for
clearness and delicate accuracy of detail. We hear
the soft beat of the breast on the frosted pane ; we

see the slender feet on the warm floor, and the eye
looking askance with mingled boldness and shyness
at the smiling and amused children. But we are
soon summoned away to the sheep-walks on the
Cheviots. All winter is driving along the darkened
air. The snow is falling, and drifting. It is the
drifting that the shepherd fears. Its effect is not
only to hide but to alter the landmarks. Scenes
familiar become foreign ; the landscape wears a
strange look ; valleys are exalted, and rough places
are made plain. At last the shepherd is completely
bewildered, and he stands disastered in the midst of
drift and snowfall. The whole moor seems to be
revolving around him, as gusts of wind lift the
surface-snow like a blanket and whirl it around.
The first realization of his danger—his destiny !—is
finely suggested. Few scenes are more pathetic than
Thomson's lost shepherd perishing in the snow.
The pathos is heightened by that little crowd of curly
heads at the cottage door or window, not many
furlongs distant, where

> his little children, peeping out
> Into the mingling storm, demand their sire
> With tears of artless innocence. Alas !
> Nor wife nor children more shall he behold,
> Nor friends, nor sacred home.

Joyous winter days of clear frost are described
with no less effective touches, among which one
remembers the swain on the frozen upland stepping
on solid crystal, and looking down curiously into the
sullen deeps of the river. But enough has been said
or suggested to show Thomson's fidelity to nature,
and the art with which he discloses the poetry of
nature. A love for nature is synonymous with
a love for Thomson.

It is scarcely possible now, at an interval of two centuries, to identify distinctly any single scene in his native Teviotdale which directly fired the heart or captivated the eye of the young poet. Neither his poems nor his letters help us much. We have a panorama of airy mountains, forests huge, and fertile valleys 'winding, deep, and green', with a more specific but still general view of Tweed—

> Pure parent stream!
> Whose pastoral banks first heard my Doric reed,
> With, sylvan Jed, thy tributary brook.

We see him, already a young Druid—the part for which, as Collins happily noted, his genius was cast— in the alleys of Marlefield woods,

> Where spreading trees a checkered scene display,
> Partly admitting and excluding day.

We have a glimpse of his boyish face at the parlour window of Southdean Manse, turned now to the bursting passage of the torrent at the side of the garden, and now to the deep-fermenting tempest brewing in the red evening sky. There is also, in a letter to a friend in Scotland, a special reference to the beloved gloom of embowering trees in some unidentified haugh near Ancram. References such as these furnish our distinctest glimpse of Thomson in Teviotdale. But, if we seldom surprise him alighted in the valley, we feel his presence over-flying the entire scene from the kaims of Ednam to the cleughs of Sou'den. This is the land of Thomson.

For the text of *The Castle of Indolence* I have followed that of the second edition, which was the last to receive the poet's revision.

I have included, with the desire of presenting

a complete edition, several pieces which have been attributed to Thomson, though the evidence for their admission is by no means satisfying. I cannot think he wrote the memorial verses on Congreve ; and the doggerel stanzas in the Scottish dialect are surely not Thomson's.

The *Juvenilia* will at least serve to show the early bent of Thomson's genius to descriptions of nature, and the unpromising character of his youthful attempts at versification. ' The accomplishment of verse ' was to him a hard, and at last an incomplete, attainment ; but his enthusiasm for his great subject, and his glowing imagination, carried him to a success which, within obvious limits, is unique of its kind. In his peculiar method of developing a scene while describing it, in the astonishing felicity of his phrases, in his happy invention of picturesque and melodious compounds, he is a master ; but his constructive skill in the use of language is sometimes unequal to the task of fitly expressing his ideas. Hence his resort to exclamations, involutions, inversions, and forced constructions which are often puzzling and occasionally ludicrous. Pages of *Liberty*—though it contains isolated passages of great force and beauty—read like a mere catalogue of notes.

It does not fall within the scheme of this edition to include the Dramas.

I do not think it necessary to adduce evidence in proof of Thomson's authorship of the national ode, which is now generally accepted as incontrovertible. The patriotic feeling was strong in his heart, and shines out in his poetry on many occasions. He was by no means an aggressive Scot. His patriotism was for Britain. It was Britannia that received

Heaven's commission to rule the waves. And he offers in *Summer* as generously sincere a tribute to the English character as Goldsmith does in *The Traveller*. Yet one likes to remember that, as he wrote to a fellow-countryman, 'Britannia includes our native kingdom of Scotland, too.'

J. L. R.

Oct., 1908.

A CHRONOLOGY

TO ELUCIDATE AND ILLUSTRATE THE LIFE AND
TIMES OF THOMSON

1666. Birth of Thomas Thomson, the poet's father.

1674. Death of Milton.

1683. Execution of Algernon Sidney ('the British Brutus').

1685. Death of Otway.

1686. Birth of Allan Ramsay.

1688. Birth of Pope.

1692. Rev. Thomas Thomson, the poet's father, appointed Minister of Ednam, Roxburghshire.

1693. Marries Beatrix, daughter of Alexander Trotter, of Widehope (a small lairdship in Roxburghshire).

1694. Birth of Voltaire.

1700. Birth, at Ednam or Widehope, of James Thomson, the poet—fourth child (third son) of his parents ; born (probably) on the 7th, baptized on the 15th of September. In the November following, his father inducted into the parish of Southdean, Roxburghshire. Birth of David Malloch (or Mallet). Death of Dryden.

1709. Birth of Johnson.

1712. Young Thomson attends a Grammar School in Jedburgh, some eight miles or so from Southdean. His acquaintance with Mr. (afterwards the Rev.) Robert Riccaltoun, farmer at Earlshaugh, begins about this time. First attempts at versifying, a year or two later.

1715. Young Thomson enters Edinburgh University.

1716. Death of his father, in February, while exorcizing a ghost. Home transferred to Edinburgh.

1719. Death of Addison.

1720. Thomson now a student of Divinity. Continues versifying, chiefly on rural subjects in the heroic couplet ; contributes to The Edinburgh Miscellany *Of a Country Life*, &c.

1721. Birth of Collins. Walpole Prime Minister (till 1742).

1724. Thomson still at the University. Adverse criticism, by the Professor of Divinity, of one of his college exercises (a discourse on the 10th portion of Psalm cxix). The turning-point of his life.

1725. End of February, Thomson sets out to seek his fortune in London : embarks at Leith, not again to see Scotland. Visits Drury Lane Theatre, and sees *Cato* acted. Death of his mother, in May. In July, acting as tutor to Lord Binning's son, at Barnet, near London. Composition of *Winter* in the following autumn and winter. Publication of Allan Ramsay's *The Gentle Shepherd.*

1726. In March, *Winter*, a thin folio of 16 pp., 405 ll., price 1*s.*, John Millan, publisher. Dyer's *Grongar Hill* published. Thomson acting as tutor in an academy in London. Acquaintance with Aaron Hill. Second edition of *Winter*, in June.

1727. Death of Sir Isaac Newton : in June, Thomson publishes a poem *To the Memory of Newton. Summer* published ; a second edition the same year. Thomson now relying on literature for his support. *Britannia* written (not published till 1729), in opposition to the peace-at-any-price policy of Walpole. The poet spends part of the summer at Marlborough Castle (the guest of the Countess of Hertford).

1728. *Spring* published by Andrew Millar. Goldsmith born.

1729. Death of Congreve : anonymous poem *To the Memory of Congreve* published ; attributed to Thomson on very unsatisfactory evidence. In September, Thomson the guest of Bubb Dodington at Eastbury. The poet busy in various ways—with the tragedy of *Sophonisba*, the completion of *The Seasons*, the publication of *Britannia*, and contributions to Ralph's *Miscellany*; among the last a *Hymn on Solitude, The Happy Man*, and a metrical version of a passage of St. Matthew's Gospel.

1730. Publication of the first collected edition of *The Seasons* (including *Autumn* and the *Hymn* for the first time) : two editions, one in quarto at a guinea, published by subscription ; the other in octavo. *Sophonisba* produced at Drury Lane, February 28th, Mrs. Oldfield taking the part of the heroine : a success on the stage, despite one weak line, and selling well when printed. Travelling tutor to young Charles Talbot, son of Mr. Charles Talbot, then Solicitor-General (soon afterwards Lord Chancellor) ; in Paris in December, where (probably) he visits Voltaire.

1731. Visits ' most of the courts and capital cities of Europe ' (Murdoch) ; in Paris in October. Visits Italy—' I long to see the fields where Virgil gathered his immortal honey,' &c. Collecting material for his poem on *Liberty.* Correspondence with Dodington—' Should you inquire after my muse, I believe she did not cross the Channel with me.' Probably wrote, however, the lines on the death of Aikman, the painter. Returns to England in December. Birth of Cowper. *The Gentleman's Magazine* established.

1733. Death of young Talbot in September ; the elder becomes Lord Chancellor in November ; soon after, Thomson appointed Secretary of Briefs in the Court of Chancery—the post a sinecure with about 300*l.* a year. Some *personal* stanzas of *The Castle of Indolence* written about this time.

1735. Publication of *Liberty* ; Parts I, II, and III, at intervals.

1736. *Liberty ;* Parts IV and V at intervals. Thomson goes to live in Kew Lane, Richmond—his residence for the rest of his life. Intimacy with Pope, whose house was only a mile off, at Twickenham. Busy with the drama—' whipping and spurring to finish a tragedy this winter.' Sends pecuniary assistance to his sisters in Edinburgh. Becomes acquainted with ' Amanda '.

1737. Death of Lord Chancellor Talbot, in February ; Thomson's memorial verses (panegyric and elegy) in June. Writing *Agamemnon.* Loss of Secretaryship. Acquaintance with George Lyttelton. Pension of 100*l.* a year from the Prince of Wales, to whom *Liberty* had been dedicated. Shenstone's *Schoolmistress* published.

1738. Thomson's Preface to Milton's *Areopagitica* appears. *Agamemnon* produced in April, Quin in the title rôle. A new edition (a reprint of octavo edition of 1730) of *The Seasons* brought out.

1739. Thomson's tragedy of *Edward and Eleonora* prohibited by the censorship.

1740. Conjointly with Malloch, *The Masque of Alfred,* containing the ode ' Rule, Britannia ', performed August 1, in Clifden Gardens, before the Prince of Wales.

1742. Young's *Night Thoughts* (Books I–III).

1743. Visits the Lytteltons, at Hagley Park, in August—' I am

come to the most agreeable place and company in the world.'
Correspondence with ' Amanda '.—' But wherever I am . . .
I never cease to think of my loveliest Miss Young. You are
part of my being ; you mix with all my thoughts.' His song,
' For ever, Fortune, wilt thou prove,' about this time. Pre-
paring, at Hagley, a revised edition of *The Seasons* with
Lyttelton's assistance.

1744. New edition of *The Seasons*, with many alterations and
additions. Lyttelton in office : he appoints Thomson Surveyor-
General of the Leeward Islands—a sinecure post, worth 300*l.*
a year clear. Death of Pope.

1745. His best drama *Tancred and Sigismunda* produced at
Drury Lane, with Garrick as Tancred. At Hagley in the
summer.

1746. Thomson makes way for his friend (and deputy), William
Paterson, in the office of Surveyor-General. At Hagley in
the autumn. Last edition of *The Seasons* published in the
poet's lifetime. Collins's *Odes* published.

1747. At Hagley in the autumn. Visits Shenstone at the
Leasowes. Busy at *Coriolanus* (nearly finished in March).

1748. Prince of Wales's displeasure with Lyttelton visited on
Lyttelton's friends—Thomson's name struck off pension list.
The Castle of Indolence, in May. Death of Thomson, after
short illness, at Richmond, August 27th. Buried in Richmond
churchyard. Collins's *Ode* in memory of Thomson—a lasting
memorial.

1749. *Coriolanus* produced, in January—the Prologue by
Lyttelton.

1753. Shiels's Life of Thomson (*Cibber's Lives of the Poets*).

1758. Death of Allan Ramsay.

1759. Birth of Burns.

1762. Murdoch's Memoir of Thomson (prefixed to an edition
of Thomson's *Works*). Monument to Thomson in West-
minster Abbey.

1781. Johnson's Life of Thomson (*Lives of the Poets*).

1791. Burns's *Address to the Shade of Thomson*.

1792. The Earl of Buchan's *Essay on the Life of the Poet Thomson*

1831. Biography of Thomson by Sir Harris Nicholas (prefixed
to the Aldine Edition of Thomson's *Works* : annotated by
P. Cunningham, 1860).

1842. An edition of *The Seasons*, with notes by Bolton Corney.

1891. Clarendon Press edition of *The Seasons* and *The Castle of Indolence*, with a biographical notice and full notes by J. Logie Robertson.

1894. *Furth in Field* (Part IV—Of the poet of *The Seasons*), by Hugh Hallburton.

1895. *James Thomson : Sa Vie et ses Œuvres* (678 pp.), by Léon Morel.

1898. *James Thomson* (in *Famous Scots* Series), by W. Bayne.

1908. *James Thomson* (in *English Men of Letters* Series), by G. C. Macaulay.

THOMSON'S FAMILY CONNEXIONS

I.—ON THE FATHER'S SIDE

[? Andrew] Thomson, a gardener, in the service of Mr. Edmonston, at Ednam, in Roxburghshire.

Thomas Thomson, born 1666, graduated M.A. 1686, licensed 1691, ordained minister of Ednam 1692; married Beatrix, daughter of Alexander Trotter, of Wide-hope, October 6, 1693:

Andrew	Alexander	Issobel	James (the poet)
(b. 1695)	(b. 1697)	(b. 1699)	(b. Sep., 1700)

These four children were born while their father was minister of Ednam. In the November following the birth of James, the Rev. Thomas Thomson was translated to the parish of Southdean, in the same county as Ednam but on the English border, and five more children were born to him there, viz., a son, John, and four daughters, Jean, Elizabeth, Margaret, and Mary.

II.—On the Mother's side

Sir John Home of Coldingknowles
(Fourth in descent from the first Baron Home, 1473)

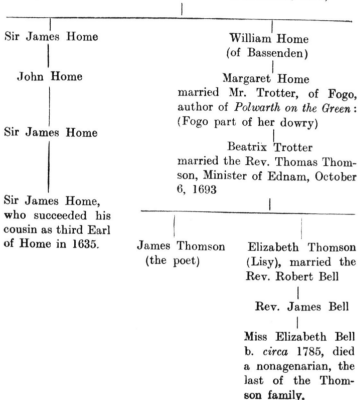

Sir James Home

John Home

Sir James Home

Sir James Home, who succeeded his cousin as third Earl of Home in 1635.

William Home
(of Bassenden)

Margaret Home
married Mr. Trotter, of Fogo, author of *Polwarth on the Green*: (Fogo part of her dowry)

Beatrix Trotter
married the Rev. Thomas Thomson, Minister of Ednam, October 6, 1693

James Thomson
(the poet)

Elizabeth Thomson
(Lisy), married the Rev. Robert Bell

Rev. James Bell

Miss Elizabeth Bell
b. *circa* 1785, died a nonagenarian, the last of the Thomson family.

CONTENTS

CONTENTS

PAGE

MISCELLANEOUS POEMS.

JUVENILIA.

THE SEASONS: A POEM

[First published in collected form in 1730, and then consisting of 4,470 ll., made up in the following way :—

Spring	.	.	1,087	ll.
Summer	.	.	1,206	
Autumn	.	.	1,269	
Winter	.	.	787	(the Quarto 781)
The Hymn	.	.	121.	

The poem as a whole was much altered for the edition of 1744, and the additions then made greatly increased the size of it, the increase being chiefly in *Summer* and *Winter*. The last edition of *The Seasons* published in the author's lifetime, in 1746, shows some further slight alterations ; with the result that the final form of *The Seasons* (including the Hymn) consists in all of 5,541 lines. The poem was inscribed to H.R.H. Frederic, Prince of Wales, in 1744.]

SPRING

[Dedicated, 1728, to the Rt. Hon. the Countess of Hertford, in a letter in which the poet writes—'As this poem grew up under your encouragement, it has therefore a natural claim to your patronage.' First published early in 1728 (1,082 ll.); last edition in author's lifetime published 1746 (1,176 ll.).]

THE ARGUMENT

The subject proposed. Inscribed to the Countess of Hartford. The Season is described as it affects the various parts of nature, ascending from the lower to the higher; and mixed with digressions arising from the subject. Its influence on inanimate matter, on vegetables, on brute animals, and last on Man; concluding with a dissuasive from the wild and irregular passion of Love, opposed to that of a pure and happy kind.*

COME, gentle Spring, ethereal mildness, come ;
And from the bosom of yon dropping cloud,
While music wakes around, veiled in a shower
Of shadowing roses, on our plains descend.

O Hartford, fitted or to shine in courts
With unaffected grace, or walk the plain

* The above is the Argument prefixed to the last edition (1746) published in the author's lifetime. It is the same as the Argument of 1730, except that in the earlier edition the Countess of Hartford is designated 'Lady Hertford'; 'This Season' appears for 'The Season'; and instead of 'pure and happy' in the concluding note we have 'purer and more reasonable' in the original form of the Argument.

5 Hertford 1728, 1729, 1730, 1738; Hartford 1744, 1746. The second edition (1729) is an exact reprint of the first (1728).

With innocence and meditation joined
In soft assemblage, listen to my song,
Which thy own season paints—when nature all
Is blooming and benevolent, like thee.   10

And see where surly Winter passes off
Far to the north, and calls his ruffian blasts :
His blasts obey, and quit the howling hill,
The shattered forest, and the ravaged vale ;
While softer gales succeed, at whose kind touch,
Dissolving snows in livid torrents lost,
The mountains lift their green heads to the sky.
  As yet the trembling year is unconfirmed,
And Winter oft at eve resumes the breeze,
Chills the pale morn, and bids his driving sleets 20
Deform the day delightless ; so that scarce
The bittern knows his time with bill engulfed
To shake the sounding marsh ; or from the shore
The plovers when to scatter o'er the heath,
And sing their wild notes to the listening waste.
  At last from Aries rolls the bounteous sun,
And the bright Bull receives him. Then no more
The expansive atmosphere is cramped with cold ;
But, full of life and vivifying soul,
Lifts the light clouds sublime, and spreads them
    thin, 30
Fleecy, and white o'er all-surrounding heaven.
  Forth fly the tepid airs ; and unconfined,
Unbinding earth, the moving softness strays.
Joyous the impatient husbandman perceives
Relenting Nature, and his lusty steers
Drives from their stalls to where the well-used plough
Lies in the furrow loosened from the frost.
There, unrefusing, to the harnessed yoke

They lend their shoulder, and begin their toil,
Cheered by the simple song and soaring lark. 40
Meanwhile incumbent o'er the shining share
The master leans, removes the obstructing clay,
Winds the whole work, and sidelong lays the glebe.
White through the neighbouring fields the sower
    stalks
With measured step, and liberal throws the grain
Into the faithful bosom of the ground :
The harrow follows harsh, and shuts the scene.
Be gracious, Heaven, for now laborious man
Has done his part. Ye fostering breezes, blow ;
Ye softening dews, ye tender showers, descend ; 50
And temper all, thou world-reviving sun,
Into the perfect year. Nor, ye who live
In luxury and ease, in pomp and pride,
Think these lost themes unworthy of your ear :
Such themes as these the rural Maro sung
To wide-imperial Rome, in the full height
Of elegance and taste, by Greece refined.
In ancient times the sacred plough employed
The kings and awful fathers of mankind ;
And some, with whom compared your insect-tribes 60
Are but the beings of a summer's day,
Have held the scale of empire, ruled the storm
Of mighty war ; then, with victorious hand,

---

49 part] due 1728-38.   51 world-reviving] influential
1728, *and so till* 1730.   55 'Twas such as these 1728-38.
56 wide-imperial Rome] the full Roman Court 1728-38 ; in all
its height 1728-38.   57 by Greece refined *added in* 1744.
    58-62 The sacred plow Employed the kings and fathers of
mankind In ancient times. And some, with whom compared
You're but the beings of a summer's day, Have held the scale of
justice, shook the lance 1728-38.
    63 victorious] descending 1728, 1730, 1738.

Disdaining little delicacies, seized
The plough, and greatly independent scorned
All the vile stores corruption can bestow.
   Ye generous Britons, venerate the plough ;
And o'er your hills and long withdrawing vales
Let Autumn spread his treasures to the sun,
Luxuriant and unbounded. As the sea   70
Far through his azure turbulent domain
Your empire owns, and from a thousand shores
Wafts all the pomp of life into your ports ;
So with superior boon may your rich soil,
Exuberant, Nature's better blessings pour
O'er every land, the naked nations clothe,
And be the exhaustless granary of a world !

   Nor only through the lenient air this change
Delicious breathes : the penetrative sun,
His force deep-darting to the dark retreat   80
Of vegetation, sets the steaming power
At large, to wander o'er the vernant earth
In various hues ; but chiefly thee, gay green !
Thou smiling Nature's universal robe !
United light and shade ! where the sight dwells
With growing strength and ever-new delight.
   From the moist meadow to the withered hill,
Led by the breeze, the vivid verdure runs,
And swells and deepens to the cherished eye.
The hawthorn whitens ; and the juicy groves   90
Put forth their buds, unfolding by degrees,

64 Disdaining] Unused to 1728, 1730, 1738.   65, 66 scorned
All the vile stores corruption can bestow] lived 1728, 1730, 1738.
67 venerate] cultivate 1728-38.   71 domain] extent 1728-38.
78 Nor thro' the lenient air alone, this change 1728-38.   81
steaming] streaming (a misprint) 1730-38.   82 verdant 1730-
38.   87 withered] brown-browed 1728-38.

Till the whole leafy forest stands display'd
In full luxuriance to the sighing gales—
Where the deer rustle through the twining brake,
And the birds sing concealed.   At once arrayed
In all the colours of the flushing year
By Nature's swift and secret-working hand,
The garden glows, and fills the liberal air
With lavish fragrance ; while the promised fruit
Lies yet a little embryo, unperceived,   100
Within its crimson folds.   Now from the town,
Buried in smoke and sleep and noisome damps,
Oft let me wander o'er the dewy fields
Where freshness breathes, and dash the trembling
   drops
From the bent bush, as through the verdant maze
Of sweet-briar hedges I pursue my walk ;
Or taste the smell of dairy ; or ascend
Some eminence, Augusta, in thy plains,
And see the country, far-diffused around,
One boundless blush, one white-empurpled shower 110
Of mingled blossoms ; where the raptured eye
Hurries from joy to joy, and, hid beneath
The fair profusion, yellow Autumn spies.
   If, brushed from Russian wilds, a cutting gale
Rise not, and scatter from his humid wings
The clammy mildew ; or, dry-blowing, breathe
Untimely frost—before whose baleful blast
The full-blown Spring through all her foliage shrinks,
Joyless and dead, a wide-dejected waste.
For oft, engendered by the hazy north,   120
Myriads on myriads, insect armies waft

104 trembling] lucid 1728-38.   105 verdant] fuming 1728-
38.   107 diary (a misprint) 1730-38.   110 snow-empurpled
1728, till 1730.   112 Hurries] Travels 1728-38.   115 humid]
foggy 1728-38.   116 clammy] bitter 1728-38.   119 Joyless
and dead, a] Into a smutty 1728-38.

Keen in the poisoned breeze, and wasteful eat
Through buds and bark into the blackened core
Their eager way. A feeble race, yet oft
The sacred sons of vengeance, on whose course
Corrosive famine waits, and kills the year.
To check this plague, the skilful farmer chaff
And blazing straw before his orchard burns;
Till, all involved in smoke, the latent foe
From every cranny suffocated falls;   130
Or scatters o'er the blooms the pungent dust
Of pepper, fatal to the frosty tribe;
Or, when the envenomed leaf begins to curl,
With sprinkled water drowns them in their nest:
Nor, while they pick them up with busy bill,
The little trooping birds unwisely scares.
Be patient, swains; these cruel-seeming winds
Blow not in vain. Far hence they keep repressed
Those deepening clouds on clouds, surcharged with
     rain,
That o'er the vast Atlantic hither borne   140
In endless train would quench the Summer blaze,
And cheerless drown the crude unripened year.

124-7 yet oft . . . this plague] scarce seen Save to the
prying eye; yet famine waits On their corrosive course and
starves the year. Sometimes o'er cities as they steer their flight,
Where rising vapour melts their wings away, Gazed by the
astonished crowd the horrid shower Descends; and hence 1728-
38. Note, however, that editions 1730-38 give ' by ' for ' to the
prying eye ', and ' kills ' for ' starves '.
     131, 132 Or onions, steaming hot, beneath his trees Exposes
1728-38.   133, 134 Not in the first editions (1728-38).   135
while they pick them up with] from their friendly task the 1728-
38.   136 The] Of 1728-38; unwisely] instinctive 1728-38.
     136 Here in the first and subsequent editions followed a passage
of 33 ll., transferred (in 1744) with alterations to Summer, ll. 287-
317,—which see.
     137-42 Not in the first editions (1728-38)

The North-east spends his rage, and, now shut up
Within his iron caves, the effusive South
Warms the wide air, and o'er the void of heaven
Breathes the big clouds with vernal showers distent.
At first a dusky wreath they seem to rise,
Scarce staining ether ; but by fast degrees,
In heaps on heaps the doubling vapour sails
Along the loaded sky, and mingling deep   150
Sits on the horizon round a settled gloom ;
Not such as wintry storms on mortals shed,
Oppressing life ; but lovely, gentle, kind,
And full of every hope and every joy,
The wish of Nature. Gradual sinks the breeze
Into a perfect calm ; that not a breath
Is heard to quiver through the closing woods,
Or rustling turn the many-twinkling leaves
Of aspen tall. The uncurling floods, diffused
In glassy breadth, seem through delusive lapse   160
Forgetful of their course. 'Tis silence all,
And pleasing expectation. Herds and flocks
Drop the dry sprig, and mute-imploring eye
The falling verdure. Hushed in short suspense,
The plumy people streak their wings with oil
To throw the lucid moisture trickling off,
And wait the approaching sign to strike at once
Into the general choir. Even mountains, vales,
And forests seem, impatient, to demand
The promised sweetness. Man superior walks   170
Amid the glad creation, musing praise
And looking lively gratitude. At last
The clouds consign their treasures to the fields,
And, softly shaking on the dimpled pool

150 deep] thick 1728-38.   166 Not in the first editions
(1728-38).   169 impatient] expansive 1728-38.   174
dimpled] dimply 1728-38.

B

Prelusive drops, let all their moisture flow
In large effusion o'er the freshened world.
The stealing shower is scarce to patter heard
By such as wander through the forest-walks,
Beneath the umbrageous multitude of leaves.
But who can hold the shade while Heaven descends
In universal bounty, shedding herbs   181
And fruits and flowers on Nature's ample lap ?
Swift fancy fired anticipates their growth ;
And, while the milky nutriment distils,
Beholds the kindling country colour round.
　Thus all day long the full-distended clouds
Indulge their genial stores, and well-showered earth
Is deep enriched with vegetable life ;
Till, in the western sky, the downward sun
Looks out effulgent from amid the flush   190
Of broken clouds, gay-shifting to his beam.
The rapid radiance instantaneous strikes
The illumined mountain, through the forest streams,
Shakes on the floods, and in a yellow mist,
Far smoking o'er the interminable plain,
In twinkling myriads lights the dewy gems.
Moist, bright, and green, the landscape laughs around.
Full swell the woods ; their every music wakes,
Mixed in wild concert, with the warbling brooks
Increased, the distant bleatings of the hills,   200
The hollow lows responsive from the vales,
Whence, blending all, the sweetened zephyr springs.
Meantime, refracted from yon eastern cloud,
Bestriding earth, the grand ethereal bow
Shoots up immense ; and every hue unfolds,

177 'Tis scarce to patter heard, the stealing shower 1728–38.
180 can] would 1728.   183 Imagination fired prevents 1728–
38.   184 milky] verdant 1728–38.   190 effulgent] illustrious 1728–38.   198 swells 1730–38.   199 consort
1728–38.   200 distant] unnumbered 1728–38.

In fair proportion running from the red
To where the violet fades into the sky.
Here, awful Newton, the dissolving clouds
Form, fronting on the sun, thy showery prism ;
And to the sage-instructed eye unfold   210
The various twine of light, by thee disclosed
From the white mingling maze. Not so the swain;
He wondering views the bright enchantment bend
Delightful o'er the radiant fields, and runs
To catch the falling glory ; but amazed
Beholds the amusive arch before him fly,
Then vanish quite away. Still night succeeds,
A softened shade, and saturated earth
Awaits the morning beam, to give to light,
Raised through ten thousand different plastic tubes,
The balmy treasures of the former day.   221
  Then spring the living herbs, profusely wild,
O'er all the deep-green earth, beyond the power
Of botanist to number up their tribes :
Whether he steals along the lonely dale
In silent search ; or through the forest, rank
With what the dull incurious weeds account,
Bursts his blind way ; or climbs the mountain-rock,
Fired by the nodding verdure of its brow.
With such a liberal hand has Nature flung   230
Their seeds abroad, blown them about in winds,

208 awful] mighty 1728-38.   209 fronting on the sun] as
they scatter round 1744.   209, 210 Are, as they scatter
round, thy numerous prism, Untwisting to the philosophic eye
1728-38.   211 disclosed] pursued 1728.   212 From the
white] Through all the 1728 ; Through the white 1730-38.   219
to light] again 1728-38.   220 Transmuted soon by Nature's
chymistry 1728-38.   221 blooming blessings 1728-38.   227
'incurious' is printed in some editions in Thomson's lifetime
with a capital initial. It does not, probably, refer to weeds.

Innumerous mixed them with the nursing mould,
The moistening current, and prolific rain.
　But who their virtues can declare ? who pierce
With vision pure into these secret stores
Of health and life and joy ? the food of man
While yet he lived in innocence, and told
A length of golden years, unfleshed in blood,
A stranger to the savage arts of life,
Death, rapine, carnage, surfeit, and disease—　240
The lord and not the tyrant of the world.
　The first fresh dawn then waked the gladdened race
Of uncorrupted man, nor blushed to see
The sluggard sleep beneath its sacred beam ;
For their light slumbers gently fumed away,
And up they rose as vigorous as the sun,
Or to the culture of the willing glebe,
Or to the cheerful tendance of the flock.
Meantime the song went round ; and dance and sport,
Wisdom and friendly talk successive stole　250
Their hours away ; while in the rosy vale
Love breathed his infant sighs, from anguish free,
And full replete with bliss—save the sweet pain
That, inly thrilling, but exalts it more.
Nor yet injurious act nor surly deed
Was known among these happy sons of heaven ;
For reason and benevolence were law.
Harmonious Nature too looked smiling on.
Clear shone the skies, cooled with eternal gales,
And balmy spirit all. The youthful sun　260
Shot his best rays, and still the gracious clouds
Dropped fatness down ; as o'er the swelling mead

236 life and health 1728–38.　　242 Then the glad morning
1728–38.　　243 man] men 1728–38.　　244 its] her 1728–38.
253, 254 Fragrant with bliss and only wept for joy 1728 ;
Replete with &c. 1730–38.

The herds and flocks commixing played secure.
This when, emergent from the gloomy wood,
The glaring lion saw, his horrid heart
Was meekened, and he joined his sullen joy.
For music held the whole in perfect peace :
Soft sighed the flute ; the tender voice was heard,
Warbling the varied heart ; the woodlands round
Applied their quire ; and winds and waters flowed 270
In consonance. Such were those prime of days.
But now those white unblemished minutes, whence
The fabling poets took their golden age,
Are found no more amid these iron times,
These dregs of life ! Now the distempered mind
Has lost that concord of harmonious powers
Which forms the soul of happiness ; and all
Is off the poise within : the passions all
Have burst their bounds ; and Reason, half extinct,
Or impotent, or else approving, sees   280
The foul disorder. Senseless and deformed,

264 This] Which 1728-38.   269 varied] joyous 1728-38.
271 those] these 1728-38.

271 Here in the first and subsequent editions down to (and
including) that of 1738 followed a passage of twenty-eight luxuri-
antly wild and even grotesque lines, which the reader will find
in the Notes at the end of the poem.

272, 273 But now whate'er these gaudy fables meant And
the white minutes that (which) they shadowed out 1728-38.

274, 275 these . . These] those . . Those 1730-38.

275, 276 Now the . . powers] in which the human mind
Has lost that harmony ineffable 1728-38.

277 forms] warms 1730-38.

281-93 Senseless and deformed . . . . object of its flame.]
This passage stood originally (1728-38) :

Anger storms at large
Without an equal cause ; and fell Revenge
Supports the falling Rage. Close Envy bites
With venomed tooth ; while weak unmanly Fear,
Full of frail fancies, loosens every power.
Even Love itself is bitterness of soul,
A pleasing anguish pining at the heart.

Convulsive Anger storms at large ; or, pale
And silent, settles into fell revenge.
Base Envy withers at another's joy,
And hates that excellence it cannot reach.
Desponding Fear, of feeble fancies full,
Weak and unmanly, loosens every power.
Even Love itself is bitterness of soul,
A pensive anguish pining at the heart ;
Or, sunk to sordid interest, feels no more   290
That noble wish, that never-cloyed desire,
Which, selfish joy disdaining, seeks alone
To bless the dearer object of its flame.
Hope sickens with extravagance ; and Grief,
Of life impatient, into madness swells,
Or in dead silence wastes the weeping hours.
These, and a thousand mixt emotions more,
From ever-changing views of good and ill,
Formed infinitely various, vex the mind
With endless storm : whence, deeply rankling, grows
The partial thought, a listless unconcern,   301
Cold, and averting from our neighbour's good ;
Then dark disgust and hatred, winding wiles,
Coward deceit, and ruffian violence.
At last, extinct each social feeling, fell

285 that excellence it cannot reach] whate'er is excellent and
good 1744.   291 noble] restless 1744 ; never-cloyed] infinite
1744.   297 mixt] new 1728.   298, 299 That from their
mixture spring, distract the mind 1728.   300 storm] tumult
1728 ; deeply rankling grows] resulting rise 1728.   300
deeply] inly 1730-44.   301 partial] selfish 1728-38.   303
hatred] malice 1728-38.   304 coward] sneaking 1728-38 ;
ruffian violence] coward villainy 1728-38.

305-7 At last unruly Hatred, lewd Reproach, Convulsive Wrath
and thoughtless Fury quick To every evil deed.   Even Nature's
self 1728.   Editions 1730-38 give this (the first text) also, except
that ' *deep-rooted* ' takes the place of ' *unruly* ', and ' quick to
deeds of vilest aim ' the place of ' quick to *every evil deed* '.

And joyless inhumanity pervades
And petrifies the heart. Nature disturbed
Is deemed, vindictive, to have changed her course.
Hence, in old dusky time, a deluge came :
When the deep-cleft disparting orb, that arched 310
The central waters round, impetuous rushed
With universal burst into the gulf,
And o'er the high-piled hills of fractured earth
Wide-dashed the waves in undulation vast,
Till, from the centre to the streaming clouds,
A shoreless ocean tumbled round the globe.
The Seasons since have, with severer sway,
Oppressed a broken world : the Winter keen
Shook forth his waste of snows; and Summer shot
His pestilential heats. Great Spring before   320
Greened all the year ; and fruits and blossoms blushed
In social sweetness on the self-same bough.
Pure was the temperate air ; an even calm
Perpetual reigned, save what the zephyrs bland
Breathed o'er the blue expanse : for then nor storms
Were taught to blow, nor hurricanes to rage ;
Sound slept the waters ; no sulphureous glooms
Swelled in the sky and sent the lightning forth ;
While sickly damps and cold autumnal fogs
Hung not relaxing on the springs of life.   330
But now, of turbid elements the sport,

309 dusky time] time, they say, 1728–38.   310 dry-crumbling Orb of Earth which 1728 ; disparting orb of earth that 1730–38.   311 imprisoned deep around 1728–38.   312, 313 With Ruin inconceivable, at once Into the gulf, and o'er the highest hills 1728–38.   317, 318 The Seasons since, as hoar tradition tells, Have kept their constant chase 1728, 1729, 1730, 1738, 1744.   319 Shook forth] Poured out 1728–38.   323 Pure] Clear 1728–38.   330 Hung not relaxing] Sat not pernicious 1728–38 ; Oppressive sat not 1744.

331–3 But now from clear to cloudy, moist to dry, And hot to cold, in restless change revolved 1728–38.

From clear to cloudy tossed, from hot to cold,
And dry to moist, with inward-eating change,
Our drooping days are dwindled down to naught,
Their period finished ere 'tis well begun.
And yet the wholesome herb neglected dies ;
Though with the pure exhilarating soul
Of nutriment and health, and vital powers,
Beyond the search of art, 'tis copious blest.
For, with hot ravine fired, ensanguined man   340
Is now become the lion of the plain,
And worse. The wolf, who from the nightly fold
Fierce drags the bleating prey, ne'er drunk her milk,
Nor wore her warming fleece : nor has the steer,
At whose strong chest the deadly tiger hangs,
E'er ploughed for him. They too are tempered high,
With hunger stung and wild necessity,
Nor lodges pity in their shaggy breast.
But man, whom Nature formed of milder clay,
With every kind emotion in his heart,   350
And taught alone to weep,—while from her lap
She pours ten thousand delicacies, herbs
And fruits, as numerous as the drops of rain
Or beams that gave them birth,—shall he, fair form !
Who wears sweet smiles, and looks erect on Heaven,
E'er stoop to mingle with the prowling herd,

335 The fleeting shadow of a Winter's sun 1728-38.
337-9 In the first edition (1728), and subsequent editions (to
1738), the original of these lines stood :—
    In lone obscurity, unprized for good,
    Although the pure exhilarating soul
    Of nutriment and health salubrious breathes,
    By heaven infused, along its secret tubes.
338, 339 and vital powers . . . . blest] salubrious, blest, And
deeply stored with wondrous vital powers 1744.
348 breasts 1728-1738.   354 And beams which gave 1728 ;
And beams that give 1730-38.

And dip his tongue in gore ? The beast of prey,
Blood-stained, deserves to bleed : but you, ye flocks,
What have ye done ? ye peaceful people, what,
To merit death ? you, who have given us milk 360
In luscious streams, and lent us your own coat
Against the Winter's cold ? And the plain ox,
That harmless, honest, guileless animal,
In what has he offended ? he, whose toil,
Patient and ever ready, clothes the land
With all the pomp of harvest ; shall he bleed,
And struggling groan beneath the cruel hands
Even of the clowns he feeds ? And that, perhaps,
To swell the riot of the autumnal feast,
Won by his labour ? This the feeling heart 370
Would tenderly suggest : but 'tis enough,
In this late age, adventurous to have touched
Light on the numbers of the Samian Sage.
High Heaven forbids the bold presumptuous strain,
Whose wisest will has fixed us in a state
That must not yet to pure perfection rise :
Besides, who knows, how, raised to higher life,
From stage to stage, the vital scale ascends ?

Now, when the first foul torrent of the brooks,

357 gore] blood 1728-38.
358 Blood-stained, deserves to bleed] 'Tis true, deserves the
fate in which he deals : Him from the thicket let the hardy
youth Provoke, and foaming through the awakened woods
With every nerve pursue 1728-38.   362 After ' the Winter's
cold ' in the earlier edition (1728-38) appeared—' Whose useful-
ness In living only lies ' : the words were dropped in edition 1744.
     365 land] fields 1728.   367 struggling] wrestling 1728-
38.   369 autumnal] gathering 1728-38.   370 This]
Thus 1728-38.   374 High Heaven] Heaven too 1744 ; forbids
the bold presumptuous] beside forbids the daring 1728-38.
     7, 378 These lines first appear in edition 1746.
     379-466 These lines, a happy afterthought, first appeared
in edition 1744 almost exactly as they stand here. A few altera-

Swelled with the vernal rains, is ebbed away,   380
And whitening down their mossy-tinctured stream
Descends the billowy foam ; now is the time,
While yet the dark-brown water aids the guile,
To tempt the trout. The well-dissembled fly,
The rod fine-tapering with elastic spring,
Snatched from the hoary steed the floating line,
And all thy slender watery stores prepare.
But let not on thy hook the tortured worm
Convulsive twist in agonizing folds ;
Which, by rapacious hunger swallowed deep,   390
Gives, as you tear it from the bleeding breast
Of the weak helpless uncomplaining wretch,
Harsh pain and horror to the tender hand.
    When with his lively ray the potent sun
Has pierced the streams and roused the finny race,
Then, issuing cheerful, to thy sport repair ;
Chief should the western breezes curling play,
And light o'er ether bear the shadowy clouds.
High to their fount, this day, amid the hills
And woodlands warbling round, trace up the brooks ;
The next, pursue their rocky-channelled maze,   401
Down to the river, in whose ample wave
Their little naiads love to sport at large.
Just in the dubious point where with the pool
Is mixed the trembling stream, or where it boils
Around the stone, or from the hollowed bank
Reverted plays in undulating flow,
There throw, nice-judging, the delusive fly ;
And, as you lead it round in artful curve,
With eye attentive mark the springing game.   410
Straight as above the surface of the flood

tions were made by the author in preparing the text for the
edition of 1746—the last to receive his attention. He died in
1748.   380 with] by 1744.

They wanton rise, or urged by hunger leap,
Then fix with gentle twitch the barbèd hook—
Some lightly tossing to the grassy bank,
And to the shelving shore slow-dragging some,
With various hand proportioned to their force.
If, yet too young and easily deceived,
A worthless prey scarce bends your pliant rod,
Him, piteous of his youth and the short space
He has enjoyed the vital light of heaven,   420
Soft disengage, and back into the stream
The speckled infant throw. But, should you lure
From his dark haunt beneath the tangled roots
Of pendent trees the monarch of the brook,
Behoves you then to ply your finest art.
Long time he, following cautious, scans the fly,
And oft attempts to seize it, but as oft
The dimpled water speaks his jealous fear.
At last, while haply o'er the shaded sun
Passes a cloud, he desperate takes the death   430
With sullen plunge. At once he darts along,
Deep-struck, and runs out all the lengthened line ;
Then seeks the farthest ooze, the sheltering weed,
The caverned bank, his old secure abode ;
And flies aloft, and flounces round the pool,
Indignant of the guile. With yielding hand,
That feels him still, yet to his furious course
Gives way, you, now retiring, following now
Across the stream, exhaust his idle rage ;
Till floating broad upon his breathless side,   440
And to his fate abandoned, to the shore
You gaily drag your unresisting prize.
    Thus pass the temperate hours : but when the sun
Shakes from his noon-day throne the scattering clouds,

422 infant] captive 1744.   425 you . . your] thee . .
thy 1744.

Even shooting listless languor through the deeps,
Then seek the bank where flowering elders crowd,
Where scattered wild the lily of the vale
Its balmy essence breathes, where cowslips hang
The dewy head, where purple violets lurk,
With all the lowly children of the shade ;   450
Or lie reclined beneath yon spreading ash
Hung o'er the steep, whence, borne on liquid wing,
The sounding culver shoots, or where the hawk,
High in the beetling cliff, his eyry builds.
There let the classic page thy fancy lead
Through rural scenes, such as the Mantuan swain
Paints in the matchless harmony of song ;
Or catch thyself the landscape, gliding swift
Athwart imagination's vivid eye ;
Or, by the vocal woods and waters lulled,   460
And lost in lonely musing, in a dream
Confused of careless solitude where mix
Ten thousand wandering images of things,
Soothe every gust of passion into peace—
All but the swellings of the softened heart,
That waken, not disturb, the tranquil mind.
    Behold yon breathing prospect bids the Muse
Throw all her beauty forth.   But who can paint
Like Nature ?   Can imagination boast,
Amid its gay creation, hues like hers ?   470
Or can it mix them with that matchless skill,

457 the matchless harmony of] immortal verse and matchless
1744.   467 Behold yon] But yonder 1728-38.
   468 In the earlier edd. (1728-38) we find here—
        Throw all her beauty forth, that daubing all
        Will be to what I gaze ; for who can paint &c.
   470 its] his 1728-38.
   471 Here followed in the original text (1728-38) the line—
        And lay them on so delicately sweet (fine)—
dropped in the later edd., 1744, 1746.   471 it] he 1728-38.

And lose them in each other, as appears
In every bud that blows ? If fancy then
Unequal fails beneath the pleasing task,
Ah, what shall language do ? ah, where find words
Tinged with so many colours and whose power,
To life approaching, may perfume my lays
With that fine oil, those aromatic gales
That inexhaustive flow continual round ?
   Yet, though successless, will the toil delight. 480
Come then, ye virgins and ye youths, whose hearts
Have felt the raptures of refining love ;
And thou, Amanda, come, pride of my song !
Formed by the Graces, loveliness itself !
Come with those downcast eyes, sedate and sweet,
Those looks demure that deeply pierce the soul,
Where, with the light of thoughtful reason mixed,
Shines lively fancy and the feeling heart :
Oh, come ! and, while the rosy-footed May
Steals blushing on, together let us tread   490
The morning dews, and gather in their prime
Fresh-blooming flowers to grace thy braided hair
And thy loved bosom, that improves their sweets.
   See where the winding vale its lavish stores,
Irriguous, spreads. See how the lily drinks
The latent rill, scarce oozing through the grass
Of growth luxuriant, or the humid bank
In fair profusion decks. Long let us walk

474 pleasing] lovely 1728–38.   478 those] these 1728–38.
483–8 These lines first appear in the edition of 1744. See
Note at the end of the poem.   490 tread] walk 1728–38.
492 thy braided] the flowing 1728; the braided 1730–38.   493
Originally (1728)—And for a breast which can improve their
sweets ; afterwards (1730–38)—And the white bosom that
improves &c.   494 its] her 1728–38.
   498 In fair profusion decks] Profusely climbs 1728–38 ;
followed by :—

Where the breeze blows from yon extended field
Of blossomed beans. Arabia cannot boast   500
A fuller gale of joy than liberal thence
Breathes through the sense, and takes the ravished soul.
Nor is the mead unworthy of thy foot,
Full of fresh verdure and unnumbered flowers,
The negligence of nature wide and wild,
Where, undisguised by mimic art, she spreads
Unbounded beauty to the roving eye.
Here their delicious task the fervent bees
In swarming millions tend. Around, athwart,
Through the soft air, the busy nations fly,   510
Cling to the bud, and with inserted tube
Suck its pure essence, its ethereal soul.
And oft with bolder wing they soaring dare
The purple heath, or where the wild thyme grows,
And yellow load them with the luscious spoil.
    At length the finished garden to the view
Its vistas opens and its alleys green.
Snatched through the verdant maze, the hurried eye
Distracted wanders ; now the bowery walk
Of covert close, where scarce a speck of day   520

Turgent in every pore
The gummy moisture shines, new lustre lends,
And feeds the spirit that diffusive round
Refreshes all the dale.

These lines were dropped in the edition of 1744.
    503 mead unworthy of thy] meadow worthless of our 1728-
38.   508 Originally (1728-38)—

'Tis here that their delicious task the bees &c.

    510 Through the soft air] This way and that 1728-38.
    512 Originally (1728-38)—

Its soul, its sweetness, and its manna suck.

And followed by—

The little chymist thus all-moving Heaven
Has taught.

    513 with . . they soaring dare] of . . he dares 1728-38.
    515 load them] loads him 1728-38.

Falls on the lengthened gloom, protracted sweeps ;
Now meets the bending sky, the river now
Dimpling along, the breezy ruffled lake,
The forest darkening round, the glittering spire,
The ethereal mountain, and the distant main.
But why so far excursive ? when at hand,
Along these blushing borders bright with dew,
And in yon mingled wilderness of flowers,
Fair-handed Spring unbosoms every grace—
Throws out the snow-drop and the crocus first,   530
The daisy, primrose, violet darkly blue,
And polyanthus of unnumbered dyes ;
The yellow wall-flower, stained with iron brown,
And lavish stock, that scents the garden round :
From the soft wing of vernal breezes shed,
Anemones ; auriculas, enriched
With shining meal o'er all their velvet leaves ;
And full ranunculus of glowing red.
Then comes the tulip-race, where beauty plays
Her idle freaks : from family diffused   540
To family, as flies the father-dust,
The varied colours run ; and, while they break
On the charmed eye, the exulting florist marks
With secret pride the wonders of his hand.

521 sweeps] darts 1728-38.   524 darkening . . glittering]
running . . rising 1728-38.   527 these . . bright with dew]
the . . dewy-bright 1728-38.

532-8 For this passage, which first appeared in the 1744
edition, there stood in the original edition (1728) and subsequent
editions (to 1738)—
    Soft-bending (dew-bending) cowslips, and of nameless dyes
    Anemonies, auriculas, a tribe
    Peculiar powdered with a shining sand,
    Renunculas, and iris many-hued.
540 idle] gayest 1728-38.   543, 544 Originally (1728-38)—
    On the charmed florist's eye, he wondering (curious) stands,
    And new-flushed glories all ecstatic marks.

No gradual bloom is wanting—from the bud
First-born of Spring to Summer's musky tribes ;
Nor hyacinths, of purest virgin white,
Low bent and blushing inward ; nor jonquils,
Of potent fragrance ; nor narcissus fair,
As o'er the fabled fountain hanging still ;   550
Nor broad carnations, nor gay-spotted pinks ;
Nor, showered from every bush, the damask-rose :
Infinite numbers, delicacies, smells,
With hues on hues expression cannot paint,
The breath of Nature, and her endless bloom.
 Hail, Source of Being ! Universal Soul
Of heaven and earth ! Essential Presence, hail !
To thee I bend the knee ; to thee my thoughts
Continual climb, who with a master-hand
Hast the great whole into perfection touched.   560
By thee the various vegetative tribes,
Wrapt in a filmy net and clad with leaves,
Draw the live ether and imbibe the dew.
By thee disposed into congenial soils,
Stands each attractive plant, and sucks, and swells
The juicy tide, a twining mass of tubes.
At thy command the vernal sun awakes
The torpid sap, detruded to the root
By wintry winds, that now in fluent dance
And lively fermentation mounting spreads   570
All this innumerous-coloured scene of things.

 As rising from the vegetable world

545, 546 First added in the edition of 1744.
 547, 548 Expanded (1744 edition) from the line—'Nor hyacinths are wanting nor junquils '—the reading of the early edition
(1728–38) ; Nor hyacinths deep-purpled, nor jonquils 1744.
 549 fair] white 1728–38.   550 Added in 1744.   551
broad . . gay-spotted] deep (striped) . . enamelled 1728–38.   552
Nor] And 1728.   556 Source of Being] Mighty Being 1728–38;
Source of Beings 1744.   572 As rising] Ascending 1728–38.

My theme ascends, with equal wing ascend,
My panting muse ; and hark, how loud the woods
Invite you forth in all your gayest trim.
Lend me your song, ye nightingales ! oh, pour
The mazy-running soul of melody
Into my varied verse ! while I deduce,
From the first note the hollow cuckoo sings,
The symphony of Spring, and touch a theme   580
Unknown to fame—the passion of the groves.
When first the soul of love is sent abroad
Warm through the vital air, and on the heart
Harmonious seizes, the gay troops begin
In gallant thought to plume the painted wing ;
And try again the long-forgotten strain,
At first faint-warbled. But no sooner grows
The soft infusion prevalent and wide
Than all alive at once their joy o'erflows
In music unconfined. Up springs the lark,   590
Shrill-voiced and loud, the messenger of morn :
Ere yet the shadows fly, he mounted sings
Amid the dawning clouds, and from their haunts
Calls up the tuneful nations. Every copse
Deep-tangled, tree irregular, and bush
Bending with dewy moisture o'er the heads
Of the coy quiristers that lodge within,
Are prodigal of harmony. The thrush
And wood-lark, o'er the kind-contending throng
Superior heard, run through the sweetest length
Of notes, when listening Philomela deigns   601
To let them joy, and purposes, in thought
Elate, to make her night excel their day.

573 My theme ascends] To higher life 1728–38.   582
When first the soul] Just as the spirit 1728–38.   585 the . .
wing] their . . wings 1728.   595 Deep-tangled] Thick-
wove and 1728, 1729, 1730, 1738, 1744.

The blackbird whistles from the thorny brake,
The mellow bullfinch answers from the grove ;
Nor are the linnets, o'er the flowering furze
Poured out profusely, silent. Joined to these
Innumerous songsters, in the freshening shade
Of new-sprung leaves, their modulations mix
Mellifluous. The jay, the rook, the daw,　　610
And each harsh pipe, discordant heard alone,
Aid the full concert ; while the stock-dove breathes
A melancholy murmur through the whole.
'Tis love creates their melody, and all
This waste of music is the voice of love,
That even to birds and beasts the tender arts
Of pleasing teaches. Hence the glossy kind
Try every winning way inventive love
Can dictate, and in courtship to their mates
Pour forth their little souls. First, wide around,　620
With distant awe, in airy rings they rove,
Endeavouring by a thousand tricks to catch
The cunning, conscious, half-averted glance
Of their regardless charmer. Should she seem
Softening the least approvance to bestow,

608, 609 Condensed (1744 edition) from the original text
(1728–38)—
　　Thousands beside, thick as the covering leaves
　　They warble under, or the nitid (nited 1730) hues
　　Which (That 1730) speck them o'er, their modulations mix.
611, 612 Originally (1728)—
　　And all these jangling pipes, when heard alone,
　　Here aid the consort (*sic*) ; while the wood-dove breathes.
Altered (in 1730, and retained on to and including 1738) as follows—
　　And each harsh pipe, discordant heard alone.
　　Here aid the consort ; while the stock-dove breathes.
614 melody] gaiety 1728–38.　　616 That] Which 1728–38.
619, 620 Originally (1728–38)—
　　　　　　　　In fluttering courtship pour
　　Their little souls before her. Wide around.
621 With distant awe] Respectful, first 1728–38.

Their colours burnish, and, by hope inspired,
They brisk advance ; then, on a sudden struck,
Retire disordered ; then again approach,
In fond rotation spread the spotted wing,
And shiver every feather with desire.   630
Connubial leagues agreed, to the deep woods
They haste away, all as their fancy leads,
Pleasure, or food, or secret safety prompts ;
That Nature's great command may be obeyed,
Nor all the sweet sensations they perceive
Indulged in vain. Some to the holly-hedge
Nestling repair, and to the thicket some ;
Some to the rude protection of the thorn
Commit their feeble offspring. The cleft tree
Offers its kind concealment to a few,   640
Their food its insects, and its moss their nests.
Others apart far in the grassy dale,
Or roughening waste, their humble texture weave
But most in woodland solitudes delight,
In unfrequented glooms, or shaggy banks,
Steep, and divided by a babbling brook
Whose murmurs soothe them all the live-long day
When by kind duty fixed. Among the roots
Of hazel, pendent o'er the plaintive stream,
They frame the first foundation of their domes— 650
Dry sprigs of trees, in artful fabric laid,
And bound with clay together. Now 'tis nought

---

629 Preceding this line, appeared in the early texts (1728-38) :
  And throwing out the last efforts of love.
First dropped in the edition of 1744.   632 all] each 1728-38.
  633 secret] latent 1728-38.   639 Resolve to trust their
young. The clefted tree 1728.   643, 644 Expanded from—
  Their humble texture weave. But most delight—
the reading of the early text (1728-38).   648 by kind duty]
for a season 1728-44.   651 fabric] manner 1728-38.

But restless hurry through the busy air,
Beat by unnumbered wings. The swallow sweeps
The slimy pool, to build his hanging house
Intent. And often, from the careless back
Of herds and flocks, a thousand tugging bills
Pluck hair and wool ; and oft, when unobserved,
Steal from the barn a straw—till soft and warm,
Clean and complete, their habitation grows. 660
As thus the patient dam assiduous sits,
Not to be tempted from her tender task
Or by sharp hunger or by smooth delight,
Though the whole loosened Spring around her blows,
Her sympathizing lover takes his stand
High on the opponent bank, and ceaseless sings
The tedious time away ; or else supplies
Her place a moment, while she sudden flits
To pick the scanty meal. The appointed time
With pious toil fulfilled, the callow young, 670
Warmed and expanded into perfect life,
Their brittle bondage break, and come to light,
A helpless family demanding food
With constant clamour. Oh, what passions then,
What melting sentiments of kindly care,
On the new parents seize ! Away they fly
Affectionate, and undesiring bear
The most delicious morsel to their young ;
Which equally distributed, again
The search begins. Even so a gentle pair, 680

653 restless hurry] hurry hurry 1728–38.
656 Originally (1728–38)—
    Ingeniously intent.   Oft from the back.
Dropped in 1744.
    659 a straw] the straw 1728–38.   661 As thus] Meantime
1728.   676 Seize the new parents' hearts, &c. 1728–38.
    680–85 Even so a gentle pair . . Oft] Expanded from the
original text (1728–38)—

By fortune sunk, but formed of generous mould,
And charmed with cares beyond the vulgar breast,
In some lone cot amid the distant woods,
Sustain'd alone by providential Heaven,
Oft, as they weeping eye their infant train,
Check their own appetites, and give them all.
　Nor toil alone they scorn : exalting love,
By the great Father of the Spring inspired,
Gives instant courage to the fearful race,
And to the simple art. With stealthy wing,　690
Should some rude foot their woody haunts molest,
Amid a neighbouring bush they silent drop,
And whirring thence, as if alarmed, deceive
The unfeeling schoolboy. Hence, around the head
Of wandering swain, the white-winged plover wheels
Her sounding flight, and then directly on
In long excursion skims the level lawn
To tempt him from her nest. The wild-duck, hence,
O'er the rough moss, and o'er the trackless waste
The heath-hen flutters, pious fraud ! to lead　700
The hot pursuing spaniel far astray.
　Be not the muse ashamed here to bemoan

So pitiful and poor
A gentle pair on providential Heaven
Cast.
　682 charmed] pierced 1744.　　685 infant] clamant 1728-38.
687 toil] pain 1744.
　687-94 Nor toil alone . . . The unfeeling schoolboy. These
lines, which first appeared in the edition of 1744, are an expansion
of the original text (1728-38)—
　　　　Nor is the courage of the fearful kind,
　　　　Nor is their cunning less should some rude foot
　　　　Their woody haunts molest : stealthy aside
　　　　Into the centre of a neighbouring bush
　　　　They drop, and whirring thence alarmed deceive
　　　　The rambling schoolboy.
　695 wandering swain] traveller 1728-38.　　700 pious fraud !]
as if hurt 1728-38.

Her brothers of the grove by tyrant man
Inhuman caught, and in the narrow cage
From liberty confined, and boundless air.
Dull are the pretty slaves, their plumage dull,
Ragged, and all its brightening lustre lost ;
Nor is that sprightly wildness in their notes,
Which, clear and vigorous, warbles from the beech.
Oh then, ye friends of love and love-taught song, 710
Spare the soft tribes, this barbarous art forbear !
If on your bosom innocence can win,
Music engage, or piety persuade.
　But let not chief the nightingale lament
Her ruined care, too delicately framed
To brook the harsh confinement of the cage.
Oft when, returning with her loaded bill,
The astonished mother finds a vacant nest,
By the hard hand of unrelenting clowns
Robbed, to the ground the vain provision falls ; 720
Her pinions ruffle, and, low-drooping, scarce
Can bear the mourner to the poplar shade ;
Where, all abandoned to despair, she sings
Her sorrows through the night, and, on the bough
Sole-sitting, still at every dying fall
Takes up again her lamentable strain
Of winding woe, till wide around the woods
Sigh to her song and with her wail resound.
　But now the feathered youth their former bounds,
Ardent, disdain ; and, weighing oft their wings, 730

708 sprightly] luscious 1728-38.　　709-13 Originally (1728-
38)—

　　That warbles from the beech.　Oh, then, desist !
　　Ye friends of harmony ;　this barbarous art
　　Forbear, if innocence and music can
　　Win on your hearts, or piety persuade.
725 Sad-sitting 1728-38.　　728 Sigh to] Sigh at 1728-38.
729 But] And 1728-38.

Demand the free possession of the sky.
This one glad office more, and then dissolves
Parental love at once, now needless grown :
Unlavish Wisdom never works in vain.
'Tis on some evening, sunny, grateful, mild,
When nought but balm is breathing through the
        woods
With yellow lustre bright, that the new tribes
Visit the spacious heavens, and look abroad
On Nature's common, far as they can see
Or wing, their range and pasture. O'er the boughs 740
Dancing about, still at the giddy verge
Their resolution fails ; their pinions still,
In loose libration stretched, to trust the void
Trembling refuse—till down before them fly
The parent-guides, and chide, exhort, command,
Or push them off. The surging air receives
The plumy burden ; and their self-taught wings
Winnow the waving element. On ground
Alighted, bolder up again they lead,
Farther and farther on, the lengthening flight ; 750
Till, vanished every fear, and every power
Roused into life and action, light in air
The acquitted parents see their soaring race,
And, once rejoicing, never know them more.
    High from the summit of a craggy cliff,
Hung o'er the deep, such as amazing frowns
On utmost Kilda's shore, whose lonely race

732 This one] But this 1728-38.   733 now needless grown :]
for needless grown, 1728-38.
    743 to trust the void] the void abrupt 1728-38.   752 light
in air] in the void 1728-38.
    753 acquitted] exoner'd 1728-38.
    755-65 These lines are an expansion of a vigorous and
picturesque passage which remained in the original text till
altered in 1744. See Note at the end of the poem.

Resign the setting sun to Indian worlds,
The royal eagle draws his vigorous young,
Strong-pounced, and ardent with paternal fire.   760
Now fit to raise a kingdom of their own,
He drives them from his fort, the towering seat
For ages of his empire—which in peace
Unstained he holds, while many a league to sea
He wings his course, and preys in distant isles.
  Should I my steps turn to the rural seat
Whose lofty elms and venerable oaks
Invite the rook, who high amid the boughs
In early Spring his airy city builds,
And ceaseless caws amusive ; there, well-pleased,   770
I might the various polity survey
Of the mixed household-kind. The careful hen
Calls all her chirping family around,
Fed and defended by the fearless cock,
Whose breast with ardour flames, as on he walks
Graceful, and crows defiance. In the pond
The finely-checkered duck before her train
Rows garrulous. The stately-sailing swan
Gives out his snowy plumage to the gale,
And, arching proud his neck, with oary feet   780
Bears forward fierce, and guards his osier-isle,
Protective of his young. The turkey nigh,
Loud-threatening, reddens ;   while   the   peacock
    spreads
His every-coloured glory to the sun,
And swims in radiant majesty along.

766 And should I wander 1728–38.   767 lofty elms . . oaks]
aged oaks . . gloom 1728–38.   768–70 Originally (1728–38) —
          Invite the noisy rook, with pleasure there—
A single line.
    781 forward] onward 1728 ; guards his osier isle] beats you
from the bank 1728–38.   785 radiant] floating 1728–38.

O'er the whole homely scene the cooing dove
Flies thick in amorous chase, and wanton rolls
The glancing eye, and turns the changeful neck.
While thus the gentle tenants of the shade
Indulge their purer loves, the rougher world   790
Of brutes below rush furious into flame
And fierce desire. Through all his lusty veins
The bull, deep-scorched, the raging passion feels.
Of pasture sick, and negligent of food,
Scarce seen he wades among the yellow broom,
While o'er his ample sides the rambling sprays
Luxuriant shoot ; or through the mazy wood
Dejected wanders, nor the enticing bud
Crops, though it presses on his careless sense.
And oft, in jealous maddening fancy wrapt,   800
He seeks the fight ; and, idly-butting, feigns
His rival gored in every knotty trunk.
Him should he meet, the bellowing war begins :
Their eyes flash fury ; to the hollowed earth,
Whence the sand flies, they mutter bloody deeds,
And, groaning deep, the impetuous battle mix :
While the fair heifer, balmy-breathing near,
Stands kindling up their rage. The trembling steed,
With this hot impulse seized in every nerve,
Nor heeds the rein, nor hears the sounding thong ; 810
Blows are not felt ; but, tossing high his head,
And by the well-known joy to distant plains

793 the raging passion feels] receives the raging fire 1728-38.
796 ample sides] brawny back 1728-38.
800, 801 Originally (editions 1728-38)—
          For, wrapt in mad imagination, he
          Roars for the fight.
802 His] A 1728-38.   806 deep] vast 1728-38.   807
balmy-breathing near] redolent in view 1728-38.   810 thong]
whip 1728-38.   In all editions (1728-46) the line is obviously
misprinted—' Nor hears the rein, nor heeds the sounding whip
(thong)'.

Attracted strong, all wild he bursts away ;
O'er rocks, and woods, and craggy mountains flies ;
And, neighing, on the aerial summit takes
The exciting gale ; then, steep-descending, cleaves
The headlong torrents foaming down the hills,
Even where the madness of the straitened stream
Turns in black eddies round : such is the force
With which his frantic heart and sinews swell. 820
   Nor undelighted by the boundless Spring
Are the broad monsters of the foaming deep :
From the deep ooze and gelid cavern roused,
They flounce and tumble in unwieldy joy.
Dire were the strain and dissonant to sing
The cruel raptures of the savage kind :
How, by this flame their native wrath sublimed,
They roam, amid the fury of their heart,
The far-resounding waste in fiercer bands,
And growl their horrid loves.   But this the theme 830
I sing enraptured to the British fair
Forbids, and leads me to the mountain-brow
Where sits the shepherd on the grassy turf,
Inhaling healthful the descending sun.
Around him feeds his many-bleating flock,
Of various cadence ; and his sportive lambs,
This way and that convolved in friskful glee,
Their frolics play.   And now the sprightly race
Invites them forth ; when swift, the signal given,

816 exciting] informing 1728-38; cleaves] stems 1728.
822, 823 Originally (1728)—
      Are the broad monsters of the deep : through all
      Their oozy caves and gelid kingdoms roused.
822 foaming] boiling 1730-44.   827-9 For the original
passage of seven lines see Note at end of the poem.   831
enraptured] transported 1728-38.
838 Originally (1728-38)—
      Their little frolics play.   And now the race.

They start away, and sweep the massy mound 840
That runs around the hill—the rampart once
Of iron war, in ancient barbarous times,
When disunited Britain ever bled,
Lost in eternal broil, ere yet she grew
To this deep-laid indissoluble state
Where wealth and commerce lift the golden head,
And o'er our labours liberty and law
Impartial watch, the wonder of a world!
What is this mighty breath, ye curious, say,
That in a powerful language, felt, not heard, 850
Instructs the fowls of heaven, and through their breast
These arts of love diffuses? What, but God?
Inspiring God! who, boundless spirit all
And unremitting energy, pervades,
Adjusts, sustains, and agitates the whole.
He ceaseless works alone, and yet alone
Seems not to work; with such perfection framed
Is this complex, stupendous scheme of things.
But, though concealed, to every purer eye
The informing Author in his works appears: 860
Chief, lovely Spring, in thee and thy soft scenes
The smiling God is seen—while water, earth,
And air attest his bounty, which exalts

840 massy] circly 1728.   846 the golden head] their
golden head 1728–38.   848 Impartial] Illustrious 1728–38.
850 Which in a language rather felt than heard 1728–38; That
in a language rather felt than heard 1744.   851 breast]
breasts 1728–38.   855 Adjusts, sustains] Subsists, adjusts 1728.
'857 with such perfection] So exquisitely 1728.   858 Stupendous scheme] amazing scene 1728; amazing scheme 1730–38
860 works] work 1730–38.

861-6 In place of these six lines the earlier editions (1728–38)
give a passage of twenty-one lines, for which the curious reader
is referred to a Note at the end of the poem.
862 is seen] appears 1728–38.   863 exalts] instils 1728–38.

The brute-creation to this finer thought,
And annual melts their undesigning hearts
Profusely thus in tenderness and joy.
 Still let my song a nobler note assume,
And sing the infusive force of Spring on man ;
When heaven and earth, as if contending, vie
To raise his being and serene his soul.	870
Can he forbear to join the general smile
Of Nature ? Can fierce passions vex his breast,
While every gale is peace, and every grove
Is melody ? Hence ! from the bounteous walks
Of flowing Spring, ye sordid sons of earth,
Hard, and unfeeling of another's woe,
Or only lavish to yourselves—away !
But come, ye generous minds, in whose wide thought,
Of all his works, Creative Bounty burns
With warmest beam, and on your open front	880
And liberal eye sits, from his dark retreat
Inviting modest Want. Nor till invoked
Can restless Goodness wait ; your active searcn
Leaves no cold wintry corner unexplored ;
Like silent-working Heaven, surprising oft
The lonely heart with unexpected good.
For you the roving spirit of the wind
Blows Spring abroad ; for you the teeming clouds
Descend in gladsome plenty o'er the world ;
And the Sun sheds his kindest rays for you,	890
Ye flower of human race ! In these green days,

864 Into the brutes this temporary thought 1728-38.
871, 872 join the general smile, &c.] smile with Nature ? Can
The stormy passions in his bosom roll 1728-38.	873 minds]
breasts 1728-38.	879, 880 burns With warmest beam] most
Divinely burns 1728-38.	882, 883 till invoked Can restless
Goodness wait] only fair And easy of approach 1728-38.	889
gladsome] buxom 1728-38.	890 sheds] spreads 1728-38 ;
kindest rays] genial blaze 1728-38.

Reviving Sickness lifts her languid head ;
Life flows afresh ; and young-eyed Health exalts
The whole creation round. Contentment walks
The sunny glade, and feels an inward bliss
Spring o'er his mind, beyond the power of kings
To purchase. Pure Serenity apace
Induces thought, and contemplation still.
By swift degrees the love of nature works,
And warms the bosom ; till at last, sublimed   900
To rapture and enthusiastic heat,
We feel the present Deity, and taste
The joy of God to see a happy world !
   These are the sacred feelings of thy heart,
Thy heart informed by reason's purer ray,
O Lyttelton, the friend ! Thy passions thus
And meditations vary, as at large,
Courting the muse, through Hagley Park you stray—
Thy British Tempè ! There along the dale   909
With woods o'erhung, and shagged with mossy rocks
Whence on each hand the gushing waters play,
And down the rough cascade white-dashing fall
Or gleam in lengthened vista through the trees,
You silent steal ; or sit beneath the shade
Of solemn oaks, that tuft the swelling mounts
Thrown graceful round by Nature's careless hand,
And pensive listen to the various voice
Of rural peace—the herds, the flocks, the birds,

892 Reviving] Sad pining 1728-38.   896 power] pride
1728.   897 To purchase. Pure] E'er to bestow. 1728.   899
swift] small 1728-38.   900 sublimed] arrived 1728-38.

903 After this line in the earlier text (1728-38) came a
notable passage of twelve lines, which anticipates something of
the teaching of Wordsworth. For this dropped passage see Note
at the end of the poem.

904-62 were first inserted in the edition of 1744.

905 purer] purest 1744.

The hollow-whispering breeze, the plaint of rills,
That, purling down amid the twisted roots   920
Which creep around, their dewy murmurs shake
On the soothed ear. From these abstracted oft,
You wander through the philosophic world ;
Where in bright train continual wonders rise
Or to the curious or the pious eye.
And oft, conducted by historic truth,
You tread the long extent of backward time,
Planning with warm benevolence of mind
And honest zeal, unwarped by party-rage,
Britannia's weal,—how from the venal gulf   930
To raise her virtue and her arts revive.
Or, turning thence thy view, these graver thoughts
The muses charm—while, with sure taste refined,
You draw the inspiring breath of ancient song,
Till nobly rises emulous thy own.
Perhaps thy loved Lucinda shares thy walk,
With soul to thine attuned. Then Nature all
Wears to the lover's eye a look of love ;
And all the tumult of a guilty world,
Tost by ungenerous passions, sinks away.   940
The tender heart is animated peace ;
And, as it pours its copious treasures forth
In varied converse, softening every theme,
You, frequent pausing, turn, and from her eyes,
Where meekened sense and amiable grace
And lively sweetness dwell, enraptured drink
That nameless spirit of ethereal joy,
Inimitable happiness ! which love
Alone bestows, and on a favoured few.
Meantime you gain the height, from whose fair brow
The bursting prospect spreads immense around ; 951
And, snatched o'er hill and dale, and wood and lawn,
And verdant field, and darkening heath between,

And villages embosomed soft in trees,
And spiry towns by surging columns marked
Of household smoke, your eye excursive roams—
Wide-stretching from the Hall in whose kind haunt
The hospitable Genius lingers still,
To where the broken landscape, by degrees
Ascending, roughens into rigid hills   960
O'er which the Cambrian mountains, like far clouds
That skirt the blue horizon, dusky rise.
Flushed by the spirit of the genial year,
Now from the virgin's cheek a fresher bloom
Shoots less and less the live carnation round ;
Her lips blush deeper sweets ; she breathes of youth ;
The shining moisture swells into her eyes
In brighter flow ; her wishing bosom heaves
With palpitations wild ; kind tumults seize
Her veins, and all her yielding soul is love.   970
From the keen gaze her lover turns away,
Full of the dear ecstatic power, and sick
With sighing languishment.   Ah then, ye fair !
Be greatly cautious of your sliding hearts :
Dare not the infectious sigh ; the pleading look,
Downcast and low, in meek submission dressed,
But full of guile.   Let not the fervent tongue,
Prompt to deceive with adulation smooth,
Gain on your purposed will.   Nor in the bower
Where woodbines flaunt and roses shed a couch,
While evening draws her crimson curtains round,
Trust your soft minutes with betraying man.   982

955 surging] dusky 1744.   956 household] rising 1744.
958 lingers] harbours 1744.   960 rigid] ridgy 1744.   962
dusky] doubtful 1744.   963 Added edition 1744.   964
Now] Hence 1728-38.   975 look] eye 1728-38.   976 In
meek submission drest deject, and low 1728-38.   977 The
earlier text (1728-38) inserts ' tempting ' before ' guile ', and omits
' fervent ' before ' tongue '.   979 will] wills 1728-38.

And let the aspiring youth beware of love,
Of the smooth glance beware ; for 'tis too late,
When on his heart the torrent-softness pours.
Then wisdom prostrate lies, and fading fame
Dissolves in air away ; while the fond soul,
Wrapt in gay visions of unreal bliss,
Still paints the illusive form, the kindling grace,
The enticing smile, the modest-seeming eye,   990
Beneath whose beauteous beams, belying Heaven,
Lurk searchless cunning, cruelty, and death :
And still, false-warbling in his cheated ear,
Her siren voice enchanting draws him on
To guileful shores and meads of fatal joy.
　　Even present, in the very lap of love
Inglorious laid—while music flows around,
Perfumes, and oils, and wine, and wanton hours—
Amid the roses fierce repentance rears
Her snaky crest : a quick-returning pang   1000
Shoots through the conscious heart, where honour
　　still
And great design, against the oppressive load
Of luxury, by fits, impatient heave.
　　But absent, what fantastic woes, aroused,
Rage in each thought, by restless musing fed,
Chill the warm cheek, and blast the bloom of life !
Neglected fortune flies ; and, sliding swift,
Prone into ruin fall his scorned affairs.
'Tis nought but gloom around : the darkened sun

984 Of the smooth glance beware] And shun the enchanting
glance 1728.   986 Then interest sinks to dirt and distant
fame 1728.   988 Is wrapt in dreams of ecstasy and bliss
1728–38.   990 enticing . . modest seeming] alluring . . full
ethereal 1728.

991–1008 For the original text (1728), which was dropped in
1730 to make way for these lines, see Note at the end of the poem.
1000 pang] twinge 1730–38.

Loses his light. The rosy-bosomed Spring 1010
To weeping fancy pines ; and yon bright arch,
Contracted, bends into a dusky vault.
All Nature fades extinct ; and she alone
Heard, felt, and seen, possesses every thought,
Fills every sense, and pants in every vein.
Books are but formal dulness, tedious friends ;
And sad amid the social band he sits,
Lonely and unattentive. From the tongue
The unfinish'd period falls : while, borne away
On swelling thought, his wafted spirit flies 1020
To the vain bosom of his distant fair ;
And leaves the semblance of a lover, fixed
In melancholy site, with head declined,
And love-dejected eyes. Sudden he starts,
Shook from his tender trance, and restless runs
To glimmering shades and sympathetic glooms,
Where the dun umbrage o'er the falling stream
Romantic hangs ; there through the pensive dusk
Strays, in heart-thrilling meditation lost,
Indulging all to love—or on the bank 1030
Thrown, amid drooping lilies, swells the breeze
With sighs unceasing, and the brook with tears.
Thus in soft anguish he consumes the day,
Nor quits his deep retirement till the moon
Peeps through the chambers of the fleecy east,
Enlightened by degrees, and in her train
Leads on the gentle hours ; then forth he walks,
Beneath the trembling languish of her beam,
With softened soul, and woos the bird of eve
To mingle woes with his ; or, while the world 1040
And all the sons of care lie hushed in sleep,

1012 Of heaven low-bends into a dusky vault 1728-38.
1018 inattentive 1728-38.   1021 vain] dear 1728; distant]
absent 1728.   1038 beam] beams 1728-38.

Associates with the midnight shadows drear,
And, sighing to the lonely taper, pours
His idly-tortured heart into the page
Meant for the moving messenger of love,
Where rapture burns on rapture, every line
With rising frenzy fired. But if on bed
Delirious flung, sleep from his pillow flies.
All night he tosses, nor the balmy power
In any posture finds ; till the grey morn   1050
Lifts her pale lustre on the paler wretch,
Exanimate by love—and then perhaps
Exhausted nature sinks a while to rest,
Still interrupted by distracted dreams
That o'er the sick imagination rise
And in black colours paint the mimic scene.
Oft with the enchantress of his soul he talks ;
Sometimes in crowds distressed ; or, if retired
To secret-winding flower-enwoven bowers,
Far from the dull impertinence of man,   1060
Just as he, credulous, his endless cares
Begins to lose in blind oblivious love,
Snatched from her yielded hand, he knows not how,
Through forests huge, and long untravelled heaths

1044 idly] sweetly 1728.   1046, 1047 Where rapture . .
frenzy fired.] Instead of this short passage, the earlier editions
(1728, 1729) give—

> But ah ! how faint, how meaningless and poor
> To what his passion swells ! which bursts the bounds
> Of every eloquence, and asks for looks,
> Where fondness flows on fondness, love on love,
> Entwisting beams with hers, and speaking more
> Than ever charmed ecstatic poet sighed
> To listening beauty, bright with conscious smiles
> And graceful vanity.

1061 credulous, his endless] kneeling, all his former 1728 ;
credulous, his thousand 1730-38.
1062 blind] vast 1728.   1063 yielded] yielding 1730-38.

With desolation brown, he wanders waste,
In night and tempest wrapt ; or shrinks aghast
Back from the bending precipice ; or wades
The turbid stream below, and strives to reach
The farther shore where, succourless and sad,
She with extended arms his aid implores,   1070
But strives in vain : borne by the outrageous flood
To distance down, he rides the ridgy wave,
Or whelmed beneath the boiling eddy sinks.
  These are the charming agonies of love,
Whose misery delights. But through the heart
Should jealousy its venom once diffuse,
'Tis then delightful misery no more,
But agony unmixed, incessant gall,
Corroding every thought, and blasting all
Love's Paradise. Ye fairy prospects, then,   1080
Ye bed of roses and ye bowers of joy,
Farewell ! Ye gleamings of departed peace,
Shine out your last ! The yellow-tinging plague
Internal vision taints, and in a night
Of livid gloom imagination wraps.
Ah then ! instead of love-enlivened cheeks,
Of sunny features, and of ardent eyes
With flowing rapture bright, dark looks succeed,
Suffused, and glaring with untender fire,
A clouded aspect, and a burning cheek   1090
Where the whole poisoned soul malignant sits,

1070 His dearer life extends her beckoning arms 1728 ; Wild
as a Bacchanal she spreads her arms 1730-38.   1073 The three
following lines were omitted from the original text in 1744—
        Then a weak, wailing, lamentable cry
        Is heard, and all in tears he wakes, again
        To tread the circle of revolving woe.
  1078 gall] rage 1728-38.   1080 The Paradise of Love 1728;
the line thus consisting of six feet.   1082 departed] departing
1728-44.   1086 Ah] Ay 1728-38.   1088 rapture] raptures
1730-38.

And frightens love away. Ten thousand fears
Invented wild, ten thousand frantic views
Of horrid rivals hanging on the charms
For which he melts in fondness, eat him up
With fervent anguish and consuming rage.
In vain reproaches lend their idle aid,
Deceitful pride, and resolution frail,
Giving false peace a moment. Fancy pours
Afresh her beauties on his busy thought,   1100
Her first endearments twining round the soul
With all the witchcraft of ensnaring love.
Straight the fierce storm involves his mind anew,
Flames through the nerves, and boils along the veins ;
While anxious doubt distracts the tortured heart :
For even the sad assurance of his fears
Were peace to what he feels. Thus the warm youth,
Whom love deludes into his thorny wilds
Through flowery-tempting paths, or leads a life
Of fevered rapture or of cruel care—   1110
His brightest aims extinguished all, and all
His lively moments running down to waste.
    But happy they ! the happiest of their kind !
Whom gentler stars unite, and in one fate
Their hearts, their fortunes, and their beings blend.
'Tis not the coarser tie of human laws,
Unnatural oft, and foreign to the mind,
That binds their peace, but harmony itself,
Attuning all their passions into love ;
Where friendship full-exerts her softest power,   1120
Perfect esteem enlivened by desire
Ineffable and sympathy of soul,
Thought meeting thought, and will preventing will,

1096 rage] pine 1728–38.   1099 Giving a moment's ease.
Reflection pours 1728–38.   1107 peace] heaven 1728.   1120
her] his 1728–38.

With boundless confidence : for nought but love
Can answer love, and render bliss secure.
Let him, ungenerous, who, alone intent
To bless himself, from sordid parents buys
The loathing virgin, in eternal care
Well-merited consume his nights and days ;
Let barbarous nations, whose inhuman love   1130
Is wild desire, fierce as the suns they feel ;
Let eastern tyrants from the light of heaven
Seclude their bosom-slaves, meanly possessed
Of a mere lifeless, violated form :
While those whom love cements in holy faith
And equal transport free as nature live,
Disdaining fear. What is the world to them,
Its pomp, its pleasure, and its nonsense all,
Who in each other clasp whatever fair
High fancy forms, and lavish hearts can wish ? 1140
Something than beauty dearer, should they look
Or on the mind or mind-illumined face ;
Truth, goodness, honour, harmony, and love,
The richest bounty of indulgent Heaven !
Meantime a smiling offspring rises round,
And mingles both their graces. By degrees
The human blossom blows ; and every day,
Soft as it rolls along, shows some new charm,
The father's lustre and the mother's bloom.
Then infant reason grows apace, and calls   1150
For the kind hand of an assiduous care.
Delightful task ! to rear the tender thought,
To teach the young idea how to shoot,
To pour the fresh instruction o'er the mind,
To breathe the enlivening spirit, and to fix
The generous purpose in the glowing breast.

1137 What is] for what's 1728-38.   1155 enlivening] inspiring 1728-38; fix] plant 1728-38.

Oh, speak the joy ! ye, whom the sudden tear
Surprises often, while you look around,
And nothing strikes your eye but sights of bliss,
All various Nature pressing on the heart—   1160
An elegant sufficiency, content,
Retirement, rural quiet, friendship, books,
Ease and alternate labour, useful life,
Progressive virtue, and approving Heaven !
These are the matchless joys of virtuous love ;
And thus their moments fly. The Seasons thus,
As ceaseless round a jarring world they roll,
Still find them happy ; and consenting Spring
Sheds her own rosy garland on their heads :
Till evening comes at last, serene and mild ;   1170
When after the long vernal day of life,
Enamoured more, as more remembrance swells
With many a proof of recollected love,
Together down they sink in social sleep ;
Together freed, their gentle spirits fly
To scenes where love and bliss immortal reign.

1157 ye] you 1728-38.   1161-5 Instead of these lines, which
first appeared in edition 1744, the first text (1728-38) gives--
          Obedient fortune and approving Heaven.
          These are the blessings of diviner love.
1169 heads] head 1728-38.   1170 serene and mild] cool,
gentle, calm 1728-38.   1172 as more remembrance swells] as
soul approaches soul 1728-38.   1173 Added in 1744.   1175,
1176 These concluding lines were added in 1744.

NOTES TO SPRING

There is no Argument prefixed to the earlier editions. But
the following interesting table of Contents appears in the second
edition (1729) :—

THE CONTENTS.

The subject—Spring. Described as a personage descending
on Earth.

Address to Lady Hartford.

Winter described as a personage resigning the dominion of the year.

Spring, yet unconfirmed.

The sun in Taurus fixes the Spring quarter.

First effects of the Spring, in softening Nature.

Plowing.

Sowing and Harrowing.

The praise of Agriculture.

Particularly applied to Britons.

Effects of the Spring in colouring the fields and unfolding the leaves.

The country in blossom.

A blight.

A philosophical account of insects producing the blight.

A Spring-shower.

The sun breaking out in the evening after the rain.

The Rainbow.

Herbs produced—the food of man in the first ages of the world.

Then, the Golden Age.

As described by the poets.

The degeneracy of mankind from that state.

On this, the Deluge and effects thereof, particularly in shortening the life of man.

Hence, a vegetable diet recommended.

The cruelty of feeding on animals.

Flowers in prospect : The difficulty of describing that delicate part of the Season.

A wildflower-piece.

A gardenflower-piece.

An apostrophe to the Supreme Being as the soul of vegetation.

Influence of the Spring on birds ; and first, of their singing.

Their courtship.

Building their nests.

Brooding, and care of their young.

Arts to secure them.

Against confining them in cages, and particularly the nightingale : her lamentation for her young.

Teaching their young to fly.

The eagle trying his at the sun.

A piece of household-fowl.

Influence of the Spring on other animals, the bull, horse, &c.

A landskip of the shepherd tending his flock with lambs frisking around him ; and a transition in praise of our present happy Constitution.

This various instinct in brutes ascribed to the continual and unbounded energy of Divine Providence.

Influence of the Spring on man, inspiring a universal benevolence, the love of mankind, and of nature.

Accounted for from that general harmony which then attunes the world.

Effects of the Spring in woman, with a caution to the fair sex.

Hence a dissuasive from the feverish, extravagant, and unchastised passion of love, in an account of its false raptures, pangs, and jealousies.

The whole concludes with the happiness of a pure mutual love, founded on friendship, conducted with honour, and confirmed by children.

LINE 5. The Countess of Hertford was a woman of some poetical taste, as shown by her own verses and by her patronage of poets. Horace Walpole accredited her with ' as much taste for the writings of others as modesty about her own '—though Johnson speaks rather contemptuously of her 'poetical operations'. It was her habit, he says, ' to invite every summer some poet into the country to hear her verses and assist her studies ; ' and he goes on to relate that when the invitation came to Thomson, in 1727, the poet disappointed her expectations by finding more delight in carousing with the Earl than in poetizing with the Countess, and therefore never received another invitation. It is extremely probable, however, that Thomson wrote part of *Spring* at Marlborough Castle, in Wiltshire, the seat of the Earl of Hertford ; and it is certain that as a poet he retained the respect and regard of the Countess as long as he lived. In 1748 we find her generously recommending to one of her friends the poem of that year—' Mr. Thomson's *Castle of Indolence.*' She died, Duchess of Somerset, in 1754.

108. Augusta ; London—so designated from the time of Constantine, early in the fourth century.

271. Here followed, in all editions from the first (in 1728) to that of 1738, the following passage of 28 ll. (withdrawn in 1744) : —

> This to the Poets gave the Golden Age ;
> When, as they sung in allegoric phrase,
> The sailor-pine had not the nations yet
> In commerce mixed ; for every country teemed
> With every thing. Spontaneous harvests waved
> Still in a sea of yellow plenty round.
> The forest was the vineyard, where, untaught
> To climb, unpruned and wild, the juicy grape

Burst into floods of wine. The knotted oak
Shook from his boughs the long, transparent streams
Of honey, creeping through the matted grass.
The uncultivated thorn a ruddy shower
Of fruitage shed on such as sat below
In blooming ease and from brown labour free,
Save what the copious gathering grateful gave.
The rivers foamed with nectar ; or diffuse,
Silent and soft, the milky maze devolved.
Nor had the spongy full-expanded fleece
Yet drunk the Tyrian dye. The stately ram
Shone through the mead in native purple clad,
Or milder saffron ; and the dancing lamb
The vivid crimson to the sun disclosed.
Nothing had power to hurt ; the savage soul,
Yet untransfused into the tyger's heart,
Burned not his bowels, nor his gamesome paw
Drove on the fleecy partners of his play :
While from the flowery brake the serpent rolled
His fairer spires, and played his pointless tongue.

In the second of these lines, for ' allegoric ', which is given in
the earlier editions (beginning in 1728), the editions 1730-38
substitute ' elevated '.

340. 'Ravine.' This form of 'rapine' (a Middle English
form) occurs in all editions, from 1728 to 1746.

483-7. These lines were introduced into the poem in 1744.
Amanda was a Miss Elizabeth Young, one of the daughters of
Captain Gilbert Young, a gentleman belonging to Dumfriesshire.
The sincerity and constancy of Thomson's affection for Miss
Young, from 1736 to 1744, are evidenced in various ways—by
contemporary report, his own correspondence and verse, and
certain lyrics which appear among his miscellaneous poems.
Mrs. Young 'constantly opposed his pretensions to her daughter ',
says Ramsay of Ochtertyre, ' saying to her one day "What!
would you marry Thomson ? He will make ballads and you will
sing them " '—from which one may infer that the poet was not
in a pecuniary position to maintain a wife. Amanda became
the wife of Admiral Campbell. We have some glimpse of her
appearance as she showed to her lover in these lines of his :—

O thou, whose tender, serious eyes
Expressive speak the mind I love,
The gentle azure of the skies,
The pensive shadows of the grove ;

as well as in the passage in *Spring* l. 483.

755-65. The original text which remained in the earlier editions (1728-38) was as follows :—

> High from the summit of a craggy cliff,
> Hung o'er the green sea grudging at its base,
> The royal eagle draws his young, resolved
> To try them at the sun. Strong-pounced, and bright
> As burnished day, they up the blue sky wind,
> Leaving dull sight below, and with fixed gaze
> Drink in their native noon : the father-king
> Claps his glad pinions, and approves the birth.

The alteration was made for edition 1744.

827-9. This short passage is a condensation of the original text of seven lines which stood as follows from 1728 to 1738 :—

> How the red lioness, her whelps forgot
> Amid the thoughtless fury of her heart ;
> The lank rapacious wolf ; the unshapely bear ;
> The spotted tyger, fellest of the fell ;
> And all the terrors of the Libyan (Lybian) swain,
> By this new flame their native wrath sublimed,
> Roam the surrounding waste in fiercer bands, &c.

861-6. Instead of these six lines the earlier editions (1728-38) give the following :—

> His grandeur in the heavens : the sun and moon,
> Whether that fires the day, or, falling, this
> Pours out a lucid softness o'er the night,
> Are but a beam from him. The glittering stars,
> By the deep ear of meditation heard,
> Still in their midnight watches sing of him.
> He nods a calm. The tempest blows his wrath,
> Roots up the forest, and o'erturns the main.
> The thunder is his voice, and the red flash
> His speedy sword of justice. At his touch
> The mountains flame. He takes the solid earth
> And rocks the nations. Nor in these alone,
> In every common instance God is seen ;
> And to the man, who casts his mental eye
> Abroad, unnoticed wonders rise. But chief
> In thee, boon Spring, and in thy softer scenes
> The smiling God appears ; while water, earth,
> And air attest his bounty, which instils
> Into the brutes this temporary thought, &c. (*two lines*).

903. This line was followed in the original text (1728-38) by the following passage of twelve lines, dropped in 1744 :—

'Tis harmony, that world-attuning power
By which all beings are adjusted, each
To all around, impelling and impelled
In endless circulation, that inspires
This universal smile.   Thus the glad skies,
The wide-rejoicing earth, the woods, the streams
With every life they hold, down to the flower
That paints the lowly vale, or insect-wing
Waved o'er the shepherd's slumber, touch the mind,
To nature tuned, with a light-flying hand
Invisible, quick-urging through the nerves
The glittering spirits in a flood of day.

In the first of these lines the first and second editions (1728
and 1729 respectively) give ' world-embracing ' for ' world-
attuning '—the latter being the reading from 1730 to 1738.

906. George, eldest son of Sir Thomas Lyttelton, of Hagley
Park, in Worcestershire.   Born in 1709, died 1773.   He wrote
Dialogues of the Dead, &c.   As a politician he opposed the policy
of Walpole, and in 1744 became one of the lords of the Treasury.
Previously he had been secretary to the Prince of Wales.   In
1755 he was Chancellor of the Exchequer, and was raised to the
peerage in 1757.   Thomson's first visit to Hagley Park was in
1743. ' Lucinda,' l. 936, refers to Mrs. Lyttelton (Lucy For-
tescue), whose death was lamented by her husband in a monody,
the tenderest and most touching of his verses.   He was a true
friend to Thomson in many ways.   In the preparation of a new
edition of *The Seasons* for 1744 the poet was indebted to him
for some suggestions.

991-1008. The original text (editions 1728, 1729) was as
follows :—

Effusing heaven ; and listens ardent still
To the small voice, where harmony and wit,
A modest, melting, mingled sweetness flow.
No sooner is the fair idea formed,
And contemplation fixes on the theme,
Than from his own creation wild he flies,
Sick of a shadow.   Absence comes apace,
And shoots his every pang into his breast.
'Tis nought, &c.

SUMMER

[Inscribed to the Right Honourable Mr. Dodington. First published in 1727 (1,146 ll.); last edition in author's lifetime published in 1746 (1,805 ll.).]

THE ARGUMENT

THE subject proposed. Invocation. Address to Mr. Dodington. An introductory reflection on the motion of the heavenly bodies ; whence the succession of the Seasons. As the face of nature in this season is almost uniform, the progress of the poem is a description of a Summer's day. *The dawn.* Sun-rising. Hymn to the sun. Forenoon. Summer insects described. *Hay-making. Sheep-shearing.* Noonday. A woodland retreat. Group of herds and flocks. A solemn grove : how it affects a contemplative mind. *A cataract, and rude scene. View of Summer in the torrid zone.* Storm of thunder and lightning. A tale. The storm over. A serene afternoon. Bathing. *Hour of walking.* Transition to the prospect of a rich, well-cultivated country ; which introduces a panegyric on Great Britain. Sunset. Evening. *Night. Summer meteors. A comet.* The whole concluding with the praise of philosophy.*

* The above is substantially the Argument of the poem in the first collected edition of *The Seasons* (1730). The notes in italics were added in 1744—all except ' A comet ', which was added in 1746. In the Argument for 1730, for ' Sun-rising ', appears ' A view of the sun rising ' ; for ' Hay-making ', appears ' Rural Prospects ' ; for ' View of Summer in the Torrid Zone ', appears ' A Digression on Foreign Summers ' ; and the note ' Rural Prospects ', of 1730, is withdrawn in 1744, as is also the note ' The Morning '—superseded by ' The Dawn '. For ' Group of herds and flocks', the 1730 edition gives 'A Group of Flocks and Herds '. The order in which the notes of the Argument come in 1730 differs considerably from the order in which they are presented above—that is, from their order in edd. 1744 and 1746.

FROM brightening fields of ether fair-disclosed,
Child of the sun, refulgent Summer comes
In pride of youth, and felt through nature's
    depth :
He comes, attended by the sultry hours
And ever-fanning breezes on his way ;
While from his ardent look the turning Spring
Averts her blushful face, and earth and skies
All-smiling to his hot dominion leaves.
  Hence let me haste into the mid-wood shade,
Where scarce a sunbeam wanders through the
    gloom,   10
And on the dark-green grass, beside the brink
Of haunted stream that by the roots of oak
Rolls o'er the rocky channel, lie at large
And sing the glories of the circling year.
  Come, Inspiration ! from thy hermit-seat,
By mortal seldom found : may fancy dare,
From thy fixed serious eye and raptured glance
Shot on surrounding Heaven, to steal one look
Creative of the poet, every power
Exalting to an ecstasy of soul.   20
  And thou, my youthful Muse's early friend,
In whom the human graces all unite—
Pure light of mind and tenderness of heart,
Genius and wisdom, the gay social sense
By decency chastised, goodness and wit

  1, 2 From southern climes, where unremitting day
      Burns overhead, illustrious Summer comes—
is the reading of the first ed. (1727).
    1 brightening] yonder 1730–38.   2 refulgent] illustrious
1727–38.   12 oak] oaks 1727.   16 fancy dare] I presume
1727.   17 eye] muse 1727–38 ; glance] eye 1730–38.   21–31
These lines are not found in the first ed. (1727). They first
appear in 1730.   21 my youthful Muse's early] the Muse's
honour and her 1730–38.

In seldom-meeting harmony combined,
Unblemished honour, and an active zeal
For Britain's glory, liberty, and man :
O Dodington ! attend my rural song,
Stoop to my theme, inspirit every line,   30
And teach me to deserve thy just applause.

With what an awful world-revolving power
Were first the unwieldy planets launched along
The illimitable void !—thus to remain,
Amid the flux of many thousand years
That oft has swept the toiling race of men,
And all their laboured monuments away,
Firm, unremitting, matchless in their course ;
To the kind-tempered change of night and day,
And of the seasons ever stealing round,   40
Minutely faithful : such the all-perfect Hand
That poised, impels, and rules the steady whole !
When now no more the alternate Twins are fired,
And Cancer reddens with the solar blaze,
Short is the doubtful empire of the night ;
And soon, observant of approaching day,
The meek-eyed morn appears, mother of dews,
At first faint-gleaming in the dappled east ;

31 just] best 1730–38.   32 an awful] a perfect 1727–38.
36 toiling] busy 1727–38.   38 Firm, unremitting] Unresisting,
changeless 1727–38.
   39–42 Instead of these lines, the first ed. (1727) gives—
      To day and night, and (with 1730–38) the delightful round
      Of seasons faithful ; not eccentric once :
      So poised and perfect is the vast machine !
The change was made in 1744, except that ' all ' was omitted
from l. 41.
   45 doubtful] uncertain 1727.   46 Edd. 1730–38 insert ' th''
before ' approaching '.   48 Mildly elucent in the streaky
east 1727. *The change was made in* 1730.

Till far o'er ether spreads the widening glow,
And, from before the lustre of her face,   50
White break the clouds away. With quickened
    step,
Brown night retires. Young day pours in apace,
And opens all the lawny prospect wide.
The dripping rock, the mountain's misty top
Swell on the sight and brighten with the dawn.
Blue through the dusk the smoking currents
    shine ;
And from the bladed field the fearful hare
Limps awkward ; while along the forest glade
The wild deer trip, and often turning gaze
At early passenger. Music awakes,   60
The native voice of undissembled joy ;
And thick around the woodland hymns arise.
Roused by the cock, the soon-clad shepherd
    leaves
His mossy cottage, where with peace he dwells,
And from the crowded fold in order drives
His flock to taste the verdure of the morn.
    Falsely luxurious, will not man awake,
And, springing from the bed of sloth, enjoy
The cool, the fragrant, and the silent hour,
To meditation due and sacred song ?   70
For is there aught in sleep can charm the wise ?
To lie in dead oblivion, losing half
The fleeting moments of too short a life—
Total extinction of the enlightened soul !

49 So in 1744. The line, added in 1730, reads—
        Till far o'er ether shoots the trembling glow.
    51 quickened] tardy 1727, 1730–38.   55 sight] eye 1727,
1730–38.   61 undissembling 1727.   68 starting 1727–38.
71 For] And 1727–38.   72 losing half] lost to all 1727.   73
Our natures boast of noble and divine 1727.

Or else, to feverish vanity alive,
Wildered, and tossing through distempered dreams !
Who would in such a gloomy state remain
Longer than nature craves ; when every muse
And every blooming pleasure wait without
To bless the wildly-devious morning walk ?   80
　But yonder comes the powerful king of day
Rejoicing in the east.　The lessening cloud,
The kindling azure, and the mountain's brow
Illumed with fluid gold, his near approach
Betoken glad.　Lo ! now, apparent all,
Aslant the dew-bright earth and coloured air,
He looks in boundless majesty abroad,
And sheds the shining day, that burnished plays
On rocks, and hills, and towers, and wandering
　　streams
High-gleaming from afar.　Prime cheerer, Light ! 90
Of all material beings first and best !
Efflux divine !　Nature's resplendent robe,
Without whose vesting beauty all were wrapt
In unessential gloom ;　and thou, O Sun !
Soul of surrounding worlds ! in whom best seen
Shines out thy Maker ! may I sing of thee ?
　'Tis by thy secret, strong, attractive force,
As with a chain indissoluble bound,
Thy system rolls entire—from the far bourne
Of utmost Saturn, wheeling wide his round   100

8 3 brow] brim 1727-38.　　8 4 Illumed] Tipt ; fluid] ethereal
1727-38.　　8 5 Lo !] And 1727-38.　　9 4 O] red 1727-38.
9 5, 9 6 In whose wide circle worlds of radiance lie, Exhaustless
Brightness ! may I sing of thee ! 1727-38.
　9 6 Following this line came in the first edd. (1727-38) a passage of five lines, which was dropped in 1744.　The reader will
find it in a Note at the end of the poem.
　1 0 0-1 0 3 For these four lines the first ed. (1727) and subsequent edd. (1730-38) give—

Of thirty years, to Mercury, whose disk
Can scarce be caught by philosophic eye,
Lost in the near effulgence of thy blaze.
  Informer of the planetary train !
Without whose quickening glance their cumbrous orbs
Were brute unlovely mass, inert and dead,
And not, as now, the green abodes of life !
How many forms of being wait on thee,
Inhaling spirit, from the unfettered mind,
By thee sublimed, down to the daily race,   110
The mixing myriads of thy setting beam !
  The vegetable world is also thine,
Parent of Seasons ! who the pomp precede
That waits thy throne, as through thy vast domain,
Annual, along the bright ecliptic road
In world-rejoicing state it moves sublime.
Meantime the expecting nations, circled gay
With all the various tribes of foodful earth,
Implore thy bounty, or send grateful up   119
A common hymn : while, round thy beaming car,
High-seen, the Seasons lead, in sprightly dance
Harmonious knit, the rosy-fingered hours,
The zephyrs floating loose, the timely rains,
Of bloom ethereal the light-footed dews,
And, softened into joy, the surly storms.
These, in successive turn, with lavish hand

Of slow-paced Saturn to the scarce-seen disk
Of Mercury lost in excessive blaze.
The change was made in 1744.
  105, 106 Without whose vital and effectual glance They'd be
but (They would be) brute, uncomfortable mass 1727–38.
  109 spirit] gladness 1727–38.   110 down to the daily] to
that day-living 1727–38.   111 setting] evening 1727.
  113–135 The original text differed from this. It will be found
(with the alterations and additions made in 1730) in a Note at
the end of the poem.

Shower every beauty, every fragrance shower,
Herbs, flowers, and fruits ; till, kindling at thy touch,
From land to land is flushed the vernal year.
　　Nor to the surface of enlivened earth,　　　　130
Graceful with hills and dales, and leafy woods,
Her liberal tresses, is thy force confined ;
But, to the bowelled cavern darting deep,
The mineral kinds confess thy mighty power.
Effulgent hence the veiny marble shines ;
Hence labour draws his tools ; hence burnished war
Gleams on the day ; the nobler works of peace
Hence bless mankind ; and generous commerce binds
The round of nations in a golden chain.
　　The unfruitful rock itself, impregned by thee,
In dark retirement forms the lucid stone.　　　141
The lively diamond drinks thy purest rays,
Collected light compact ; that, polished bright,
And all its native lustre let abroad,
Dares, as it sparkles on the fair one's breast,
With vain ambition emulate her eyes.
At thee the ruby lights its deepening glow,
And with a waving radiance inward flames.
From thee the sapphire, solid ether, takes

136-9 These lines had no place in the first ed. (1727).　In
the ed. of 1730, when the addition was made, they read—
　　　Hence labour draws his tools ; hence waving war
　　　Flames on the day ; hence busy commerce binds
　　　The round of nations in a golden chain ;
　　　And hence the sculptured palace sumptuous shines
　　　With glittering silver and refulgent gold.
142 Not in the first edd. (1727-38) ; added in 1744.
145, 146 Instead of these two lines the first ed. (1727) gives
only—' Shines proudly on the bosoms of the Fair ! '　This
remained the reading till 1744.
147 its] his 1727-38.　　　　148 A bleeding radiance grateful
to the view 1727-38.　The change was made in 1744.

Its hue cerulean ; and, of evening tinct,   150
The purple-streaming amethyst is thine
With thy own smile the yellow topaz burns ;
Nor deeper verdure dyes the robe of Spring,
When first she gives it to the southern gale,
Than the green emerald shows. But, all combined,
Thick through the whitening opal play thy beams ;
Or, flying several from its surface, form
A trembling variance of revolving hues
As the site varies in the gazer's hand.
The very dead creation from thy touch   160
Assumes a mimic life. By thee refined,
In brighter mazes the relucent stream
Plays o'er the mead. The precipice abrupt,
Projecting horror on the blackened flood,
Softens at thy return. The desert joys
Wildly through all his melancholy bounds.
Rude ruins glitter ; and the briny deep,
Seen from some pointed promontory's top
Far to the blue horizon's utmost verge,
Restless reflects a floating gleam. But this,   170
And all the much-transported Muse can sing,
Are to thy beauty, dignity, and use
Unequal far, great delegated Source
Of light and life and grace and joy below !
How shall I then attempt to sing of Him
Who, Light Himself, in uncreated light
Invested deep, dwells awfully retired
From mortal eye or angel's purer ken ;
Whose single smile has, from the first of time,

150 Its] His 1727–38.   159 varies] changes 1727.   162
brisker measures 1727–38.   163 Frisks 1727–38.   169, 170
For these lines the original text from 1727 to 1738 gives—
          Reflects from every fluctuating wave
          A glance extensive as the day. But these.

Filled overflowing all those lamps of heaven   180
That beam for ever through the boundless sky :
But, should He hide his face, the astonished sun
And all the extinguished stars would, loosening, reel
Wide from their spheres, and chaos come again.
  And yet, was every faltering tongue of man,
Almighty Father ! silent in thy praise,
Thy works themselves would raise a general voice ;
Even in the depth of solitary woods,
By human foot untrod, proclaim thy power ;
And to the quire celestial Thee resound,   190
The eternal cause, support, and end of all !
  To me be Nature's volume broad displayed ;
And to peruse its all-instructing page,
Or, haply catching inspiration thence,
Some easy passage, raptured, to translate,
My sole delight ; as through the falling glooms
Pensive I stray, or with the rising dawn
On fancy's eagle-wing excursive soar.

  Now, flaming up the heavens, the potent sun
Melts into limpid air the high-raised clouds   200
And morning fogs that hovered round the hills

181 boundless] immeasured 1727.   183 reel] start 1744.
186 Father] Poet 1727-38 ; Maker 1744.   187-91 The
original text (1727) reads—
      Thy matchless works in each exalted line,
      And all the full harmonic universe,
      Would, tuneful or expressive, Thee attest,
      The cause, the glory, and the end of all.
The edd. 1730-38 give the original text except that ' tuneful ' is
changed to ' vocal '.
  192 broad] wide 1727-38   193 its all-instructing] the broad
illumined 1727-38.   197 stray . . dawn] muse . . day 1727-
38.   199 Now . . potent] Fierce . . piercing 1727-38.
200 Melts into limpid] Attenuates to 1727.   201 fogs] mists
1727-44 ; round] o'er 1744.

In parti-coloured bands ; till wide unveiled
The face of nature shines from where earth seems,
Far-stretched around, to meet the bending sphere.
Half in a blush of clustering roses lost,
Dew-dropping Coolness to the shade retires ;
There, on the verdant turf or flowery bed,
By gelid founts and careless rills to muse ;
While tyrant Heat, dispreading through the sky
With rapid sway, his burning influence darts   210
On man and beast and herb and tepid stream.
Who can unpitying see the flowery race,
Shed by the morn, their new-flushed bloom resign
Before the parching beam ? So fade the fair,
When fevers revel through their azure veins.
But one, the lofty follower of the sun,
Sad when he sets, shuts up her yellow leaves,
Drooping all night ; and, when he warm returns,
Points her enamoured bosom to his ray.
Home from his morning task the swain retreats,
His flock before him stepping to the fold ;   221
While the full-uddered mother lows around
The cheerful cottage then expecting food,
The food of innocence and health ! The daw,
The rook, and magpie, to the grey-grown oaks
(That the calm village in their verdant arms,
Sheltering, embrace) direct their lazy flight ;
Where on the mingling boughs they sit embowered
All the hot noon, till cooler hours arise.
Faint underneath the household fowls convene ;   230
And, in a corner of the buzzing shade,

202 wide] all 1727–38.   207, 208 Added in 1744.   209
While] And 1727–38.   210 With rapid sway] By sharp
degrees 1727–38 ; darts] rains 1727–38.   216 Edd. 1727 and
1730–38 omit 'lofty' and after 'sun' insert 'they say'.   218
Drooping] Weeping 1727–38.   230 household] homely 1727–38.

The house-dog with the vacant greyhound lies
Out-stretched and sleepy. In his slumbers one
Attacks the nightly thief, and one exults
O'er hill and dale ; till, wakened by the wasp,
They starting snap. Nor shall the muse disdain
To let the little noisy summer-race
Live in her lay and flutter through her song :
Not mean though simple—to the sun allied,
From him they draw their animating fire.   240
Waked by his warmer ray, the reptile young
Come winged abroad, by the light air upborne,
Lighter, and full of soul. From every chink
And secret corner, where they slept away
The wintry storms, or rising from their tombs
To higher life, by myriads forth at once
Swarming they pour, of all the varied hues
Their beauty-beaming parent can disclose.
Ten thousand forms, ten thousand different tribes
People the blaze. To sunny waters some   250
By fatal instinct fly ; where on the pool
They sportive wheel, or, sailing down the stream,
Are snatched immediate by the quick-eyed trout
Or darting salmon. Through the green-wood glade
Some love to stray ; there lodged, amused, and fed
In the fresh leaf. Luxurious, others make

232 vacant] employless 1727–38.   236 starting] bootless
1727–38.   240 they draw their animating fire] their high
descent direct they draw 1727–38.   243 soul] life 1727–38.
245-8 The original text (1727–38) reads—
    The wintry glooms, by myriads all at once
    Swarming they pour, green, speckled, yellow, grey,
    Black, azure, brown, more than the assisted eye
    Of poring virtuoso can discern.
The change was made in 1744.
253 quick-eyed] springing 1727–38.   254 Or darting salmon]
Often beguiled. Some 1727–38.   255 Some love] Delight
1727–38.

The meads their choice, and visit every flower
And every latent herb : for the sweet task
To propagate their kinds, and where to wrap
In what soft beds their young, yet undisclosed,   260
Employs their tender care. Some to the house,
The fold, and dairy hungry bend their flight ;
Sip round the pail, or taste the curdling cheese :
Oft, inadvertent, from the milky stream
They meet their fate ; or, weltering in the bowl,
With powerless wings around them wrapt, expire.
But chief to heedless flies the window proves
A constant death ; where, gloomily retired,
The villain spider lives, cunning and fierce,
Mixture abhorred ! Amid a mangled heap   270
Of carcases in eager watch he sits,
O'erlooking all his waving snares around.
Near the dire cell the dreadless wanderer oft
Passes ; as oft the ruffian shows his front.
The prey at last ensnared, he dreadful darts
With rapid glide along the leaning line ;
And, fixing in the wretch his cruel fangs,
Strikes backward grimly pleased : the fluttering wing
And shriller sound declare extreme distress,
And ask the helping hospitable hand.   280
Resounds the living surface of the ground :
Nor undelightful is the ceaseless hum
To him who muses through the woods at noon,

258–61 The original text (1727–38) reads—
            But careful still
      To shun the mazes of the sounding bee
      As o'er the blooms he sweeps.
264 from the milky] by the boiling 1727–38.   265 They
meet their fate] They're (Are) pierced to death 1727–38.   272
O'er-looking] Surveying 1727.   273 Near the dire cell] Within
an inch 1727–38.   277 wretch] fly 1727–38.   281 Resounds]
Echoes 1727–38.   282 ceaseless hum] humming sound 1727.

Or drowsy shepherd as he lies reclined,
With half-shut eyes, beneath the floating shade
Of willows grey, close-crowding o'er the brook.
  Gradual from these what numerous kinds descend,
Evading even the microscopic eye !
Full Nature swarms with life ; one wondrous mass
Of animals, or atoms organized   290
Waiting the vital breath when Parent-Heaven
Shall bid his spirit blow. The hoary fen
In putrid streams emits the living cloud
Of pestilence. Through subterranean cells,
Where searching sunbeams scarce can find a way,
Earth animated heaves. The flowery leaf
Wants not its soft inhabitants. Secure
Within its winding citadel the stone
Holds multitudes. But chief the forest boughs,
That dance unnumbered to the playful breeze, 300
The downy orchard, and the melting pulp
Of mellow fruit the nameless nations feed
Of evanescent insects. Where the pool
Stands mantled o'er with green, invisible
Amid the floating verdure millions stray.
Each liquid too, whether it pierces, soothes,
Inflames, refreshes, or exalts the taste,
With various forms abounds. Nor is the stream
Of purest crystal, nor the lucid air,
Though one transparent vacancy it seems,   310
Void of their unseen people. These, concealed
By the kind art of forming Heaven, escape
The grosser eye of man : for, if the worlds
In worlds inclosed should on his senses burst,

287–317 This passage (with alterations) was transferred in
1744 from its original place in *Spring* (1727–38). See note to
l. 136 in *Spring*. The original form of the passage, before its
transference, will be found in a Note at the end of the poem.

From cates ambrosial and the nectared bowl
He would abhorrent turn ; and in dead night,
When Silence sleeps o'er all, be stunned with noise.
Let no presuming impious railer tax
Creative Wisdom, as if aught was formed
In vain, or not for admirable ends.   320
Shall little haughty Ignorance pronounce
His works unwise, of which the smallest part
Exceeds the narrow vision of her mind ?
As if upon a full-proportioned dome,
On swelling columns heaved, the pride of art '
A critic fly, whose feeble ray scarce spreads
An inch around, with blind presumption bold
Should dare to tax the structure of the whole.
And lives the man whose universal eye   329
Has swept at once the unbounded scheme of things,
Marked their dependence so and firm accord,
As with unfaltering accent to conclude
That this availeth nought ?   Has any seen
The mighty chain of beings, lessening down
From infinite perfection to the brink
Of dreary nothing, desolate abyss !
From which astonished thought recoiling turns ?
Till then, alone let zealous praise ascend

323 her] his 1727–38.   324-8 Originally (1727)—
     So on the concave of a sounding dome,
     On swelling columns heaved, the pride of Art,
     Wanders a critic fly : his feeble ray
     Extends an inch around, yet, blindly bold,
     He dares dislike the structure of the whole.
The text of edd. 1730–38 is exactly the same as the text of
1727, excepting only that the passage begins with ' Thus ' in
place of ' So '.
   337 Instead of this line the original text (1727–38) gives—
     Recoiling giddy thought : or with sharp glance,
     Such as remotely wafting spirits use,
     Surveyed (Beheld) the glories of the little world ?

And hymns of holy wonder to that Power
Whose wisdom shines as lovely on our minds   340
As on our smiling eyes his servant-sun.
   Thick in yon stream of light, a thousand ways,
Upward and downward, thwarting and convolved,
The quivering nations sport ; till, tempest-winged,
Fierce Winter sweeps them from the face of day.
Even so luxurious men, unheeding, pass
An idle summer life in fortune's shine,
A season's glitter ! Thus they flutter on
From toy to toy, from vanity to vice ;
Till, blown away by death, oblivion comes   350
Behind and strikes them from the book of life.

   Now swarms the village o'er the jovial mead—
The rustic youth, brown with meridian toil,
Healthful and strong ; full as the summer rose
Blown by prevailing suns, the ruddy maid,
Half naked, swelling on the sight, and all
Her kindled graces burning o'er her cheek.
Even stooping age is here ; and infant hands
Trail the long rake, or, with the fragrant load
O'ercharged, amid the kind oppression roll.   360
Wide flies the tedded grain ; all in a row

339 holy] heavenly 1727–38.   344 nations] Kingdoms 1727–38; till, tempest-winged] with tempest-wing 1727–38.   345 Fierce] Till 1727–38.   348 After ' A season's glitter ! ' the original text (1727–38) gives—

                 In soft-circling robes,
     Which the hard hand of Industry has wrought,
     The human insects glow, by Hunger fed,
     And cheered by toiling Thirst, they roll about.

349 toy, from] trifle 1730–38.

352–70 This description of hay-making did not appear in the first ed. (1727) : it will be found in edd. 1730–38, with a few variations, noted below.

355 ruddy] blooming 1730–38.   360 kind] soft 1730–38.

Advancing broad, or wheeling round the field,
They spread their breathing harvest to the sun,
That throws refreshful round a rural smell ;
Or, as they rake the green-appearing ground,
And drive the dusky wave along the mead,
The russet hay-cock rises thick behind
In order gay : while heard from dale to dale,
Waking the breeze, resounds the blended voice
Of happy labour, love, and social glee.   370
Or, rushing thence, in one diffusive band
They drive the troubled flocks, by many a dog
Compelled, to where the mazy-running brook
Forms a deep pool, this bank abrupt and high,
And that fair-spreading in a pebbled shore.
Urged to the giddy brink, much is the toil,
The clamour much of men and boys and dogs
Ere the soft, fearful people to the flood
Commit their woolly sides. And oft the swain,
On some impatient seizing, hurls them in :   380
Emboldened then, nor hesitating more,
Fast, fast they plunge amid the flashing wave,
And, panting, labour to the farther shore.
Repeated this, till deep the well-washed fleece
Has drunk the flood, and from his lively haunt
The trout is banished by the sordid stream.
Heavy and dripping, to the breezy brow
Slow move the harmless race ; where, as they spread
Their swelling treasures to the sunny ray,
Inly disturbed, and wondering what this wild   390
Outrageous tumult means, their loud complaints
The country fill ; and, tossed from rock to rock,

363 their breathing] the breathing 1744 ; the tawny 1730–38.
364 throws] casts 1730–38.   367 Rises the russet hay-cock
1730–38.   371–431 This long passage, descriptive of sheep-
shearing, was added in ed. 1744.   377 dogs 1746 ; dog 1744.

Incessant bleatings run around the hills.
At last, of snowy white the gathered flocks
Are in the wattled pen innumerous pressed,
Head above head ; and, ranged in lusty rows,
The shepherds sit, and whet the sounding shears.
The housewife waits to roll her fleecy stores,
With all her gay-drest maids attending round.
One, chief, in gracious dignity enthroned,　400
Shines o'er the rest, the pastoral queen, and rays
Her smiles sweet-beaming on her shepherd-king ;
While the glad circle round them yield their souls
To festive mirth, and wit that knows no gall.
Meantime, their joyous task goes on apace :
Some mingling stir the melted tar, and some,
Deep on the new-shorn vagrant's heaving side
To stamp his master's cipher ready stand ;
Others the unwilling wether drag along ;
And, glorying in his might, the sturdy boy　410
Holds by the twisted horns the indignant ram.
Behold where bound, and of its robe bereft
By needy man, that all-depending lord,
How meek, how patient, the mild creature lies !
What softness in its melancholy face,
What dumb complaining innocence appears !
Fear not, ye gentle tribes ! 'tis not the knife
Of horrid slaughter that is o'er you waved ;
No, 'tis the tender swain's well-guided shears,
Who having now, to pay his annual care,　420
Borrowed your fleece, to you a cumbrous load,
Will send you bounding to your hills again.
　A simple scene ! yet hence Britannia sees
Her solid grandeur rise : hence she commands
The exalted stores of every brighter clime,
The treasures of the sun without his rage :
Hence, fervent all with culture, toil, and arts,

Wide glows her land : her dreadful thunder hence
Rides o'er the waves sublime, and now, even now,
Impending hangs o'er Gallia's humbled coast ; 430
Hence rules the circling deep, and awes the world.

'Tis raging noon ; and, vertical, the sun
Darts on the head direct his forceful rays.
O'er heaven and earth, far as the ranging eye
Can sweep, a dazzling deluge reigns ; and all
From pole to pole is undistinguished blaze.
In vain the sight dejected to the ground
Stoops for relief ; thence hot ascending steams
And keen reflection pain. Deep to the root
Of vegetation parched, the cleaving fields 440
And slippery lawn an arid huo disclose,
Blast fancy's blooms, and wither even the soul.
Echo no more returns the cheerful sound
Of sharpening scythe : the mower, sinking, heaps
O'er him the humid hay, with flowers perfumed ;
And scarce a chirping grasshopper is heard

433 Originally (1727–38)—
Shoots through the expanding air a torrid gleam.
434 ranging] darted 1727–38. 435 sweep] pierce 1727–38.
437 Originally (1727–38)—
Down to the dusty earth the sight o'erpowered.
438 Edd. 1727–38 insert ' but ' before ' thence ' and omit
' hot '. The change was made in 1744. Edd. 1730–38 give
'streams '—a misprint for 'steams '.
439 After ' reflection pain the original text (1727–38) gives
the following lines, struck out or altered in 1744 :—
Burnt to the heart
Are the refreshless fields : their arid hue
Adds a new fever to the sickening soul :
And o'er their slippery surface wary treads
The foot of thirsty pilgrim, often dipt
In a cross rill presenting to his wish
A living draught : he feels before he drinks.
443 No more the woods return the sandy sound 1727 ; Echo no
more returns the sandy sound 1730–38. 445 humid] tedded 1727.

Through the dumb mead. Distressful nature pants.
The very streams look languid from afar,
Or, through the unsheltered glade, impatient seem
To hurl into the covert of the grove.   450
All-conquering heat, oh, intermit thy wrath !
And on my throbbing temples potent thus
Beam not so fierce ! Incessant still you flow,
And still another fervent flood succeeds,
Poured on the head profuse. In vain I sigh,
And restless turn, and look around for night :
Night is far off ; and hotter hours approach.
Thrice happy he, who on the sunless side
Of a romantic mountain, forest-crowned,
Beneath the whole collected shade reclines ;   460
Or in the gelid caverns, woodbine-wrought
And fresh bedewed with ever-spouting streams,
Sits coolly calm ; while all the world without,
Unsatisfied and sick, tosses in noon.
Emblem instructive of the virtuous man,
Who keeps his tempered mind serene and pure,
And every passion aptly harmonized
Amid a jarring world with vice inflamed.

447 the dumb] all the 1727.   447 After this line came in
ed. 1727—
        The desert singes ; and the stubborn rock,
        Split to the centre, sweats at every pore—
repeated with ' singes ' altered to ' reddens ', in edd. 1730–38 ;
and struck out in edd. 1744–46.
    449, 450 Originally (1727–38)—
        Or through the fervid glade impetuous hurl
        Into the shelter of the crackling grove.
    451 All-conquering] Prevailing 1727.   452 throbbing] aching
1727.   453 fierce] hard 1727–38.   455 sigh] groan 1727.
    457 After this line a passage of seven lines appeared in the
first ed. (1727), and with slight alterations was continued in
edd. 1730–38.   It is given (with the alterations) in a Note
at the end of the poem.   458 who] that 1744.   467 every
passion] all his passions 1727–38.

Welcome, ye shades ! ye bowery thickets, hail !
Ye lofty pines ! ye venerable oaks !   470
Ye ashes wild, resounding o'er the steep !
Delicious is your shelter to the soul
As to the hunted hart the sallying spring
Or stream full-flowing, that his swelling sides
Laves as he floats along the herbaged brink.
Cool through the nerves your pleasing comfort
    glides ;
The heart beats glad ; the fresh-expanded eye
And ear resume their watch ; the sinews knit ;
And life shoots swift through all the lightened
    limbs
Around the adjoining brook, that purls along 480
The vocal grove, now fretting o'er a rock,
Now scarcely moving through a reedy pool,
Now starting to a sudden stream, and now
Gently diffused into a limpid plain,
A various group the herds and flocks compose,
Rural confusion ! On the grassy bank
Some ruminating lie, while others stand
Half in the flood and, often bending, sip
The circling surface. In the middle droops
The strong laborious ox, of honest front,   490
Which incomposed he shakes ; and from his sides
The troublous insects lashes with his tail,
Returning still. Amid his subjects safe
Slumbers the monarch-swain, his careless arm
Thrown round his head on downy moss sustained ;

471 Ye] With 1727.   476 Cool] Cold 1727-38; comfort
glides] comforts glide 1727.   477 fresh-expanded eye] misty
eyes refulge 1727.   478 And ear] The ears 1727.   479 all
the lightened limbs] every active limb 1727 ; every lightened
limb 1730-38.   480 Around . . purls] All in . . shrills
1727-38.   492 troublous] busy 1727.

Here laid his scrip with wholesome viands filled,
There, listening every noise, his watchful dog.
    Light fly his slumbers, if perchance a flight
Of angry gad-flies fasten on the herd,
That startling scatters from the shallow brook   500
In search of lavish stream. Tossing the foam,
They scorn the keeper's voice, and scour the plain
Through all the bright severity of noon ;
While from their labouring breasts a hollow moan
Proceeding runs low-bellowing round the hills.
    Oft in this season too, the horse, provoked,
While his big sinews full of spirits swell,
Trembling with vigour, in the heat of blood
Springs the high fence, and, o'er the field effused,
Darts on the gloomy flood with steadfast eye   510
And heart estranged to fear : his nervous chest,
Luxuriant and erect, the seat of strength,
Bears down the opposing stream ; quenchless his
        thirst,
He takes the river at redoubled draughts,
And with wide nostrils, snorting, skims the wave.
    Still let me pierce into the midnight depth
Of yonder grove, of wildest largest growth,
That, forming high in air a woodland quire,
Nods o'er the mount beneath. At every step,
Solemn and slow the shadows blacker fall,   520
And all is awful listening gloom around.
    These are the haunts of meditation, these
The scenes where ancient bards the inspiring breath
Ecstatic felt, and, from this world retired,
Conversed with angels and immortal forms,

497 And there his sceptre-crook and watchful dog 1727-38.
499 gad-flies] hornets 1727-38.   518 That high embowering in the middle air 1727-38.   521 listening] silent
1727-38.

On gracious errands bent—to save the fall
Of virtue struggling on the brink of vice ;
In waking whispers and repeated dreams
To hint pure thought, and warn the favoured soul,
For future trials fated, to prepare ;   530
To prompt the poet, who devoted gives
His muse to better themes ; to soothe the pangs
Of dying worth, and from the patriot's breast
(Backward to mingle in detested war,
But foremost when engaged) to turn the death ;
And numberless such offices of love,
Daily and nightly, zealous to perform.
　Shook sudden from the bosom of the sky,
A thousand shapes or glide athwart the dusk
Or stalk majestic on. Deep-roused, I feel   540
A sacred terror, a severe delight,
Creep through my mortal frame ; and thus, methinks,
A voice, than human more, the abstracted ear
Of fancy strikes—' Be not of us afraid,
Poor kindred man ! thy fellow-creatures, we
From the same Parent-Power our beings drew,
The same our Lord and laws and great pursuit.
Once some of us, like thee, through stormy life
Toiled tempest-beaten ere we could attain
This holy calm, this harmony of mind,   550
Where purity and peace immingle charms.

526 gracious] heavenly 1727–38.   533 worth] saints 1727–
38.   538 sky] air 1727.   540 Deep-roused] harrowed
1727 ; Aroused 1730–38.   541 a severe] and severe 1727,
1744.   543, 544 In the first ed. (1727)—
　　Those hollow accents, floating on my ear,
　　Pronounce distinct ;
and in edd. 1730–38—
　　Those accents murmured in the abstracted ear
　　Pronounce distinct.
546 Parent] bounteous 1727.

D

Then fear not us ; but with responsive song,
Amid these dim recesses, undisturbed
By noisy folly and discordant vice,
Of Nature sing with us, and Nature's God.
Here frequent, at the visionary hour,
When musing midnight reigns or silent noon,
Angelic harps are in full concert heard,
And voices chaunting from the wood-crown'd hill,
The deepening dale, or inmost sylvan glade :   560
A privilege bestow'd by us alone
On contemplation, or the hallow'd ear
Of poet swelling to seraphic strain.'
  And art thou, Stanley, of that sacred band ?
Alas ! for us too soon ! Though raised above
The reach of human pain, above the flight
Of human joy, yet with a mingled ray
Of sadly pleased remembrance, must thou feel
A mother's love, a mother's tender woe—
Who seeks thee still in many a former scene,   570
Seeks thy fair form, thy lovely beaming eyes,
Thy pleasing converse, by gay lively sense
Inspired, where moral wisdom mildly shone
Without the toil of art, and virtue glowed
In all her smiles without forbidding pride.
But, O thou best of parents ! wipe thy tears ;

552 not us] us not 1730–38 ; responsive] commutual 1727.
  553 Amid] Oft in 1727–38.   556–61 Instead of these lines
the original text (1727–38) gives—
> And frequent at the middle waste of night,
> Or all day long, in deserts still, are heard,
> Now here, now there, now wheeling in mid-sky
> Around or underneath, aerial sounds
> Sent from angelic harps and voices joined—
> A happiness bestowed by us alone &c.

564–84 This address to the shade of Miss Stanley (a young
lady of Thomson's acquaintance, who died at the age of eighteen,
in 1738) first appeared in the ed. of 1744.

Or rather to parental Nature pay
The tears of grateful joy, who for a while
Lent thee this younger self, this opening bloom
Of thy enlightened mind and gentle worth.   580
Believe the muse—the wintry blast of death
Kills not the buds of virtue ; no, they spread
Beneath the heavenly beam of brighter suns
Through endless ages into higher powers.
　Thus up the mount, in airy vision rapt,
I stray, regardless whither ; till the sound
Of a near fall of water every sense
Wakes from the charm of thought : swift-shrinking
　　back,
I check my steps and view the broken scene.
　Smooth to the shelving brink a copious flood   590
Rolls fair and placid ; where, collected all
In one impetuous torrent, down the steep
It thundering shoots, and shakes the country round.
At first, an azure sheet, it rushes broad ;
Then, whitening by degrees as prone it falls,
And from the loud-resounding rocks below
Dashed in a cloud of foam, it sends aloft
A hoary mist and forms a ceaseless shower.
Nor can the tortured wave here find repose ;
But, raging still amid the shaggy rocks,   600
Now flashes o'er the scattered fragments, now

585 airy vision rapt] visionary muse 1727-38.   586 sound]
stun 1727-38.   589 check my steps] stand aghast 1727-38.
　590 shelving . . copious flood] giddy . . lucid stream 1727;
shaggy . . spreading flood 1730-38. This line was preceded in
the first ed. (1727) by the lines—
　　Like one who flows in joy, when all at once
　　Misfortune hurls him down the hill of life.
　591-606 The earlier edd.—both the ed. of 1727 and those of
1730-38—present something very different from this. See Note
at the end of the poem.

Aslant the hollow channel rapid darts ;
And, falling fast from gradual slope to slope,
With wild infracted course and lessened roar
It gains a safer bed, and steals at last
Along the mazes of the quiet vale.
Invited from the cliff, to whose dark brow
He clings, the steep-ascending eagle soars
With upward pinions through the flood of day,
And, giving full his bosom to the blaze,   610
Gains on the Sun ; while all the tuneful race,
Smit by afflictive noon, disordered droop
Deep in the thicket, or, from bower to bower
Responsive, force an interrupted strain.
The stock-dove only through the forest coos,
Mournfully hoarse ; oft ceasing from his plaint,
Short interval of weary woe ! again
The sad idea of his murdered mate,
Struck from his side by savage fowler's guile,
Across his fancy comes ; and then resounds   620
A louder song of sorrow through the grove.
Beside the dewy border let me sit,
All in the freshness of the humid air,

607 The following five lines introduced in the first ed. (1727)
the passage beginning here :—
  With the rough prospect tired I turn my eyes
  Where in long visto the soft-murmuring main
  Darts a green lustre trembling through the trees ;
  Or to yon silver-streaming threads of light,
  A showery beauty beaming through the boughs.
They appear in edd. 1730-38 also, but with the following alterations : for ' eyes ' in l. 1, ' gaze ' ; for ' visto ', ' vista ', ; and,
in the last line, for ' beauty ', ' radiance '. They were dropped
in 1744.
 607 cliff . . brow] rock . . cliff 1727-38. 609 flood of
day] attractive gleam 1727-38. 611 tuneful] feathery 1727-
38. 612 Smit by] Smote by 1727 ; Smote with 1730-38.
615 stock] wood 1727 ; through the forest] in the centre 1727.

There on that hollowed rock, grotesque and wild,
An ample chair moss-lined, and over head
By flowering umbrage shaded ; where the bee
Strays diligent, and with the extracted balm
Of fragrant woodbine loads his little thigh.
  Now, while I taste the sweetness of the shade,
While Nature lies around deep-lulled in noon,   630
Now come, bold fancy, spread a daring flight
And view the wonders of the torrid zone :
Climes unrelenting ! with whose rage compared,
Yon blaze is feeble and yon skies are cool.
  See how at once the bright effulgent sun,
Rising direct, swift chases from the sky
The short-lived twilight, and with ardent blaze
Looks gaily fierce o'er all the dazzling air !
He mounts his throne ; but kind before him sends,
Issuing from out the portals of the morn,   640
The general breeze to mitigate his fire
And breathe refreshment on a fainting world.
Great are the scenes, with dreadful beauty crowned
And barbarous wealth, that see, each circling year,
Returning suns and double seasons pass ;
Rocks rich in gems, and mountains big with mines,
That on the high equator ridgy rise,
Whence many a bursting stream auriferous plays ;
Majestic woods of every vigorous green,
Stage above stage high waving o'er the hills,   650
Or to the far horizon wide-diffused,
A boundless deep immensity of shade.

624 There, on that rock, by nature's chisel carved 1727–38.
626 flowering .. shaded, where] weaving .. hung, through which
1727.   627 balm] sweet 1727–38.   628 fragrant wood-
bine] honeysuckle 1727–38.   629–897 These lines appear for
the first time in ed. 1744, or in ed. 1746.   The later additions
are pointed out below.

Here lofty trees, to ancient song unknown,
The noble sons of potent heat and floods
Prone-rushing from the clouds, rear high to heaven
Their thorny stems, and broad around them throw
Meridian gloom. Here, in eternal prime,
Unnumbered fruits of keen delicious taste
And vital spirit drink, amid the cliffs   659
And burning sands that bank the shrubby vales,
Redoubled day, yet in their rugged coats
A friendly juice to cool its rage contain.
   Bear me, Pomona! to thy citron groves ;
To where the lemon and the piercing lime,
With the deep orange glowing through the green,
Their lighter glories blend. Lay me reclined
Beneath the spreading tamarind, that shakes,
Fanned by the breeze, its fever-cooling fruit.
Deep in the night the massy locust sheds   669
Quench my hot limbs ; or lead me through the maze,
Embowering endless, of the Indian fig ;
Or, thrown at gayer ease on some fair brow,
Let me behold, by breezy murmurs cooled,
Broad o'er my head the verdant cedar wave,
And high palmettos lift their graceful shade.
Oh, stretched amid these orchards of the sun,
Give me to drain the cocoa's milky bowl,
And from the palm to draw its freshening wine !
More bounteous far than all the frantic juice
Which Bacchus pours. Nor, on its slender twigs 680
Low-bending, be the full pomegranate scorned ;
Nor, creeping through the woods, the gelid race
Of berries. Oft in humble station dwells

669-75 These seven lines were added in 1746.   676 Oh] Or
1744.   677 Give me to] O let me 1744.   678 Added in
1746.

Unboastful worth, above fastidious pomp.
Witness, thou best Anana, thou the pride
Of vegetable life, beyond whate'er
The poets imaged in the golden age :
Quick let me strip thee of thy tufty coat,
Spread thy ambrosial stores, and feast with Jove!
  From these the prospect varies. Plains immense
Lie stretched below, interminable meads   691
And vast savannas, where the wandering eye,
Unfixt, is in a verdant ocean lost.
Another Flora there, of bolder hues
And richer sweets beyond our garden's pride,
Plays o'er the fields, and showers with sudden hand
Exuberant spring—for oft these valleys shift
Their green-embroidered robe to fiery brown,
And swift to green again, as scorching suns
Or streaming dews and torrent rains prevail.   700
Along these lonely regions, where, retired
From little scenes of art, great Nature dwells
In awful solitude, and naught is seen
But the wild herds that own no master's stall,
Prodigious rivers roll their fattening seas ;
On whose luxuriant herbage, half-concealed,
Like a fallen cedar, far diffused his train,
Cased in green scales, the crocodile extends.
The flood disparts : behold ! in plaited mail
Behemoth rears his head. Glanced from his side,
The darted steel in idle shivers flies :   711
He fearless walks the plain, or seeks the hills,
Where, as he crops his varied fare, the herds,
In widening circle round, forget their food
And at the harmless stranger wondering gaze.
  Peaceful beneath primeval trees that cast

688 tufty] spiny 1744.

Their ample shade o'er Niger's yellow stream,
And where the Ganges rolls his sacred wave,
Or mid the central depth of blackening woods,
High-raised in solemn theatre around,   720
Leans the huge elephant—wisest of brutes !
Oh, truly wise ! with gentle might endowed,
Though powerful not destructive ! Here he sees
Revolving ages sweep the changeful earth,
And empires rise and fall ; regardless he
Of what the never-resting race of men
Project : thrice happy, could he 'scape their guile
Who mine, from cruel avarice, his steps,
Or with his towery grandeur swell their state,
The pride of kings ! or else his strength pervert,   730
And bid him rage amid the mortal fray,
Astonished at the madness of mankind.
   Wide o'er the winding umbrage of the floods,
Like vivid blossoms glowing from afar,
Thick-swarm the brighter birds. For nature's hand,
That with a sportive vanity has decked
The plumy nations, there her gayest hues
Profusely pours. But, if she bids them shine
Arrayed in all the beauteous beams of day,
Yet, frugal still, she humbles them in song.   740
Nor envy we the gaudy robes they lent
Proud Montezuma's realm, whose legions cast
A boundless radiance waving on the sun,
While Philomel is ours, while in our shades,
Through the soft silence of the listening night,
The sober-suited songstress trills her lay.
   But come, my muse, the desert-barrier burst,
A wild expanse of lifeless sand and sky ;
And, swifter than the toiling caravan,
Shoot o'er the vale of Sennar ; ardent climb   750
The Nubian mountains, and the secret bounds

Of jealous Abyssinia boldly pierce.
Thou art no ruffian, who beneath the mask
Of social commerce com'st to rob their wealth;
No holy fury thou, blaspheming Heaven,
With consecrated steel to stab their peace,
And through the land, yet red from civil wounds,
To spread the purple tyranny of Rome.
Thou, like the harmless bee, mayst freely range
From mead to mead bright with exalted flowers, 760
From jasmine grove to grove; may'st wander gay
Through palmy shades and aromatic woods
That grace the plains, invest the peopled hills,
And up the more than Alpine mountains wave.
There on the breezy summit, spreading fair
For many a league, or on stupendous rocks,
That from the sun-redoubling valley lift,
Cool to the middle air, their lawny tops,
Where palaces and fanes and villas rise,
And gardens smile around and cultured fields, 770
And fountains gush, and careless herds and flocks
Securely stray—a world within itself,
Disdaining all assault : there let me draw
Ethereal soul, there drink reviving gales
Profusely breathing from the spicy groves
And vales of fragrance, there at distance hear
The roaring floods and cataracts that sweep
From disembowelled earth the virgin gold,
And o'er the varied landscape restless rove,
Fervent with life of every fairer kind. 780
A land of wonders ! which the sun still eyes
With ray direct, as of the lovely realm
Enamoured, and delighting there to dwell.
  How changed the scene ! In blazing height of noon,
The sun, oppressed, is plunged in thickest gloom.
Still horror reigns, a dreary twilight round,

Of struggling night and day malignant mixed.
For to the hot equator crowding fast,
Where, highly rarefied, the yielding air
Admits their stream, incessant vapours roll,   790
Amazing clouds on clouds continual heaped ;
Or whirled tempestuous by the gusty wind,
Or silent borne along, heavy and slow,
With the big stores of steaming oceans charged.
Meantime, amid these upper seas, condensed
Around the cold aerial mountain's brow,
And by conflicting winds together dashed,
The Thunder holds his black tremendous throne ;
From cloud to cloud the rending Lightnings rage ;
Till, in the furious elemental war   800
Dissolved, the whole precipitated mass
Unbroken floods and solid torrents pours.
   The treasures these, hid from the bounded search
Of ancient knowledge, whence with annual pomp,
Rich king of floods ! o'erflows the swelling Nile.
From his two springs in Gojam's sunny realm
Pure-welling out, he through the lucid lake
Of fair Dambea rolls his infant stream.
There, by the Naiads nursed, he sports away
His playful youth amid the fragrant isles   810
That with unfading verdure smile around.
Ambitious thence the manly river breaks,
And, gathering many a flood, and copious fed
With all the mellowed treasures of the sky,
Winds in progressive majesty along :
Through splendid kingdoms now devolves his maze,
Now wanders wild o'er solitary tracts
Of life-deserted sand ; till, glad to quit
The joyless desert, down the Nubian rocks
From thundering steep to steep he pours his urn, 820
And Egypt joys beneath the spreading wave.

His brother Niger too, and all the floods
In which the full-formed maids of Afric lave
Their jetty limbs, and all that from the tract
Of woody mountains stretched thro' gorgeous
  Ind
Fall on Cormandel's coast or Malabar ;
From Menam's orient stream that nightly shines
With insect-lamps, to where Aurora sheds
On Indus' smiling banks the rosy shower—
All, at this bounteous season, ope their urns   830
And pour untoiling harvest o'er the land.
  Nor less thy world, Columbus, drinks refreshed
The lavish moisture of the melting year.
Wide o'er his isles the branching Oronoque
Rolls a brown deluge, and the native drives
To dwell aloft on life-sufficing trees—
At once his dome, his robe, his food, and arms.
Swelled by a thousand streams, impetuous hurled
From all the roaring Andes, huge descends
The mighty Orellana.   Scarce the muse   840
Dares stretch her wing o'er this enormous mass
Of rushing water ; scarce she dares attempt
The sea-like Plata, to whose dread expanse,
Continuous depth, and wondrous length of course
Our floods are rills.   With unabated force
In silent dignity they sweep along,
And traverse realms unknown, and blooming wilds,
And fruitful deserts—worlds of solitude
Where the sun smiles and seasons teem in vain,
Unseen and unenjoyed.   Forsaking these,   850
O'er peopled plains they fair-diffusive flow
And many a nation feed, and circle safe
In their soft bosom many a happy isle,
The seat of blameless Pan, yet undisturbed
By Christian crimes and Europe's cruel sons.

Thus pouring on they proudly seek the deep,
Whose vanquish'd tide, recoiling from the shock,
Yields to this liquid weight of half the globe ;
And Ocean trembles for his green domain.
  But what avails this wondrous waste of wealth,
This gay profusion of luxurious bliss,   861
This pomp of Nature ? what their balmy meads,
Their powerful herbs, and Ceres void of pain ?
By vagrant birds dispersed and wafting winds,
What their unplanted fruits ? what the cool draughts,
The ambrosial food, rich gums, and spicy health
Their forests yield ? their toiling insects what,
Their silky pride and vegetable robes ?
Ah ! what avail their fatal treasures, hid
Deep in the bowels of the pitying earth,   870
Golconda's gems, and sad Potosi's mines
Where dwelt the gentlest children of the Sun ?
What all that Afric's golden rivers roll,
Her odorous woods, and shining ivory stores ?
Ill-fated race ! the softening arts of peace,
Whate'er the humanizing muses teach,
The godlike wisdom of the tempered breast,
Progressive truth, the patient force of thought,
Investigation calm whose silent powers
Command the world, the light that leads to Heaven,
Kind equal rule, the government of laws,   885
And all-protecting freedom which alone
Sustains the name and dignity of man—
These are not theirs. The parent sun himself
Seems o'er this world of slaves to tyrannize,
And, with oppressive ray the roseate bloom
Of beauty blasting, gives the gloomy hue
And feature gross—or, worse, to ruthless deeds.
Mad jealousy, blind rage, and fell revenge

863 herbs] herds 1744.

Their fervid spirit fires. Love dwells not there, 890
The soft regards, the tenderness of life,
The heart-shed tear, the ineffable delight
Of sweet humanity : these court the beam
Of milder climes—in selfish fierce desire
And the wild fury of voluptuous sense
There lost. The very brute creation there
This rage partakes, and burns with horrid fire.
  Lo ! the green serpent, from his dark abode,
Which even imagination fears to tread,
At noon forth-issuing, gathers up his train   900
In orbs immense, then, darting out anew,
Seeks the refreshing fount, by which diffused
He throws his folds ; and while, with threatening
        tongue
And deathful jaws erect, the monster curls
His flaming crest, all other thirst appalled
Or shivering flies, or checked at distance stands,
Nor dares approach. But still more direful he,
The small close-lurking minister of fate,
Whose high-concocted venom through the veins
A rapid lightning darts, arresting swift   910
The vital current. Formed to humble man,
This child of vengeful Nature ! There, sublimed
To fearless lust of blood, the savage race

898–912 This is an expansion of the original text (1727–38),
which reads as follows :—

> Here the green serpent gathers up his train
> In orbs immense ; then, darting out anew,
> Progressive rattles through the withered brake,
> And, lolling frightful, guards the scanty fount,
> If fount there be : or, of diminished size,
> But mighty mischief, on the unguarded swain
> Steals full of rancour.

912–38 This passage, beginning 'There, sublimed', is an
expansion of the original text (1727–38), which will be found
in a Note at the end of the poem.

Roam, licensed by the shading hour of guilt
And foul misdeed, when the pure day has shut
His sacred eye. The tiger, darting fierce
Impetuous on the prey his glance has doomed ;
The lively-shining leopard, speckled o'er
With many a spot, the beauty of the waste ;
And, scorning all the taming arts of man,   920
The keen hyena, fellest of the fell—
These, rushing from the inhospitable woods
Of Mauritania, or the tufted isles
That verdant rise amid the Libyan wild,
Innumerous glare around their shaggy king
Majestic stalking o'er the printed sand ;
And with imperious and repeated roars
Demand their fated food. The fearful flocks
Crowd near the guardian swain ; the nobler herds,
Where round their lordly bull in rural ease   930
They ruminating lie, with horror hear
The coming rage. The awakened village starts ;
And to her fluttering breast the mother strains
Her thoughtless infant. From the pirate's den,
Or stern Morocco's tyrant fang escaped,
The wretch half wishes for his bonds again ;
While, uproar all, the wilderness resounds
From Atlas eastward to the frighted Nile.
    Unhappy he ! who, from the first of joys,
Society, cut off, is left alone   940
Amid this world of death ! Day after day,
Sad on the jutting eminence he sits,
And views the main that ever toils below ;
Still fondly forming in the farthest verge,

936 bonds] bounds 1744.   941 Day after day] Ceaseless
he sits 1727–38.   942 jutting] rocky 1727 ; he sits] and views
1727–38.   943 And views the] The rolling 1727–38.

Where the round ether mixes with the wave,
Ships, dim-discovered, dropping from the clouds ;
At evening, to the setting sun he turns
A mournful eye, and down his dying heart
Sinks helpless ; while the wonted roar is up,
And hiss continual through the tedious night.   950
Yet here, even here, into these black abodes
Of monsters, unappalled, from stooping Rome
And guilty Caesar, Liberty retired,
Her Cato following through Numidian wilds—
Disdainful of Campania's gentle plains
And all the green delights Ausonia pours,
When for them she must bend the servile knee,
And, fawning, take the splendid robber's boon.
   Nor stop the terrors of these regions here.
Commissioned demons oft, angels of wrath,   960
Let loose the raging elements. Breathed hot
From all the boundless furnace of the sky,
And the wide glittering waste of burning sand,
A suffocating wind the pilgrim smites
With instant death. Patient of thirst and toil,
Son of the desert ! even the camel feels,
Shot through his withered heart, the fiery blast.
Or from the black-red ether, bursting broad,
Sallies the sudden whirlwind. Straight the sands,
Commoved around, in gathering eddies play ;   970
Nearer and nearer still they darkening come ;
Till, with the general all-involving storm

945 round] blue 1727.   948 mournful] watery 1727.
954 With Cato leading 1727–38.   955 gentle] fertile 1727–38.
956 Ausonia pours] of Italy 1727–38.   958 splendid robber's
boon] blessings once her own 1727–38.

959–1051 This long passage of nearly 100 lines is not found
in ed. 1738, or any previous ed. : it was inserted in the poem in
1744. A line of it here and there, but in a different connexion,
may, however, be found in the first ed. (1727).

Swept up, the whole continuous wilds arise ;
And by their noon-day fount dejected thrown,
Or sunk at night in sad disastrous sleep,
Beneath descending hills the caravan
Is buried deep. In Cairo's crowded streets
The impatient merchant, wondering, waits in vain,
And Mecca saddens at the long delay.
  But chief at sea, whose every flexile wave   980
Obeys the blast, the aerial tumult swells.
In the dread ocean, undulating wide,
Beneath the radiant line that girts the globe,
The circling typhon, whirled from point to point,
Exhausting all the rage of all the sky,
And dire ecnephia reign. Amid the heavens,
Falsely serene, deep in a cloudy speck
Compressed, the mighty tempest brooding dwells.
Of no regard, save to the skilful eye,
Fiery and foul, the small prognostic hangs   990
Aloft, or on the promontory's brow
Musters its force. A faint deceitful calm,
A fluttering gale, the demon sends before
To tempt the spreading sail. Then down at once
Precipitant descends a mingled mass
Of roaring winds and flame and rushing floods.
In wild amazement fixed the sailor stands.
Art is too slow. By rapid fate oppressed,
His broad-winged vessel drinks the whelming tide,
Hid in the bosom of the black abyss.   1000
With such mad seas the daring Gama fought,
For many a day and many a dreadful night
Incessant labouring round the stormy Cape,—
By bold ambition led, and bolder thirst
Of gold. For then from ancient gloom emerged
The rising world of trade : the genius then
Of navigation, that in hopeless sloth

Had slumbered on the vast Atlantic deep
For idle ages, starting, heard at last
The Lusitanian Prince, who, heaven-inspired,   1010
To love of useful glory roused mankind,
And in unbounded commerce mixed the world.
  Increasing still the terrors of these storms,
His jaws horrific armed with threefold fate,
Here dwells the direful shark. Lured by the scent
Of steaming crowds, of rank disease, and death,
Behold ! he rushing cuts the briny flood,
Swift as the gale can bear the ship along ;
And from the partners of that cruel trade
Which spoils unhappy Guinea of her sons   1020
Demands his share of prey—demands themselves.
The stormy fates descend : one death involves
Tyrants and slaves ; when straight, their mangled
    limbs
Crashing at once, he dyes the purple seas
With gore, and riots in the vengeful meal.
  When o'er this world, by equinoctial rains
Flooded immense, looks out the joyless sun,
And draws the copious steam from swampy fens,
Where putrefaction into life ferments
And breathes destructive myriads, or from woods,
Impenetrable shades, recesses foul,   1031
In vapours rank and blue corruption wrapt,
Whose gloomy horrors yet no desperate foot
Has ever dared to pierce ; then wasteful forth
Walks the dire power of pestilent disease.
A thousand hideous fiends her course attend,
Sick nature blasting, and to heartless woe
And feeble desolation, casting down
The towering hopes and all the pride of man :
Such as of late at Carthagena quenched   1040
The British fire. You, gallant Vernon, saw

The miserable scene ; you, pitying, saw
To infant-weakness sunk the warrior's arm ;
Saw the deep-racking pang, the ghastly form,
The lip pale-quivering, and the beamless eye
No more with ardour bright ; you heard the groans
Of agonizing ships from shore to shore,
Heard, nightly plunged amid the sullen waves,
The frequent corse, while, on each other fixed
In sad presage, the blank assistants seemed   1050
Silent to ask whom fate would next demand.

What need I mention those inclement skies
Where frequent o'er the sickening city, plague,
The fiercest child of Nemesis divine,
Descends ? From Ethiopia's poisoned woods,
From stifled Cairo's filth, and fetid fields
With locust armies putrefying heaped,
This great destroyer sprung. Her awful rage
The brutes escape : Man is her destined prey,
Intemperate man ! and o'er his guilty domes   1060
She draws a close incumbent cloud of death ;
Uninterrupted by the living winds,
Forbid to blow a wholesome breeze ; and stained
With many a mixture by the Sun suffused
Of angry aspect. Princely wisdom then
Dejects his watchful eye ; and from the hand
Of feeble justice ineffectual drop
The sword and balance ; mute the voice of joy,
And hushed the clamour of the busy world.
Empty the streets, with uncouth verdure clad ;   1070

1055-61 The first ed. (1727) gives only the one line here—
        Collects a close incumbent night of death—
a reading which was continued to 1738. In 1744 the present
text was inserted.
    1067 feeble . . drop] drooping . . falls 1727-38.   1069
clamour] murmur 1730-38 ; clamour 1727.

Into the worst of deserts sudden turned
The cheerful haunt of men—unless, escaped
From the doomed house, where matchless horror
  reigns,
Shut up by barbarous fear, the smitten wretch
With frenzy wild breaks loose, and, loud to Heaven
Screaming, the dreadful policy arraigns,
Inhuman and unwise. The sullen door,
Yet uninfected, on its cautious hinge
Fearing to turn, abhors society :
Dependents, friends, relations, Love himself,   1080
Savaged by woe, forget the tender tie,
The sweet engagement of the feeling heart.
But vain their selfish care : the circling sky,
The wide enlivening air is full of fate ;
And, struck by turns, in solitary pangs
They fall, unblest, untended, and unmourned.
Thus o'er the prostrate city black despair
Extends her raven wing ; while, to complete
The scene of desolation stretched around,
The grim guards stand, denying all retreat,   1090
And give the flying wretch a better death.
  Much yet remains unsung : the rage intense
Of brazen-vaulted skies, of iron fields,
Where drought and famine starve the blasted year ;
Fired by the torch of noon to tenfold rage,

1071-88 The original text (1727) is given in a Note at the end
of the poem. The text of edd. 1730-38, which differs considerably
from the first text, is also given.   1089 stretched] wide 1727-38.
  1090 Denying all retreat, the grim guards stand 1727-38.
1091 And] To 1727.   1092-1102 Instead of these lines the
original text (from 1727 to 1738) gives—
      Much of the force of foreign Summers still,
      Of growling hills that shoot the pillared flame,
      Of earthquake, and pale famine could I sing ;
      But equal scenes of horror call me home.

The infuriate hill that shoots the pillared flame ;
And, roused within the subterranean world,
The expanding earthquake, that resistless shakes
Aspiring cities from their solid base,
And buries mountains in the flaming gulf.   1100
But 'tis enough ; return, my vagrant muse ;
A nearer scene of horror calls thee home.

Behold, slow-settling o'er the lurid grove
Unusual darkness broods, and, growing, gains
The full possession of the sky, surcharged
With wrathful vapour, from the secret beds
Where sleep the mineral generations drawn.
Thence nitre, sulphur, and the fiery spume
Of fat bitumen, steaming on the day,
With various-tinctured trains of latent flame,   1110
Pollute the sky, and in yon baleful cloud,
A reddening gloom, a magazine of fate,
Ferment ; till, by the touch ethereal roused,
The dash of clouds, or irritating war
Of fighting winds, while all is calm below,
They furious spring. A boding silence reigns
Dread through the dun expanse—save the dull sound
That from the mountain, previous to the storm,
Rolls o'er the muttering earth, disturbs the flood,

1103 Behold] For now 1727-38.   1105 full] whole 1727 ;
broad 1730-38.   1106 secret beds] damp abrupt 1727-38.

1108-16 The original text (from 1727 to 1738) stood as
follows :—

    Thence nitre, sulphur, vitriol on the day
    Stream, and fermenting in yon baneful cloud
    Extensive o'er the world, a reddening gloom,
    In dreadful promptitude to spring await
    The high command. A boding silence, &c.

' Stream ' in the second line here is, however, corrected to ' Steam '
in edd. 1730-38.

1117 Dread through] Through all 1727.   1119 muttering]
trembling 1727-38.

And shakes the forest-leaf without a breath   1120
Prone to the lowest vale the aerial tribes
Descend : the tempest-loving raven scarce
Dares wing the dubious dusk. In rueful gaze
The cattle stand, and on the scowling heavens
Cast a deploring eye—by man forsook,
Who to the crowded cottage hies him fast,
Or seeks the shelter of the downward cave.
'Tis listening fear and dumb amazement all :
When to the startled eye the sudden glance
Appears far south, eruptive through the cloud,   1130
And, following slower, in explosion vast
The thunder raises his tremendous voice.
At first, heard solemn o'er the verge of heaven,
The tempest growls ; but as it nearer comes,
And rolls its awful burden on the wind,
The lightnings flash a larger curve, and more
The noise astounds, till overhead a sheet
Of livid flame discloses wide, then shuts
And opens wider, shuts and opens still
Expansive, wrapping ether in a blaze.   1140
Follows the loosened aggravated roar,
Enlarging, deepening, mingling, peal on peal
Crushed horrible, convulsing heaven and earth.
   Down comes a deluge of sonorous hail,

1120 shakes] stirs 1727–38.   1128 'Tis dumb amaze and
listening terror all 1727–38.   1129 startled .. sudden] quicker ..
livid 1727–38.   1130 eruptive] emissive 1727–38.   1131 And
by the powerful breath of God inflate 1727–38.   1133–5 In
the original text (from 1727 to 1738) one line only is given :—
     At first low-muttering ; but at each approach.
The change was made to the present text in 1744.
   1138 livid] various 1727–38.   1144 Following this line
comes in the first text (1727–38) the passage—
     In the white heavenly magazines congealed,
     And often fatal to the unsheltered head
     Of man or rougher beast.

Or prone-descending rain. Wide-rent, the clouds
Pour a whole flood ; and yet, its flame unquenched,
The unconquerable lightning struggles through,
Ragged and fierce, or in red whirling balls,
And fires the mountains with redoubled rage.   1149
Black from the stroke, above, the smouldering pine
Stands a sad shattered trunk ; and, stretched below,
A lifeless group the blasted cattle lie :
Here the soft flocks, with that same harmless look
They wore alive, and ruminating still
In fancy's eye ; and there the frowning bull,
And ox half-raised.   Struck on the castled cliff,

Thereafter followed in the first ed. (1727)—
         The sluicy rain
     In one unbroken flood descends ; and yet
     The unconquerable, &c.
   1145 ' Or prone-descending rain ' was first added in 1744.
' Wide-rent, the clouds ', &c. was added in 1730.   1146 flame]
rage 1730-38.   1147 inconquerable 1730-38.   1148 After
this line came in the first text (1727-38) the passage—
     And strikes the shepherd as he shuddering sits
     Presaging ruin in the rocky clift.
     His inmost marrow feels the gliding flame :
     He dies ! and, like a statue grimed with age,
     His live dejected posture still remains,
     His russet singed and rent his hanging hat,
     Against his crook his sooty cheek reclined,
     While, whining at his feet, his half-stunned dog,
     Importunately kind and fearful, pats
     On his insensate master for relief.
In the second line of this dropped passage, edd. 1730-38 give
' mid ' for ' in '.
   1150 smouldering] mountain 1727-38.
   1151 For this line in edd. 1727 to 1738 we have—
     A leaning shattered trunk stands scathed to heaven,
     The talk of future ages ! and below.
   1156-68 Instead of these lines, which first appeared in ed.
1744, the first text (1727-38) gives the following :—
     [And ox half-raised.]   A little farther burns
     The guiltless cottage, and the haughty dome

SUMMER 95

The venerable tower and spiry fane
Resign their aged pride. The gloomy woods
Start at the flash, and from their deep recess
Wide-flaming out, their trembling inmates shake. 1160
Amid Carnarvon's mountains rages loud
The repercussive roar : with mighty crush,
Into the flashing deep, from the rude rocks
Of Penmanmaur heaped hideous to the sky
Tumble the smitten cliffs ; and Snowdon's peak,
Dissolving, instant yields his wintry load.
Far seen, the heights of heathy Cheviot blaze,
And Thulè bellows through her utmost isles.

Guilt hears appalled, with deeply troubled thought ;
And yet not always on the guilty head   1170
Descends the fated flash. Young Celadon
And his Amelia were a matchless pair,
With equal virtue formed and equal grace
The same, distinguished by their sex alone :
Hers the mild lustre of the blooming morn,
And his the radiance of the risen day.
They loved : but such their guileless passion was
As in the dawn of time informed the heart

> Stoops to the base. The uprooted forest flies
> Aloft in air, or, flaming out, displays
> The savage haunts, by day unpierced before.
> Scarred is the mountain's brow, and from the cliff
> Tumbles the smitten rock. The desert shakes,
> And gleams, and grumbles, through his deepest dens.

Edd. 1730 to 1738 give, at ll. 3, 4 of this passage, the variation, ' In
one immediate flash The forest falls ', and, at l. 5, ' unpierced by day.'
1169 In place of this line, which first appeared in ed. 1730,
came in the original text [1727] a long passage of twenty-four
lines, which the reader will find in a Note at the end of the poem.
Edd. 1730–38 print ' dubious hears ' for ' hears appalled '. The
change was made in 1744.
1171 Falls the devoted 1727–38.   1172 were a matchless
pair] an unrivalled twain 1727.   1175 blooming] unfolding
1727.   1178 informed] alarmed 1727–38.

Of innocence and undissembling truth.
'Twas friendship heightened by the mutual wish,   1180
The enchanting hope and sympathetic glow
Beamed from the mutual eye. Devoting all
To love, each was to each a dearer self,
Supremely happy in the awakened power
Of giving joy. Alone amid the shades,
Still in harmonious intercourse they lived
The rural day, and talked the flowing heart,
Or sighed and looked unutterable things.
So passed their life, a clear united stream,
By care unruffled ; till, in evil hour,   1190
The tempest caught them on the tender walk,
Heedless how far and where its mazes strayed,
While with each other blest, creative Love
Still bade eternal Eden smile around.
Heavy with instant fate, her bosom heaved
Unwonted sighs, and, stealing oft a look
Of the big gloom, on Celadon her eye
Fell tearful, wetting her disordered cheek.
In vain assuring love and confidence
In Heaven repressed her fear ; it grew, and shook   1200
Her frame near dissolution. He perceived
The unequal conflict, and, as angels look
On dying saints, his eyes compassion shed,
With love illumined high. ' Fear not,' he said,
' Sweet innocence ! thou stranger to offence
And inward storm ! he, who yon skies involves

1182 Beamed . . mutual] struck . . charmful 1727–38.   1186
harmonious] angelic 1727.   1189 So] Thus 1727–38.
   1192–5 For these lines the earlier text (1727–38) gives only—
        Heedless how far. Her breast, presageful heaved.
   1198 all her glowing cheek 1727.   1204 Mingled with
matchless love 1727.   1205 Sweet] Fair 1727.   1206
enwraps yon skies 1727.

In frowns of darkness, ever smiles on thee
With kind regard. O'er thee the secret shaft
That wastes at midnight, or the undreaded hour
Of noon, flies harmless : and that very voice,   1210
Which thunders terror through the guilty heart,
With tongues of seraphs whispers peace to thine.
'Tis safety to be near thee sure, and thus
To clasp perfection ! ' From his void embrace,
Mysterious Heaven ! that moment to the ground,
A blackened corse, was struck the beauteous maid.
But who can paint the lover, as he stood
Pierced by severe amazement, hating life,
Speechless, and fixed in all the death of woe ?
So, faint resemblance ! on the marble tomb   1220
The well-dissembled mourner stooping stands,
For ever silent and for ever sad.
As from the face of Heaven the shattered clouds
Tumultuous rove, the interminable sky
Sublimer swells, and o'er the world expands

1208 kind] full 1727–38.   1211 guilty] sinner's 1727 ; conscious 1730–38.   1215 to the ground] in a heap 1727–38.
1216 Of pallid ashes fell 1727–38.   1218 Pierced] Struck
1727–38.   1223 each shattered cloud 1727.

1223 Immediately preceding this line came, in the first ed.
(1727), a passage of eleven lines, which the reader will find in a
Note at the end of the poem.

1224 rove, the interminable sky] roves, the unfathomable
blue 1727 ; rove, the interminable blue 1730–38.

1225, 1226 Instead of these two lines the first ed. (1727) gives—
following ' the unfathomable blue '—

    That constant joy to every finer eye,
    That rapture ! swells into the general arch
    Which copes the nations.—On the lilied bank
    Where a brook quivers, often, careless thrown,
    Up the wide scene I've gazed whole hours away
    With growing wonder, while the sun declined,
    As now, forth breaking from the blotting storm.
Edd. 1730–38 give only—

A purer azure. Nature from the storm
Shines out afresh ; and through the lightened air
A higher lustre and a clearer calm
Diffusive tremble ; while, as if in sign
Of danger past, a glittering robe of joy,   1230
Set off abundant by the yellow ray,
Invests the fields, yet dropping from distress.
  'Tis beauty all, and grateful song around,
Joined to the low of kine, and numerous bleat
Of flocks thick-nibbling through the clovered vale.
And shall the hymn be marred by thankless man,
Most-favoured, who with voice articulate
Should lead the chorus of this lower world ?
Shall he, so soon forgetful of the hand
That hushed the thunder, and serenes the sky, 1240
Extinguished feel that spark the tempest waked,
That sense of powers exceeding far his own,
Ere yet his feeble heart has lost its fears ?
  Cheered by the milder beam, the sprightly youth
Speeds to the well-known pool, whose crystal depth
A sandy bottom shows. Awhile he stands
Gazing the inverted landscape, half afraid

> Delightful swell into the general arch
> That copes the nations. Nature from the storm &c.

1227 Nature shines out, and through, &c. 1727.   1229
while] and 1727.   1230 robe] face 1727.   1231 yellow]
level 1727.   1232 fields, yet dropping] Earth yet weeping
1727.   1239 hand] past 1727.   1240-43 For these four
lines the first ed. (1727) gives—

> After the tempest, puff his transient vows,
> And a new dance of vanity begin
> Scarce ere the pant forsakes his feeble heart ?

Edd. 1730 to 1738 give—

> That hushed the thunder and expands the sky,
> After the tempest puff his idle vows,
> And a new dance of vanity begin,
> Scarce ere the pant forsake the feeble heart ?

1244 milder] setting 1727-38.

To meditate the blue profound below;
Then plunges headlong down the circling flood.
His ebon tresses and his rosy cheek   1250
Instant emerge; and through the obedient wave,
At each short breathing by his lip repelled,
With arms and legs according well, he makes,
As humour leads, an easy-winding path;
While from his polished sides a dewy light
Effuses on the pleased spectators round.
This is the purest exercise of health,
The kind refresher of the summer heats;
Nor, when cold winter keens the brightening flood,
Would I weak-shivering linger on the brink.   1260
Thus life redoubles, and is oft preserved
By the bold swimmer, in the swift illapse
Of accident disastrous. Hence the limbs
Knit into force; and the same Roman arm
That rose victorious o'er the conquered earth
First learned, while tender, to subdue the wave.
Even from the body's purity the mind
Receives a secret sympathetic aid.
Close in the covert of an hazel copse,

1248 After this line in the first ed. (1727) came—
         Till disenchanted by the ruffling gale—
which was struck out in 1730.
    1249 Then] He 1727; circling] closing 1727.   1251
obedient] glassy 1727; flexile 1730-38.   1255 polished . .
dewy] snowy . . humid 1727.   1259 Nor when the brook
pellucid Winter keens 1727-38.   1264 the] that 1727.   1265
That rose] Which stretched 1727.   1268 Strictly allied
receives a secret aid 1727.
    1268 The passage of twelve lines ending here followed the
episode of Damon and Musidora, which first appeared in the
ed. of 1730, and was retained down to 1738. In 1744 the episode
underwent a great alteration.
    1269-72 For these lines the first text of the episode of
Damon and Musidora (1730-38) gives—

Where, winded into pleasing solitudes,   1270
Runs out the rambling dale, young Damon sat
Pensive, and pierced with love's delightful pangs.
There to the stream that down the distant rocks
Hoarse-murmuring fell, and plaintive breeze that
      played
Among the bending willows, falsely he
Of Musidora's cruelty complained.
She felt his flame ; but deep within her breast,
In bashful coyness or in maiden pride,
The soft return concealed ; save when it stole
In side-long glances from her downcast eye,   1280
Or from her swelling soul in stifled sighs.
Touched by the scene, no stranger to his vows,
He framed a melting lay to try her heart ;
And, if an infant passion struggled there,
To call that passion forth.   Thrice happy swain !
A lucky chance, that oft decides the fate
Of mighty monarchs, then decided thine !
For, lo ! conducted by the laughing Loves,
This cool retreat his Musidora sought :
Warm in her cheek the sultry season glowed ;   1290
And, robed in loose array, she came to bathe
Her fervent limbs in the refreshing stream.
What shall he do ?   In sweet confusion lost,

'Twas then, beneath a secret waving shade
Where, winded into lovely solitudes,
Runs out the rambling dale, that Damon sat,
Thoughtful and fixed in philosophic muse.

1273–89 Instead of these lines the original text of this
episode (1730–38) gives only seven lines, which are printed
in a Note at the end of the poem.

1290 her] their 1730–38.   1291 she] they 1730–38.

1292 Her] Their 1730–38.   After this line in the original
version (1730–38) came ten lines (struck out in 1744) which
the reader will find in a Note at the end of the poem.   They were
superseded by the passage here given, ending ' Of Ida ', l. 1305.

And dubious flutterings, he a while remained.
A pure ingenuous elegance of soul,
A delicate refinement, known to few,
Perplexed his breast and urged him to retire :
But love forbade. Ye prudes in virtue, say,
Say, ye severest, what would you have done ?
Meantime, this fairer nymph than ever blest   1300
Arcadian stream, with timid eye around
The banks surveying, stripped her beauteous limbs
To taste the lucid coolness of the flood.
Ah ! then, not Paris on the piny top
Of Ida panted stronger, when aside
The rival goddesses the veil divine
Cast unconfined, and gave him all their charms,
Than, Damon, thou ; as from the snowy leg
And slender foot the inverted silk she drew ;
As the soft touch dissolved the virgin zone ;   1310
And, through the parting robe, the alternate breast,
With youth wild-throbbing, on thy lawless gaze
In full luxuriance rose. But, desperate youth,
How durst thou risk the soul-distracting view
As from her naked limbs of glowing white,
Harmonious swelled by nature's finest hand,
In folds loose-floating fell the fainter lawn,
And fair exposed she stood, shrunk from herself,
With fancy blushing, at the doubtful breeze

1305 Of Ida] Nor Paris 1730–38.   1308 After ' thou ' in
the original version (1730–38) came—
        ' the stoic now no more,
      But man deep-felt.'
1309 she] they 1730–38.
1313–16 For these four lines the original version (1730–38)
gives the following two—
      Luxuriant rose ; yet more enamoured still
      When from their naked limbs of glowing white.
1318 she . . herself] they . . themselves 1730–38.

Alarmed, and starting like the fearful fawn ?   1320
Then to the flood she rushed : the parted flood
Its lovely guest with closing waves received ;
And every beauty softening, every grace
Flushing anew, a mellow lustre shed—
As shines the lily through the crystal mild,
Or as the rose amid the morning dew,
Fresh from Aurora's hand, more sweetly glows.
While thus she wantoned, now beneath the wave
But ill-concealed, and now with streaming locks,
That half-embraced her in a humid veil,   1330
Rising again, the latent Damon drew
Such maddening draughts of beauty to the soul
As for a while o'erwhelmed his raptured thought
With luxury too daring. Checked, at last,
By love's respectful modesty, he deemed
The theft profane, if aught profane to love
Can e'er be deemed, and, struggling from the shade,
With headlong hurry fled : but first these lines,
Traced by his ready pencil, on the bank   1339

1320 Alarmed] Aroused 1730–38. After this line in the original
version of the episode came the three lines—
    So stands the statue that enchants the world,
    Her full proportions such, and bashful so
    Bends ineffectual from the roving eye.
See ll. 1347–9 *infra*.
    1321 she] they 1730–38.   1322 Its lovely guest] The plunging
fair 1730–38.   1324 anew] afresh 1730–38.   1327 Puts
on a warmer glow. In various play 1730–38.   1328 she] they
1730–38.   1330 her] them 1730–38.   1332 maddening
draughts of] draughts of love and 1730–38.   1333 The original
version (1730–38) ended here as follows :—
    As put his harsh philosophy to flight,
    The joyless search of long-deluded years ;
    And Musidora fixing in his heart
    Informed and humanized him into man.
Here followed in the original version, ' This is the purest exercise ',
&c. See l. 1257 *supra*.

With trembling hand he threw—'Bathe on, my fair,
Yet unbeheld save by the sacred eye
Of faithful love : I go to guard thy haunt ;
To keep from thy recess each vagrant foot
And each licentious eye.' With wild surprise,
As if to marble struck, devoid of sense,
A stupid moment motionless she stood :
So stands the statue that enchants the world ;
So, bending, tries to veil the matchless boast,
The mingled beauties of exulting Greece.
Recovering, swift she flew to find those robes   1350
Which blissful Eden knew not ; and, arrayed
In careless haste, the alarming paper snatched.
But, when her Damon's well-known hand she saw,
Her terrors vanished, and a softer train
Of mixed emotions, hard to be described,
Her sudden bosom seized : shame void of guilt,
The charming blush of innocence, esteem
And admiration of her lover's flame,
By modesty exalted, even a sense
Of self-approving beauty stole across   1360
Her busy thought. At length, a tender calm
Hushed by degrees the tumult of her soul ;
And on the spreading beech, that o'er the stream
Incumbent hung, she with the sylvan pen
Of rural lovers this confession carved,
Which soon her Damon kissed with weeping joy :
' Dear youth ! sole judge of what these verses mean,
By fortune too much favoured, but by love,
Alas ! not favoured less, be still as now
Discreet : the time may come you need not fly.' 1370
   The Sun has lost his rage : his downward orb
Shoots nothing now but animating warmth

1371-1437. This long passage first appeared in 1744. The
reference at l. 1427 is to Pope's last illness. He died in 1744.

And vital lustre ; that with various ray,
Lights up the clouds, those beauteous robes of heaven,
Incessant rolled into romantic shapes,
The dream of waking fancy ! Broad below,
Covered with ripening fruits, and swelling fast
Into the perfect year, the pregnant earth
And all her tribes rejoice. Now the soft hour
Of walking comes for him who lonely loves   1380
To seek the distant hills, and there converse
With nature, there to harmonize his heart,
And in pathetic song to breathe around
The harmony to others. Social friends,
Attuned to happy unison of soul—
To whose exulting eye a fairer world,
Of which the vulgar never had a glimpse,
Displays its charms ; whose minds are richly fraught
With philosophic stores, superior light ;
And in whose breast enthusiastic burns   1390
Virtue, the sons of interest deem romance—
Now called abroad, enjoy the falling day :
Now to the verdant portico of woods,
To nature's vast Lyceum, forth they walk ;
By that kind school where no proud master reigns,
The full free converse of the friendly heart,
Improving and improved. Now from the world,
Sacred to sweet retirement, lovers steal,
And pour their souls in transport, which the sire
Of love approving hears, and calls it good.   1400
Which way, Amanda, shall we bend our course ?
The choice perplexes. Wherefore should we choose ?
All is the same with thee. Say, shall we wind
Along the streams ? or walk the smiling mead ?
Or court the forest glades ? or wander wild
Among the waving harvests ? or ascend,
While radiant Summer opens all its pride,

Thy hill, delightful Shene ?   Here let us sweep
The boundless landscape ;   now the raptured eye,
Exulting swift, to huge Augusta send,   1410
Now to the sister hills that skirt her plain,
To lofty Harrow now, and now to where
Majestic Windsor lifts his princely brow.
In lovely contrast to this glorious view,
Calmly magnificent, then will we turn
To where the silver Thames first rural grows.
There let the feasted eye unwearied stray ;
Luxurious, there, rove through the pendent woods
That nodding hang o'er Harrington's retreat ;
And, stooping thence to Ham's embowering walks, 1420
Beneath whose shades, in spotless peace retired,
With her the pleasing partner of his heart,
The worthy Queensberry yet laments his Gay,
And polished Cornbury woos the willing muse,
Slow let us trace the matchless vale of Thames ;
Fair-winding up to where the muses haunt
In Twit'nam's bowers, and for their Pope implore
The healing god ; to royal Hampton's pile,
To Clermont's terraced height, and Esher's groves,
Where in the sweetest solitude, embraced   1430
By the soft windings of the silent Mole,
From courts and senates Pelham finds repose.
Enchanting vale ! beyond whate'er the muse
Has of Achaia or Hesperia sung !
O vale of bliss ! O softly-swelling hills !
On which the power of cultivation lies,
And joys to see the wonders of his toil.
   Heavens ! what a goodly prospect spreads around,

1438   And what a pleasing (various) prospect lies around !
1727-38.   The passage beginning here followed (in the editions
preceding that of 1744) the passage ending at l. 628 of the
present text.

Of hills, and dales, and woods, and lawns, and spires,
And glittering towns, and gilded streams, till all 1440
The stretching landskip into smoke decays !
Happy Britannia ! where the Queen of Arts,
Inspiring vigour, Liberty, abroad
Walks unconfined even to thy farthest cots,
And scatters plenty with unsparing hand.
 Rich is thy soil, and merciful thy clime ;
Thy streams unfailing in the Summer's drought ;
Unmatched thy guardian-oaks ; thy valleys float
With golden waves ; and on thy mountains flocks
Bleat numberless ; while, roving round their sides,
Bellow the blackening herds in lusty droves.   1451
Beneath, thy meadows glow, and rise unquelled
Against the mower's scythe. On every hand
Thy villas shine. Thy country teems with wealth ;
And Property assures it to the swain,
Pleased and unwearied in his guarded toil.
 Full are thy cities with the sons of art ;
And trade and joy, in every busy street,
Mingling are heard : even Drudgery himself,
As at the car he sweats, or, dusty, hews   1460
The palace stone, looks gay. Thy crowded ports,
Where rising masts an endless prospect yield,
With labour burn, and echo to the shouts
Of hurried sailor, as he hearty waves
His last adieu, and, loosening every sheet,
Resigns the spreading vessel to the wind.
 Bold, firm, and graceful, are thy generous youth,
By hardship sinewed, and by danger fired,
Scattering the nations where they go ; and first

1439 dales] vales 1727–38.   1440 glittering towns] towns
betwixt 1727–38.   1444 Walks through the land of heroes
unconfined 1727–38.   1446 clime] skies 1727–38.   1452
glow] flame 1727–38.   1456 guarded] certain 1727.

Or in the listed plain or stormy seas.   1470
Mild are thy glories too, as o'er the plans
Of thriving peace thy thoughtful sires preside—
In genius and substantial learning, high ;
For every virtue, every worth, renowned ;
Sincere, plain-hearted, hospitable, kind,
Yet like the mustering thunder when provoked,
The dread of tyrants, and the sole resource
Of those that under grim oppression groan.
   Thy sons of glory many ! Alfred thine,
In whom the splendour of heroic war,   1480
And more heroic peace, when governed well,
Combine ; whose hallowed name the Virtues saint,
And his own muses love ; the best of kings !
With him thy Edwards and thy Henrys shine,
Names dear to fame ; the first who deep impressed
On haughty Gaul the terror of thy arms,
That awes her genius still. In statesmen thou,
And patriots, fertile. Thine a steady More,
Who, with a generous though mistaken zeal,
Withstood a brutal tyrant's useful rage ;   1490
Like Cato firm, like Aristides just,

1470 in . . stormy] on (in). . wintry 1727-38. 1471 plans]
arts 1727.   1477 dread] scourge 1727.   1478 those that]
such as 1727-38.   1479 Alfred thine] Thine a More 1730-38.
   1479-1579 This passage of 101 lines, containing a list of
England's worthies, was a gradual growth. The first ed. of
Summer (1727) included only nine names. In edd. 1730-38
we find two of these nine withdrawn (those of Tillotson and
Barrow) and eight other worthies added to the list. The list
was still further increased in edd. 1744, 1746. The text of the
original ed. (1727), consisting of only 23 lines, followed by a short
passage of 13 lines in honour of the worthies of Scotland—afterwards expanded and transferred to *Autumn*—will be found in
a Note at the end of the poem.
   1480-90 Added in 1744.   1491 Like . . like] As . . as
1730-38.

Like rigid Cincinnatus nobly poor—
A dauntless soul erect, who smil'd on death.
Frugal and wise, a Walsingham is thine ;
A Drake, who made thee mistress of the deep,
And bore thy name in thunder round the world.
Then flamed thy spirit high. But who can speak
The numerous worthies of the maiden reign ?
In Raleigh mark their every glory mixed—
Raleigh, the scourge of Spain ! whose breast with all
The sage, the patriot, and the hero burned.   1501
Nor sunk his vigour when a coward reign
The warrior fettered, and at last resigned,
To glut the vengeance of a vanquished foe.
Then, active still and unrestrained, his mind
Explored the vast extent of ages past,
And with his prison-hours enriched the world ;
Yet found no times, in all the long research,
So glorious, or so base, as those he proved,
In which he conquered, and in which he bled.   1510
Nor can the muse the gallant Sidney pass,
The plume of war ! with early laurels crowned,
The lover's myrtle and the poet's bay.
A Hampden too is thine, illustrious land !
Wise, strenuous, firm, of unsubmitting soul,
Who stemmed the torrent of a downward age
To slavery prone, and bade thee rise again,
In all thy native pomp of freedom bold.

1505, 1506 In place of these two lines the text of 1730–38
gives only—
    Then deep through fate his mind retorted saw &c.
  1511–13 These three lines followed in edd. 1730–38 the com-
pliment to Hampden which ends in the present text at l. 1518.
  1512 early laurels] every laurel 1730–38.   1514, 1515 In
place of these two lines the text of 1730–38 gives only—
    A Hampden thine, of unsubmitting soul.
  1518 bold] fierce 1730–38.

Bright at his call thy age of men effulged ;
Of men on whom late time a kindling eye   1520
Shall turn, and tyrants tremble while they read.
Bring every sweetest flower, and let me strew
The grave where Russel lies, whose tempered blood,
With calmest cheerfulness for thee resigned,
Stained the sad annals of a giddy reign
Aiming at lawless power, though meanly sunk
In loose inglorious luxury. With him
His friend, the British Cassius, fearless bled ;
Of high determined spirit, roughly brave,
By ancient learning to the enlighten'd love   1530
Of ancient freedom warmed. Fair thy renown
In awful sages and in noble bards ;
Soon as the light of dawning Science spread
Her orient ray, and waked the Muses' song.
Thine is a Bacon, hapless in his choice,
Unfit to stand the civil storm of state,
And, through the smooth barbarity of courts,
With firm but pliant virtue forward still
To urge his course : him for the studious shade
Kind Nature formed, deep, comprehensive, clear, 1540

1519-24 These six lines, introduced in 1744, took the place of
the following four which will be found in edd. 1730-38 :—
    Nor him of later name, firm to the cause
    Of Liberty, her rough determined friend,
    The British Brutus ; whose united blood
    With, Russel, thine, thou patriot wise and calm
1527 luxury] sloth 1730-38.
1527-50 Instead of these lines (commencing ' With him ')
the text of edd. 1730-38 gives only the following :—
        High thy renown
    In sages too. far as the sacred light
    Of science spreads, and wakes the muse's song.
    Thine is a Bacon, formed of happy mould
    When Nature smiled, deep, comprehensive, clear,
    Exact, and elegant, in one rich soul
    Plato, the Stagyrite, and Tully joined.

Exact, and elegant ; in one rich soul,
Plato, the Stagyrite, and Tully joined.
The great deliverer he, who, from the gloom
Of cloistered monks and jargon-teaching schools,
Led forth the true philosophy, there long
Held in the magic chain of words and forms
And definitions void : he led her forth,
Daughter of Heaven ! that, slow-ascending still,
Investigating sure the chain of things,
With radiant finger points to Heaven again.　　1550
The generous Ashley thine, the friend of man,
Who scanned his nature with a brother's eye,
His weakness prompt to shade, to raise his aim,
To touch the finer movements of the mind,
And with the moral beauty charm the heart.
Why need I name thy Boyle, whose pious search,
Amid the dark recesses of his works,
The great Creator sought ?　And why thy Locke,
Who made the whole internal world his own ?
Let Newton, pure intelligence, whom God　　1560
To mortals lent to trace his boundless works
From laws sublimely simple, speak thy fame
In all philosophy.　For lofty sense,
Creative fancy, and inspection keen
Through the deep windings of the human heart,
Is not wild Shakespeare thine and nature's boast ?

1556-8 What need I name thy Boyle, whose pious search
　　　Still sought the great Creator in His works,
　　　By sure experience led ? And why thy Locke—
1730-38.
　1560-63 In edd. 1727-38 the text reads—
　　　Let comprehensive Newton speak thy fame
　　　In all philosophy.
　1563-6 In edd. 1727-38 the text is—
　　　　　　For solemn song
　　Is not wild Shakespeare nature's boast and thine ?

Is not each great, each amiable muse
Of classic ages in thy Milton met ?
A genius universal as his theme,
Astonishing as chaos, as the bloom   1570
Of blowing Eden fair, as heaven sublime!
Nor shall my verse that elder bard forget,
The gentle Spenser, fancy's pleasing son ;
Who, like a copious river, poured his song
O'er all the mazes of enchanted ground :
Nor thee, his ancient master, laughing sage,
Chaucer, whose native manners-painting verse,
Well moralized, shines through the Gothic cloud
Of time and language o'er thy genius thrown.
May my song soften as thy daughters I,   1580
Britannia, hail ! for beauty is their own,
The feeling heart, simplicity of life,
And elegance, and taste ; the faultless form,
Shaped by the hand of harmony ; the cheek,
Where the live crimson, through the native white
Soft-shooting, o'er the face diffuses bloom
And every nameless grace ; the parted lip,
Like the red rosebud moist with morning dew,
Breathing delight ; and, under flowing jet,
Or sunny ringlets, or of circling brown,   1590

1567-71 The first text of this passage (1727-38), altered
in 1744, reads as follows :—
        And every greatly amiable muse
        Of elder ages in thy Milton met ?
        His was the treasure of two thousand years
        Seldom indulged to man ; a godlike mind
        Unlimited and various as his theme,
        Astonishing as chaos, as the bloom
        Of blowing Eden fair, soft as the talk
        Of our grandparents, and as heaven sublime.
1572-9 These lines were added in 1744.   1579 thy] his
1744.   1582 First added in 1730 ; not in the original text
of 1727.

The neck slight-shaded and the swelling breast ;
The look resistless, piercing to the soul,
And by the soul informed, when, dressed in love,
She sits high-smiling in the conscious eye.
  Island of bliss ! amid the subject seas
That thunder round thy rocky coasts, set up,
At once the wonder, terror, and delight,
Of distant nations, whose remotest shore
Can soon be shaken by thy naval arm ;
Not to be shook thyself, but all assaults   1600
Baffling, like thy hoar cliffs the loud sea-wave.
  O Thou, by whose almighty nod the scale
Of empire rises, or alternate falls,
Send forth the saving Virtues round the land
In bright patrol—white Peace, and social Love ;
The tender-looking Charity, intent
On gentle deeds, and shedding tears through smiles ;
Undaunted Truth, and Dignity of mind ;
Courage, composed and keen ; sound Temperance,
Healthful in heart and look ; clear Chastity,   1610
With blushes reddening as she moves along,
Disordered at the deep regard she draws ;
Rough Industry ; Activity untired,
With copious life informed, and all awake :
While in the radiant front superior shines
That first paternal virtue, Public Zeal,
Who throws o'er all an equal, wide survey,
And, ever musing on the common weal,
Still labours glorious with some great design.

1594 sweet-smiling in the lovely eye 1727.
1617 throws] casts 1727–38.   1619 great] brave 1727–38.
1619 After the passage ending here the first ed. and edd. 1730–
38 give a text of many lines (withdrawn in 1744) which the
reader will find (with their variations) at the end of the poem,
in the Notes, pp. 127, 128.

Low walks the sun, and broadens by degrees, 1620
Just o'er the verge of day. The shifting clouds
Assembled gay, a richly-gorgeous train,
In all their pomp attend his setting throne.
Air, earth, and ocean smile immense. And now,
As if his weary chariot sought the bowers
Of Amphitritè and her tending nymphs,
(So Grecian fable sung) he dips his orb ;
Now half-immersed ; and now, a golden curve,
Gives one bright glance, then total disappears.
For ever running an enchanted round, 1630
Passes the day, deceitful, vain, and void ;
As fleets the vision o'er the formful brain,
This moment hurrying wild the impassioned soul,
The next in nothing lost. 'Tis so to him,
The dreamer of this earth, an idle blank—
A sight of horror to the cruel wretch,
Who, all day long in sordid pleasure rolled,

1620-29 These lines (with variations) are found in the first
ed. (1727), about 200 ll. from the end. The variations are given
below.　　　1621 shifting] rising 1727-38.
　1622 That shift perpetual in his vivid train 1727-38.
　1623-27 Instead of these lines the original text 1727-38 gives—
　　Their dewy (watery) mirrors numberless opposed,
　　Unfold the hidden riches of his ray,
　　And chase a change of colours round the sky.
　　'Tis all one blush from east to west ; and now,
　　Behind the dusky earth, he dips his orb.
　1630 This line is not in the first ed. (1727) ; it first appears in
ed. 1730.　　1631 deceitful, vain, and void] illusive and perplext
1727 ; deceitful, tedious, void 1730-38.　　1633 wild] all 1727-38.
1635 an idle] a cheerless 1727-38.　　1636 cruel] ungodly 1727.
1637-41 For these lines the first text (1727) gives—
　　The hard, the lewd, the cruel, and the false,
　　Who all day long have made the widow weep,
　　And snatched the morsel from her orphan's mouth
　　To give their dogs : but to the harmonious mind, &c. ;
while edd. 1730-38 give—

Himself an useless load, has squandered vile
Upon his scoundrel train what might have cheered
A drooping family of modest worth.   1640
But to the generous, still-improving mind
That gives the hopeless heart to sing for joy,
Diffusing kind beneficence around
Boastless as now descends the silent dew—
To him the long review of ordered life
Is inward rapture only to be felt.
    Confessed from yonder slow-extinguished clouds,
All ether softening, sober Evening takes
Her wonted station in the middle air,
A thousand shadows at her beck. First this   1650
She sends on earth ; then that of deeper dye
Steals soft behind ; and then a deeper still,
In circle following circle, gathers round
To close the face of things. A fresher gale
Begins to wave the wood and stir the stream,
Sweeping with shadowy gust the fields of corn,
While the quail clamours for his running mate.
Wide o'er the thistly lawn, as swells the breeze,
A whitening shower of vegetable down
Amusive floats. The kind impartial care   1660
Of Nature naught disdains : thoughtful to feed
Her lowest sons, and clothe the coming year,
From field to field the feathered seeds she wings.
    His folded flock secure, the shepherd home

> Who, rolling in inhuman pleasure deep,
> The whole day long has made the widow pine,
> And snatched the morsel from her orphan's mouth
> To give his dogs : but to the tuneful mind, &c.

1642 That gives] Who makes 1727-38.   1648 All ether
softening] The sky begreying 1727 ; All ether saddening 1730-38.
1653 circle following circle] well adjusted circles 1727.   1654 A
fresher gale] The expected breeze 1727 ; A fresher breeze 1730-38.
1658-63 A condensation of twelve lines in the first text (of 1727),
which the reader will find in a Note at the end of the poem.

Hies, merry-hearted ; and by turns relieves
The ruddy milk-maid of her brimming pail—
The beauty whom perhaps his witless heart,
Unknowing what the joy-mixed anguish means,
Sincerely loves, by that best language shown
Of cordial glances and obliging deeds.   1670
Onward they pass, o'er many a panting height
And valley sunk and unfrequented ; where
At fall of eve the fairy people throng,
In various game and revelry to pass
The summer night, as village stories tell.
But far about they wander from the grave
Of him whom his ungentle fortune urged
Against his own sad breast to lift the hand
Of impious violence. The lonely tower
Is also shunned ; whose mournful chambers hold, 1680
So night-struck fancy dreams, the yelling ghost.
    Among the crooked lanes, on every hedge,
The Glow-worm lights his gem ; and, through the dark,
A moving radiance twinkles. Evening yields

1669 Loves fond, by that sincerest language shown 1727-38.
1675 The] A 1727.   1677 urged] forced 1727.
   1678, 1679 Against himself to lift the hated hand
                  Of violence—1727-38.
There followed here in the original text (from 1727 to 1738) the
short passage—
               By man (men) cast out from life
           And, after death, to which they drove his hope,
           Into the broad way-side—
dropped in 1744.
   1679 lonely] ruined 1727-38.   1680 mournful] unblest
1727 ; hoary 1730-38.   1681 So night-struck fancy dreams]
Nightly, sole habitant 1727.
   1681 Here in the first ed. (1727) followed a passage of fourteen
lines (1007-20) descriptive of wild-fire, which will be found in a
Note at the end of the poem.
   1683 gem] lamp 1727-38.   1684, 1685 Twinkles a moving
gem. On Evening's heel Night follows fast 1727-38.

The world to Night ; not in her winter robe
Of massy Stygian woof, but loose arrayed
In mantle dun.   A faint erroneous ray,
Glanced from the imperfect surfaces of things,
Flings half an image on the straining eye ;
While wavering woods, and villages, and streams, 1690
And rocks, and mountain-tops that long retained
The ascending gleam are all one swimming scene,
Uncertain if beheld.   Sudden to heaven
Thence weary vision turns ; where, leading soft
The silent hours of love, with purest ray
Sweet Venus shines ; and, from her genial rise,
When daylight sickens, till it springs afresh,
Unrivalled reigns, the fairest lamp of night.
As thus the effulgence tremulous I drink,   '
With cherished gaze, the lambent lightnings shoot 1700
Across the sky, or horizontal dart
In wondrous shapes—by fearful murmuring crowds

1687 faint . . ray] few . . rays 1727.   1689 Flings] Fling
1727.   1693 Doubtful if seen ; whence posting Vision turns
1727 ; Sudden Vision turns 1730–38.   1694-8 For these lines
the original text (1727-38) gives—

> To heaven, where Venus in the starry front
> Shines eminent, and from her genial rise,
> When daylight sickens, till it springs afresh,
> Sheds influence on earth to love and life
> And every form of vegetation kind.

1700 cherished gaze] fixed peruse 1727 ; glad peruse 1730–38.
1702-29 Instead of these twenty-seven lines the text of edd.
1730–38 gives only the following eight :—

> O'er half the nations, in a minute's space
> Conglobed or long.   Astonishment succeeds
> And silence, ere the various talk begin.
> The vulgar stare : amazement is their joy
> And mystic faith,—a fond sequacious herd !
> But scrutinous Philosophy looks deep
> With piercing eye into the latent cause,
> Nor can she swallow what she does not see.

Portentous deemed. Amid the radiant orbs
That more than deck, that animate the sky,
The life-infusing suns of other worlds,
Lo ! from the dread immensity of space
Returning with accelerated course,
The rushing comet to the sun descends ;
And, as he sinks below the shading earth,
With awful train projected o'er the heavens,   1710
The guilty nations tremble. But, above
Those superstitious horrors that enslave
The fond sequacious herd, to mystic faith
And blind amazement prone, the enlightened few,
Whose godlike minds philosophy exalts,
The glorious stranger hail. They feel a joy
Divinely great ; they in their powers exult,
That wondrous force of thought, which mounting spurns
This dusky spot, and measures all the sky ;
While, from his far excursions through the wilds 1720
Of barren ether, faithful to his time,
They see the blazing wonder rise anew,
In seeming terror clad, but kindly bent
To work the will of all-sustaining love—
From his huge vapoury train perhaps to shake
Reviving moisture on the numerous orbs
Through which his long ellipsis winds, perhaps
To lend new fuel to declining suns,
To light up worlds, and feed the eternal fire.
   With thee, serene Philosophy, with thee,   1730
And thy bright garland, let me crown my song !
Effusive source of evidence and truth !
A lustre shedding o'er the ennobled mind,
Stronger than summer-noon, and pure as that

The first three of these lines appear in the first ed. (1727) and
are followed by thirty-two more, which are given in a Note at the
end of the poem.   1731 bright garland] high praises 1727–38.

Whose mild vibrations soothe the parted soul,
New to the dawning of celestial day.
Hence through her nourished powers, enlarged by thee,
She springs aloft, with elevated pride,
Above the tangling mass of low desires,
That bind the fluttering crowd ; and, angel-winged,
The heights of science and of virtue gains,   1741
Where all is calm and clear ; with Nature round,
Or in the starry regions or the abyss,
To reason's and to fancy's eye displayed—
The first up-tracing, from the dreary void,
The chain of causes and effects to Him,
The world-producing Essence, who alone
Possesses being ; while the last receives
The whole magnificence of heaven and earth,
And every beauty, delicate or bold,   1750
Obvious or more remote, with livelier sense,
Diffusive painted on the rapid mind.
    Tutored by thee, hence Poetry exalts
Her voice to ages ; and informs the page
With music, image, sentiment, and thought,
Never to die ; the treasure of mankind,
Their highest honour, and their truest joy !
    Without thee what were unenlightened man ?
A savage, roaming through the woods and wilds
In quest of prey ; and with the unfashioned fur 1760
Rough-clad ; devoid of every finer art
And elegance of life. Nor happiness

1735 Which gently vibrates on the eye of Saint 1727.   1738
springs aloft] soaring spurns 1727-38.   1739 The tangling
mass of cares and 1727-38.   1742 clear] bright 1727.   1745
dreary void] vast inane 1727-38.   1747 Who absolutely in
Himself alone 1727; Who, all-sustaining in Himself alone 1730-38.
1752 A world swift-painted on the attentive mind 1727-38.
1758 unenlightened] unassisted 1727-38.   1761 finer] honest
1727-38.   1762 happiness] home nor joy 1727-38.

Domestic, mixed of tenderness and care,
Nor moral excellence, nor social bliss,
Nor guardian law were his ; nor various skill
To turn the furrow, or to guide the tool
Mechanic ; nor the heaven-conducted prow
Of Navigation bold, that fearless braves
The burning line or dares the wintry pole,
Mother severe of infinite delights !   1770
Nothing, save rapine, indolence, and guile,
And woes on woes, a still-revolving train !
Whose horrid circle had made human life
Than non-existence worse : but, taught by thee,
Ours are the plans of policy and peace ;
To live like brothers, and, conjunctive all,
Embellish life.   While thus laborious crowds
Ply the tough oar, Philosophy directs
The ruling helm ; or, like the liberal breath
Of potent heaven, invisible, the sail   1780
Swells out, and bears the inferior world along.
    Nor to this evanescent speck of earth
Poorly confined : the radiant tracts on high
Are her exalted range ; intent to gaze
Creation through ; and, from that full complex
Of never-ending wonders, to conceive
Of the Sole Being right, who spoke the word,

1765 Nor law were his, nor property, nor swain 1727-38.
    1766-9 For these four lines the original text (1727) gives only—
        To turn the furrow, nor mechanic hand
        Hardened to toil, nor servant prompt, nor trade ;
and later edd. (1730-38) follow the first text, substituting only
' sailor bold ' for ' servant prompt '.
    1772 a still-revolving train] to render human life 1727, the next
line being omitted.   1772, 1773 So in edd. 1730-38.   1775
plans] Arts 1727.   1779 The ruling] Star-led the 1727-38.
1780 potent] urgent 1727-38 ; sail] sails 1727-38.   1783 the]
those 1727.   1785 full] round 1727.   1786 ending] ceasing 1727.

And Nature moved complete. With inward view,
Thence on the ideal kingdom swift she turns
Her eye ; and instant, at her powerful glance,   790
The obedient phantoms vanish or appear ;
Compound, divide, and into order shift,
Each to his rank, from plain perception up
To the fair forms of fancy's fleeting train ;
To reason then, deducing truth from truth,
And notion quite abstract ; where first begins
The world of spirits, action all, and life
Unfettered and unmixed. But here the cloud,
So wills Eternal Providence, sits deep.
Enough for us to know that this dark state,   1800
In wayward passions lost and vain pursuits,
This infancy of being, cannot prove
The final issue of the works of God,
By boundless love and perfect wisdom formed,
And ever rising with the rising mind.

1788 moved complete . . inward] circled . . inflected 1727.
1790 virtual glance 1727-38.   1791 or] and 1727.   1794,
1795 These lines were added, the former in ed. 1744, the latter
in ed. 1746. They are not in any of the earlier edd.   1796
And] To 1727-38. 1798 Unfettered] Immediate 1727-38.   1800
to know] we know 1727-38.   1804 By love and wisdom inex-
pressive formed 1727-38.

NOTES TO SUMMER

The general scheme of this part of *The Seasons* is the description
(with digressions) of a typical summer's day from dawn to midnight.

LINE 29. George Bubb Dodington, born 1691, entered Parliament 1715, Member for Bridgewater 1722-54 ; he was a Lord of
the Treasury when Thomson first knew him, in 1726 or 1727.
He took the name of Dodington with the fine estate of Eastbury
in 1720, inherited from his maternal uncle. In 1761 he was
raised to the peerage as Lord Melcombe : he died the year after.

He has been called ' the last of the Patrons '. Thomson's eulogy of him is very extravagant ; but there is no doubt that the poet felt honoured by intimacy with him,—an intimacy which he long retained.

96. After this line came in the first ed. (1727) the following passage, dropped in 1730 :—

> Who would the blessings first and last recount
> That in a full effusion from thee flow
> As soon might number at the height of noon
> The rays that radiate from thy cloudless sphere,
> An universal glory darting round.

113-35. The original text (first ed., 1727) was as follows :—

> Parent of Seasons ! from whose rich-stained rays,
> Reflected various, various colours rise :
> The freshening mantle of the youthful year ;
> The wild embroidery of the watery vale ;
> With all that chears the eye and charms the heart.
>
> The branching grove thy lusty product stands,
> To quench the fury of thy noon-career ;
> And crowd a shade for the retreating swain,
> When on his russet fields you look direct.
>
> Fruit is thy bounty too, with juice replete,   10
> Acid or mild ; and from thy ray receives
> A flavour pleasing to the taste of man ;
> By thee concocted, blushes ; and, by thee
> Fully matured, into the verdant lap
> Of Industry the mellow plenty falls.
>
> Extensive harvests wave at thy command,
> And the bright ear, consolidate by thee,
> Bends, unwithholding, to the reaper's hand.
>
> Even Winter speaks thy power, whose every blast
> O'ercast with tempest, or severely sharp   20
> With breathing frost, is eloquent of thee,
> And makes us languish for thy vernal gleams.
>
> Shot to the bowels of the teeming earth,
> The ripening oar (sic) confesses all thy flame.
> [The unfruitful rock itself, impregned &c.].

The text of edd. 1730-38 differed only slightly from this : they gave for l. 7—

> Diffused and deep, to quench the summer noon ;

and for ' flame ' at the end of l. 24 they substituted ' power '.

287-317. The substance of this passage originally appeared in

Spring (1728-38), from which it was transferred (with alterations)
in 1744 : the original text was as follows :—
These are not idle philosophic dreams ;
Full nature swarms with life. The unfaithful fen
In putrid steams emits the living cloud
Of pestilence. Through subterranean cells,
Where searching sunbeams never found a way,
Earth animated heaves. The flowery leaf
Wants not its soft inhabitants. The stone,
Hard as it is, in every winding pore
Holds multitudes. But chief the forest-boughs,
Which dance unnumbered to the inspiring breeze,
The downy orchard, and the melting pulp
Of mellow fruit the nameless nations feed
Of evanescent insects. Where the pool
Stands mantled o'er with green, invisible
Amid the floating verdure millions stray.
Each liquid too, whether of acid taste,
Milky, or strong, with various forms abounds.
Nor is the lucid stream, nor the pure air,
Though one transparent vacancy they seem,
Devoid of theirs. Even animals subsist
On animals, in infinite descent ;
And all so fine adjusted that the loss
Of the least species would disturb the whole.
Stranger than this the inspective glass confirms,
And to the curious gives the amazing scenes
Of lessening life—by Wisdom kindly hid
From eye and ear of man ; for if at once
The worlds in worlds enclosed were pushed to light,
Seen by his sharpened eye, and by his ear
Intensely bended heard, from the choice cate,
The freshest viands, and the brightest wines,
He'd turn abhorrent, and in dead of night,
When silence sleeps o'er all, be stunned with noise.
457.   Here followed in the first ed. (1727) a passage of seven
lines, viz. :—
Who shall endure !—The too resplendent scene
Already darkens on the dizzy eye ;
And double objects dance : unreal sounds
Sing round the ears : a weight of sultry dew
Hangs, deathful, on the limbs : shiver the nerves :
The supple sinews sink ; and on the heart,
Misgiving, Horror lays his heavy hand.

This passage was continued in edd. 1730-38 with the following alterations:—*Line* 1, shall *became* can ; *line* 2, eye *became* sight; *line* 4, round the ears *became* deep around. The passage was dropped in 1744.

564. Elizabeth Stanley, died 1738, at the age of eighteen. Thomson wrote the verses for her epitaph, which will be found among his miscellaneous pieces. The prose part of the epitaph, in Holyrood Church, Southampton, informs the reader that she joined to beauty, modesty, and gentleness ' all the fortitude, elevation, and vigour of mind that ever exalted the most heroical man '. Her mother, the daughter of Sir Hans Sloane, was an early friend of Thomson's.

591-606. The text of the earliest ed. (1727) is as follows :—

Rolls unsuspecting, till surprised 'tis thrown
In loose meanders through the trackless air ;
Now a blue watery sheet, anon dispersed
A hoary mist, then gathered in again
A darted stream aslant the hollow rock,
This way and that tormented, dashing thick
From steep to steep with wild infracted course,
And restless roaring to the humble vale.

The following alterations appear in edd. 1730-38 :—

In line 1, Rolls fair and placid ; till collected all.

For line 2, *the following* :—

In one big glut, as sinks the shelving ground,
The impetuous torrent, tumbling down the steep,
Thunders, and shakes the astonished country round.

641. *The general breeze.* Which blows constantly between the tropics from the east, or the collateral points, the north-east and south-east ; caused by the pressure of the rarefied air on that before it, according to the diurnal motion of the sun from east to west.—T.

645. *Returning suns and double seasons.* In all places between the tropics the sun, as he passes and repasses in his annual motion, is twice a year perpendicular, which produces this effect.—T.

710. *Behemoth.* The hippopotamus, or river-horse.—T.

738. *But, if she bids them shine.* In all the regions of the torrid zone the birds, though more beautiful in their plumage, are observed to be less melodious than ours.—T.

827. *Menam's orient stream.* The river that runs through Siam : on whose banks a vast multitude of those insects called fireflies make a beautiful appearance in the night.—T.

840. *The mighty Orellana.* The river of the Amazons.—T.

912-38. This passage, beginning ' There sublimed ', is an expansion of the original (1727) text, which stood as follows :—

> Here the savage race
> Roam, licensed by the shading hour of blood
> And foul misdeed, when the pure day has shut
> His sacred eye. The rabid tiger, then,
> The fiery panther, and the whiskered pard,
> Bespeckled fair, the beauty of the waste,
> In dire divan surround their shaggy king
> Majestic stalking o'er the burning sand
> With planted step, while an obsequious crowd
> Of grinning forms at humble distance wait.
> These, all together joined, from darksome caves
> Where o'er gnawed bones they slumbered out the day,
> By supreme hunger smit, and thirst intense,
> At once their mingling voices raise to heaven ;
> And, with imperious and repeated roars
> Demanding food, the wilderness resounds
> From Atlas eastward to the frighted Nile.

The alteration of this text (which remained verbally unchanged from 1727 down to 1738) was made for the ed. of 1744.

984. *The circling typhon ;* 986 *And dire ecnephia.* Terms for particular storms or hurricanes known only between the tropics.—T.

987. *a cloudy speck.* Called by sailors the ox-eye, being in appearance at first no bigger.—T.

1001. *the daring Gama.* Vasco de Gama, the first that sailed round Africa, by the Cape of Good Hope, to the East Indies.—T.

1010. *The Lusitanian Prince.* Don Henry, third son to John the First, King of Portugal. His strong genius to the discovery of new countries was the source of all the modern improvements in navigation.—T.

1055. *Ethiopia's poisoned woods.* These are the causes supposed to be the first origin of the Plague, in Doctor Mead's elegant book on that subject.—T.

1071-88. The original text (1727) was as follows :—

> And ranged at open noon by beasts of prey
> And birds of bloody beak : while, all night long,
> In spotted troops the recent ghosts complain.
> Demanding but the covering grave. Meantime
> Locked is the deaf door to distress ; even friends,
> And relatives endeared for many a year,
> Savaged by woe, forget the social tie,
> The blest engagement of the yearning heart,
> And sick in solitude successive die
> Untended and unmourned. And to complete, &c.

The text of 1730–38 was as follows :—

> And ranged at open noon by beasts of prey
> And birds of bloody beak. The sullen door
> No visit knows, nor hears the wailing voice
> Of fervent want. Even soul-attracted friends
> And relatives endeared for many a year,
> Savaged by woe, forget the social tie,
> The close engagement of the kindred heart,
> And sick in solitude successive die
> Untended and unmourned. While to complete, &c.

1169. For this line, which (with a slight variation) first appeared in 1730, came, in the original text (1727), the following passage of twenty-four lines :—

> Now swells the triumph of the virtuous man ;
> And this outrageous elemental fray
> To him a dread magnificence appears,
> The glory of that Power he calls his friend,
> Sole honourable name !—but woe to him
> Who, of infuriate malice, and confirmed
> In vice long-practised, is a foe to man,
> His brother, and at variance with his God.
> He thinks the tempest weaves around his head ;
> Loudens the roar to him, and in his eye
> The bluest vengeance glares. The oppressor who
> Unpitying heard the wailings of distress,
> Galled by the scourge, now shrinks at other sounds.
> Hid are the Neros of the earth—in vain
> Like children hid in sport. Chief in the breast
> Of solitary atheist wildness reigns
> Licentious,—vanished every quaint conceit
> And impious jest with which he used to pelt
> Superior reason—anguish in his look—
> And supplication lifts his hand. He'd pray
> If his hard heart would flow. At last he runs,
> Precipitant, and entering just the cave,
> The messenger-of-justice glancing comes
> With swifter sweep behind, and trips his heel.

1223. Preceding this line a passage of eleven lines appears in the first ed. (1727) :—

> Heard indistinct the far-off thunder peals,—
> From suffering earth commissioned o'er the main
> Where the black tempest, pressing on the pool,
> Heaves the dead billows to the bursting clouds.
> Dire is the fate of those who, reeling high

From wave to wave, even at the very source
Of lightning feel the undissipated flame ;
Or, should they in a watery vale escape,
If on their heads the forceful spout descends
And drives the dizzy vessel down the deep
Till in the oozy bottom stuck profound !

This passage was dropped in 1730.

1273-89. For these lines the original text of this episode of
Damon and Musidora gives only the following seven lines :—

Damon ! who still amid the savage woods
And lonely lawns the force of beauty scorned,
Firm and to false philosophy devote.
The brook ran babbling by, and, sighing weak,
The breeze among the bending willows played,
When Sacharissa to the cool retreat
With Amoret and Musidora stole.

1292. After this line, came in the original version (1730-38)
the following ten lines—superseded in 1744 by the passage of the
final text ending ' Of Ida ', at l. 1305 :—

Tall and majestic Sacharissa rose,
Superior trading (sic), as on Ida's top
(So Grecian bards in wanton fable sung)
High shone the sister and the wife of Jove.
Another Pallas Musidora seemed,
Meek-eyed, sedate, and gaining every look
A surer conquest of the sliding heart ;
While, like the Cyprian goddess, Amoret,
Delicious dressed in rosy-dimpled smiles,
And all one softness, melted on the sense.

1347. *the statue that enchants the world.* The Venus of Medici.
—T.

1408. *delightful Shene.* The old name of Richmond, signify-
ing in Saxon shining or splendour.—T.

1411. *the sister hills.* Highgate and Hampstead.—T.

1479-1579. This passage of 101 lines was gradually expanded
from the original text (1727) of twenty-three lines :—

Hence mayst thou boast a Bacon and a More ;
Nor cease to vie them with the noblest names
Of ancient times, or patriot or sage.
And for the strength and elegance of truth
A Barrow and a Tillotson are thine ;
A Locke inspective into human minds
And all the unnoticed world that passes there.
Nor be thy Boyle forgot, who, while he lived,

Seraphic sought the Eternal through his works
By sure experience led, and, when he died,
Still bid his bounty argue for his God—
Worthy of riches he ! But what needs more ?
Let comprehensive Newton speak thy fame
In all philosophy. For solemn song
Is not wild Shakespear Nature's boast and thine ?
And every greatly amiable muse
Of elder ages in thy Milton met ?
His was the treasure of two thousand years,
Seldom indulged to man, a god-like mind—
Unlimited and various as his theme,
Astonishing as Chaos, as the bloom
Of blowing Eden fair, soft as the talk
Of our grandparents, and as Heaven sublime.

This was followed (1727) by a short passage of thirteen lines in honour of the worthies of Scotland—afterwards (1730) expanded and transferred to *Autumn* :—

And should I northward turn my filial eye
Beyond the Tweed, pure parent-stream ! to where
The Hyperborean ocean furious foams
O'er Orca or Betubium's highest peak,
Rapt I might sing thy Caledonian sons,
A gallant, warlike, unsubmitting race !
Nor less in learning versed, soon as he took
Before the Gothic rage his western flight ;
Wise in the council, at the banquet gay ;
The pride of honour burning in their breasts,
And glory, not to their own realms confined
But into foreign countries shooting far,
As over Europe bursts the Boreal Morn.

1528. *the British Cassius*. Algernon Sidney.—T.

1551. *The generous Ashley*. Anthony Ashley Cooper, Earl of Shaftesbury.—T.

1619. Here followed in edd. 1727-38 a passage of many lines (considerably increased in 1730, and with some alterations on the original version of 1727)—withdrawn from the poem in 1744. The passage with its addition and alterations is here reproduced :—

Thus far transported by my country's love,
Nobly digressive from my theme, I've aimed
To sing her praises in ambitious verse,—
While slightly to recount I simply meant
The various summer-horrors which infest
Kingdoms that scorch below severer suns :

Kingdoms on which direct the flood of day
Oppressive falls, and gives the gloomy hue
And feature gross; or, worse, to ruthless deeds
Wan jealousy, red rage, and fell revenge
Their hasty spirit prompts. Ill-fated race !
Although the treasures of the sun be theirs,
Rocks rich in gems, and mountains big with mines,
Whence over sands of gold the Niger rolls
His amber wave,—while on his balmy banks,
Or in the spicy Abyssinian vales,
The citron, orange and pomegranate drink
Intolerable day, yet in their coats
A cooling juice contain. Peaceful beneath
Leans the huge elephant, and in his shade
A multitude of beauteous creatures play,
And birds of bolder note rejoice around.

And oft amid their aromatic groves,
Touched by the torch of noon, the gummy bark
Smouldering begins to roll the dusky wreath.
Instant, so swift the ruddy ruin spreads,
A cloud of incense shadows all the land,
And o'er a thousand thundering trees at once
Riots with lawless rage the running blaze—
But chiefly if fomenting winds assist
And doubling blend the circulating waves
Of flames tempestuous, or directly on
Far-streaming drives them through the forest's length.

But other views await—where heaven above
Glows like an arch of brass, and all below,
The earth a mass of rusty iron lies—
Of fruits and flowers and every verdure spoilt—
Barren and bare, a joyless weary waste,
Thin-cottaged, and in time of trying need
Abandoned by the vanished brook, like one
Of fading fortune by his treacherous friend.

Such are thy horrid deserts, Barca ; such,
Zaara, thy hot interminable sands,
Continuous, rising often with the blast
Till the sun sees no more, and unknit earth,
Shook by the south into the darkened air,
Falls in new hilly kingdoms o'er the waste.

The above lines are the text of the first ed., reproduced in
1730-38 with ' mine ' for ' mines ' at l. 13, ' should ' for ' if ' at

l. 30, ' The brown-burnt earth a mass of iron ' for ' The earth
a mass of rusty iron ' at l. 36, and ' inhospitable ' for ' interminable '
at l. 43. The following lines, enclosed within square brackets,
were added in 1730 :—

[Hence, late exposed, if distant fame says true,
A smothered city from the sandy wave
Emergent rose ; with olive-fields around,
Fresh woods, reclining herds, and silent flocks,
Amusing all, and incorrupted seen.
For by the nitrous penetrating salts,
Mixed copious with the sand, pierced and preserved,.
Each object hardens gradual into stone,
Its posture fixes, and its colour keeps.
The statue-folk within unnumbered crowd
The streets, in various attitudes surprised
By sudden fate, and live on every face
The passions caught beyond the sculptor's art.
Here leaning soft the marble-lovers stand,
Delighted even in death, and each for each
Feeling alone, with that expressive look
Which perfect nature only knows to give.
And there the father agonizing bends
Fond o'er his weeping wife and infant train—
Aghast and trembling though they know not why.
The stiffened vulgar stretch their arms to heaven,
With horror staring ; while, in council deep
Assembled full, the hoary-headed sires
Sit sadly thoughtful of the public fate ;—
As when old Rome, beneath the raging Gaul
Sunk her proud turrets, resolute on death,
Around the forum sat the grey divan
Of senators majestic, motionless,
With ivory staves, and in their awful robes
Dressed like the falling fathers of mankind :
Amazed and shivering from the solemn sight
The red barbarians shrunk, and deemed them gods.]

The concluding part of this long, dropped passage appears in all
the early edd. (from 1727 to 1738) :—

'Tis here that Thirst has fixed his dry domain,
And walks his wide malignant round in search
Of pilgrim lost ; or on the Merchant's tomb
Triumphant sits, who for a single cruse
Of unavailing water paid so dear :
Nor could the gold his hard associate save.

Thomson appended the following note to 'the Merchant's tomb':—In the desert of Araoan are two tombs with inscriptions on them importing that the persons there interred were a rich merchant and a poor carrier who had died of thirst, and that the former had given to the latter ten thousand ducats for one cruse of water. [Thomson's form of 'cruse', in both text and note, is 'cruise'.]

1658-63. This passage is a condensation of twelve lines which appeared in the earlier edd. (1727 and 1728), were dropped altogether in 1730, and—in a condensed form—restored in 1744. It was an unhappy restoration : the poet had already described the face of things as closed by the deepening darkness ; now he introduces what must have been invisible—a whitening shower of thistle-down. The twelve lines of 1727 are given here :—

Wide-wafting o'er the lawn, the thistly down
Plays in the fickle air ; now seems to fall,
And now, high-soaring over head, an arch
Amusive forms ; then, slanting down, eludes
The grasp of idle swain. But, should the west
A little swell the breeze, the woolly shower,
Blown in a white confusion through the dusk,
Falls o'er the face unfelt, and, settling slow,
Mantles the twilight plain. And yet even here,
As through all nature in her lowest forms,
A fine contrivance lies, to wing the seed
By this light plumage into distant vales.

1681. Here followed a passage of fourteen lines in the first ed. (1727),—transferred, with alterations, in 1730 to *Autumn*. Its original form was as follows :—

Struck from the roots of slimy rushes, blue
The wildfire scatters round ; or, gathered, trails
A length of flame deceitful o'er the moss ;
Whither, entangled in the maze of night,
While the damp desert breathes his fogs around,
The traveller decoyed is quite absorpt,
Rider and horse, into the miry gulf,
Leaving his wife and family involved
In sorrowful conjecture. Other times,
Sent by the quick-eyed angel of the night,
Innoxious on the unstartling horse's mane.
The meteor sits, and shows the narrow path
That winding leads through pits of death, or else
Directs him how to take the dangerous ford.

For ll. 4-6 of the above the edd. of 1730-38 give—

Whither decoyed by the fantastic blaze,
Now sunk and now renewed, he's quite absorpt;

for ll. 8, 9, they give—

While still from day to day his pining wife
And plaintive children his return await
In wild conjecture lost. At other times;

in l. 10, for 'quick-eyed angel' they give 'better genius'; in
l. 11, for 'on the unstartling', they give 'gleaming on the'
and in l. 14, for 'Directs' they give 'Instructs'. It may also
be noted that they give 'root' for 'roots' in the first line.

The final form of this passage on wildfire appeared in 1744, and
differs only from the form of 1730-38 in giving 'lost' for 'sunk'
and 'amid' for 'into' at the lines descriptive of the traveller's
absorption in the mire.

1700-29. The first ed. (1727) gives the following long passage,
which was afterwards (1730) transferred, with variations, to
Autumn :—

[The lambent lightnings shoot
Across the sky, or horizontal dart
O'er half the nations in a minute's space,
Conglobed or long. Astonishment succeeds,
And silence, ere the various talk begins.]

That instant, flashing noiseless from the north,
A thousand meteors stream, ensweeping first
The lower skies, then all at once converge
High to the crown of heaven, and, all at once
Relapsing quick, as quickly reascend   10
And mix and thwart, extinguish and renew,
All ether coursing in a maze of light.

From eye to eye contagious through the crowd
The panic runs, and into wondrous shapes
The appearance throws : armies in meet array
Throng with aerial spears and steeds of fire,
Till, the long lines of full-extended war
In bleeding fight commixed, the sanguine flood
Rolls a broad slaughter o'er the plains of heaven.

As the mad people scan the fancied scene,   20
On all sides swells the superstitious din
Incontinent, and busy frenzy talks
Of blood and battle, cities overturned
And late at night in swallowing earthquake sunk
Or painted hideous with ascending flame,

Of blights that blacken the white-bosomed spring,
And tempest shaking autumn into chaff
Till famine empty-handed starves the year,
Of pestilence and every great distress,
Empires subversed when ruling fate has struck   30
The unalterable hour : even Nature's self
Is deemed to totter on the brink of time.

Not so the man of philosophic eye
And inspect sage ; the waving brightness he
Curious surveys, inquisitive to know
The causes and materials yet unfixed
Of this appearance beautiful and new.
(First ed. of *Summer*, ll. 1044–75.)

The above passage (except the first five lines) was transferred
to *Autumn* in the edition of 1730, and remained in the text up
to 1738, where it will be found as numbered from l. 1005 to l. 1034 :
the transferred passage shows the following variations :—

l. 6 Oft in this season, silent from the north

l. 7 A blaze of meteors shoots, &c.

l. 13 From look to look, &c.

l. 20 As thus they scan the visionary scene,

ll. 26, 27 (*omitted*).

l. 28 Of sallow famine, inundation, storm ;

The ed. of 1744 repeats the text of 1730–38 with one variation
at l. 25, viz.—Or hideous wrapt in fierce ascending flame ; also
at l. 8 ' they ' for ' then ', and at l. 16 ' Thronged ' for ' Throng '.

AUTUMN

[Inscribed to the Rt. Hon. Arthur Onslow, Esq., Speaker of the House of Commons. First published in 1730 (1,269 ll.) ; last edition in author's lifetime published 1746 (1373 ll.).]

THE ARGUMENT

THE subject proposed. Addressed to Mr. Onslow. A prospect of the fields ready for harvest. *Reflections in praise of industry raised by that view.* Reaping. A tale *relative to it.* A harvest storm. Shooting and hunting ; their barbarity. A ludicrous account of foxhunting. A view of an orchard. Wall fruit. A vineyard. A description of fogs, frequent in the latter part of Autumn ; whence a digression, inquiring into the rise of fountains and rivers. Birds of season considered, that now shift their habitation. The prodigious number of them that cover the northern and western isles of Scotland. Hence a view of the country. A prospect of the discoloured, fading woods. After a gentle dusky day, moonlight. Autumnal meteors. Morning ; to which succeeds a calm, pure, *sunshiny* day, such as usually shuts up the season. The harvest being gathered in, the country dissolved in joy. The whole concludes with a panegyric on a philosophical country life.*

CROWNED with the sickle and the wheaten sheaf
While Autumn nodding o'er the yellow plain
Comes jovial on, the Doric reed once more
Well-pleased I tune. Whate'er the Wintry frost
Nitrous prepared, the various-blossomed Spring
Put in white promise forth, and Summer-suns
Concocted strong, rush boundless now to view,
Full, perfect all, and swell my glorious theme.

* The above is the original Argument (1730) enlarged for the ed. of 1744. The additions to the original are in italics. For 'sunshiny' the original Argument gives 'sunshine'.

Onslow ! the muse, ambitious of thy name
To grace, inspire, and dignify her song,   10
Would from the public voice thy gentle ear
A while engage. Thy noble cares she knows,
The patriot-virtues that distend thy thought,
Spread on thy front, and in thy bosom glow ;
While listening senates hang upon thy tongue,
Devolving through the maze of eloquence
A roll of periods, sweeter than her song.
But she too pants for public virtue; she,
Though weak of power, yet strong in ardent will,
Whene'er her country rushes on her heart,   20
Assumes a bolder note, and fondly tries
To mix the patriot's with the poet's flame.

When the bright Virgin gives the beauteous days,
And Libra weighs in equal scales the year,
From heaven's high cope the fierce effulgence shook
Of parting Summer, a serener blue,
With golden light enlivened, wide invests
The happy world. Attempered suns arise
Sweet-beamed, and shedding oft through lucid
     clouds
A pleasing calm ; while broad and brown, below, 30
Extensive harvests hang the heavy head.
Rich, silent, deep they stand ; for not a gale
Rolls its light billows o'er the bending plain ;
A calm of plenty ! till the ruffled air
Falls from its poise, and gives the breeze to blow.
Rent is the fleecy mantle of the sky ;
The clouds fly different ; and the sudden sun
By fits effulgent gilds the illumined field,

14 bosom] conduct 1730-38.   27 enlivened] irradiate 1730-
38.   31 Extensive] Unbounded 1730-38.

And black by fits the shadows sweep along—
A gaily chequered, heart-expanding view,   40
Far as the circling eye can shoot around,
Unbounded tossing in a flood of corn.
  These are thy blessings, Industry, rough power !
Whom labour still attends, and sweat, and pain ;
Yet the kind source of every gentle art
And all the soft civility of life :
Raiser of human kind ! by nature cast
Naked and helpless out amid the woods
And wilds to rude inclement elements ;
With various seeds of art deep in the mind   50
Implanted, and profusely poured around
Materials infinite ; but idle all,
Still unexerted, in the unconscious breast
Slept the lethargic powers ; Corruption still
Voracious swallowed what the liberal hand
Of Bounty scattered o'er the savage year.
And still the sad barbarian roving mixed
With beasts of prey ; or for his acorn meal
Fought the fierce tusky boar—a shivering wretch !
Aghast and comfortless when the bleak north,   60
With winter charged, let the mixed tempest fly,
Hail, rain, and snow, and bitter-breathing frost.
Then to the shelter of the hut he fled,
And the wild season, sordid, pined away ;
For home he had not : home is the resort
Of love, of joy, of peace and plenty, where,
Supporting and supported, polished friends
And dear relations mingle into bliss.
But this the rugged savage never felt,

40 heart-expanding] wide-extended 1730-38   42 Un-
bounded] Convolved and 1730-38.   50 With various powers
of deep efficiency 1730-38.   60 bleak] red 1730-38.

Even desolate in crowds ; and thus his days   70
Rolled heavy, dark, and unenjoyed along—
A waste of time ! till Industry approached,
And roused him from his miserable sloth ;
His faculties unfolded ; pointed out
Where lavish Nature the directing hand
Of Art demanded ; showed him how to raise
His feeble force by the mechanic powers,
To dig the mineral from the vaulted earth,
On what to turn the piercing rage of fire,
On what the torrent, and the gathered blast ;   80
Gave the tall ancient forest to his axe ;
Taught him to chip the wood, and hew the stone,
Till by degrees the finished fabric rose ;
Tore from his limbs the blood-polluted fur,
And wrapt them in the woolly vestment warm,
Or bright in glossy silk, and flowing lawn ;
With wholesome viands filled his table, poured
The generous glass around, inspired to wake
The life-refining soul of decent wit ;
Nor stopped at barren bare necessity ;   90
But, still advancing bolder, led him on
To pomp, to pleasure, elegance, and grace ;
And, breathing high ambition through his soul,
Set science, wisdom, glory in his view,
And bade him be the lord of all below.
    Then gathering men their natural powers combined,
And formed a public ; to the general good
Submitting, aiming, and conducting all.
For this the patriot-council met, the full,
The free, and fairly represented whole ;   100

91 Following this line in the original text (1730–38) came—
        By hardy patience and experience slow—
dropped in 1744.

For this they planned the holy guardian laws,
Distinguished orders, animated arts,
And, with joint force Oppression chaining, set
Imperial Justice at the helm, yet still
To them accountable : nor slavish dreamed
That toiling millions must resign their weal
And all the honey of their search to such
As for themselves alone themselves have raised.
Hence every form of cultivated life
In order set, protected, and inspired   110
Into perfection wrought. Uniting all,
Society grew numerous, high, polite,
And happy. Nurse of art, the city reared
In beauteous pride her tower-encircled head ;
And, stretching street on street, by thousands drew,
From twining woody haunts, or the tough yew
To bows strong-straining, her aspiring sons.
Then commerce brought into the public walk
The busy merchant ; the big warehouse built ;
Raised the strong crane ; choked up the loaded street
With foreign plenty ; and thy stream, O Thames, 121
Large, gentle, deep, majestic, king of floods !

101 they planned] devised 1730–38.   113 reared] rose
1730–38.   114 This line does not appear in the original text.
It was added in 1744.   115 drew] led 1730–38.   118 Here
followed in the original text (1730–38) a passage of six lines,
dropped in 1744 :—
          'Twas nought but labour—the whole dusky group
          Of clustering houses and of mingling men—
          Restless design and execution strong ;
          In every street the sounding hammer plied
          His massy task, while the corrosive file
          In flying touches formed the fine machine.
121 on thee, thou Thames 1730–38.   122 After this line
came in the original text (1730–44)—
          Than whom no river heaves a fuller tide—
dropped in 1746.

F

Chose for his grand resort. On either hand,
Like a long wintry forest, groves of masts
Shot up their spires ; the bellying sheet between
Possessed the breezy void ; the sooty hulk
Steered sluggish on ; the splendid barge along
Rowed regular to harmony ; around,
The boat light-skimming stretched its oary wings ;
While deep the various voice of fervent toil   130
From bank to bank increased ; whence, ribbed with
        oak
To bear the British thunder, black, and bold,
The roaring vessel rushed into the main.
    Then too the pillared dome magnific heaved
Its ample roof ; and luxury within
Poured out her glittering stores. The canvas smooth,
With glowing life protuberant, to the view
Embodied rose ; the statue seemed to breathe
And soften into flesh beneath the touch
Of forming art, imagination-flushed.   140
    All is the gift of industry,—whate'er
Exalts, embellishes, and renders life
Delightful. Pensive Winter, cheered by him,
Sits at the social fire, and happy hears
The excluded tempest idly rave along ;
His hardened fingers deck the gaudy Spring ;
Without him Summer were an arid waste ;
Nor to the Autumnal months could thus transmit
Those full, mature, immeasurable stores
That, waving round, recall my wandering song.   150

    Soon as the morning trembles o'er the sky,
And unperceived unfolds the spreading day,
Before the ripened field the reapers stand

123 Chose] Seized 1730-38.   135 Its] His 1730-38.

In fair array, each by the lass he loves,
To bear the rougher part and mitigate
By nameless gentle offices her toil.
At once they stoop, and swell the lusty sheaves ;
While through their cheerful band the rural talk,
The rural scandal, and the rural jest
Fly harmless, to deceive the tedious time   160
And steal unfelt the sultry hours away.
Behind the master walks, builds up the shocks,
And, conscious, glancing oft on every side
His sated eye, feels his heart heave with joy.
The gleaners spread around, and here and there,
Spike after spike, their sparing harvest pick.
Be not too narrow, husbandmen ! but fling
From the full sheaf with charitable stealth
The liberal handful. Think, oh ! grateful think
How good the God of harvest is to you,   170
Who pours abundance o'er your flowing fields,
While these unhappy partners of your kind
Wide-hover round you, like the fowls of heaven,
And ask their humble dole. The various turns
Of fortune ponder ; that your sons may want
What now with hard reluctance faint ye give.

The lovely young Lavinia once had friends ;
And fortune smiled deceitful on her birth.
For, in her helpless years deprived of all,
Of every stay save innocence and Heaven,   180
She, with her widowed mother, feeble, old,
And poor, lived in a cottage far retired

158 through their cheerful band] bandied round and round
1730–38.   160 harmless] hearty 1730–38.   161 steal
unfelt] cheerly steal 1730–38.   163 on every side] this way
and that 1730–38.   182 far retired] lost far up 1730–38.

Among the windings of a woody vale ;
By solitude and deep surrounding shades,
But more by bashful modesty, concealed.
Together thus they shunned the cruel scorn
Which virtue, sunk to poverty, would meet
From giddy fashion and low-minded pride ;
Almost on nature's common bounty fed,
Like the gay birds that sung them to repose,   190
Content, and careless of to-morrow's fare.
Her form was fresher than the morning-rose
When the dew wets its leaves ; unstained and pure
As is the lily or the mountain-snow.
The modest virtues mingled in her eyes,
Still on the ground dejected, darting all
Their humid beams into the blooming flowers :
Or when the mournful tale her mother told,
Of what her faithless fortune promised once,
Thrilled in her thought, they, like the dewy star   200
Of evening, shone in tears.   A native grace
Sat fair-proportioned on her polished limbs,
Veiled in a simple robe, their best attire,
Beyond the pomp of dress ; for loveliness
Needs not the foreign aid of ornament,
But is when unadorned adorned the most.
Thoughtless of beauty, she was beauty's self,
Recluse amid the close-embowering woods.

184-8 For these five lines, added in 1744, the original text
(1730-38) gives only—
        Safe from the cruel blasting arts of man.
    196 dejected] deject and *second ed.* 1730.   198 mournful
tale] stories that 1730-38.   199 promised] flattered 1730-38.
    203 After ' simple robe ' came in the first text (1730-38) the
words ' for loveliness Needs not &c.' The addition, ' their best
attire, Beyond the pomp of dress ', was made in 1744.
    208-16 For these lines, introduced in 1744, the original text
gives only—

As in the hollow breast of Apennine,
Beneath the shelter of encircling hills,   210
A myrtle rises, far from human eye,
And breathes its balmy fragrance o'er the wild—
So flourished blooming, and unseen by all,
The sweet Lavinia ; till at length, compelled
By strong necessity's supreme command,
With smiling patience in her looks she went
To glean Palemon's fields. The pride of swains
Palemon was, the generous and the rich,
Who led the rural life in all its joy
And elegance, such as Arcadian song   220
Transmits from ancient uncorrupted times,
When tyrant custom had not shackled man,
But free to follow nature was the mode.
He then, his fancy with autumnal scenes
Amusing, chanced beside his reaper-train
To walk, when poor Lavinia drew his eye ;
Unconscious of her power, and turning quick
With unaffected blushes from his gaze—
He saw her charming, but he saw not half
The charms her downcast modesty concealed.   230
That very moment love and chaste desire
Sprung in his bosom, to himself unknown ;
For still the world prevailed, and its dread laugh,
Which scarce the firm philosopher can scorn,
Should his heart own a gleaner in the field ;
And thus in secret to his soul he sighed :

Recluse among the woods,—if city-dames
Will deign their faith. And thus she went compelled
By strong necessity with as serene
And pleased a look as patience can put on.
  210 encircling] embowering 1744.   221 incorrupted
1730–38.

' What pity that so delicate a form,
By beauty kindled, where enlivening sense
And more than vulgar goodness seem to dwell,
Should be devoted to the rude embrace   240
Of some indecent clown ! She looks, methinks,
Of old Acasto's line ; and to my mind
Recalls that patron of my happy life,
From whom my liberal fortune took its rise,—
Now to the dust gone down, his houses, lands,
And once fair-spreading family dissolved.
'Tis said that in some lone, obscure retreat,
Urged by remembrance sad and decent pride,
Far from those scenes which knew their better
    days,
His aged widow and his daughter live ;   250
Whom yet my fruitless search could never find.
Romantic wish, would this the daughter were ! '
  When, strict inquiring, from herself he found
She was the same, the daughter of his friend,
Of bountiful Acasto, who can speak
The mingled passions that surprised his heart
And through his nerves in shivering transport ran ?
Then blazed his smothered flame, avowed and bold
And, as he viewed her ardent o'er and o'er,
Love, gratitude, and pity wept at once.   260
Confused and frightened at his sudden tears,
Her rising beauties flushed a higher bloom,
As thus Palemon, passionate and just,
Poured out the pious rapture of his soul :

237, 238 For these lines the first text (1730-38) gives—
    By beauty kindled, and harmonious shaped,
    Where sense sincere and goodness seemed to dwell.
  247 'Tis said . . lone] I've heard . . waste 1730-38.   255
Of] The 1730-38.   256 mingled passions] mingling passion
1730-38.   259 viewed] run 1730-38.

' And art thou then Acasto's dear remains ?
She whom my restless gratitude has sought
So long in vain ? O yes ! the very same,
The softened image of my noble friend,
Alive his every feature, every look,
More elegantly touched. Sweeter than Spring !   270
Thou soul surviving blossom from the root
That nourished up my fortune ! say, ah where,
In what sequestered desert, hast thou drawn
The kindest aspect of delighted Heaven ?
Into such beauty spread, and blown so fair ?
Though poverty's cold wind and crushing rain
Beat keen and heavy on thy tender years.
Oh, let me now into a richer soil
Transplant thee safe, where vernal suns and showers
Diffuse their warmest, largest influence ;   280
And of my garden be the pride and joy !
It ill befits thee, oh, it ill befits
Acasto's daughter—his, whose open stores,
Though vast, were little to his ampler heart,
The father of a country—thus to pick
The very refuse of those harvest-fields
Which from his bounteous friendship I enjoy.
Then throw that shameful pittance from thy hand,
But ill applied to such a rugged task ;
The fields, the master, all, my fair, are thine ;   290
If, to the various blessings which thy house

270 Sweeter] Fairer 1730-38.   275 fair] white 1730-38.
287 His bounty taught to gain, and right enjoy 1730-38.
    290-93 For these lines, which first appeared in ed. 1744, the
original text (1730-38) gives—
        With harvest shining all these fields are thine ;
        And, if my wishes may presume so far,
        Their master too, who then indeed were blest
        To make the daughter of Acasto so.

Has on me lavish'd, thou wilt add that bliss,
That dearest bliss, the power of blessing thee ! '
Here ceased the youth : yet still his speaking eye
Expressed the sacred triumph of his soul,
With conscious virtue, gratitude, and love
Above the vulgar joy divinely raised.
Nor waited he reply. Won by the charm
Of goodness irresistible, and all
In sweet disorder lost, she blushed consent.   300
The news immediate to her mother brought,
While, pierced with anxious thought, she pined away
The lonely moments for Lavinia's fate,
Amazed, and scarce believing what she heard,
Joy seized her wither'd veins, and one bright gleam
Of setting life shone on her evening hours,—
Not less enraptured than the happy pair ;
Who flourished long in tender bliss, and reared
A numerous offspring, lovely like themselves,
And good, the grace of all the country round.   310

Defeating oft the labours of the year,
The sultry south collects a potent blast.
At first, the groves are scarcely seen to stir
Their trembling tops ; and a still murmur runs
Along the soft-inclining fields of corn.
But, as the aerial tempest fuller swells,
And in one mighty stream, invisible,
Immense, the whole excited atmosphere
Impetuous rushes o'er the sounding world—
Strained to the root, the stooping forest pours   320
A rustling shower of yet untimely leaves.
High-beat, the circling mountains eddy in,
From the bare wild, the dissipated storm,

292 lavished on me 1744.   308 tender] mutual 1730-38.

And send it in a torrent down the vale.
Exposed, and naked to its utmost rage,
Through all the sea of harvest rolling round,
The billowy plain floats wide ; nor can evade,
Though pliant to the blast, its seizing force—
Or whirled in air or into vacant chaff
Shook waste. And sometimes too a burst of rain, 330
Swept from the black horizon, broad descends
In one continuous flood. Still over head
The mingling tempest weaves its gloom, and still
The deluge deepens ; till the fields around
Lie sunk and flatted in the sordid wave.
Sudden the ditches swell ; the meadows swim.
Red from the hills innumerable streams
Tumultuous roar, and high above its banks
The river lift—before whose rushing tide
Herds, flocks, and harvests, cottages, and swains 340
Roll mingled down; all that the winds had spared
In one wild moment ruined, the big hopes
And well-earned treasures of the painful year.
Fled to some eminence, the husbandman
Helpless beholds the miserable wreck
Driving along ; his drowning ox, at once
Descending with his labours scattered round,
He sees ; and instant o'er his shivering thought
Comes winter unprovided, and a train
Of clamant children dear. Ye masters, then 350
Be mindful of the rough laborious hand
That sinks you soft in elegance and ease ;
Be mindful of those limbs in russet clad
Whose toil to yours is warmth and graceful pride ;

327 floats] boils 1730–38. 333 mingling tempest weaves]
glomerating tempest grows 1730–38 ; mingling tempest waves
1744. 339 rushing tide] weighty rush 1730–38.

And oh, be mindful of that sparing board
Which covers yours with luxury profuse,
Makes your glass sparkle, and your sense rejoice ;
Nor cruelly demand what the deep rains
And all-involving winds have swept away !

Here the rude clamour of the sportsman's joy, 360
The gun fast-thundering and the winded horn,
Would tempt the Muse to sing the rural game,—
How, in his mid career, the spaniel, struck
Stiff by the tainted gale, with open nose
Outstretched and finely sensible, draws full,
Fearful, and cautious on the latent prey ·
As in the sun the circling covey bask
Their varied plumes, and, watchful every way,
Through the rough stubble turn the secret eye.
Caught in the meshy snare, in vain they beat   370
Their idle wings, entangled more and more :
Nor, on the surges of the boundless air
Though borne triumphant, are they safe ; the gun,
Glanced just, and sudden, from the fowler's eye,
O'ertakes their sounding pinions, and again
Immediate brings them from the towering wing
Dead to the ground ; or drives them wide-dispersed,
Wounded and wheeling various down the wind.
   These are not subjects for the peaceful muse,
Nor will she stain with such her spotless song—   380
Then most delighted when she social sees
The whole mixed animal creation round

361 fast] thick 1730-38.   362 the rural game] a rural game
1730; the rural game *second ed.* 1730.   368 and, watchful]
watchful, and 1730-38. 369 turned 1730-38.   371 idle] useless
1730-38.   377 wide] else 1730-38   380 her spotless
theme with such 1730-38.   381 social] smiling 1730-38.

Alive and happy. 'Tis not joy to her,
This falsely cheerful barbarous game of death,
This rage of pleasure which the restless youth
Awakes, impatient, with the gleaming morn ;
When beasts of prey retire that all night long,
Urged by necessity, had ranged the dark,
As if their conscious ravage shunned the light
Ashamed. Not so the steady tyrant, man,   390
Who, with the thoughtless insolence of power
Inflamed beyond the most infuriate wrath
Of the worst monster that e'er roamed the waste,
For sport alone pursues the cruel chase
Amid the beamings of the gentle days.
Upbraid, ye ravening tribes, our wanton rage,
For hunger kindles you, and lawless want ;
But lavish fed, in Nature's bounty rolled,
To joy at anguish, and delight in blood,
Is what your horrid bosoms never knew.   400
    Poor is the triumph o'er the timid hare !
Scared from the corn, and now to some lone seat
Retired—the rushy fen, the ragged furze
Stretched o'er the stony heath, the stubble chapped,
The thistly lawn, the thick entangled broom,
Of the same friendly hue the withered fern,
The fallow ground laid open to the sun
Concoctive, and the nodding sandy bank
Hung o'er the mazes of the mountain brook.
Vain is her best precaution ; though she sits   410
Concealed with folded ears, unsleeping eyes

388 ranged] roamed 1730–38.   392 wrath] rage 1730–38.
393 roamed] howled 1730–38.   394 pursues . . chase] takes
up . . tract 1730–38.   396 Upbraid us not, ye wolves! ye
tigers fell ! 1730–38 ; ye ravening tribes, upbraid our wanton
rage 1744.   399 joy . . delight] laugh . . rejoice 1730–38.
402 Scared] Shook 1730–38.

By Nature raised to take the horizon in,
And head couched close betwixt her hairy feet
In act to spring away. The scented dew
Betrays her early labyrinth ; and deep,
In scattered sullen openings, far behind,
With every breeze she hears the coming storm
But, nearer and more frequent as it loads
The sighing gale, she springs amazed, and all
The savage soul of game is up at once—   420
The pack full-opening various, the shrill horn
Resounded from the hills, the neighing steed
Wild for the chase, and the loud hunter's shout—
O'er a weak, harmless, flying creature, all
Mixed in mad tumult and discordant joy.
    The stag, too, singled from the herd, where long
He ranged the branching monarch of the shades,
Before the tempest drives. At first, in speed
He sprightly puts his faith, and, roused by fear,
Gives all his swift aerial soul to flight.   430
Against the breeze he darts, that way the more
To leave the lessening murderous cry behind.
Deception short ! though, fleeter than the winds
Blown o'er the keen-aired mountain by the North,
He bursts the thickets, glances through the glades,
And plunges deep into the wildest wood.
If slow, yet sure, adhesive to the track
Hot-steaming, up behind him come again
The inhuman rout, and from the shady depth
Expel him, circling through his every shift.   440
He sweeps the forest oft ; and sobbing sees
The glades, mild opening to the golden day,
Where in kind contest with his butting friends
He wont to struggle, or his loves enjoy.

429 fear-aroused 1730-44.   437 tract 1730-38.   438 comes
1730-44.   440 Expels 1744.   444 wont] went 1730-38.

Oft in the full-descending flood he tries
To lose the scent, and lave his burning sides—
Oft seeks the herd ; the watchful herd, alarmed,
With selfish care avoid a brother's woe.
What shall he do ? His once so vivid nerves,
So full of buoyant spirit, now no more   450
Inspire the course ; but fainting, breathless toil
Sick seizes on his heart : he stands at bay,
And puts his last weak refuge in despair.
The big round tears run down his dappled face ;
He groans in anguish ; while the growling pack,
Blood-happy, hang at his fair jutting chest,
And mark his beauteous chequered sides with gore.
  Of this enough. But, if the sylvan youth,
Whose fervent blood boils into violence,
Must have the chase, behold, despising flight,   460
The roused up lion, resolute and slow,
Advancing full on the protended spear
And coward band that circling wheel aloof.
Slunk from the cavern and the troubled wood,
See the grim wolf ; on him his shaggy foe
Vindictive fix, and let the ruffian die :
Or, growling horrid, as the brindled boar
Grins fell destruction, to the monster's heart
Let the dart lighten from the nervous arm.
  These Britain knows not ; give, ye Britons, then 470
Your sportive fury pitiless to pour
Loose on the nightly robber of the fold.
Him, from his craggy winding haunts unearthed,

448 With quick consent avoid the infectious maze 1730-38.
450 spirit, now] soul, inspire 1730-38.   451 The fainting
course ; but wrenching, breathless toil 1730-38.   466 and let
the ruffian die] for murder is his trade 1730-38.   467 Or]
And 1730-38.   468 fell] near 1730-38.
  472 nightly robber . . fold] sly destroyer . . flock 1730-38.

Let all the thunder of the chase pursue.
Throw the broad ditch behind you ; o'er the hedge
High bound resistless ; nor the deep morass
Refuse, but through the shaking wilderness
Pick your nice way ; into the perilous flood
Bear fearless, of the raging instinct full ;
And, as you ride the torrent, to the banks   480
Your triumph sound sonorous, running round
From rock to rock, in circling echo tost ;
Then scale the mountains to their woody tops ;
Rush down the dangerous steep ; and o'er the
      lawn,
In fancy swallowing up the space between,
Pour all your speed into the rapid game.
For happy he who tops the wheeling chase ;
Has every maze evolved, and every guile
Disclosed ; who knows the merits of the pack ;
Who saw the villain seized, and dying hard   490
Without complaint, though by an hundred mouths
Relentless torn : O glorious he beyond
His daring peers, when the retreating horn
Calls them to ghostly halls of grey renown,
With woodland honours graced—the fox's fur
Depending decent from the roof, and spread
Round the drear walls, with antic figures fierce,
The stag's large front : he then is loudest heard
When the night staggers with severer toils,
With feats Thessalian Centaurs never knew,   500
And their repeated wonders shake the dome
    But first the fuelled chimney blazes wide ;

476 High-bound (*hyphenated*) 1730–46.   483 scale . . to]
snatch . . by 1730–38.
    492, 493 At once tore merciless. Thrice happy he !
        At hour of dusk, while &c. 1730–38.
    500 This line was added in 1744.

The tankards foam ; and the strong table groans
Beneath the smoking sirloin, stretched immense
From side to side, in which with desperate knife
They deep incision make, and talk the while
Of England's glory, ne'er to be defaced
While hence they borrow vigour ; or, amain
Into the pasty plunged, at intervals,
If stomach keen can intervals allow,   510
Relating all the glories of the chase.
Then sated Hunger bids his brother Thirst
Produce the mighty bowl : the mighty bowl,
Swelled high with fiery juice, steams liberal round
A potent gale, delicious as the breath
Of Maia to the love-sick shepherdess
On violets diffused, while soft she hears
Her panting shepherd stealing to her arms.
Nor wanting is the brown October, drawn
Mature and perfect from his dark retreat   520
Of thirty years ; and now his honest front
Flames in the light refulgent, not afraid
Even with the vineyard's best produce to vie.
To cheat the thirsty moments, whist a while
Walks his grave round beneath a cloud of smoke,
Wreathed fragrant from the pipe ; or the quick dice,
In thunder leaping from the box, awake
The sounding gammon ; while romp-loving miss
Is hauled about in gallantry robust.
    At last these puling idlenesses laid   530

505 on which with fell intent 1730–38.   511 Relating how
it ran and how it fell 1730–38.   515 delicious] reviving
1730–38.   519 october (*with a small o*) 1730–38.   522 not
afraid] nor ashamed 1730–38.   523 To vie it with the vineyards best produce 1730–38.   524 whist] whisk 1744; Perhaps
a while amusive thoughtful Whisk 1730–38.   525 grave] dull
1744; Walks gentle round 1730–38.

Aside, frequent and full, the dry divan
Close in firm circle ; and set ardent in
For serious drinking. Nor evasion sly
Nor sober shift is to the puking wretch
Indulged apart ; but earnest brimming bowls
Lave every soul, the table floating round,
And pavement faithless to the fuddled foot.
Thus as they swim in mutual swill, the talk,
Vociferous at once from twenty tongues,   539
Reels fast from theme to theme—from horses, hounds,
To church or mistress, politics or ghost—
In endless mazes, intricate, perplext.
Meantime, with sudden interruption, loud
The impatient catch bursts from the joyous heart.
That moment touched is each congenial soul ;
And, opening in a full-mouthed cry of joy,
The laugh, the slap, the jocund curse goes round ;
While, from their slumbers shook, the kennelled hounds
Mix in the music of the day again.
As when the tempest, that has vexed the deep   550
The dark night long, with fainter murmurs falls ;
So gradual sinks their mirth. Their feeble tongues,
Unable to take up the cumbrous word,
Lie quite dissolved. Before their maudlin eyes,
Seen dim and blue, the double tapers dance,
Like the sun wading through the misty sky.
Then, sliding soft, they drop. Confused above,
Glasses and bottles, pipes and gazetteers,
As if the table even itself was drunk,

535 apart] askew 1730-38.   539 Vociferous . . . from]
Vociferate . . by 1730-38.   545 each congenial] every kindred
1730-44.   551 falls murmuring towards morn 1730-38.   552
So their mirth gradual sinks 1730-38.   557 soft] sweet 1730-
38 ; Confused] O'erturned 1730-38.   558, 559 These two
lines were added in 1744.

Lie a wet broken scene : and wide, below, 560
Is heaped the social slaughter—where astride
The lubber Power in filthy triumph sits,
Slumbrous, inclining still from side to side,
And steeps them drenched in potent sleep till morn.
Perhaps some doctor of tremendous paunch,
Awful and deep, a black abyss of drink,
Outlives them all ; and, from his buried flock
Retiring, full of rumination sad,
Laments the weakness of these latter times.
But if the rougher sex by this fierce sport 570
Is hurried wild, let not such horrid joy
E'er stain the bosom of the British fair.
Far be the spirit of the chase from them !
Uncomely courage, unbeseeming skill,
To spring the fence, to reign the prancing steed,
The cap, the whip, the masculine attire
In which they roughen to the sense and all
The winning softness of their sex is lost.
In them 'tis graceful to dissolve at woe ;
With every motion, every word, to wave 580
Quick o'er the kindling cheek the ready blush ;
And from the smallest violence to shrink
Unequal, then the loveliest in their fears ;
And, by this silent adulation soft,
To their protection more engaging man.
O may their eyes no miserable sight,
Save weeping lovers, see ! a nobler game,

560 Lies the wet broken scene, and stretched below 1730-38.
561 Each way the drunken slaughter 1730-38.   562 in filthy
triumph] himself triumphant 1730-38.   564 drenched in
potent] silent all, in 1730-38.   569 The five lines ending
here were added in 1744.   570 fierce] red 1730-38.   571 Is]
Are 1730-44.   579 Before this line, in the original text (1730-
38), came a line, dropped in 1744,—
        Made up of blushes, tenderness, and fears.

Through love's enchanting wiles pursued, yet fled,
In chase ambiguous. May their tender limbs
Float in the loose simplicity of dress !   590
And, fashioned all to harmony, alone
Know they to seize the captivated soul,
In rapture warbled from love-breathing lips ;
To teach the lute to languish ; with smooth step,
Disclosing motion in its every charm,
To swim along and swell the mazy dance ;
To train the foliage o'er the snowy lawn ;
To guide the pencil, turn the tuneful page ;
To lend new flavour to the fruitful year,
And heighten nature's dainties ; in their race   600
To rear their graces into second life ;
To give society its highest taste ;
Well-ordered home man's best delight to make ;
And, by submissive wisdom, modest skill,
With every gentle care-eluding art,
To raise the virtues, animate the bliss,
Even charm the pains to something more than joy,
And sweeten all the toils of human life :
This be the female dignity and praise.

      Ye swains, now hasten to the hazel-bank,   610
Where down yon dale the wildly-winding brook
Falls hoarse from steep to steep. In close array,
Fit for the thickets and the tangling shrub,
Ye virgins, come. For you their latest song
The woodlands raise ; the clustering nuts for you
The lover finds amid the secret shade ;

      593 the radiant lip 1730-38.   598 guide . . tuneful] play
. . instructive 1730-38.   599 lend] give 1730-38.   605
gentle care-eluding] kinder, care-elusive 1730-38.   606 virtues
. . bliss] glory . . joys 1730-38.   607 This line was added
in 1744.   615 the clustered nut 1730-38.

And, where they burnish on the topmost bough,
With active vigour crushes down the tree ;
Or shakes them ripe from the resigning husk,
A glossy shower and of an ardent brown   620
As are the ringlets of Melinda's hair—
Melinda ! form'd with every grace complete,
Yet these neglecting, above beauty wise,
And far transcending such a vulgar praise.

Hence from the busy joy-resounding fields,
In cheerful error let us tread the maze
Of Autumn unconfined ; and taste, revived,
The breath of orchard big with bending fruit.
Obedient to the breeze and beating ray,
From the deep-loaded bough a mellow shower   630
Incessant melts away. The juicy pear
Lies in a soft profusion scattered round.
A various sweetness swells the gentle race,
By Nature's all-refining hand prepared,
Of tempered sun, and water, earth, and air,
In ever-changing composition mixed.
Such, falling frequent through the chiller night,
The fragrant stores, the wide-projected heaps
Of apples, which the lusty-handed year
Innumerous o'er the blushing orchard shakes.   640
A various spirit, fresh, delicious, keen,
Dwells in their gelid pores, and active points
The piercing cider for the thirsty tongue—

617 And] Or 1730–38.   627 taste, revived] vital taste
1730–38.   633 After this line in the original text (1730–44)
came—
        In species different, but in kind the same—
dropped in 1746.
    636 every-changing (a *misprint*) 1744.   637, 638 For these
two lines the first text (1730–38) gives only—
        So fares it with those wide-projected heaps &c.

Thy native theme, and boon inspirer too,
Phillips, Pomona's bard! the second thou
Who nobly durst in rhyme-unfettered verse
With British freedom sing the British song—
How from Silurian vats high-sparkling wines
Foam in transparent floods, some strong to cheer
The wintry revels of the labouring hind,   650
And tasteful some to cool the summer hours.

In this glad season, while his sweetest beams
The Sun sheds equal o'er the meekened day,
Oh, lose me in the green delightful walks
Of, Dodington, thy seat, serene and plain ;
Where simple Nature reigns ; and every view
Diffusive spreads the pure Dorsetian downs
In boundless prospect—yonder shagged with wood,
Here rich with harvest, and there white with flocks !
Meantime the grandeur of thy lofty dome   660
Far-splendid seizes on the ravished eye.
New beauties rise with each revolving day ;
New columns swell ; and still the fresh Spring finds
New plants to quicken, and new groves to green.
Full of thy genius all, the Muses' seat !
Where, in the secret bower and winding walk,
For virtuous Young and thee they twine the bay.
Here wandering oft, fired with the restless thirst
Of thy applause, I solitary court
The inspiring breeze, and meditate the book   670
Of Nature, ever open, aiming thence
Warm from the heart to learn the moral song.

645 Pomona's] facetious 1730–38.   652 sweetest] last, best
1730–38.   654 delightful] majestic 1730–38.   667–9 For
these three lines the first text (1730–38) gives the following two :—
    They twine the bay for thee. Here oft alone,
    Fired by the thirst of thy applause, I court &c.
672 Warm from the heart] Heart-taught like thine 1730–38.

And, as I steal along the sunny wall,
Where Autumn basks, with fruit empurpled deep,
My pleasing theme continual prompts my thought—
Presents the downy peach, the shining plum
With a fine bluish mist of animals
Clouded, the ruddy nectarine, and dark
Beneath his ample leaf the luscious fig.
The vine too here her curling tendrils shoots,   680
Hangs out her clusters glowing to the south,
And scarcely wishes for a warmer sky.

Turn we a moment fancy's rapid flight
To vigorous soils and climes of fair extent,
Where, by the potent sun elated high,
The vineyard swells refulgent on the day,
Spreads o'er the vale, or up the mountain climbs
Profuse, and drinks amid the sunny rocks,
From cliff to cliff increased, the heightened blaze.
Low bend the weighty boughs. The clusters clear, 690
Half through the foliage seen, or ardent flame
Or shine transparent ; while perfection breathes
White o'er the turgent film the living dew.
As thus they brighten with exalted juice,
Touched into flavour by the mingling ray,
The rural youth and virgins o'er the field,
Each fond for each to cull the autumnal prime,

673-5 The first text (1730-38) is, punctuation and all, as
follows :—
      And, as I steal along, the sunny wall,
      Where *Autumn* basks, with fruit empurpled deep,
      My theme still urges in my vagrant thought ;—
apparently meaning that the fruit-covered wall reminded him of
his subject.
   676 shining plum] purple plumb 1730-38.   681 glowing]
swelling 1730-38.   686 swells] heaves 1730-38.   690
weighty] gravid 1730- 8.

Exulting rove, and speak the vintage nigh.
Then comes the crushing swain ; the country floats,
And foams unbounded with the mashy flood,   700
That, by degrees fermented, and refined,
Round the raised nations pours the cup of joy—
The claret smooth, red as the lip we press
In sparkling fancy while we drain the bowl,
The mellow-tasted burgundy, and, quick
As is the wit it gives, the gay champagne.

Now, by the cool declining year condensed,
Descend the copious exhalations, checked
As up the middle sky unseen they stole,
And roll the doubling fogs around the hill.   710
No more the mountain, horrid, vast, sublime,
Who pours a sweep of rivers from his sides,
And high between contending kingdoms rears
The rocky long division, fills the view
With great variety ; but, in a night
Of gathering vapour, from the baffled sense
Sinks dark and dreary. Thence expanding far,
The huge dusk gradual swallows up the plain :
Vanish the woods : the dim-seen river seems,
Sullen and slow, to roll the misty wave.   720
Even in the height of noon oppressed, the sun
Sheds, weak and blunt, his wide-refracted ray ;
Whence glaring oft, with many a broadened orb,
He frights the nations. Indistinct on earth,

703 red] deep 1730-38.   713 high between . . . rears] deep
betwixt . . . lays 1730-38.   714 Here, after ' long division ',
the original text (1730-38) gives—
                   While aloft
     His piny top is, lessening, lost in air ;
     No more his thousand prospects fill the view
     With great variety &c.
717 Sink dark and total. Nor alone immersed 1730-38.

Seen through the turbid air, beyond the life
Objects appear, and, wildered, o'er the waste
The shepherd stalks gigantic ; till at last,
Wreathed dun around, in deeper circles still
Successive closing, sits the general fog
Unbounded o'er the world, and, mingling thick,   730
A formless grey confusion covers all.
As when of old (so sung the Hebrew bard)
Light, uncollected, through the Chaos urged
Its infant way, nor order yet had drawn
His lovely train from out the dubious gloom.

  These roving mists, that constant now begin
To smoke along the hilly country, these,
With weighty rains and melted Alpine snows,
The mountain-cisterns fill—those ample stores
Of water, scooped among the hollow rocks,   740
Whence gush the streams, the ceaseless fountains play,
And their unfailing wealth the rivers draw.
Some sages say, that, where the numerous wave
For ever lashes the resounding shore,
Drilled through the sandy stratum, every way,
The waters with the sandy stratum rise ;
Amid whose angles infinitely strained,
They joyful leave their jaggy salts behind,

728 dun] close 1730–38.   729 closing] floating 1730–38.
735 His endless train forth from &c. 1730–38. 738 With mighty
rains, the skilled in nature say 1730–38.   739 ample stores]
grand reserves 1730–38.   740 rock (*erratum*) 1744.
  742 wealth] stores 1730–38. Following this line in the original
text (1730–38) came a long passage of 17 lines, which the reader
will find in a Note at the end of the poem. It was dropped in 1744.
  743–5 The original text (1730–38) reads—
      And thus some sages deep-exploring teach
      That where the hoarse innumerable wave
      Eternal lashes the resounding shore,
      Sucked through the &c.
  748 They leave each saline particle behind 1730–38.

And clear and sweeten as they soak along.
Nor stops the restless fluid, mounting still,   750
Though oft amidst the irriguous vale it springs ;
But, to the mountain courted by the sand,
That leads it darkling on in faithful maze,
Far from the parent main, it boils again
Fresh into day, and all the glittering hill
Is bright with spouting rills. But hence this vain
Amusive dream ! why should the waters love
To take so far a journey to the hills,
When the sweet valleys offer to their toil
Inviting quiet and a nearer bed ?   760
Or if, by blind ambition led astray,
They must aspire, why should they sudden stop
Among the broken mountain's rushy dells.
And, ere they gain its highest peak, desert
The attractive sand that charmed their course so long ?
Besides, the hard agglomerating salts,
The spoil of ages, would impervious choke
Their secret channels, or by slow degrees,
High as the hills, protrude the swelling vales :
Old ocean too, sucked through the porous globe,   770
Had long ere now forsook his horrid bed,
And brought Deucalion's watery times again.
　　Say, then, where lurk the vast eternal springs
That, like creating Nature, lie concealed
From mortal eye, yet with their lavish stores
Refresh the globe and all its joyous tribes ?
O thou pervading genius, given to man

751 oft amidst the irriguous vale] here and there in lowly
plains 1730-38.
756-835 This long passage of eighty lines beginning ' But hence
this vain ' was introduced into the text in 1744, displacing eleven
lines which had appeared in the early edd. (1730-38).　The displaced lines are given in a Note at the end of the poem.

To trace the secrets of the dark abyss !
Oh ! lay the mountains bare, and wide display
Their hidden structure to the astonished view ;   780
Strip from the branching Alps their piny load,
The huge incumbrance of horrific woods
From Asian Taurus, from Imaus stretched
Athwart the roving Tartar's sullen bounds ;
Give opening Hemus to my searching eye,
And high Olympus pouring many a stream !
Oh, from the sounding summits of the north,
The Dofrine Hills, through Scandinavia rolled
To farthest Lapland and the frozen main ;
From lofty Caucasus, far seen by those   790
Who in the Caspian and black Euxine toil ;
From cold Riphaean rocks, which the wild Russ
Believes the stony girdle of the world ;
And all the dreadful mountains wrapt in storm
Whence wide Siberia draws her lonely floods ;
Oh, sweep the eternal snows ! Hung o'er the deep,
That ever works beneath his sounding base,
Bid Atlas, propping heaven, as poets feign,
His subterranean wonders spread ! Unveil
The miny caverns, blazing on the day,   800
Of Abyssinia's cloud-compelling cliffs,
And of the bending Mountains of the Moon !
O'ertopping all these giant-sons of earth,
Let the dire Andes, from the radiant Line
Stretched to the stormy seas that thunder round
The Southern Pole, their hideous deeps unfold !
Amazing scene ! Behold ! the glooms disclose !
I see the rivers in their infant beds !
Deep, deep I hear them labouring to get free !
I see the leaning strata, artful ranged ;   810
The gaping fissures, to receive the rains,
The melting snows, and ever-dripping fogs.

Strowed bibulous above I see the sands,
The pebbly gravel next, the layers then
Of mingled moulds, of more retentive earths,
The guttured rocks and mazy-running clefts,
That, while the stealing moisture they transmit,
Retard its motion, and forbid its waste.
Beneath the incessant weeping of these drains,
I see the rocky siphons stretched immense,   820
The mighty reservoirs, of hardened chalk
Or stiff compacted clay capacious formed :
O'erflowing thence, the congregated stores,
The crystal treasures of the liquid world,
Through the stirred sands a bubbling passage burst,
And, welling out around the middle steep
Or from the bottoms of the bosomed hills
In pure effusion flow. United thus,
The exhaling sun, the vapour-burdened air,
The gelid mountains, that to rain condensed   830
These vapours in continual current draw,
And send them o'er the fair-divided earth
In bounteous rivers to the deep again,
A social commerce hold, and firm support
The full-adjusted harmony of things.

When Autumn scatters his departing gleams,
Warned of approaching Winter, gathered, play
The swallow-people ; and, tossed wide around,
O'er the calm sky in convolution swift
The feathered eddy floats, rejoicing once   840
Ere to their wintry slumbers they retire,
In clusters clung beneath the mouldering bank,
And where, unpierced by frost, the cavern sweats :
Or rather, into warmer climes conveyed,

836 When] While 1730-38.   843 And where the cavern
sweats,—as sages dream 1730-38

With other kindred birds of season, there
They twitter cheerful, till the vernal months
Invite them welcome back—for thronging now
Innumerous wings are in commotion all.
Where the Rhine loses his majestic force
In Belgian plains, won from the raging deep   850
By diligence amazing and the strong
Unconquerable hand of liberty,
The stork-assembly meets, for many a day
Consulting deep and various ere they take
Their arduous voyage through the liquid sky.
And now, their route designed, their leaders chose,
Their tribes adjusted, cleaned their vigorous wings,
And many a circle, many a short essay,
Wheeled round and round, in congregation full
The figured flight ascends, and, riding high   860
The aerial billows, mixes with the clouds.
   Or, where the Northern Ocean in vast whirls
Boils round the naked melancholy isles
Of farthest Thule, and the Atlantic surge
Pours in among the stormy Hebrides,
Who can recount what transmigrations there
Are annual made ? what nations come and go ?
And how the living clouds on clouds arise,
Infinite wings ! till all the plume-dark air
And rude resounding shore are one wild cry ?   870
   Here the plain harmless native his small flock
And herd diminutive of many hues
Tends on the little island's verdant swell,
The shepherd's sea-girt reign ; or, to the rocks
Dire-clinging, gathers his ovarious food ;
Or sweeps the fishy shore ; or treasures up
The plumage, rising full, to form the bed

855 arduous] plumy 1730–38.   870 rude] white 1730–38.

Of luxury. And here a while the muse,
High hovering o'er the broad cerulean scene,
Sees Caledonia in romantic view—   880
Her airy mountains from the waving main
Invested with a keen diffusive sky,
Breathing the soul acute ; her forests huge,
Incult, robust, and tall, by Nature's hand
Planted of old ; her azure lakes between,
Poured out extensive, and of watery wealth
Full ; winding deep and green, her fertile vales,
With many a cool translucent brimming flood
Washed lovely, from the Tweed (pure parent-stream,
Whose pastoral banks first heard my Doric reed,   890
With, silvan Jed, thy tributary brook)
To where the north-inflated tempest foams
O'er Orca's or Betubium's highest peak—
Nurse of a people, in misfortune's school
Trained up to hardy deeds, soon visited
By Learning, when before the Gothic rage
She took her western flight; a manly race
Of unsubmitting spirit, wise, and brave,
Who still through bleeding ages struggled hard
(As well unhappy Wallace can attest,   900
Great patriot-hero ! ill requited chief !)
To hold a generous undiminished state,
Too much in vain ! Hence, of unequal bounds

878–949 This passage is a development of thirteen lines which
originally appeared in *Summer*. See *Summer*, Note to ll. 1479–
1579.
  881 waving] gelid 1730–38.
  890, 891 These two lines were added in 1744. The ed. of that
year, however, gave ' waked ' altered in 1746 to ' heard '.
  893 Orca's] Orca 1730–38.
  897 manly] generous 1730–38.   900, 901 These two
bracketed lines were added in 1744.   902 generous] hapless
1730–38.   903 unequal] ignoble 1730–38.

Impatient, and by tempting glory borne
O'er every land, for every land their life
Has flowed profuse, their piercing genius planned,
And swelled the pomp of peace their faithful toil :
As from their own clear north in radiant streams
Bright over Europe bursts the boreal morn.
  Oh ! is there not some patriot in whose power 910
That best, that godlike luxury is placed,
Of blessing thousands, thousands yet unborn,
Through late posterity ? some, large of soul,
To cheer dejected Industry, to give
A double harvest to the pining swain,
And teach the labouring hand the sweets of toil ?
How, by the finest art, the native robe
To weave ; how, white as Hyperborean snow,
To form the lucid lawn ; with venturous oar
How to dash wide the billow ; nor look on, 920
Shamefully passive, while Batavian fleets
Defraud us of the glittering finny swarms
That heave our friths and crowd upon our shores ;
How all-enlivening trade to rouse, and wing
The prosperous sail from every growing port,
Uninjured, round the sea-encircled globe ;
And thus, in soul united as in name,
Bid Britain reign the mistress of the deep ?
  Yes, there are such. And full on thee, Argyle,
Her hope, her stay, her darling, and her boast, 930
From her first patriots and her heroes sprung,
Thy fond imploring Country turns her eye ;
In thee, with all a mother's triumph, sees
Her every virtue, every grace combined,

926 Uninjured] Unchallenged 1730-38.
927, 928 And thus united Britain Britain make
          Entire, the imperial Mistress of the deep
second ed. 1730.

Her genius, wisdom, her engaging turn,
Her pride of honour, and her courage tried,
Calm and intrepid, in the very throat
Of sulphurous war, on Tenier's dreadful field.
Nor less the palm of peace enwreathes thy brow :
For, powerful as thy sword, from thy rich tongue 940
Persuasion flows, and wins the high debate ;
While mixed in thee combine the charm of youth,
The force of manhood, and the depth of age.
Thee, Forbes, too, whom every worth attends,
As truth sincere, as weeping friendship kind,
Thee, truly generous, and in silence great,
Thy country feels through her reviving arts,
Planned by thy wisdom, by thy soul informed ;
And seldom has she felt a friend like thee.

But see the fading many-coloured woods,   950
Shade deepening over shade, the country round
Imbrown ; a crowded umbrage, dusk and dun,
Of every hue from wan declining green
To sooty dark. These now the lonesome muse,
Low-whispering, lead into their leaf-strown walks,
And give the season in its latest view.
Meantime, light shadowing all, a sober calm
Fleeces unbounded ether ; whose least wave

935 engaging] politest 1730-38.
939 Instead of this line, which first appeared in 1744, the
original text (1730-38) gives the following six lines :—
    While thick around the deadly tempest flew.
    And when the trumpet, kindling war no more,
    Pours not the flaming squadrons o'er the field,
    But, fruitful of fair deeds and mutual faith,
    Kind peace unites the jarring world again,
    Let the deep olive through thy laurels twine.
949 a] the 1730-38.   956-63 These lines are an expansion
of a passage in the first ed. of *Winter*, ll. 29-33.   (See p. 228 of
this book.)

Stands tremulous, uncertain where to turn
The gentle current ; while, illumined wide,   960
The dewy-skirted clouds imbibe the sun,
And through their lucid veil his softened force
Shed o'er the peaceful world. Then is the time
For those whom wisdom and whom nature charm
To steal themselves from the degenerate crowd,
And soar above this little scene of things—
To tread low-thoughted vice beneath their feet,
To soothe the throbbing passions into peace,
And woo lone Quiet in her silent walks.

   Thus solitary, and in pensive guise,   970
Oft let me wander o'er the russet mead,
And through the saddened grove, where scarce is heard
One dying strain to cheer the woodman's toil.
Haply some widowed songster pours his plaint
Far in faint warblings through the tawny copse ;
While congregated thrushes, linnets, larks,
And each wild throat whose artless strains so late
Swelled all the music of the swarming shades,
Robbed of their tuneful souls, now shivering sit
On the dead tree, a dull despondent flock,   980
With not a brightness waving o'er their plumes,
And naught save chattering discord in their note.
Oh, let not, aimed from some inhuman eye,

962 lucid veil his softened] uvid pores his tempered 1730–38.
   963–75 This passage, beginning ' Then is the time ', formed part
of the first ed. (1726) of *Winter* (ll. 33–45). With a few slight
alterations they were transferred to *Autumn*, where they appear
in the first ed. (1730) of that poem. The variations are indicated
below.
   968 To lay their passions in a gentle calm *Winter*, first ed. 1726.
970 Thus] Now *Winter*, first ed. 1726.   972 And . . saddened]
Or . . pining *Winter*, first ed. 1726.   974 Sad Philomel, perchance, pours forth her plaint *Winter*, first ed. 1726.   975
Far through the withering copse *Winter*, first ed. 1726.

The gun the music of the coming year
Destroy, and harmless, unsuspecting harm,
Lay the weak tribes, a miserable prey!
In mingled murder fluttering on the ground!
  The pale descending year, yet pleasing still,
A gentler mood inspires; for now the leaf
Incessant rustles from the mournful grove,   990
Oft startling such as studious walk below,
And slowly circles through the waving air.
But, should a quicker breeze amid the boughs
Sob, o'er the sky the leafy deluge streams;
Till, choked and matted with the dreary shower,
The forest-walks, at every rising gale,
Roll wide the wither'd waste, and whistle bleak.
Fled is the blasted verdure of the fields;
And, shrunk into their beds, the flowery race
Their sunny robes resign. Even what remained   1000
Of bolder fruits falls from the naked tree;
And—woods, fields, gardens, orchards, all around—
The desolated prospect thrills the soul.
  He comes! he comes! in every breeze the Power
Of Philosophic Melancholy comes!
His near approach the sudden-starting tear,
The glowing cheek, the mild dejected air,
The softened feature, and the beating heart,
Pierced deep with many a virtuous pang, declare.
O'er all the soul his sacred influence breathes;   1010
Inflames imagination; through the breast
Infuses every tenderness; and far

994 deluge] ruin 1730–38.   1000 'Their sunny robes resign'
occurs in *Winter*, first ed., l. 60.   1001 bolder *in all edd., from
1730 to 1746.*   1010 the] his 1730.   1011 breast] sense
1730–38.   Preceding this line in the first text (1730–38) came—
    In all the bosom triumphs, all the nerves—
dropped in ed. 1744.

Beyond dim earth exalts the swelling thought.
Ten thousand thousand fleet ideas, such
As never mingled with the vulgar dream,
Crowd fast into the mind's creative eye.
As fast the correspondent passions rise,
As varied, and as high—devotion raised
To rapture, and divine astonishment ;
The love of nature unconfined, and, chief,   1020
Of human race ; the large ambitious wish
To make them blest ; the sigh for suffering worth
Lost in obscurity ; the noble scorn
Of tyrant pride ; the fearless great resolve ;
The wonder which the dying patriot draws,
Inspiring glory through remotest time ;
The awakened throb for virtue and for fame ;
The sympathies of love and friendship dear,
With all the social offspring of the heart.
       Oh ! bear me then to vast embowering shades, 1030
To twilight groves, and visionary vales,
To weeping grottoes, and prophetic glooms ;
Where angel forms athwart the solemn dusk,
Tremendous, sweep, or seem to sweep along ;
And voices more than human, through the void
Deep-sounding, seize the enthusiastic ear.

1015 vulgar] Vulgar's 1730-38.   1021 race] kind 1730-38.
1023 noble] indignant 1730-38.   1024 tyrant] mighty 1730-
38.   1025 which] that 1730-38.   1027 awakened throb]
arousing pant 1730-38.

1030-36 This passage was (with variations) transferred from
the first ed. (1726) of *Winter*, ll. 74-9. The original form was as
follows :—

Oh ! bear me then to high embowering shades,
To twilight groves and visionary vales,
To weeping grottos and to hoary caves [prophetic
    glooms, (second ed.)]
Where angel-forms are seen, and voices heard,
Sighed in low whispers, that abstract the soul
From outward sense far into worlds remote.

G

Or is this gloom too much ?   Then lead, ye Powers
That o'er the garden and the rural seat
Preside, which, shining through the cheerful land
In countless numbers, blest Britannia sees—   1040
Oh ! lead me to the wide extended walks,
The fair majestic paradise of Stowe !
Not Persian Cyrus on Ionia's shore
E'er saw such sylvan scenes, such various art
By genius fired, such ardent genius tamed
By cool judicious art, that in the strife
All-beauteous Nature fears to be outdone.
And there, O Pitt ! thy country's early boast,
There let me sit beneath the sheltered slopes,
Or in that Temple where, in future times,   1050
Thou well shalt merit a distinguished name,
And, with thy converse blest, catch the last smiles
Of Autumn beaming o'er the yellow woods.
While there with thee the enchanted round I walk,
The regulated wild, gay fancy then
Will tread in thought the groves of Attic land ;
Will from thy standard taste refine her own,
Correct her pencil to the purest truth
Of nature, or, the unimpassioned shades
Forsaking, raise it to the human mind.   1060
Oh, if hereafter she with juster hand
Shall draw the tragic scene, instruct her thou
To mark the varied movements of the heart,
What every decent character requires,
And every passion speaks !   Oh, through her strain
Breathe thy pathetic eloquence, that moulds
The attentive senate, charms, persuades, exalts,
Of honest zeal the indignant lightning throws,
And shakes Corruption on her venal throne !

1037–81 These forty-five lines were added in 1744.   1048
' Pit ' is Thomson's form of the name, both in 1744 and in 1746.

While thus we talk, and through Elysian vales 1070
Delighted rove, perhaps a sigh escapes—
What pity, Cobham ! thou thy verdant files
Of ordered trees shouldst here inglorious range,
Instead of squadrons flaming o'er the field,
And long-embattled hosts ! when the proud foe,
The faithless vain disturber of mankind,
Insulting Gaul, has roused the world to war ;
When keen, once more, within their bounds to press
Those polished robbers, those ambitious slaves,
The British youth would hail thy wise command, 1080
Thy tempered ardour and thy veteran skill.

The western sun withdraws the shortened day ;
And humid evening, gliding o'er the sky,

1082 And now the western sun withdraws the day 1730-38.

1082-1102 These lines are, substantially, a transference from
the first ed. (1726) of *Winter*, ll. 80-96.   Their original form was
as follows :—

> Now, when the western sun withdraws the day,
> And humid evening, gliding o'er the sky,
> In her chill progress checks the straggling beams
> And robs them of their gathered vapoury prey—
> [And their moist captives frees ; where waters ooze
> (*second ed.*)]
> Where marshes stagnate and where rivers wind
> Cluster the rolling fogs, and swim along
> The dusky-mantled lawn ; then slow descend
> Once more to mingle with their watery friends.
> The vivid stars shine out in radiant [brightened (*second
> ed.*)] files,
> And boundless ether glows, till the fair moon
> Shows her broad visage in the crimsoned east ;
> Now, stooping, seems to kiss the passing cloud,
> Now, o'er the pure cerulean rides sublime ;
> Wide the pale deluge floats with silver waves
> O'er the skied mountain to the low-laid vale,
> From the white rocks with dim reflection gleams,
> And faintly glitters through the waving shades.

1083 gliding] gilding (*a misprint*) 1730-38.

In her chill progress, to the ground condensed
The vapours throws. Where creeping waters ooze,
Where marshes stagnate, and where rivers wind,
Cluster the rolling fogs, and swim along
The dusky-mantled lawn. Meanwhile the moon,
Full-orbed and breaking through the scattered clouds,
Shows her broad visage in the crimsoned east. 1090
Turned to the sun direct, her spotted disk
(Where mountains rise, umbrageous dales descend,
And caverns deep, as optic tube descries)
A smaller earth, gives all his blaze again,
Void of its flame, and sheds a softer day.
Now through the passing cloud she seems to stoop,
Now up the pure cerulean rides sublime.
Wide the pale deluge floats, and streaming mild
O'er the skied mountain to the shadowy vale,
While rocks and floods reflect the quivering gleam, 1100
The whole air whitens with a boundless tide
Of silver radiance trembling round the world.
    But when, half blotted from the sky, her light
Fainting, permits the starry fires to burn
With keener lustre through the depth of heaven ;
Or quite extinct her deadened orb appears,
And scarce appears, of sickly beamless white ;
Oft in this season, silent from the north
A blaze of meteors shoots—ensweeping first
The lower skies, they all at once converge 1110
High to the crown of heaven, and, all at once
Relapsing quick, as quickly re-ascend,

1085 The ascending vapour throws.   Where waters ooze
1730-38.   1093 caverns deep] oceans roll 1730-44.   1094
smaller] lesser 1730-38 ; his] its 1744.

    1108-37 The original of these lines first appeared in the first
ed. (1727) of *Summer*. See Note to ll. 1700-29 of *Summer*,—
where (p. 131) the original text is given. 1110 they] then 1730-38.

And mix and thwart, extinguish and renew,
All ether coursing in a maze of light.
From look to look, contagious through the crowd,
The panic runs, and into wondrous shapes
The appearance throws—armies in meet array,
Thronged with aerial spears and steeds of fire ;
Till, the long lines of full-extended war
In bleeding fight commixed, the sanguine flood   1120
Rolls a broad slaughter o'er the plains of heaven.
As thus they scan the visionary scene,
On all sides swells the superstitious din,
Incontinent ; and busy frenzy talks
Of blood and battle ; cities overturned,
And late at night in swallowing earthquake sunk,
Or hideous wrapt in fierce ascending flame ;
Of sallow famine, inundation, storm ;
Of pestilence, and every great distress ;
Empires subversed, when ruling fate has struck
The unalterable hour : even nature's self   1131
Is deemed to totter on the brink of time.
Not so the man of philosophic eye
And inspect sage : the waving brightness he
Curious surveys, inquisitive to know
The causes and materials, yet unfixed,
Of this appearance beautiful and new.

Now black and deep the night begins to fall,
A shade immense ! Sunk in the quenching gloom,
Magnificent and vast, are heaven and earth.   1140
Order confounded lies, all beauty void,
Distinction lost, and gay variety
One universal blot—such the fair power

1118 thronged] throng 1730–38.   1127 hideous wrapt in
fierce] painted hideous with 1730–38.   1139 A solid shade
immense. Sunk in the gloom 1730–38.

Of light to kindle and create the whole.
Drear is the state of the benighted wretch
Who then bewildered wanders through the dark
Full of pale fancies and chimeras huge ;
Nor visited by one directive ray
From cottage streaming or from airy hall.
Perhaps, impatient as he stumbles on,   1150
Struck from the root of slimy rushes, blue
The wild-fire scatters round, or, gathered, trails
A length of flame deceitful o'er the moss ;
Whither decoyed by the fantastic blaze,
Now lost and now renewed, he sinks absorbed,
Rider and horse, amid the miry gulf—
While still, from day to day, his pining wife
And plaintive children his return await,
In wild conjecture lost. At other times,
Sent by the better genius of the night,   1160
Innoxious, gleaming on the horse's mane,
The meteor sits, and shows the narrow path
That winding leads through pits of death, or else
Instructs him how to take the dangerous ford.

The lengthened night elapsed, the morning shines

1150–64 The original of these lines first appeared in the first
ed. (1727) of *Summer*. They are substantially (and almost
verbally, but with variations) the same as the original—which
the reader will find in a Note to *Summer*, l. 1681.

1155 lost . . he sinks] sunk . . he's quite 1730–38.   1156
amid] into 1730–38.   1165–71 The original of these lines
appeared in the first ed. (1726) of *Winter*, ll. 97–103 :—

All night abundant dews unnoted fall
And at return of morning silver o'er
[That, lighted by the morning's ray, impearl (*second ed.*)]
The face of mother Earth. From every branch
Depending tremble the translucent gems,
And quivering [twinkling (*second ed.*)] seem to fall away,
    yet cling,

Serene, in all her dewy beauty bright,
Unfolding fair the last autumnal day.
And now the mounting sun dispels the fog ;
The rigid hoar-frost melts before his beam ;
And, hung on every spray, on every blade 1170
Of grass, the myriad dew-drops twinkle round.
Ah, see where, robbed and murdered, in that pit
Lies the still-heaving hive ! at evening snatched,
Beneath the cloud of guilt-concealing night,
And fixed o'er sulphur—while, not dreaming ill,
The happy people in their waxen cells
Sat tending public cares and planning schemes
Of temperance for Winter poor ; rejoiced
To mark, full-flowing round, their copious stores.
Sudden the dark oppressive steam ascends ; 1180
And, used to milder scents, the tender race
By thousands tumbles from their honeyed domes,
Convolved and agonizing in the dust.
And was it then for this you roamed the spring,
Intent from flower to flower ? for this you toiled
Ceaseless the burning summer-heats away ?
For this in Autumn searched the blooming waste,
Nor lost one sunny gleam ? for this sad fate ?
O man ! tyrannic lord ! how long, how long
Shall prostrate nature groan beneath your rage, 1190
Awaiting renovation ? When obliged,
Must you destroy ? Of their ambrosial food
Can you not borrow, and in just return
Afford them shelter from the wintry winds ?
Or, as the sharp year pinches, with their own
Again regale them on some smiling day ?

And sparkle in the sun, whose rising eye,
With fogs bedimmed, portends a beauteous day.
1175 fixed . . not] whelmed . . un- 1730–38.   1182 tumble
1730–38.

See where the stony bottom of their town
Looks desolate and wild,—with here and there
A helpless number, who the ruined state
Survive, lamenting weak, cast out to death!   1200
Thus a proud city, populous and rich.
Full of the works of peace, and high in joy,
At theatre or feast, or sunk in sleep
(As late, Palermo, was thy fate) is seized
By some dread earthquake, and convulsive hurled
Sheer from the black foundation, stench-involved,
Into a gulf of blue sulphureous flame.

Hence every harsher sight! for now the day,
O'er heaven and earth diffused, grows warm and high ;
Infinite splendour! wide-investing all.   1210
How still the breeze! save what the filmy threads
Of dew evaporate brushes from the plain.
How clear the cloudless sky! how deeply tinged
With a peculiar blue! the ethereal arch
How swelled immense! amid whose azure throned,
The radiant sun how gay! how calm below
The gilded earth! the harvest-treasures all
Now, gathered in, beyond the rage of storms,
Sure to the swain ; the circling fence shut up ;
And instant Winter's utmost rage defied—   1220
While, loose to festive joy, the country round
Laughs with the loud sincerity of mirth,
Shook to the wind their cares. The toil-strung youth,
By the quick sense of music taught alone,
Leaps wildly graceful in the lively dance.
Her every charm abroad, the village-toast,

1197 See where] Hard by 1730-38.
1220 Winter bid to do his worst 1730-38.
1223, 1224 Care shook away. The toil-invigorate youth,
        Not needing the melodious impulse much
1730-38.

Young, buxom, warm, in native beauty rich,
Darts not-unmeaning looks ; and, where her eye
Points an approving smile, with double force
The cudgel rattles, and the wrestler twines.   1230
Age too shines out ; and, garrulous, recounts
The feats of youth. Thus they rejoice ; nor think
That with to-morrow's sun their annual toil
Begins again the never-ceasing round.

Oh ! knew he but his happiness, of men
The happiest he ! who far from public rage
Deep in the vale, with a choice few retired,
Drinks the pure pleasures of the rural life.
What though the dome be wanting, whose proud gate
Each morning vomits out the sneaking crowd   1240
Of flatterers false, and in their turn abused ?
Vile intercourse ! What though the glittering robe,
Of every hue reflected light can give,
Or floating loose or stiff with massy gold,
The pride and gaze of fools, oppress him not ?
What though, from utmost land and sea purveyed,
For him each rarer tributary life
Bleeds not, and his insatiate table heaps
With luxury and death ? What though his bowl
Flames not with costly juice ; nor, sunk in beds 1250
Oft of gay care, he tosses out the night,
Or melts the thoughtless hours in idle state ?
What though he knows not those fantastic joys
That still amuse the wanton, still deceive ;
A face of pleasure, but a heart of pain ;
Their hollow moments undelighted all ?

1230 wrestler twines] struggle twists 1730–38.   1249 bowl]
wine 1730–38.   1250 Flows not from brighter gems 1730–38.
1252 Or thoughtless sleeps at best in idle state 1730–38.   1253
he knows not those] deprived of these 1730–38.

Sure peace is his ; a solid life, estranged
To disappointment and fallacious hope—
Rich in content, in Nature's bounty rich,
In herbs and fruits ; whatever greens the spring 1260
When heaven descends in showers, or bends the bough
When summer reddens and when autumn beams,
Or in the wintry glebe whatever lies
Concealed and fattens with the richest sap :
These are not wanting ; nor the milky drove,
Luxuriant spread o'er all the lowing vale ;
Nor bleating mountains ; nor the chide of streams
And hum of bees, inviting sleep sincere
Into the guiltless breast beneath the shade,
Or thrown at large amid the fragrant hay ;   1270
Nor aught besides of prospect, grove, or song,
Dim grottoes, gleaming lakes, and fountain clear.
Here too dwells simple truth, plain innocence,
Unsullied beauty, sound unbroken youth
Patient of labour—with a little pleased,
Health ever-blooming, unambitious toil,
Calm contemplation, and poetic ease.
    Let others brave the flood in quest of gain,
And beat for joyless months the gloomy wave.
Let such as deem it glory to destroy   1280
Rush into blood, the sack of cities seek—
Unpierced, exulting in the widow's wail,
The virgin's shriek, and infant's trembling cry.
Let some, far distant from their native soil,
Urged or by want or hardened avarice,
Find other lands beneath another sun.
Let this through cities work his eager way
By legal outrage and established guile,
The social sense extinct ; and that ferment

1271 beside 1730-44.   1273 dwells] lives 1730-38.   1287
eager] ardent 1730-38.

Mad into tumult the seditious herd,   1290
Or melt them down to slavery. Let these
Ensnare the wretched in the toils of law,
Fomenting discord, and perplexing right,
An iron race ! and those of fairer front,
But equal inhumanity, in courts,
Delusive pomp, and dark cabals delight ;
Wreathe the deep bow, diffuse the lying smile,
And tread the weary labyrinth of state.
While he, from all the stormy passions free
That restless men involve, hears, and but hears,
At distance safe, the human tempest roar,   1301
Wrapped close in conscious peace. The fall of kings,
The rage of nations, and the crush of states
Move not the man who, from the world escaped,
In still retreats and flowery solitudes
To Nature's voice attends from month to month,
And day to day, through the revolving year—
Admiring, sees her in her every shape ;
Feels all her sweet emotions at his heart ;
Takes what she liberal gives, nor thinks of more. 1310
He, when young Spring protrudes the bursting gems,
Marks the first bud, and sucks the healthful gale
Into his freshened soul ; her genial hours
He full enjoys ; and not a beauty blows
And not an opening blossom breathes in vain.
In Summer he, beneath the living shade,
Such as o'er frigid Tempe wont to wave,
Or Haemus cool, reads what the muse, of these
Perhaps, has in immortal numbers sung ;
Or what she dictates writes ; and oft, an eye   1320

1296 And slippery pomp delight, in dark cabals 1730-38.
1306 day to day 1730-38.   1307 month to month 1730-38.
1309 sweet] fine 1730-38.   1314 full] quite 1730-38.   1317
o'er . . . wave] from . . . fall 1730-38.

Shot round, rejoices in the vigorous year.
When Autumn's yellow lustre gilds the world
And tempts the sickled swain into the field,
Seized by the general joy his heart distends,
With gentle throes ; and, through the tepid gleams
Deep musing, then he best exerts his song.
Even Winter wild to him is full of bliss.
The mighty tempest, and the hoary waste
Abrupt and deep, stretched o'er the buried earth,
Awake to solemn thought. At night the skies,　1330
Disclosed and kindled by refining frost,
Pour every lustre on the exalted eye.
A friend, a book the stealing hours secure,
And mark them down for wisdom. With swift wing,
O'er land and sea imagination roams ;
Or truth, divinely breaking on his mind,
Elates his being, and unfolds his powers ;
Or in his breast heroic virtue burns.
The touch of kindred, too, and love he feels—
The modest eye whose beams on his alone　　1340
Ecstatic shine, the little strong embrace
Of prattling children, twined around his neck,
And emulous to please him, calling forth
The fond parental soul. Nor purpose gay,
Amusement, dance, or song, he sternly scorns :
For happiness and true philosophy
Are of the social still and smiling kind.
This is the life which those who fret in guilt
And guilty cities never knew—the life
Led by primeval ages uncorrupt　　　　1350
When angels dwelt, and God himself, with man !

1326 he] the 1730.　　　1332 exalted] astonished 1730–38.
1339 love and kindred too 1730–38.　　1347 Still are and have
been of the 1730–38.　　1351 When God himself and Angels
dwelt with men ! 1730–38.

O Nature ! all-sufficient ! over all
Enrich me with the knowledge of thy works ;
Snatch me to heaven ; thy rolling wonders there,
World beyond world, in infinite extent
Profusely scattered o'er the blue immense,
Show me ; their motions, periods, and their laws
Give me to scan ; through the disclosing deep
Light my blind way : the mineral strata there ;
Thrust blooming thence the vegetable world ;   1360
O'er that the rising system, more complex,
Of animals ; and, higher still, the mind,
The varied scene of quick-compounded thought,
And where the mixing passions endless shift ;
These ever open to my ravished eye—
A search, the flight of time can ne'er exhaust !
But, if to that unequal—if the blood
In sluggish streams about my heart forbid
That best ambition—under closing shades
Inglorious lay me by the lowly brook,   1370
And whisper to my dreams. From thee begin,
Dwell all on thee, with thee conclude my song ;
And let me never, never stray from thee !

1356 blue] void 1730-44.   1361 ' the ' omitted in second
ed. 1730.   1368 forbids 1730-38.

NOTES TO AUTUMN

LINE 9. *Onslow*. Born 1691 ; chosen Speaker of the House of
Commons 1727, and remained Speaker for the long period of
thirty-four years ; died 1768. Thomson's eulogy is scarcely
overcharged ; but it was Onslow's integrity that most won the
respect of all political parties.

416. *sullen openings*. Referring to the barking of dogs in the
chase.

506. *and talk the while*. The grammar here can be saved only
by regarding ' talk ' as a noun.

595. Meaning 'disclosing every charm of motion'; otherwise, a mistake for ' disclosing charm in every motion '.

702. *raised* (*nations*). Probably a Scotticism for 'excited by wine '.

742. After this line in the original text (1730-38) came the following seventeen lines, dropped in 1744 :—

But is this equal to the vast effect ?
Is thus the Volga filled ? the rapid Rhine ?
The broad Euphrates ? all the unnumbered floods
That large refresh the fair-divided earth,
And in the rage of summer never cease
To send a thundering torrent to the main ?

What though the sun draws from the steaming deep
More than the rivers pour ? How much again
O'er the vext surge in bitter-driving showers
Frequent returns let the wet sailor say :
And on the thirsty down, far from the burst
Of springs, how much to their reviving fields
And feeding flocks let lonely shepherds sing.
But sure 'tis no weak variable cause
That keeps at once ten thousand thousand floods
Wide-wandering o'er the world. so fresh and clear,
For ever flowing and for ever full.

756-835. For these eighty lines the original text (1730-38) gives only—

The vital stream
Hence, in its subterranean passage, gains
From the washed mineral that restoring power
And salutary virtue which anew
Strings every nerve, calls up the kindling soul
Into the healthful cheek and joyous eye :
And whence the royal maid, Amelia, blooms
With new-flushed graces,—yet reserved to bless
Beyond a crown some happy prince, and shine
In all her mother's matchless virtues dressed
The Carolina of another land.

786. *high Olympus*. The mountain called by that name in the lesser Asia.—T.

793. *the stony girdle of the world*. The Moscovites call the Riphean mountains Weliki Camenypoys, that is, the great stony girdle ; because they suppose them to encompass the whole Earth.—T.

802. *the bending Mountains of the Moon.* A range of mountains in Africa that surround almost all Monomotapa.—T.

893. *Orca's or Betubium's highest peak.* Orca is for Orkney; and Betubium is Duncansbay Head, the Berubium of Ptolemy.

929. John, Duke of Argyll and Greenwich. He was born in 1678, served with distinction under Marlborough in Flanders, and is commonly known in Scotland as ' The Good Duke of Argyll '. It was of him that Pope wrote—

'Argyll, the state's whole thunder born to wield
And shake alike the senate and the field ! '

He died in 1743.

944. Duncan Forbes, of Culloden, Lord President of the Court of Session, in Scotland. Born 1685 ; Lord Advocate 1725; Lord President 1737. Died 1747.

1004–29. Compare Tennyson's unrhymed lyric, ' Tears, idle tears ', in *The Princess.*

1050. The Temple of Virtue in Stowe Gardens.—T.

Stowe was the seat of Lord Cobham (l. 1072), cousin to Lyttelton It was at Lyttelton's seat, Hagley Park, that Thomson first met Pitt (the elder—but then only commencing his political career).

WINTER

[Originally (in 1726) dedicated by letter 'To the Right Honourable Sir Spencer Compton'; in 1730 simply inscribed 'to the Right Honourable the Lord Wilmington'. Compton was created Baron Wilmington in January, 1728,—Earl in May, 1730.]

THE ARGUMENT

THE subject proposed. Address to the Earl of Wilmington. First approach of Winter. According to the natural course of the season, various storms described. Rain. Wind. Snow. The driving of the snows : a man perishing among them; *whence reflections on the wants and miseries of human life.* The wolves descending from the Alps and Apennines. A winter evening described : as spent by philosophers ; by the country people ; in the city. Frost. A view of Winter within the polar circle. A thaw. The whole concluding with moral reflections on a future state.*

* The above is, substantially, the Argument of the poem in the first collected edition of *The Seasons* (1730). The words in italics were added in 1744. In the Argument for 1730 appears the note 'A short digression into Russia', withdrawn in 1744; and the passage on the wolves is noted as 'The wolves in Italy'. Other differences in the Argument of 1730 are merely verbal— 'Lord Wilmington' for 'the Earl of Wilmington', 'order' for 'course', 'its effects' for 'a view of Winter', and 'philosophical' for 'moral'.

WINTER

[First published in March, 1726 (405 ll.); second ed. also in 1726 (463 ll.); ed. of 1730—not the Quarto—the first collected ed. of *The Seasons* (787 ll.); final ed. in Author's lifetime, in 1746 (1,069 ll.).]

SEE, Winter comes to rule the varied year,
Sullen and sad, with all his rising train—
Vapours, and clouds, and storms. Be these my theme ;
These, that exalt the soul to solemn thought
And heavenly musing. Welcome, kindred glooms !
Cogenial horrors, hail ! With frequent foot,
Pleased have I, in my cheerful morn of life,
When nursed by careless solitude I lived
And sung of Nature with unceasing joy,
Pleased have I wandered through your rough domain ;
Trod the pure virgin-snows, myself as pure ;   11
Heard the winds roar, and the big torrent burst ;
Or seen the deep-fermenting tempest brewed
In the grim evening-sky. Thus passed the time,
Till through the lucid chambers of the south
Looked out the joyous Spring—looked out and smiled.

To thee, the patron of this first essay,
The Muse, O Wilmington ! renews her song.
Since has she rounded the revolving year :
Skimm'd the gay Spring ; on eagle-pinions borne,
Attempted through the Summer-blaze to rise ;   21
Then swept o'er Autumn with the shadowy gale.
And now among the Wintry clouds again,
Rolled in the doubling storm, she tries to soar,

6 Cogenial] Wished, wintry *first ed.* (1726); cogenial *from* 1730.   10 domains *first ed.* (1726); domain *from* 1730. 14 grim] red *first ed.* (1726); grim 1744.   15 lucid] opening *first ed.* (1726); lucid 1730.   17 this] her 1730–44.   17–40 This passage was introduced in 1730 on the publication of the first collected ed. of *The Seasons*.

To swell her note with all the rushing winds,
To suit her sounding cadence to the floods;
As is her theme, her numbers wildly great.
Thrice happy, could she fill thy judging ear
With bold description and with manly thought!
Nor art thou skilled in awful schemes alone,   30
And how to make a mighty people thrive;
But equal goodness, sound integrity,
A firm, unshaken, uncorrupted soul
Amid a sliding age, and burning strong,
Not vainly blazing, for thy country's weal,
A steady spirit, regularly free—
These, each exalting each, the statesman light
Into the patriot; these, the public hope
And eye to thee converting, bid the Muse
Record what envy dares not flattery call.   40

Now, when the cheerless empire of the sky
To Capricorn the Centaur-Archer yields,
And fierce Aquarius stains the inverted year—
Hung o'er the farthest verge of heaven, the sun
Scarce spreads o'er ether the dejected day.
Faint are his gleams, and ineffectual shoot
His struggling rays in horizontal lines
Through the thick air; as clothed in cloudy storm,

30 For this line the original (1730–38) gives—
    For thee the Graces smoothe, thy softer thoughts
    The Muses tune; nor art thou skilled alone
    In awful schemes, the management of States &c.
38 these] and 1730–38.   41–4 Edd. 1730 to 1738 read—
    When Scorpio gives to Capricorn the sway,
    And fierce Aquarius fouls the inverted year,
    Retiring to the verge of heaven the sun &c.
41–71 For these lines there is in the first text of *Winter* a
long passage of nearly 100 ll. that were withdrawn in 1730 and
utilized elsewhere in the collected *Seasons*. Thomson's use of
them is noted as it occurs. See the first *Winter*, p. 228.
48 clothed in cloudy storm] at dull distance seen 1730–38.

Weak, wan, and broad, he skirts the southern
   sky ;
And, soon descending, to the long dark night,   50
Wide-shading all, the prostrate world resigns.
Nor is the night unwished ; while vital heat,
Light, life, and joy the dubious day forsake.
Meantime, in sable cincture, shadows vast,
Deep-tinged and damp, and congregated clouds,
And all the vapoury turbulence of heaven
Involve the face of things. Thus Winter falls,
A heavy gloom oppressive o'er the world,
Through Nature shedding influence malign,
And rouses up the seeds of dark disease.   60
The soul of man dies in him, loathing life,
And black with more than melancholy views.
The cattle droop ; and o'er the furrowed land,
Fresh from the plough, the dun discoloured flocks,
Untended spreading, crop the wholesome root.
Along the woods, along the moorish fens,
Sighs the sad genius of the coming storm ;
And up among the loose disjointed cliffs
And fractured mountains wild, the brawling brook
And cave, presageful, send a hollow moan,   70
Resounding long in listening fancy's ear.
   Then comes the father of the tempest forth,
Wrapt in black glooms. First, joyless rains obscure
Drive through the mingling skies with vapour foul,
Dash on the mountain's brow, and shake the woods

62, 63 And black with horrid views. The cattle droop
     The conscious head, and o'er &c. 1730–38.
  64 Fresh] Red 1730–38.   72 *So from* 1730 ;
For see ! where Winter comes himself confest *first ed.* (1726) ;
Winter ! who rides along the darkened air *second ed.* (1726).
  73 Striding the gloomy blast. First rains obscure 1726–38.
74 vapour foul] tempest foul 1726 ; vapour vile 1730–38.   75
Dash] Beat 1726 ; dash *from* 1730.

That grumbling wave below. The unsightly plain
Lies a brown deluge; as the low-bent clouds
Pour flood on flood, yet unexhausted still
Combine, and, deepening into night, shut up
The day's fair face. The wanderers of heaven, 80
Each to his home, retire; save those that love
To take their pastime in the troubled air,
Or skimming flutter round the dimply pool.
The cattle from the untasted fields return
And ask, with meaning low, their wonted stalls,
Or ruminate in the contiguous shade.
Thither the household feathery people crowd,
The crested cock, with all his female train,
Pensive and dripping; while the cottage-hind
Hangs o'er the enlivening blaze, and taleful there 90
Recounts his simple frolic: much he talks,
And much he laughs, nor recks the storm that blows
Without, and rattles on his humble roof.
Wide o'er the brim, with many a torrent swelled,
And the mixed ruin of its banks o'erspread,
At last the roused-up river pours along:
Resistless, roaring, dreadful, down it comes,
From the rude mountain and the mossy wild,
Tumbling through rocks abrupt, and sounding far;
Then o'er the sanded valley floating spreads, 100

76 grumbling .. unsightly] sounding .. dreary *first ed.* (1726);
sounding .. unsightly *second ed.* (1726); *as above* 1730.
77-9 Lies overwhelmed and lost. The bellying clouds
    Combine and, deepening into night, shut up 1726
as above, 1730.
83 Or] And *first ed.* (1726); pool] flood 1726, pool *from* 1730.
89 and wet. Meanwhile the cottage-swain 1726-38. 94, 95
These lines do not appear in the edd. 1726: they are found (with
'ruins' for 'ruin') in 1730. 96 roused-up river] muddy
deluge 1726. 97 In the first edd. (1726-38) a semicolon sepa-
rated 'roaring' from 'dreadful'. 98 rude] chapt 1726-38.

Calm, sluggish, silent ; till again, constrained
Between two meeting hills, it bursts a way
Where rocks and woods o'erhang the turbid stream ;
There, gathering triple force, rapid and deep,
It boils, and wheels, and foams, and thunders through.

Nature ! great parent ! whose unceasing hand
Rolls round the Seasons of the changeful year,
How mighty, how majestic are thy works !
With what a pleasing dread they swell the soul,
That sees astonished, and astonished sings !   110
Ye too, ye winds ! that now begin to blow
With boisterous sweep, I raise my voice to you.
Where are your stores, ye powerful beings ! say,
Where your aerial magazines reserved
To swell the brooding terrors of the storm ?
In what far-distant region of the sky,
Hushed in deep silence, sleep you when 'tis calm ?

When from the pallid sky the Sun descends,
With many a spot, that o'er his glaring orb
Uncertain wanders, stained ; red fiery streaks   120
Begin to flush around. The reeling clouds
Stagger with dizzy poise, as doubting yet
Which master to obey ; while, rising slow,
Blank in the leaden-coloured east, the moon

102 Betwixt . . a way *first ed.* (1726) and 1730 ; Betwixt . .
away *second ed.* (1726) ; Between . . a way 1744, 1746.   106
unceasing] directing 1726 ; continual 1730–38.   111 Ye] You
1726.   113 powerful] viewless 1726 ; subtile 1730–38.   115
Against the day of tempest perilous 1726–38.   116 In what
untravelled country of the air 1726 ; *as above* 1730.   117
deep] still 1726 ; dead 1730–44.   118, 119 Added in 1744.
120 Late in the lowring sky red fiery streaks 1726–38.   Before
1744 the paragraph opened with this line.   121 around] about
1726–38.   122 poise] aim 1726 ; poise *from* 1730.   124 Blank]
Sad *first ed.* (1726) ; Blank *second ed.* (1726).

Wears a wan circle round her blunted horns.
Seen through the turbid, fluctuating air,
The stars obtuse emit a shivering ray ;
Or frequent seem to shoot athwart the gloom,
And long behind them trail the whitening blaze.
Snatched in short eddies, plays the withered leaf ;
And on the flood the dancing feather floats.   131
With broadened nostrils to the sky upturned,
The conscious heifer snuffs the stormy gale.
Even, as the matron, at her nightly task,
With pensive labour draws the flaxen thread,
The wasted taper and the crackling flame
Foretell the blast. But chief the plumy race,
The tenants of the sky, its changes speak.
Retiring from the downs, where all day long   139
They picked their scanty fare, a blackening train
Of clamorous rooks thick-urge their weary flight,
And seek the closing shelter of the grove.
Assiduous, in his bower, the wailing owl
Plies his sad song. The cormorant on high
Wheels from the deep, and screams along the land.
Loud shrieks the soaring hern ; and with wild wing
The circling sea-fowl cleave the flaky clouds.
Ocean, unequal pressed, with broken tide
And blind commotion heaves ; while from the shore,
Eat into caverns by the restless wave,   150
And forest-rustling mountain comes a voice
That, solemn-sounding, bids the world prepare.

125 her blunted horns] her sullied orb 1726–38 ; wan] black
erratum for bleak *first ed.* (1726).
126–45 Introduced in 1744—except l. 127 and l. 130, which
occur in edd. 1730–38 ; in the latter line, however, ' fluttering
straw ' was used for ' withered leaf '.
146 with wild wing] screaming wild 1730–38.   147 cleave
the flaky clouds] rise ; while from the shore 1730–38.   148, 149
From ' Ocean ' to ' heaves ' was added in 1744.

Then issues torth the storm with sudden burst,
And hurls the whole precipitated air
Down in a torrent. On the passive main
Descends the ethereal force, and with strong gust
Turns from its bottom the discoloured deep.
Through the black night that sits immense around,
Lashed into foam, the fierce-conflicting brine
Seems o'er a thousand raging waves to burn.   160
Meantime the mountain-billows, to the clouds
In dreadful tumult swelled, surge above surge,
Burst into chaos with tremendous roar,
And anchored navies from their stations drive
Wild as the winds, across the howling waste
Of mighty waters : now the inflated wave
Straining they scale, and now impetuous shoot
Into the secret chambers of the deep,
The wintry Baltic thundering o'er their head.
Emerging thence again, before the breath   170
Of full-exerted heaven they wing their course,

153 sudden burst] loud control *first ed.*, mad control *second ed.*
(1726), *and on to* 1738.

154, 155 And the thin fabric of the pillared air O'erturns at
once. Prone on the uncertain main *first ed.* (1726) ; *also second ed.*
(1726) *and on to* 1738, *except that* ' passive ' *takes the place of*
' uncertain '.

156 with strong gust] ploughs its waves 1726.   157 With
dreadful rift *first ed.* ; In frightful furrows *second ed.* (1726).

157-175 These lines did not appear in the earlier texts. For
the original text, which they displaced, see ll. 165-72 of the first
ed., given at the end of the poem. For the text of the second ed.
(1726) see Note at p. 232.

158 Through the loud night that bids the waves arise 1730-38.

160 Seems, as it sparkles, all around to burn 1730-38.

161-3 Edd. 1730-38 give —
    Meantime whole oceans, heaving to the clouds,
    And in broad billows rolling gathered seas,
    Surge over surge, burst in a general roar &c.

166 inflated] hilly 1730-38.   169 wintry] full-blown **1730-38.**

And dart on distant coasts—if some sharp rock
Or shoal insidious break not their career,
And in loose fragments fling them floating round.
  Nor less at land the loosened tempest reigns.
The mountain thunders, and its sturdy sons
Stoop to the bottom of the rocks they shade.
Lone on the midnight steep, and all aghast,
The dark wayfaring stranger breathless toils,
And, often falling, climbs against the blast.   180
Low waves the rooted forest, vexed, and sheds
What of its tarnished honours yet remain—
Dashed down and scattered, by the tearing wind's
Assiduous fury, its gigantic limbs.
Thus struggling through the dissipated grove,
The whirling tempest raves along the plain ;
And, on the cottage thatched or lordly roof
Keen-fastening, shakes them to the solid base.
Sleep frighted flies ; and round the rocking dome,
For entrance eager, howls the savage blast.   190
Then too, they say, through all the burdened air
Long groans are heard, shrill sounds, and distant sighs,
That, uttered by the demon of the night,
Warn the devoted wretch of woe and death.

172 coast 1730–38.   173 shoal] sand 1730–38.
175 For this line edd. 1730–38 give the following four lines :—
    Nor raging here alone unreined at sea,
    To land the tempest bears ; and o'er the cliff,
    Where screams the seamew, foaming unconfined,
    Fierce swallows up the long-resounding shore.
176 thunders and] growls and all 1726–38.   178 the . . steep]
its . . side 1726–38.   180 The first and second edd. (1726) omit
' often falling '—thus giving an imperfect line.   182 tarnished
. . remain] leafy . . remains 1726.   183, 184 These lines
are not in the early edd.   They are found in 1730.   187 roof]
dome 1726.   189, 190 and round &c.] the hollow chimney
howls, The windows rattle, and the hinges creak. 1726.   193
uttered] murmured 1726.

Huge uproar lords it wide.   The clouds, commixed
With stars swift-gliding, sweep along the sky.
All Nature reels :   till Nature's King, who oft
Amid tempestuous darkness dwells alone,
And on the wings of the careering wind
Walks dreadfully serene, commands a calm ;   200
Then straight air, sea, and earth are hushed at once.
   As yet 'tis midnight deep.   The weary clouds,
Slow-meeting, mingle into solid gloom.
Now, while the drowsy world lies lost in sleep,
Let me associate with the serious Night,
And Contemplation, her sedate compeer ;
Let me shake off the intrusive cares of day,
And lay the meddling senses all aside.
   Where now, ye lying vanities of life !
Ye ever-tempting, ever-cheating train !   210
Where are you now ?   and what is your amount ?
Vexation, disappointment, and remorse.
Sad, sickening thought !   and yet deluded man,
A scene of crude disjointed visions past,
And broken slumbers, rises still resolved,
With new-flushed hopes, to run the giddy round.
   Father of light and life !   thou Good Supreme !
O teach me what is good !   teach me Thyself !
Save me from folly, vanity, and vice,
From every low pursuit ;   and feed my soul   220
With knowledge, conscious peace, and virtue pure—
Sacred, substantial, never-fading bliss !

195 Huge] Wide *first ed.* (1726).
197-201 This passage first appeared in the second ed. (1726).
The text of the first ed. (1726) was as follows :—
    All Nature reels.   But hark !   The Almighty speaks :
    Instant the chidden storm begins to pant
    And dies at once into a noiseless calm.
202 midnight's reign 1726 ; midnight waste *second ed.* 1726-38.
205 serious] low-browed 1726.   209 Where] And 1726-38.

The keener tempests come : and, fuming dun
From all the livid east or piercing north,
Thick clouds ascend, in whose capacious womb
A vapoury deluge lies, to snow congealed.
Heavy they roll their fleecy world along,
And the sky saddens with the gathered storm.
Through the hushed air the whitening shower descends,
At first thin-wavering ; till at last the flakes   230
Fall broad and wide and fast, dimming the day
With a continual flow. The cherished fields
Put on their winter-robe of purest white.
'Tis brightness all ; save where the new snow melts
Along the mazy current. Low the woods
Bow their hoar head ; and, ere the languid sun
Faint from the west emits his evening ray,
Earth's universal face, deep-hid and chill,
Is one wild dazzling waste, that buries wide
The works of man. Drooping, the labourer-ox   240
Stands covered o'er with snow, and then demands
The fruit of all his toil. The fowls of heaven,

223 This line is not in the earlier text (1726).   224 From
all] Lo ! from *first ed.* ; Dun from *second ed.* (1726).   228
gathered] impending 1726.   232 The cherished fields] Sudden
the fields 1730-38.   232-4 The first ed. gives—
              See ! sudden hoared
The woods beneath the stainless burden bow,
Blackening along the mazy stream it melts.
The second ed. gives—
              Blackening they melt
Along the mazy stream. The leafless woods
Bow their hoar' heads. And ere &c.
   235 Low the woods] The leafless woods 1730-38.   236, 237
First introduced in second ed. (1726) ; ' heads ' to 1744.
   239 wide] deep 1744.   239, 240 For these two lines the
first and second edd. (1726) give only—
       Is all one dazzling waste. The labourer-ox ;
and edd. 1730-38 give—
       Is one wild dazzling waste, &c.

Tamed by the cruel season, crowd around
The winnowing store, and claim the little boon
Which Providence assigns them. One alone,
The redbreast, sacred to the household gods,
Wisely regardful of the embroiling sky,
In joyless fields and thorny thickets leaves
His shivering mates, and pays to trusted man
His annual visit. Half afraid, he first   250
Against the window beats ; then brisk alights
On the warm hearth ; then, hopping o'er the floor,
Eyes all the smiling family askance,
And pecks, and starts, and wonders where he is—
Till, more familiar grown, the table-crumbs
Attract his slender feet. The foodless wilds
Pour forth their brown inhabitants. The hare,
Though timorous of heart, and hard beset
By death in various forms, dark snares, and dogs,
And more unpitying men, the garden seeks,   260
Urged on by fearless want. The bleating kind
Eye the bleak heaven, and next the glistening earth,
With looks of dumb despair ; then, sad-dispersed,
Dig for the withered herb through heaps of snow.
  Now, shepherds, to your helpless charge be kind :

245 Which . . assigns them.] That . . allows. 1726-38. The
lines on the redbreast are not in the first ed. : they were introduced in the second ed. (1726), beginning thus :—
              The redbreast sole,
        Wisely regardful &c.
The variations are noted below. In the Quarto ed. of *The Seasons*
(1730), only four of the ten lines on the redbreast appear ; in the
octavo of the same year, the whole ten.
  246 sacred to the household gods *not in the original* (*second ed.*,
1726) : added 1744.   249 mates, and pays] fellows, and
original (*second ed.*, 1726), *to* 1738.   250 His annual visit
pays : new to the dome *original* (*second ed.*, 1726) *to* 1738.
252 then] and *second ed.* (1726) *to* 1738.   262 Heavens 1726.
263 sad-dispersed] sad, dispersed 1726-38.

Baffle the raging year, and fill their pens
With food at will ; lodge them below the storm,
And watch them strict : for, from the bellowing east,
In this dire season, oft the whirlwind's wing
Sweeps up the burden of whole wintry plains   270
In one wide waft, and o'er the hapless flocks,
Hid in the hollow of two neighbouring hills,
The billowy tempest whelms ; till, upward urged,
The valley to a shining mountain swells,
Tipt with a wreath high-curling in the sky.
　　As thus the snows arise, and, foul and fierce,
All Winter drives along the darkened air,
In his own loose-revolving fields the swain
Disastered stands ; sees other hills ascend,
Of unknown joyless brow ; and other scenes,   280
Of horrid prospect, shag the trackless plain ;
Nor finds the river nor the forest, hid
Beneath the formless wild ; but wanders on
From hill to dale, still more and more astray—
Impatient flouncing through the drifted heaps,
Stung with the thoughts of home : the thoughts of
　　　home
Rush on his nerves and call their vigour forth
In many a vain attempt.　How sinks his soul !
What black despair, what horror fills his heart,

267 storm] blast *first ed.* (1726).　　271 wide waft] fierce
blast 1726 ; hapless] unhappy 1726.　　272 Hid] Lodged *first
ed.* (1726).　　273 upwards 1726-38.　　275 That curls its
wreaths amid the freezing sky 1726.

276-423 These lines do not appear in the first ed. (March, 1726) ;
a passage of 39 ll., descriptive of the Bear and Wolves, was introduced in the second ed. (June, 1726).　The passage descriptive
of the Bear *in Russian wilds* will be found in a Note at the end
of the poem ; another passage, descriptive of the Bear *in Siberian*
wilds (as given in edd. 1730-38), will also be found at the same
place.　See also ll. 827-33, and ll. 895-7, *infra.*

283 formless wild] white abrupt 1730-38.

When, for the dusky spot which fancy feigned   290
His tufted cottage rising through the snow,
He meets the roughness of the middle waste,
Far from the track and blest abode of man ;
While round him night resistless closes fast,
And every tempest, howling o'er his head,
Renders the savage wilderness more wild.
Then throng the busy shapes into his mind
Of covered pits, unfathomably deep,
A dire descent! beyond the power of frost ;
Of faithless bogs ; of precipices huge,   300
Smoothed up with snow ; and (what is land unknown,
What water) of the still unfrozen spring,
In the loose marsh or solitary lake,
Where the fresh fountain from the bottom boils.
These check his fearful steps ; and down he sinks
Beneath the shelter of the shapeless drift,
Thinking o'er all the bitterness of death,
Mixed with the tender anguish nature shoots
Through the wrung bosom of the dying man—
His wife, his children, and his friends unseen.   310
In vain for him the officious wife prepares
The fire fair-blazing and the vestment warm ;
In vain his little children, peeping out
Into the mingling storm, demand their sire
With tears of artless innocence. Alas !
Nor wife nor children more shall he behold,
Nor friends, nor sacred home. On every nerve
The deadly Winter seizes, shuts up sense,
And, o'er his inmost vitals creeping cold,
Lays him along the snows a stiffened corse,   320
Stretched out, and bleaching in the northern blast.

290 which] that 1730-38.   293 track] tract 1730-38.   302
spring] eye 1730-38.   314 storm] rack 1730-38.   319 inmost]
stronger 1730-38.   321 Unstretched 1730-38.

Ah ! little think the gay licentious proud,
Whom pleasure, power, and affluence surround—
They, who their thoughtless hours in giddy mirth,
And wanton, often cruel, riot waste—
Ah ! little think they, while they dance along,
How many feel, this very moment, death
And all the sad variety of pain ;
How many sink in the devouring flood,
Or more devouring flame ; how many bleed,   330
By shameful variance betwixt man and man ;
How many pine in want, and dungeon-glooms,
Shut from the common air and common use
Of their own limbs ; how many drink the cup
Of baleful grief, or eat the bitter bread
Of misery ; sore pierced by wintry winds,
How many shrink into the sordid hut
Of cheerless poverty ; how many shake
With all the fiercer tortures of the mind,
Unbounded passion, madness, guilt, remorse—   340
Whence, tumbled headlong from the height of life,
They furnish matter for the tragic muse ;
Even in the vale, where wisdom loves to dwell,
With friendship, peace, and contemplation joined,
How many, racked with honest passions, droop
In deep retired distress ; how many stand
Around the death-bed of their dearest friends,
And point the parting anguish ! Thought fond man
Of these, and all the thousand nameless ills
That one incessant struggle render life,   350
One scene of toil, of suffering, and of fate,

347 Following this line came (edd. 1730–38)—
   Like wailing pensive ghosts awaiting theirs,—
dropped in 1744.
   348 anguish ! Thought] pang ! Thought but 1730–38.   351
suffering] anguish 1730–38.

Vice in his high career would stand appalled,
And heedless rambling Impulse learn to think ;
The conscious heart of Charity would warm,
And her wide wish Benevolence dilate ;
The social tear would rise, the social sigh ;
And, into clear perfection, gradual bliss,
Refining still, the social passions work.
    And here can I forget the generous band
Who, touched with human woe, redressive searched 360
Into the horrors of the gloomy jail ?
Unpitied and unheard where misery moans,
Where sickness pines, where thirst and hunger
    burn,
And poor misfortune feels the lash of vice ;
While in the land of liberty—the land
Whose every street and public meeting glow
With open freedom—little tyrants raged,
Snatched the lean morsel from the starving mouth,
Tore from cold wintry limbs the tattered weed,
Even robbed them of the last of comforts, sleep, 370
The free-born Briton to the dungeon chained
Or, as the lust of cruelty prevailed,
At pleasure marked him with inglorious stripes,
And crushed out lives, by secret barbarous ways,
That for their country would have toiled or bled.
O great design ! if executed well,
With patient care and wisdom-tempered zeal.
Ye sons of mercy ! yet resume the search ;
Drag forth the legal monsters into light,

359 band] few 1730–38.   360 searched] sought 1730–38.
366 glows 1730–38.   369 weed] robe 1730–38.   374 secret
barbarous] various nameless 1730–38.
  376-8 Hail, patriot band ! who, scorning secret scorn,
      When justice and when mercy led the way, 1730–38.
  379 Dragged the detected, &c., 1730–38.

Wrench from their hands Oppression's iron rod,   380
And bid the cruel feel the pains they give.
Much still untouched remains ; in this rank age,
Much is the patriot's weeding hand required.
The toils of law—what dark insidious men
Have cumbrous added to perplex the truth
And lengthen simple justice into trade—
How glorious were the day that saw these broke,
And every man within the reach of right !

By wintry famine roused, from all the tract
Of horrid mountains which the shining Alps,   390
And wavy Apennines, and Pyrenees
Branch out stupendous into distant lands,
Cruel as death, and hungry as the grave !
Burning for blood, bony, and gaunt, and grim !
Assembling wolves in raging troops descend ;
And, pouring o'er the country, bear along,
Keen as the north-wind sweeps the glossy snow.
All is their prize. They fasten on the steed,
Press him to earth, and pierce his mighty heart.

380 Wrenched . . hand 1730–38.   381 bid . . give] bade
. gave 1730–38.   382 Preceding this line edd. 1730–38 give
the following two lines (dropped in 1744) :—
    Yet stop not here ! let all the land rejoice,
    And make the blessing unconfined as great.
388 Following this line, appeared in ed. 1730 a passage of 16 ll.,
given on p. 243.   389–92 For these lines appeared in the original
(second ed., June, 1726), and remained on to 1738, the following :—
    Or from the cloudy Alps and Appenine (*sic*)
    Capt with grey mists and everlasting snows,
    Where nature in stupendous ruin lies,
    And from the leaning rock on either side
    Gush out those streams that classic song renowns, &c.
391 Appenines 1746.   395 raging] torrent *second ed.* (1726)
to 1738.   396 Instead of this line the second ed. (1726) gives—
    And spread wide-wasting desolation round.
    Nought may their course withstand. They bear along, &c.

Nor can the bull his awful front defend, 400
Or shake the murdering savages away.
Rapacious, at the mother's throat they fly,
And tear the screaming infant from her breast.
The godlike face of man avails him naught.
Even Beauty, force divine! at whose bright glance
The generous lion stands in softened gaze,
Here bleeds, a hapless undistinguished prey.
But if, apprised of the severe attack,
The country be shut up, lured by the scent,
On churchyards drear (inhuman to relate!) 410
The disappointed prowlers fall, and dig
The shrouded body from the grave ; o'er which,
Mixed with foul shades and frighted ghosts, they howl.

Among those hilly regions, where, embraced
In peaceful vales, the happy Grisons dwell,
Oft, rushing sudden from the loaded cliffs,
Mountains of snow their gathering terrors roll.
From steep to steep, loud thundering, down they come,
A wintry waste in dire commotion all ;
And herds, and flocks, and travellers, and swains, 420
And sometimes whole brigades of marching troops,
Or hamlets sleeping in the dead of night,
Are deep beneath the smothering ruin whelmed.

Now, all amid the rigours of the year,
In the wild depth of winter, while without
The ceaseless winds blow ice, be my retreat,
Between the groaning forest and the shore,
Beat by the boundless multitude of waves,
A rural, sheltered, solitary scene ;

412 grave] tomb *second ed.* (1726) *to* 1738.   414–23 **These**
lines were introduced in ed. 1744.   426 ice] keen 1726, *both*
first and second edd.   427, 428 These two lines are not in
the edd. of 1726 ; they appear in edd. 1730–38, with 'a' for
'the' in the second line.

H

Where ruddy fire and beaming tapers join   430
To cheer the gloom. There studious let me sit,
And hold high converse with the mighty dead—
Sages of ancient time, as gods revered,
As gods beneficent, who blessed mankind
With arts and arms, and humanized a world.
Roused at the inspiring thought, I throw aside
The long-lived volume, and deep-musing hail
The sacred shades that slowly rising pass
Before my wondering eyes. First Socrates,
Who, firmly good in a corrupted state,   440
Against the rage of tyrants single stood,
Invincible ! calm reason's holy law,
That voice of God within the attentive mind,
Obeying, fearless or in life or death :
Great moral teacher ! wisest of mankind !
Solon the next, who built his commonweal
On equity's wide base ; by tender laws
A lively people curbing, yet undamped
Preserving still that quick peculiar fire,
Whence in the laurelled field of finer arts,   450
And of bold freedom, they unequalled shone,
The pride of smiling Greece and human-kind.
Lycurgus then, who bowed beneath the force

431 To chase the cheerless gloom : there let me sit 1726-38.
440-45 For these lines the edd. of 1726 give only—
     Truth's early champion, martyr for his God ;
the edd. 1730-38 give—
     Whose simple question to the folded heart
     Stole unperceived, and from the maze of thought
     Evolved the secret truth,—a god-like man !
446 commonwealth 1730-38.
447 wide] firm 1726.   The passage beginning here ' by tender
laws ', and going on to the end of l. 452, was introduced in 1744.
453-529 The readings of the first ed., the second, and the edd.
of 1730-38 differ from this, and from each other : they are all
given in a Note at the end of the poem.

Of strictest discipline, severely wise,
All human passions. Following him I see,
As at Thermopylae he glorious fell,
The firm devoted chief, who proved by deeds
The hardest lesson which the other taught.
Then Aristides lifts his honest front ;
Spotless of heart, to whom the unflattering voice
Of freedom gave the noblest name of Just ;   461
In pure majestic poverty revered ;
Who, even his glory to his country's weal
Submitting, swelled a haughty rival's fame.
Reared by his care, of softer ray appears
Cimon, sweet-souled ; whose genius, rising strong,
Shook off the load of young debauch ; abroad
The scourge of Persian pride, at home the friend
Of every worth and every splendid art ;
Modest and simple in the pomp of wealth.   470
Then the last worthies of declining Greece,
Late-called to glory, in unequal times,
Pensive appear. The fair Corinthian boast,
Timoleon, tempered happy, mild, and firm,
Who wept the brother while the tyrant bled ;
And, equal to the best, the Theban pair,
Whose virtues, in heroic concord joined,
Their country raised to freedom, empire, fame.
He too, with whom Athenian honour sunk,
And left a mass of sordid lees behind,—   480
Phocion the Good ; in public life severe,
To virtue still inexorably firm ;
But when, beneath his low illustrious roof,
Sweet peace and happy wisdom smoothed his brow,
Not friendship softer was, nor love more kind.
And he, the last of old Lycurgus' sons,
The generous victim to that vain attempt
To save a rotten state—Agis, who saw

Even Sparta's self to servile avarice sunk.
The two Achaian heroes close the train— 490
Aratus, who a while relumed the soul
Of fondly lingering liberty in Greece ;
And he, her darling, as her latest hope,
The gallant Philopoemen, who to arms
Turned the luxurious pomp he could not cure,
Or toiling in his farm, a simple swain,
Or bold and skilful thundering in the field.
  Of rougher front, a mighty people come,
A race of heroes! in those virtuous times
Which knew no stain, save that with partial flame 500
Their dearest country they too fondly loved.
Her better founder first, the Light of Rome,
Numa, who softened her rapacious sons ;
Servius, the king who laid the solid base
On which o'er earth the vast republic spread.
Then the great consuls venerable rise :
The public father who the private quelled,
As on the dread tribunal, sternly sad ;
He, whom his thankless country could not lose,
Camillus, only vengeful to her foes ; 510
Fabricius, scorner of all-conquering gold,
And Cincinnatus, awful from the plough ;
Thy willing victim, Carthage! bursting loose
From all that pleading Nature could oppose,
From a whole city's tears, by rigid faith
Imperious called, and honour's dire command ;
Scipio, the gentle chief, humanely brave,
Who soon the race of spotless glory ran,
And, warm in youth, to the poetic shade
With friendship and philosophy retired ; 520
Tully, whose powerful eloquence a while
Restrained the rapid fate of rushing Rome ;
Unconquered Cato, virtuous in extreme ;

And thou, unhappy Brutus, kind of heart,
Whose steady arm, by awful virtue urged,
Lifted the Roman steel against thy friend.
Thousands besides the tribute of a verse
Demand ; but who can count the stars of heaven ?
Who sing their influence on this lower world ?
  Behold, who yonder comes ! in sober state,   530
Fair, mild, and strong as is a vernal sun :
'Tis Phoebus' self, or else the Mantuan swain !
Great Homer too appears, of daring wing,
Parent of song ! and equal by his side,
The British Muse ; join'd hand in hand they walk,
Darkling, full up the middle steep to fame.
Nor absent are those shades, whose skilful touch
Pathetic drew the impassioned heart, and charmed
Transported Athens with the moral scene ;
Nor those who, tuneful, waked the enchanting lyre. 540
  First of your kind ! society divine !
Still visit thus my nights, for you reserved,

530 Behold] But see 1730-38.   530-40 The first ed. (1726)
gives—
      But see who yonder comes ! nor comes alone,
      With sober state and of majestic mien,
      The sister-muses in his train—'Tis he !
      Maro, the best of poets, and of men !
      Great Homer, too, appears, of daring wing !
      Parent of Song ! and equal, by his side,
      The British muse : joined hand in hand, they walk
      Darkling, nor miss their way to fame's ascent.
For the fourth of these lines the second ed. (June, 1726) gives—
      Maro ! the glory of the poet's art !
537 touch] hand 1744.   537-40 Edd. 1730-38 give—
      Nor absent are those tuneful shades, I ween,
      Taught by the graces, whose enchanting touch
      Shakes every passion from the various string ;
      Nor those who solemnize the moral scene.
541 Society divine ! immortal minds ! 1726.

And mount my soaring soul to thoughts like yours.
Silence, thou lonely power ! the door be thine ;
See on the hallowed hour that none intrude,
Save a few chosen friends, who sometimes deign
To bless my humble roof, with sense refined,
Learning digested well, exalted faith,
Unstudied wit, and humour ever gay.
Or from the Muses' hill will Pope descend,   550
To raise the sacred hour, to bid it smile,
And with the social spirit warm the heart ;
For, though not sweeter his own Homer sings,
Yet is his life the more endearing song.
    Where art thou, Hammond ? thou the darling pride,
The friend and lover of the tuneful throng !
Ah ! why, dear youth, in all the blooming prime
Of vernal genius, where, disclosing fast,
Each active worth, each manly virtue lay,
Why wert thou ravished from our hope so soon ? 560
What now avails that noble thirst of fame,
Which stung thy fervent breast ? that treasured store
Of knowledge, early gained ? that eager zeal
To serve thy country, glowing in the band
Of youthful patriots who sustain her name ?
What now, alas ! that life-diffusing charm
Of sprightly wit ? that rapture for the muse,
That heart of friendship, and that soul of joy,
Which bade with softest light thy virtues smile ?
Ah ! only showed to check our fond pursuits,   570
And teach our humbled hopes that life is vain.

543 thoughts] deeds 1726–38.   546 who] that 1744.
546, 547 Save Lycidas the friend, with sense refined 1726–38.
550–54 These lines are not in the earlier texts. The only variation in the text of edd. 1730–38 is ' make ' for ' bid ', l. 551.
555–71 This passage was added after the death of Hammond in
1742 : it first appeared in ed. 1744.

Thus in some deep retirement would I pass
The winter-glooms with friends of pliant soul,
Or blithe or solemn, as the theme inspired :
With them would search if nature's boundless frame
Was called, late-rising, from the void of night,
Or sprung eternal from the Eternal Mind ;
Its life, its laws, its progress, and its end.
Hence larger prospects of the beauteous whole
Would gradual open on our opening minds ;   580
And each diffusive harmony unite
In full perfection to the astonished eye.
Then would we try to scan the moral world,
Which, though to us it seems embroiled, moves on
In higher order, fitted and impelled
By wisdom's finest hand, and issuing all
In general good. The sage historic muse
Should next conduct us through the deeps of time,
Show us how empire grew, declined, and fell
In scattered states ; what makes the nations smile, 590
Improves their soil, and gives them double suns ;
And why they pine beneath the brightest skies
In nature's richest lap. As thus we talked,
Our hearts would burn within us, would inhale
That portion of divinity, that ray
Of purest heaven, which lights the public soul
Of patriots and of heroes. But, if doomed
In powerless humble fortune to repress

572–652 These eighty-one lines are not in the earlier text : they
occur in edd. 1730–38. 573 pliant soul] various turn 1730–38.
575 nature's boundless] this unbounded 1730–38. 576 Of
nature rose from unproductive night 1730–38. 577 Mind]
Cause 1730–38. 578 life] springs 1730–38. 583 Then . .
try to scan] Thence . . plunge into 1730–38. 584 to us it
seems embroiled] more seemingly perplexed 1730–38. 587
general] universal ; The sage historic muse] Historic truth 1730–
38. 589 Show . . declined] Point . . revolved 1730–38. 596
public soul] glorious flame 1730–38.

These ardent risings of the kindling soul,
Then, even superior to ambition, we   600
Would learn the private virtues—how to glide
Through shades and plains along the smoothest stream
Of rural life : or, snatched away by hope
Through the dim spaces of futurity,
With earnest eye anticipate those scenes
Of happiness and wonder, where the mind,
In endless growth and infinite ascent,
Rises from state to state, and world to world.
But, when with these the serious thought is foiled,
We, shifting for relief, would play the shapes   610
Of frolic fancy ; and incessant form
Those rapid pictures, that assembled train
Of fleet ideas, never joined before,
Whence lively wit excites to gay surprise,
Or folly-painting humour, grave himself,
Calls laughter forth, deep-shaking every nerve.

Meantime the village rouses up the fire ;
While, well attested, and as well believed,
Heard solemn, goes the goblin-story round,
Till superstitious horror creeps o'er all.   620
Or frequent in the sounding hall they wake
The rural gambol. Rustic mirth goes round—
The simple joke that takes the shepherd's heart,
Easily pleased ; the long loud laugh sincere ;

609 thought] soul 1730-38.   612-15 For these four lines
edd. 1730-38 give the following six :—
 Unnumbered pictures, fleeting o'er the brain,
 Yet rapid still renewed, and poured immense
 Into the mind, unbounded without space—
 The great, the new, the beautiful ; or mixed—
 Burlesque and odd, the risible and gay ;
 Whence vivid wit, and humour, droll of face, &c.
616 Calls] Call 1730-38.

The kiss, snatched hasty from the sidelong maid
On purpose guardless, or pretending sleep ;
The leap, the slap, the haul ; and, shook to notes
Of native music, the respondent dance.
Thus jocund fleets with them the winter-night.
   The city swarms intense. The public haunt,   630
Full of each theme and warm with mixed discourse,
Hums indistinct. The sons of riot flow
Down the loose stream of false enchanted joy
To swift destruction. On the rankled soul
The gaming fury falls ; and in one gulf
Of total ruin, honour, virtue, peace,
Friends, families, and fortune headlong sink.
Up springs the dance along the lighted dome,
Mixed and evolved a thousand sprightly ways.
The glittering court effuses every pomp ;   640
The circle deepens ; beamed from gaudy robes,
Tapers, and sparkling gems, and radiant eyes,
A soft effulgence o'er the palace waves—
While, a gay insect in his summer shine,
The fop, light-fluttering, spreads his mealy wings.
   Dread o'er the scene the ghost of Hamlet stalks ;
Othello rages ; poor Monimia mourns ;
And Belvidera pours her soul in love.
Terror alarms the breast ; the comely tear
Steals o'er the cheek : or else the comic muse   650
Holds to the world a picture of itself,
And raises sly the fair impartial laugh.
Sometimes she lifts her strain, and paints the scenes

638 Up springs] Rises 1730-38.   641, 642 For these two
lines edd. 1730-38 give only one line—
    The circle deepens ; rained from radiant eyes, &c.
644 a gay insect in his] thick as insects in the 1730-38.
649 Assenting terror shakes ; the silent tear 1730-38 ;
    Deep-thrilling terror shakes ; the comely tear 1744.
653-5 Added in 1744 to introduce what immediately follows.

Of beauteous life—whate'er can deck mankind,
Or charm the heart, in generous Bevil showed.

O thou, whose wisdom, solid yet refined,
Whose patriot virtues, and consummate skill
To touch the finer springs that move the world,
Joined to whate'er the graces can bestow,
And all Apollo's animating fire   660
Give thee with pleasing dignity to shine
At once the guardian, ornament, and joy
Of polished life—permit the rural muse,
O Chesterfield, to grace with thee her song.
Ere to the shades again she humbly flies,
Indulge her fond ambition, in thy train
(For every muse has in thy train a place)
To mark thy various full-accomplished mind—
To mark that spirit which with British scorn
Rejects the allurements of corrupted power;   670
That elegant politeness which excels,
Even in the judgement of presumptuous France,
The boasted manners of her shining court;
That wit, the vivid energy of sense,
The truth of nature, which with Attic point,
And kind well-tempered satire, smoothly keen,
Steals through the soul and without pain corrects.
Or, rising thence with yet a brighter flame,
O let me hail thee on some glorious day,
When to the listening senate ardent crowd   680
Britannia's sons to hear her pleaded cause!
Then, dressed by thee, more amiably fair,
Truth the soft robe of mild persuasion wears;
Thou to assenting reason giv'st again
Her own enlightened thoughts; called from the heart,

656–90 These complimentary lines to Chesterfield were added
in 1744. Bevil suggests Chesterfield.

The obedient passions on thy voice attend ;
And even reluctant party feels a while
Thy gracious power, as through the varied maze
Of eloquence, now smooth, now quick, now strong,
Profound and clear, you roll the copious flood.   690

   To thy loved haunt return, my happy muse :
For now, behold ! the joyous Winter days,
Frosty, succeed ; and through the blue serene,
For sight too fine, the ethereal nitre flies,
Killing infectious damps, and the spent air
Storing afresh with elemental life.
Close crowds the shining atmosphere ; and binds
Our strengthened bodies in its cold embrace,
Constringent ; feeds, and animates our blood ;
Refines our spirits, through the new-strung nerves 700
In swifter sallies darting to the brain—
Where sits the soul, intense, collected, cool,
Bright as the skies, and as the season keen.
All nature feels the renovating force
Of Winter—only to the thoughtless eye
In ruin seen.   The frost-concocted glebe
Draws in abundant vegetable soul,
And gathers vigour for the coming year ;
A stronger glow sits on the lively cheek
Of ruddy fire ; and luculent along   710
The purer rivers flow : their sullen deeps,

691, 692 Added in 1744, to make the transition from Chesterfield to the subject proper easier and less abrupt.   693 Clear
frost succeeds, and through the blue serene 1726–38.

   695–987 For this long passage of almost 300 lines the original
text (first ed. 1726) gives 22 lines, the second ed. (June, 1726)
gives 23.   For these early readings see ll. 303–24 of the original
text at the end of the poem.

   706 ruin . . frost-concocted] desolation . . vacant 1730–38.

Transparent, open to the shepherd's gaze,
And murmur hoarser at the fixing frost.
   What art thou, frost ? and whence are thy keen
    stores
Derived, thou secret all-invading power,
Whom even the illusive fluid cannot fly ?
Is not thy potent energy, unseen,
Myriads of little salts, or hooked, or shaped
Like double wedges, and diffused immense
Through water, earth, and ether ? Hence at eve, 720
Steamed eager from the red horizon round,
With the fierce rage of Winter deep suffused,
An icy gale, oft shifting, o'er the pool
Breathes a blue film, and in its mid-career
Arrests the bickering stream. The loosened ice,
Let down the flood and half dissolved by day,
Rustles no more ; but to the sedgy bank
Fast grows, or gathers round the pointed stone,
A crystal pavement, by the breath of heaven
Cemented firm ; till, seized from shore to shore, 730
The whole imprisoned river growls below.
Loud rings the frozen earth, and hard reflects
A double noise ; while, at his evening watch,
The village-dog deters the nightly thief ;
The heifer lows ; the distant waterfall
Swells in the breeze ; and with the hasty tread
Of traveller the hollow-sounding plain
Shakes from afar. The full ethereal round,
Infinite worlds disclosing to the view,
Shines out intensely keen, and, all one cope   740
Of starry glitter, glows from pole to pole.
From pole to pole the rigid influence falls

712 Transparent] Amazing 1730–38.   722 fierce] still 1730
–38.   731 imprisoned] detruded 1730–38.   737 hollow-]
many 1730–38.

Through the still night incessant, heavy, strong,
And seizes nature fast. It freezes on,
Till morn, late-rising o'er the drooping world,
Lifts her pale eye unjoyous. Then appears
The various labour of the silent night—
Prone from the dripping eave, and dumb cascade,
Whose idle torrents only seem to roar,
The pendent icicle ; the frost-work fair,   750
Where transient hues and fancied figures rise ;
Wide-spouted o'er the hill the frozen brook,
A livid tract, cold-gleaming on the morn ;
The forest bent beneath the plumy wave ;
And by the frost refined the whiter snow
Incrusted hard, and sounding to the tread
Of early shepherd, as he pensive seeks
His pining flock, or from the mountain top,
Pleased with the slippery surface, swift descends.
    On blithesome frolics bent, the youthful swains, 760
While every work of man is laid at rest,
Fond o'er the river crowd, in various sport

750 pendant *in all edd.* (1726-46).   751 This line was
followed in edd. 1730-38 by the line—
          The liquid kingdom all to solid turned ;
dropped in 1744.
    752 hill . . frozen] brow . . frozed (*a misprint* ?) 1730-38.
    762-78 For these seventeen lines the text of edd. 1730-38 gives
the following ten :—
          Fond o'er the river rush, and shuddering view
          The doubtful deeps below. Or where the lake
          And long canal the cerule plain extend,
          The city pours her thousands, swarming all,
          From every quarter : and with him who slides,
          Or skating sweeps swift as the winds along
          In circling poise, or else disordered falls—
          His feet, illuded, sprawling to the sky,
          While the laugh rages round—from end to end,
          Increasing still, resounds the crowded scene.

And revelry dissolved ; where, mixing glad,
Happiest of all the train ! the raptured boy
Lashes the whirling top. Or, where the Rhine
Branched out in many a long canal extends,
From every province swarming, void of care,
Batavia rushes forth ; and, as they sweep
On sounding skates a thousand different ways
In circling poise swift as the winds along,   770
The then gay land is maddened all to joy.
Nor less the northern courts, wide o'er the snow,
Pour a new pomp. Eager, on rapid sleds,
Their vigorous youth in bold contention wheel
The long-resounding course. Meantime, to raise
The manly strife, with highly blooming charms,
Flushed by the season, Scandinavia's dames
Or Russia's buxom daughters glow around.

  Pure, quick, and sportful is the wholesome day ;
But soon elapsed. The horizontal sun   780
Broad o'er the south hangs at his utmost noon ;
And ineffectual strikes the gelid cliff.
His azure gloss the mountain still maintains,
Nor feels the feeble touch. Perhaps the vale
Relents awhile to the reflected ray ;
Or from the forest falls the clustered snow,
Myriads of gems, that in the waving gleam
Gay-twinkle as they scatter. Thick around
Thunders the sport of those who with the gun,
And dog impatient bounding at the shot,   790
Worse than the season desolate the fields,
And, adding to the ruins of the year,
Distress the footed or the feathered game.

783 The mountain still his azure gloss maintains 1730–38.
787 in the waving gleam] by the breeze diffused 1730–38.
788 as they scatter.] through the gleam. Heard 1730–38

But what is this ? Our infant Winter sinks
Divested of his grandeur should our eye
Astonished shoot into the frigid zone,
Where for relentless months continual night
Holds o'er the glittering waste her starry reign.
There, through the prison of unbounded wilds,
Barred by the hand of nature from escape,   800
Wide roams the Russian exile. Naught around
Strikes his sad eye but deserts lost in snow,
And heavy-loaded groves, and solid floods
That stretch athwart the solitary vast
Their icy horrors to the frozen main,
And cheerless towns far distant—never blessed,
Save when its annual course the caravan
Bends to the golden coast of rich Cathay,
With news of human-kind. Yet there life glows ;
Yet, cherished there, beneath the shining waste 810
The furry nations harbour—tipt with jet,
Fair ermines spotless as the snows they press ;
Sables of glossy black ; and, dark-embrowned,
Or beauteous freakt with many a mingled hue,
Thousands besides, the costly pride of courts.
There, warm together pressed, the trooping deer
Sleep on the new-fallen snows ; and, scarce his head
Raised o'er the heapy wreath, the branching elk
Lies slumbering sullen in the white abyss.
The ruthless hunter wants nor dogs nor toils,   820

794–903 For these 110 lines the text of 1730–38 gives only the
following five :—
    But what is this ? these infant tempests what ?
    The mockery of Winter ! Should our eye
    Astonished shoot into the frozen zone
    Where more than half the joyless year is night,
    And, failing gradual, life at last goes out.
820, 821 Nor dogs nor toils they want, nor with the dread
        Of sounding bows the ruthless hunter drives 1744.

Nor with the dread of sounding bows he drives
The fearful flying race—with ponderous clubs,
As weak against the mountain-heaps they push
Their beating breast in vain, and piteous bray,
He lays them quivering on the ensanguined snows,
And with loud shouts rejoicing bears them home.
There, through the piny forest half-absorpt,
Rough tenant of these shades, the shapeless bear,
With dangling ice all horrid, stalks forlorn ;
Slow-paced, and sourer as the storms increase,   830
He makes his bed beneath the inclement drift,
And, with stern patience, scorning weak complaint,
Hardens his heart against assailing want.
　Wide o'er the spacious regions of the north,
That see Boötes urge his tardy wain,
A boisterous race, by frosty Caurus pierced,
Who little pleasure know and fear no pain,
Prolific swarm. They once relumed the flame
Of lost mankind in polished slavery sunk ;
Drove martial horde on horde, with dreadful sweep 840
Resistless rushing o'er the enfeebled south,
And gave the vanquished world another form.
Not such the sons of Lapland : wisely they
Despise the insensate barbarous trade of war ;
They ask no more than simple Nature gives ;
They love their mountains and enjoy their storms.
No false desires, no pride-created wants,
Disturb the peaceful current of their time,
And through the restless ever-tortured maze

827-33 The original of these lines will be found in the second ed.
(1726).　The reader will find it in a Note (to l. 276 *supra*) given at
the end of the poem.　There also is given the reading of edd.
1730-38.　The final form of the text of this picturesque passage
appears for the first time in the ed. of 1744.
　848 time] days 1744.

Of pleasure or ambition bid it rage.   850
Their reindeer form their riches. These their tents,
Their robes, their beds, and all their homely wealth
Supply, their wholesome fare, and cheerful cups.
Obsequious at their call, the docile tribe
Yield to the sled their necks, and whirl them swift
O'er hill and dale, heaped into one expanse
Of marbled snow, or, far as eye can sweep,
With a blue crust of ice unbounded glazed.
By dancing meteors then, that ceaseless shake
A waving blaze refracted o'er the heavens,   860
And vivid moons, and stars that keener play
With doubled lustre from the radiant waste,
Even in the depth of polar night they find
A wondrous day—enough to light the chase
Or guide their daring steps to Finland fairs.
Wished spring returns ; and from the hazy south,
While dim Aurora slowly moves before,
The welcome sun, just verging up at first,
By small degrees extends the swelling curve ;
Till, seen at last for gay rejoicing months,   870
Still round and round his spiral course he winds,
And, as he nearly dips his flaming orb,
Wheels up again and re-ascends the sky.
In that glad season, from the lakes and floods,
Where pure Niëmi's fairy mountains rise,
And fringed with roses Tenglio rolls his stream,
They draw the copious fry. With these at eve
They cheerful-loaded to their tents repair,
Where, all day long in useful cares employed,
Their kind unblemished wives the fire prepare.   880
Thrice happy race ! by poverty secured
From legal plunder and rapacious power,
In whom fell interest never yet has sown
The seeds of vice, whose spotless swains ne'er knew

Injurious deed, nor, blasted by the breath
Of faithless love, their blooming daughters woe.
Still pressing on, beyond Tornêa's lake,
And Hecla flaming through a waste of snow,
And farthest Greenland, to the pole itself,
Where, failing gradual, life at length goes out,   890
The muse expands her solitary flight ;
And, hovering o'er the wild stupendous scene,
Beholds new seas beneath another sky.
Throned in his palace of cerulean ice,
Here Winter holds his unrejoicing court ;
And through his airy hall the loud misrule
Of driving tempest is for ever heard :
Here the grim tyrant meditates his wrath ;
Here arms his winds with all-subduing frost ;
Moulds his fierce hail, and treasures up his snows, 900
With which he now oppresses half the globe.
Thence winding eastward to the Tartar's coast,
She sweeps the howling margin of the main ;
Where, undissolving from the first of time,
Snows swell on snows amazing to the sky ;
And icy mountains high on mountains piled
Seem to the shivering sailor from afar,
Shapeless and white, an atmosphere of clouds.
Projected huge and horrid o'er the surge,
Alps frown on Alps ; or, rushing hideous down, 910
As if old Chaos was again returned,
Wide-rend the deep and shake the solid pole.

890 The original form of this line will be found in ed. 1730.
See footnote to l. 794 *supra*.
895–7 The original form of these lines occurs in the second ed.
(June, 1726). It is repeated in edd. 1730–38. Their present form
was taken in 1744. See *supra* Note to l. 276.
904 Where] There 1730–38.   909 surge] main 1730–38.
912 Shake the firm pole and make an ocean boil. 1730–38.

Ocean itself no longer can resist
The binding fury ; but, in all its rage
Of tempest taken by the boundless frost,
Is many a fathom to the bottom chained,
And bid to roar no more—a bleak expanse
Shagged o'er with wavy rocks, cheerless, and void
Of every life, that from the dreary months
Flies conscious southward. Miserable they !   920
Who, here entangled in the gathering ice,
Take their last look of the descending sun ;
While, full of death and fierce with tenfold frost,
The long long night, incumbent o'er their heads,
Falls horrible ! Such was the Briton's fate,
As with first prow (what have not Britons dared ?)
He for the passage sought, attempted since
So much in vain, and seeming to be shut
By jealous nature with eternal bars.
In these fell regions, in Arzina caught,   930
And to the stony deep his idle ship
Immediate sealed, he with his hapless crew,
Each full exerted at his several task,
Froze into statues—to the cordage glued
The sailor, and the pilot to the helm.
   Hard by these shores, where scarce his freezing
     stream

After this line came in edd. 1730–38 the following six lines,
dropped in 1744 :—
    Whence heaped abrupt along the howling shore,
    And into various shapes (as fancy leans)
    Worked by the wave, the crystal pillars heave,
    Swells the blue portico, the Gothic dome
    Shoots fretted up, and birds and beasts and men
    Rise into mimic life, and sink by turns.
  913 The restless deep itself cannot resist 1730–38.
  936, 937 For these two lines edd. 1730–38 give only one line—
    Hard by these shores the last of mankind live.
The change was made in 1744.

Rolls the wild Oby, live the last of men ;
And, half enlivened by the distant sun,
That rears and ripens man as well as plants,
Here human nature wears its rudest form.   940
Deep from the piercing Season sunk in caves,
Here by dull fires and with unjoyous cheer
They waste the tedious gloom: immersed in furs
Doze the gross race—nor sprightly jest, nor song,
Nor tenderness they know, nor aught of life
Beyond the kindred bears that stalk without—
Till Morn at length, her roses drooping all,
Sheds a long twilight brightening o'er their fields
And calls the quivered savage to the chase.
    What cannot active government perform,   950
New-moulding man ?   Wide-stretching from these
        shores,
A people savage from remotest time,
A huge neglected empire, one vast mind
By heaven inspired from Gothic darkness called.
Immortal Peter ! first of monarchs ! He
His stubborn country tamed,—her rocks, her fens,
Her floods, her seas, her ill-submitting sons ;
And, while the fierce barbarian he subdued,
To more exalted soul he raised the man.
Ye shades of ancient heroes, ye who toiled   960
Through long successive ages to build up
A labouring plan of state, behold at once
The wonder done ! behold the matchless prince !
Who left his native throne, where reigned till then
A mighty shadow of unreal power ;

938 half] scarce 1730–38.   940 wears its rudest form] just
begins to dawn 1730–38.   944 Doze] Lie 1730–38.
    947, 948 The edd. 1730–38 give—
        Till long-expected morning looks at length
        Faint on their fields (where Winter reigns alone).
    950–87 Added in 1744.

Who greatly spurned the slothful pomp of courts ;
And, roaming every land, in every port
His sceptre laid aside, with glorious hand
Unwearied plying the mechanic tool,
Gathered the seeds of trade, of useful arts,　　970
Of civil wisdom, and of martial skill.
Charged with the stores of Europe home he goes !
Then cities rise amid the illumined waste ;
O'er joyless deserts smiles the rural reign ;
Far-distant flood to flood is social joined ;
The astonished Euxine hears the Baltic roar ;
Proud navies ride on seas that never foamed
With daring keel before ; and armies stretch
Each way their dazzling files, repressing here
The frantic Alexander of the north,　　980
And awing there stern Othman's shrinking sons.
Sloth flies the land, and ignorance and vice,
Of old dishonour proud : it glows around,
Taught by the royal hand that roused the whole,
One scene of arts, of arms, of rising trade—
For, what his wisdom planned and power enforced,
More potent still his great example showed.

Muttering, the winds at eve with blunted point
Blow hollow-blustering from the south.　Subdued,
The frost resolves into a trickling thaw.　　990
Spotted the mountains shine : loose sleet descends,
And floods the country round.　The rivers swell,

988–90 In the first ed. (March, 1726)—
　　　But hark ! the mighty winds with hollow voice
　　　Blow blustering from the south : the frost subdued
　　　Gradual resolves into a weeping thaw.
　　988 blunted point] hoarser voice *second ed.* (June, 1726) *and all
edd. down to* 1738.　　989 Blow, blustering, from the South.　The
Frost subdued 1726–38.　　990 Gradual resolves into a trickling
thaw *second ed. to ed. of* 1738; a weeping thaw *first ed. only.*

Of bonds impatient. Sudden from the hills,
O'er rocks and woods, in broad brown cataracts,
A thousand snow-fed torrents shoot at once ;
And, where they rush, the wide-resounding plain
Is left one slimy waste. Those sullen seas,
That wash'd the ungenial pole, will rest no more
Beneath the shackles of the mighty north,
But, rousing all their waves, resistless heave.   1000
And, hark ! the lengthening roar continuous runs
Athwart the rifted deep : at once it bursts,
And piles a thousand mountains to the clouds.
Ill fares the bark, with trembling wretches charged,
That, tossed amid the floating fragments, moors
Beneath the shelter of an icy isle,
While night o'erwhelms the sea, and horror looks
More horrible. Can human force endure
The assembled mischiefs that besiege them round ?—
Heart-gnawing hunger, fainting weariness,   1010
The roar of winds and waves, the crush of ice,
Now ceasing, now renewed with louder rage,
And in dire echoes bellowing round the main.

993-7 For these lines the first ed. (March, 1726) gives only—
    Impatient for the day. Those sullen seas.
The expansion was made in the second ed. (June, 1726), beginning—
    Impatient for the day. Broke from the hills, &c.,
as in the final text. The reading of the second ed. remained
down to 1738.

   1004 with trembling wretches charged] the wretches' last
resort 1726-38.   1005 tossed] lost 1726-38.   1008 force]
hearts 1726 ; force 1730 *onwards*.   1010 Heart-gnawing]
Unlistening 1726 ; Heart-gnawing 1730 *onwards*.

   1013 And bellowing round the main : nations, remote *first and
second edd.* (1726) ; *followed by*—
    Shook from their midnight slumbers, deem they hear
    Portentous thunder in the troubled (*first ed.* ; gelid
      second ed.) sky.
The final reading was given in 1730.

More to embroil the deep, Leviathan
And his unwieldy train in dreadful sport
Tempest the loosened brine ; while through the gloom
Far from the bleak inhospitable shore,
Loading the winds, is heard the hungry howl
Of famished monsters, there awaiting wrecks.
Yet Providence, that ever-waking Eye,   1020
Looks down with pity on the feeble toil
Of mortals lost to hope, and lights them safe
Through all this dreary labyrinth of fate.

'Tis done ! Dread Winter spreads his latest glooms,
And reigns tremendous o'er the conquered year.
How dead the vegetable kingdom lies !
How dumb the tuneful ! Horror wide extends
His desolate domain. Behold, fond man !
See here thy pictured life ; pass some few years,
Thy flowering Spring, thy Summer's ardent strength,
Thy sober Autumn fading into age,   1031
And pale concluding Winter comes at last
And shuts the scene. Ah ! whither now are fled

1015 dreadful] horrid 1726-38.   1017 bleak] dire 1726
bleak *since* 1730.
   1018-19 The lion's rage, the wolf's sad howl is heard
         And all the fell society of night *first ed*
         At once is heard the united hungry howl
         Of all the fell society of night *second ed.*
The final text since 1730.
   1021 feeble] fruitless 1726-38.   1024 spreads &c.] has
subdued the year 1726-38.   1025 conquered year] desert
plains 1726-38.   1028 desolate domain. Behold] solitary
empire. Now 1726; solitary empire. Here 1730-38; melancholy
empire. Here 1744.   1029 See here] Behold 1726-44.   1030
Summer's ardent] short-lived summer's 1726.
   1032-3 comes at last And shuts the scene. Ah ! whither]
shuts thy scene, And shrouds thee in the grave. Where 1726.
The final text was reached in 1730.

Those dreams of greatness ? those unsolid hopes
Of happiness ? those longings after fame ?
Those restless cares ? those busy bustling days ?
Those gay-spent festive nights ? those veering
        thoughts,
Lost between good and ill, that shared thy life ?
All now are vanished ! Virtue sole survives—
Immortal, never-failing friend of man,   1040
His guide to happiness on high. And see !
'Tis come, the glorious morn ! the second birth
Of heaven and earth ! awakening nature hears
The new-creating word, and starts to life
In every heightened form, from pain and death
For ever free. The great eternal scheme,
Involving all, and in a perfect whole
Uniting, as the prospect wider spreads,
To reason's eye refined clears up apace.
Ye vainly wise ! ye blind presumptuous ! now,   1050
Confounded in the dust, adore that Power
And Wisdom—oft arraigned : see now the cause
Why unassuming worth in secret lived

1037 gay-spent festive nights] nights of secret guilt 1726.
1038 Lost between] Fluttering 'twixt 1726.   1040 mankind's
never-failing friend 1726–38.   1044 The new-creating word]
The almighty trumpet's voice 1726.
    1045–8 So since 1730. The original text (1726) was—
        Renewed unfading. Now the eternal scheme,
        That dark perplexity, that mystic maze,
        Which sight could never trace nor heart conceive,
        To reason's eye, &c.
    1050, 1051 For these two lines the original text (1726) is
as follows :—
        Angels and men astonished pause, and dread
        To travel through the depths of Providence,
        Untried, unbounded. Ye vain Learnèd, see,
        And, prostrate in the dust, adore that power, &c.
    1053, 1054 conscious worth, oppressed in secret long Mourned
unregarded 1726.

And died neglected : why the good man's share
In life was gall and bitterness of soul :
Why the lone widow and her orphans pined
In starving solitude ; while luxury
In palaces lay straining her low thought
To form unreal wants : why heaven-born truth
And moderation fair wore the red marks   1060
Of superstition's scourge ; why licensed pain,
That cruel spoiler, that embosomed foe,
Embittered all our bliss. Ye good distressed !
Ye noble few ! who here unbending stand
Beneath life's pressure, yet bear up a while,
And what your bounded view, which only saw
A little part, deemed evil is no more :
The storms of wintry time will quickly pass,
And one unbounded Spring encircle all.

1058 straining] prompting 1726 ; prompting his 1730-38.
1059 truth] faith 1726.   1060 moderation fair] charity, prime
grace ! 1726.   1061 persecution's 1726.   1065 pressure]
pressures 1726 ; bear up a while] a little while 1726-44.   1066,
1067 And what you reckon evil is no more 1730-38.

1068-9 So since 1730. For the reading of the last four lines
in edd. of 1726, see the original *Winter* at p. 238.

NOTE BY THE EDITOR.

I give here a reprint of the text of the first *Winter*, carefully taken from the folio copy of sixteen pages now in the Advocates' Library, Edinburgh. I have only corrected the four errata to which, on the back of his title-page, Thomson drew his readers' attention. I have also discarded the long 's'. In other respects —such as peculiarities of spelling, punctuation, use of capitals and italics—I present the text as published in March, 1726.

The lines are numbered for the sake of reference; and I also accompany the text with the variations which appeared in the second edition, published only a few months after the first.

WINTER.

A

POEM.

By *JAMES THOMSON*, A.M.

———————————————— *Rapidus Sol*
Nondum Hyemem contingit Equis. Jam præterit æstas.
V I R G.

————*Glacialis* HYEMS *canos hirsuta Capillos.*
O V I D.

L O N D O N:
Printed for J. MILLAN, at *Locke's-Head*, in *Shug-Lane*,
near the Upper End of the *Hay-Market;* and Sold by
J. ROBERTS, in *Warwick-Lane*, and N. BLANDFORD,
at the *London-Gazette, Charing-Cross.* MDCCXXVI.
(Price One Shilling.)

WINTER.

A POEM

SEE! WINTER comes, to rule the varied Year,
Sullen, and sad; with all his rising Train,
Vapours, and *Clouds,* and *Storms :* Be these my Theme,
These, that exalt the Soul to solemn Thought,
And heavenly musing. Welcome kindred Glooms!
Wish'd, wint'ry, Horrors, hail!—With frequent Foot,
Pleas'd, have I, in my cheerful Morn of Life,
When, nurs'd by careless *Solitude,* I liv'd,
And sung of Nature with unceasing Joy,
10 Pleas'd, have I wander'd thro' your rough Domains;
Trod the pure, virgin, Snows, myself as pure :
Heard the Winds roar, and the big Torrent burst:
Or seen the deep, fermenting, Tempest brew'd,
In the red, evening, Sky.—Thus pass'd the Time,
Till, thro' the opening Chambers of the South,
Look'd out the joyous *Spring,* look'd out, and smil'd.

THEE too, Inspirer of the toiling Swain!
Fair AUTUMN, yellow rob'd! I'll sing of thee,
Of thy last, temper'd,[1] Days, and sunny [2] Calms;   [1] equal
20 When all the golden *Hours* are on the Wing,   [2] clouded
Attending thy Retreat, and round thy Wain,
Slow-rolling, onward to the Southern Sky.

BEHOLD![3] the well-pois'd *Hornet,* hovering, hangs,   [3] Mark
With quivering Pinions, in the genial Blaze;   how
Flys off, in airy Circles : then returns,
And hums, and dances to the beating Ray.
Nor shall the Man, that, musing, walks alone,
And, heedless, strays within his radiant Lists,
Go unchastis'd away.—Sometimes, a Fleece
30 Of Clouds, wide-scattering, with a lucid Veil,
Soft,[4] shadow o'er th' unruffled Face of Heaven;   [4] Light
And, thro' their dewy Sluices, shed the Sun,
With temper'd Influence down. Then is the Time,

For those, whom *Wisdom*, and whom *Nature* **charm,**
To steal themselves from the degenerate Croud,
And soar above this *little* Scene of Things :
To tread low-thoughted *Vice* beneath their Feet :
To lay their Passions in a gentle Calm,[1]
And woo lone *Quiet*, in her silent *Walks*.

40 Now, solitary, and in pensive Guise,
Oft, let me wander o'er the russet Mead,
Or thro' the pining Grove ; where scarce is heard
One dying Strain, to chear the *Woodman's* Toil :
Sad *Philomel*, perchance, pours forth her Plaint,[2]
Far, thro' the withering Copse. Mean while, the Leaves,
That, late, the Forest clad with lively Green,
Nipt by the drizzly Night, and Sallow-hu'd,
Fall, wavering, thro' the Air ; or shower amain,
Urg'd by the Breeze, that sobs amid the Boughs.
50 Then listening *Hares* forsake the rusling Woods,
And, starting at the frequent Noise, escape
To the rough Stubble, and the rushy Fen.
Then *Woodcocks*, o'er the fluctuating Main,
That glimmers to the Glimpses of the Moon,
Stretch their long Voyage to the woodland Glade
Where, wheeling with uncertain Flight, they mock
The nimble *Fowler's* Aim.—Now *Nature* droops ;
Languish the living Herbs, with pale Decay :
And all the *various Family* of Flowers
60 Their sunny Robes resign. The falling Fruits,
Thro' the still Night, forsake the Parent-Bough,
That, in the first, grey, Glances of the Dawn,
Looks wild, and wonders at the wintry Waste.

THE *Year*, yet pleasing, but declining fast,
Soft, o'er the secret Soul, in gentle Gales,
A Philosophic Melancholly breathes,
And bears the swelling Thought aloft to Heaven.
Then forming *Fancy* rouses to conceive,
What never mingled with the Vulgar's Dream :
70 Then wake the tender *Pang*, the pitying *Tear*,
The *Sigh* for suffering Worth, the *Wish* prefer'd
For Humankind, the *Joy* to see them bless'd,
And all the *Social Off-spring* of the Heart !

OH ! bear me then to high, embowering, Shades ;

[1] To soothe the throbbing passions into peace,

[2] Haply some widowed songster pours his plaint,

To twilight Groves, and visionary Vales ;
To weeping Grottos, and to hoary Caves [1] ;   [1] prophetic
Where Angel-Forms are seen, and Voices heard,   Glooms
Sigh'd in low Whispers, that abstract the Soul,
From outward Sense, far into Worlds remote.

80 Now, when the Western Sun withdraws the Day,
And humid *Evening*, gliding o'er the Sky,
In her chill Progress, checks the straggling Beams,
And robs them of their gather'd, vapoury, Prey,[2]   [2] And their
Where Marshes stagnate, and where Rivers wind,   moist
Cluster the rolling *Fogs*, and swim along   captives
The dusky-mantled Lawn : then slow descend,   frees ;
Once more to mingle with their *Watry Friends*.   where
                                     waters
THE vivid Stars shine out, in radiant [3] Files ;   ooze,
And boundless *Ether* glows, till the fair Moon   [3] brighten-
90 Shows her broad Visage, in the crimson'd East ; ing
Now, stooping, seems to kiss the passing Cloud :
Now, o'er the pure *Cerulean*, rides sublime.
Wide the pale Deluge floats, with silver Waves,
O'er the sky'd Mountain, to the low-laid Vale ;
From the white Rocks, with dim Reflexion, gleams,
And faintly glitters thro' the waving Shades.

ALL Night, abundant Dews, unnoted, fall,
And, at Return of Morning, silver o'er [4]   [4] That,
The Face of Mother-Earth ; from every Branch lighted
100 Depending, tremble the translucent Gems,   by the
And, quivering, seem to fall away, yet cling,   Morn-
And sparkle in the Sun, whose rising Eye,   ing's ray,
With Fogs bedim'd, portends a beauteous Day. impearl

Now, giddy [5] Youth, whom headlong Passions fire, [5] roving
Rouse the wild Game, and stain the guiltless Grove,
With Violence, and Death ; yet call it Sport,
To scatter Ruin thro' the Realms of *Love*,
And *Peace*, that thinks no ill : But These, the *Muse*,
Whose Charity, unlimited, extends
110 As wide as *Nature* works, disdains to sing,
Returning to her nobler Theme in view—
                                     [6] Winter !
FOR see ! where *Winter* comes, himself, confest, [6] who
Striding the gloomy Blast. First Rains obscure rides
Drive thro' the mingling Skies, with Tempest foul; along the
Beat on the Mountain's Brow, and shake the Woods, darken'd
                                     air,

That, sounding, wave below. The dreary ¹ Plain   ¹ unsightly
Lies overwhelm'd, and lost. The bellying Clouds
Combine, and deepening into Night, shut up
The Day's fair Face. The Wanderers of Heaven,
120 Each to his Home, retire ; save those that love
To take their Pastime in the troubled Air,
And, skimming, flutter round the dimply Flood.
The Cattle, from th' untasted Fields, return,
And ask, with Meaning low,² their wonted Stalls ;   ² meaning
Or ruminate in the contiguous Shade :   Low
Thither, the houshold, feathery, People croud,
The crested Cock, with all his female Train,
Pensive, and wet. Mean while, the Cottage-Swain
Hangs o'er th' enlivening Blaze, and, taleful, there,
130 Recounts his simple Frolic : Much he talks,
And much he laughs, nor recks the Storm that blows
Without, and rattles on his humble Roof.

At last, the muddy Deluge pours along,
Resistless, roaring ; dreadful down it comes
From the chapt Mountain, and the mossy Wild,
Tumbling thro' Rocks abrupt, and sounding far :
Then o'er the sanded Valley, floating, spreads,
Calm, sluggish, silent ; till again constrain'd,
Betwixt two meeting Hills, it bursts a Way,³   ³ away
140 Where Rocks, and Woods o'erhang the turbid Stream.
There gathering triple Force, rapid, and deep,
It boils, and wheels, and foams, and thunders thro'.

Nature ! great Parent ! whose directing Hand
Rolls round the Seasons of the changeful Year,
How mighty ! how majestick are thy Works !
With what a pleasing Dread they swell the Soul,
That sees, astonish'd ! and, astonish'd sings !
You too, ye *Winds !* that now begin to blow,
With boisterous Sweep, I raise my Voice to you.
150 Where are your Stores, ye viewless *Beings !* say ?
Where your aerial Magazines reserv'd,
Against the Day of Tempest perilous ?
In what untravel'd Country of the Air,
Hush'd in still Silence, sleep you, when 'tis calm ?

Late, in the louring Sky, red, fiery, Streaks
Begin to flush about ; the reeling Clouds
Stagger with dizzy Aim, as doubting yet

Which Master to obey : while rising, slow
Sad, in the Leaden-colour'd East, the Moon
160 Wears a bleak Circle round her sully'd Orb.
Then issues forth the Storm, with loud Control,
And the thin Fabrick of the pillar'd Air
O'erturns, at once. Prone, on th' uncertain[1] Main, [1] passive
Descends th' Etherial Force, and plows its Waves,
With dreadful Rift : from the mid-Deep, appears,
Surge after Surge, the rising, wat'ry, War.
Whitening, the angry Billows rowl immense,
And roar their Terrors, through the shuddering Soul
Of feeble Man, amidst their Fury caught,
170 And, dash'd upon his Fate : Then, o'er the Cliff,
Where dwells the *Sea-Mew*, unconfin'd, they fly,
And, hurrying, swallow up the steril Shore.

THE Mountain growls ; and all its sturdy *Sons*
Stoop to the Bottom of the Rocks they shade :
Lone, on its Midnight-Side, and all aghast,
The dark, way-faring, *Stranger*, breathless, toils,
And climbs against the Blast—
Low, waves the rooted Forest, vex'd, and sheds
What of its leafy Honours yet remains.
180 Thus, struggling thro' the dissipated Grove,
The whirling Tempest raves along the Plain ;
And, on the Cottage thacht, or lordly Dome,
Keen-fastening, shakes 'em to the solid Base.
Sleep, frighted, flies ; the hollow Chimney howls,
The Windows rattle, and the Hinges creak.

THEN, too, they say, thro' all the burthen'd Air,
Long Groans are heard, shrill Sounds, and distant Sighs
That, murmur'd by the *Demon* of the Night,
Warn the devoted *Wretch* of Woe, and Death !
190 Wild Uproar lords it wide : the Clouds commixt,
With Stars, swift-gliding, sweep along the Sky.
All Nature reels.—But hark ! The *Almighty* speaks :

165-8 For these four lines the second edition gives—
  In frightful furrows : from the brawling Deep,
  Heav'd to the Clouds, the watry *Tumult* comes.
  Rumbling, the wind-swoln Billows rowl immense,
  And, on th'evanish'd vessel bursting fierce,
  Their Terrors thunder thro' the prostrate Soul
192-4 For these the second edition gives—
  Till Nature's KING, who oft
  Amid tempestuous Darkness dwells alone,

Instant, the chidden Storm begins to pant,
And dies, at once, into a noiseless Calm.

As yet, 'tis Midnight's Reign; the weary Clouds,
Slow-meeting, mingle into solid Gloom:
Now, while the drousy World lies lost in Sleep,
Let me associate with the low-brow'd *Night*,
And *Contemplation*, her sedate Compeer;
200 Let me shake off th' intrusive Cares of Day,
And lay the medling Senses all aside.

AND now, ye lying *Vanities* of Life!
You ever-tempting, ever-cheating Train!
Where are you now? and what is your Amount?
Vexation, Disappointment, and Remorse.
Sad, sickening, Thought! and yet, deluded Man,
A Scene of wild,[1] disjointed, Visions past,   [1] crude
And broken Slumbers, rises, still resolv'd,
With new-flush'd Hopes, to run your giddy Round.

210 FATHER of Light, and Life! Thou *Good Supreme!*
O! teach me what is   ood! teach me thy self!
Save me from Folly, Vanity and Vice,
From every low Pursuit! and feed my Soul,
With Knowledge, conscious Peace, and Vertue pure,
Sacred, substantial, never-fading Bliss!

Lo![2] from the livid East, or piercing North,   [2] Dun
Thick Clouds ascend, in whose capacious Womb,
A vapoury Deluge lies, to Snow congeal'd:
Heavy, they roll their fleecy World along;
220 And the Sky saddens with th' impending Storm.
Thro' the hush'd Air, the whitening Shower descends,
At first, thin-wavering; till, at last, the Flakes
Fall broad, and wide, and fast, dimming the Day,
With a continual Flow. See! sudden, hoar'd,
The Woods beneath the stainless Burden bow,
Blackning, along the mazy Stream it melts;

And on the Wings of the careering Wind
Walks dreadfully serene, commands a Calm:
And strait Earth, Sea, and Air are hush'd at once.
224–6 For these the second edition gives—
Blackening, they melt
Along the mazy Stream. The leafless Woods
Bow their hoar Heads. And, ere the languid Sun
Faint from the West emit his evening Ray,

I

Earth's universal Face, deep-hid, and chill,
Is all one, dazzling, Waste. The Labourer-Ox
Stands cover'd o'er with Snow, and then demands
230 The Fruit of all his Toil. The Fowls of Heaven,
Tam'd by the cruel Season, croud around
The winnowing Store, and claim the little Boon,
That *Providence* allows. The foodless Wilds
Pour forth their brown *Inhabitants ;* the Hare,
Tho' timorous of Heart, and hard beset
By Death, in various Forms, dark Snares, and Dogs,
And more unpitying Men, the Garden seeks,
Urg'd on by *fearless* Want. The bleating Kind
Eye the bleak Heavens, and next, the glistening Earth,
240 With Looks of dumb Despair ; then sad, dispers'd,
Dig, for the wither'd Herb, thro' Heaps of Snow.

Now, *Shepherds,* to your helpless Charge be kind ;
Baffle the raging Year, and fill their Penns
With Food, at will : lodge them below the Blast,[1]   [1] Storm
And watch them strict ; for from the bellowing East,
In this dire Season, oft the Whirlwind's Wing
Sweeps up the Burthen of whole wintry Plains,
In one fierce Blast, and o'er th' unhappy Flocks,
Lodged in the Hollow of two neighbouring Hills,
250 The billowy Tempest whelms ; till, upwards urg'd,
The Valley to a shining Mountain swells,
That curls its Wreaths amid the freezing Sky.

Now, all amid the Rigours of the Year,
In the wild Depth of Winter, while without
The ceaseless Winds blow keen, be my Retreat
A rural, shelter'd, solitary, Scene ;
Where ruddy Fire, and beaming Tapers join
To chase the chearless Gloom : there let' me sit,
And hold high Converse with the mighty Dead,
260 *Sages* of ancient Time, as Gods rever'd,
As Gods beneficent, who blest Mankind,
With Arts, and Arms, and humaniz'd a World.
Rous'd at th' inspiring Thought—I throw aside
The long-liv'd Volume, and, deep-musing, hail

238 After ' Providence allows ' the lines on the redbreast were introduced. For them, see Note at p. 195.
252 After this line, came, in the second edition, a passage of twelve
lines, given on p. 243 ; followed by another passage, on Wolves, for
which see Note at p. 200.

The sacred *Shades*, that, slowly-rising, pass
Before my wondering Eyes—First, *Socrates*,
Truth's early Champion, Martyr for his God :
Solon, the next, who built his Commonweal,
On Equity's firm Base : *Lycurgus*, then,
270 Severely good, and him of rugged *Rome*,
Numa, who soften'd *her* rapacious *Sons*.
Cimon, sweet-soul'd, and *Aristides* just.
Unconquer'd *Cato*, virtuous in Extreme ;
With that attemper'd *Heroe, mild, and firm,
Who wept the Brother, while the Tyrant bled.
Scipio, the humane Warriour, gently brave,
Fair Learning's Friend ; who early sought the Shade,
To dwell, with *Innocence*, and *Truth*, retir'd.
And, equal to the best, the *Theban*, *He*
280 Who, *single*, rais'd his Country into Fame.
Thousands behind, the Boast of *Greece* and *Rome*,
Whom *Vertue* owns, the Tribute of a Verse
Demand, but who can count the Stars of Heaven ?
Who sing their Influence on this lower World ?
But see who yonder comes ! nor comes alone,
With *sober* State, and of *majestic* Mien,
The Sister-Muses in his Train—'Tis He !
Maro ! the best of Poets, and of Men ![1]
Great *Homer* too appears, of *daring* Wing !
290 *Parent* of Song ! and *equal*, by his Side,
The *British Muse*, join'd Hand in Hand, they walk,
Darkling, nor miss their Way to Fame's Ascent.

[1] the Glory of the Poet's Art.

Society divine ! Immortal Minds !
Still visit thus my Nights, for *you* reserv'd,
And mount my soaring Soul to Deeds like yours.
Silence ! thou lonely *Power !* the Door be thine :
See, on the hallow'd Hour, that none intrude,
Save *Lycidas*, the Friend, with Sense refin'd,
Learning digested well, exalted Faith,
300 Unstudy'd Wit, and Humour ever gay.

CLEAR Frost succeeds, and thro' the blew Serene,
For Sight too fine, th' Ætherial Nitre flies,
To bake the Glebe, and bind the slip'ry Flood.
This of the wintry Season is the Prime ;

273 This line is taken two lines lower in the second edition.

*Timoleon.

Pure are the Days, and lustrous are the Nights,
Brighten'd [1] with starry Worlds, till then unseen.   [1] Radiant
Mean while, the Orient, darkly red, breathes forth
An Icy Gale, that, in its mid Career,
Arrests the bickering Stream.   The nightly Sky,
310 And all her glowing Constellations pour
Their rigid Influence down : It freezes on
Till Morn, late-rising, o'er the drooping World,
Lifts her pale Eye, unjoyous :   then appears
The various Labour of the silent Night,
The pendant Isicle, the Frost-Work fair,
Where thousand [2] Figures rise, the crusted Snow,   [2] fancy'd
Tho' white, made whiter, by the fining North.
On blithsome Frolic bent, the youthful Swains,
While every Work of Man is laid at Rest,
320 Rush o'er the watry Plains, and, shuddering, view
The fearful Deeps below :   or with the Gun,
And faithful Spaniel, range the ravag'd Fields,
And, adding to the Ruins of the Year,
Distress the Feathery, or the Footed *Game.*

BUT hark !   the nightly Winds, with hollow Voice,
Blow, blustering, from the South—the Frost subdu'd,
Gradual, resolves into a weeping [3] Thaw.   [3] trickling
Spotted, the Mountains shine :   loose Sleet descends,
And floods the Country round :   the Rivers swell,
330 Impatient for the Day.—Those sullen Seas,
That wash th' ungenial Pole, will rest no more,
Beneath the Shackles of the mighty North ;
But, rousing all their Waves, resistless heave,—
And hark !—the length'ning Roar, continuous, runs
Athwart the rifted Main ;   at once, it bursts,
And piles a thousand Mountains to the Clouds !
Ill fares the Bark, the Wretches' last Resort,
That, lost amid the floating Fragments, moors

317 This line is followed in the second edition by—
    And Gem-besprinkled in the Mid-Day Beam.
325 In the second edition—
    Muttering, the Winds, at Eve, with hoarser voice.
330 After 'Day', the following passage was added in the second
edition—
            Broke from the Hills,
    O'er Rocks and Woods, in broad, brown Cataracts
    A thousand Snow-fed Torrents shoot at once ;
    And, where they rush, the wide-resounding plain
    Is left one slimy Waste.

Beneath the Shelter of an Icy Isle;
340 While Night o'erwhelms the Sea, and Horror looks
More horrible. Can human Hearts endure
Th' assembled *Mischiefs*, that besiege them round:
Unlist'ning *Hunger*, fainting *Weariness*,
The *Roar* of Winds, and Waves, the *Crush* of Ice,
Now, ceasing, now, renew'd, with louder Rage,
And bellowing round the Main: Nations remote,
Shook from their Midnight-Slumbers, deem they hear
Portentous Thunder, in the troubled¹ Sky.   ¹ gelid
More to embroil the Deep, Leviathan,
350 And his unweildy Train, in horrid Sport,
Tempest the loosen'd Brine; while, thro' the Gloom,
Far, from the dire, unhospitable Shore,
The Lyon's Rage, the Wolf's sad Howl is heard,
And all the fell Society of Night.
Yet, *Providence*, that ever-waking *Eye*
Looks down, with Pity, on the fruitless Toil
Of Mortals, lost to Hope, and *lights* them safe,
Thro' all this dreary Labyrinth of Fate.

'TIS done!—Dread WINTER has subdued the Year,
360 And reigns, tremenduous, o'er the desart Plains!
How dead the Vegetable Kingdom lies!
How dumb the Tuneful! *Horror* wide extends
His solitary Empire.—Now, fond *Man!*
Behold thy pictur'd life: Pass some few Years,
Thy flow'ring SPRING, Thy short-liv'd SUMMER's Strength,
Thy sober AUTUMN, fading into Age,
And pale, concluding, WINTER shuts thy Scene,
And shrouds *Thee* in the Grave—where now, are fled
Those Dreams of Greatness? those unsolid Hopes
370 Of Happiness? those Longings after Fame?
Those restless Cares? those busy, bustling Days?
Those Nights of secret Guilt? those veering Thoughts,
Flutt'ring 'twixt Good, and Ill, that shar'd thy Life?
All, now, are vanish'd! *Vertue*, sole, survives,
Immortal, Mankind's never-failing Friend,
His Guide to Happiness on high—and see!
'Tis come, the Glorious *Morn!* the second Birth
Of Heaven, and Earth!—awakening *Nature* hears

353 In the second edition—
         At once, is heard th' united, hungry, Howl
      [Of all the fell, &c.]

Th' Almighty Trumpet's Voice, and starts to Life,
380 Renew'd, unfading. Now, th' Eternal *Scheme*,
That Dark Perplexity, that Mystic Maze,
Which Sight cou'd never trace, nor Heart conceive,
To *Reason's* Eye, refin'd, clears up apace.
Angels, and Men, astonish'd, pause—and dread
To travel thro' the Depths of Providence,
Untry'd, unbounded. Ye vain *Learned !* see,
And, prostrate in the Dust, adore that *Power*,
And *Goodness*, oft arraign'd. See now the Cause,
Why conscious *Worth*, oppress'd, in secret long
390 Mourn'd, unregarded : Why the *Good Man's* Sha[re]
In Life, was Gall, and Bitterness of Soul :
Why the lone *Widow*, and her *Orphans*, pin'd,
In starving Solitude ; while *Luxury*,
In Palaces, lay prompting her low Thought,
To form unreal Wants : why Heaven-born *Faith*,
And *Charity*, prime Grace ! wore the *red* Marks
Of *Persecution's* Scourge : Why licens'd *Pain*,
That cruel *Spoiler*, that embosom'd *Foe*,
Imbitter'd all our Bliss. Ye Good *Distrest !*
400 Ye Noble *Few !* that, here, unbending, stand
Beneath Life's Pressures—yet a little while,
And all your Woes are past. *Time* swiftly fleets,
And wish'd *Eternity*, approaching, brings
Life undecaying, Love without Allay,
Pure flowing Joy, and Happiness sincere.

THE END.

NOTES TO WINTER

The following Preface by Thomson was written for the second edition of *Winter*, and continued to be printed with separate editions of that poem ; but was dropped in 1730, when the first collected edition of *The Seasons* appeared : it constitutes Thomson's apology for poesy, or rather his vindication of poetry :—

I am neither ignorant nor concerned how much one may suffer in the opinion of several persons of great gravity and character by the study and pursuit of poetry.

Although there may seem to be some appearance of reason for the present contempt of it as managed by the most part of our modern writers, yet that any man should seriously declare against that divine art is really amazing. It is declaring against the most charming power of imagination, the most exalting force of thought, the most affecting touch of sentiment—in a word, against the very soul of all learning and politeness. It is affronting the universal taste of mankind, and declaring against what has charmed the listening world from Moses down to Milton. In fine, it is even declaring against the sublimest passages of the inspired writings themselves, and what seems to be the peculiar language of heaven.

The truth of the case is this : These weak-sighted gentlemen cannot bear the strong light of poetry and the finer and more amusing scene of things it displays. But must those therefore whom heaven has blessed with the discerning eye shut it to keep them company ?

It is pleasant enough, however, to observe frequently in these enemies of poetry an awkward imitation of it. They sometimes have their little brightnesses when the opening glooms will permit. Nay, I have seen their heaviness on some occasions deign to turn friskish, and witty, in which they make just such another figure as Æsop's Ass when he began to fawn. To complete the absurdity, they would even in their efforts against Poetry fain be poetical : like those gentlemen that reason with a great deal of zeal and severity against reason.

That there are frequent and notorious abuses of Poetry is as true as that the best things are most liable to that misfortune ; but is there no end of that clamorous argument against the use of things from the abuse of them ? and yet, I hope, that no man who has the least sense of shame in him will fall into it after the present sulphureous attacker of the stage.

To insist no further on this head, let poetry once more be restored to her ancient truth and purity ; let her be inspired from heaven, and in return her incense ascend thither ; let her exchange her low, venal, trifling, subjects for such as are fair, useful, and magnificent ; and let her execute these so as at once to please, instruct, surprise, and astonish : and then of necessity the most inveterate ignorance, and prejudice, shall be struck dumb; and poets yet become the delight and wonder of mankind.

But this happy period is not to be expected, till some long-wished, illustrious man of equal power and beneficence rise on the wintry world of letters : one of a genuine and unbounded greatness and generosity of mind ; who, far above all the pomp and pride of fortune, scorns the little addressful flatterer ; pierces through the disguised designing villain ; discountenances all the reigning fopperies of a tasteless age : and who, stretching his views into late futurity, has the true interest of virtue, learning, and mankind entirely at heart—a character so nobly desirable that to an honest heart it is almost incredible so few should have the ambition to deserve it.

Nothing can have a better influence towards the revival of poetry than the choosing of great and serious subjects, such as at once amuse the fancy, enlighten the head, and warm the heart. These give a weight and dignity to the poem ; nor is the pleasure— I should say rapture—both the writer and the reader feels unwarranted by reason or followed by repentant disgust. To be able to write on a dry, barren theme is looked upon by some as the sign of a happy, fruitful genius :—fruitful indeed ! like one of the pendant gardens in Cheapside, watered every morning by the hand of the Alderman himself. And what are we commonly entertained with on these occasions save forced unaffecting fancies, little glittering prettinesses, mixed turns of wit and expression, which are as widely different from native poetry as buffoonery is from the perfection of human thinking ? A genius fired with the charms of truth and nature is tuned to a sublimer pitch, and scorns to associate with such subjects.

I cannot more emphatically recommend this poetical ambition than by the four following lines from Mr. Hill's poem, called *The Judgment Day*, which is so singular an instance of it :—

> For me, suffice it to have taught my Muse,
> The tuneful Triflings of her tribe to shun ;
> And rais'd her warmth such heavenly themes to chuse,
> As, in past ages, the best garlands won.

I know no subject more elevating, more amusing ; more ready to awake the poetical enthusiasm, the philosophical reflection, and the moral sentiment, than the works of Nature. Where can we meet with such variety, such beauty, such magnificence ? All that enlarges and transports the soul ! What more inspiring than a calm, wide survey of them ? In every dress nature is greatly charming—whether she puts on the crimson robes of the morning, the strong effulgence of noon, the sober suit of the evening, or the deep sables of blackness and tempest ! How gay looks the Spring ! how glorious the Summer ! how pleasing the Autumn ! and how venerable the Winter !—But there is no thinking of these things without breaking out into poetry ; which is, by-the-by, a plain and undeniable argument of their superior excellence.

For this reason the best, both ancient, and modern, Poets have been passionately fond of retirement, and solitude. The wild romantic country was their delight. And they seem never to have been more happy, than when, lost in unfrequented fields, far from the little busy world, they were at leisure, to meditate, and sing the Works of Nature.

The book of Job, that noble and ancient poem, which, even, strikes so forcibly through a mangling translation, is crowned with a description of the grand works of Nature ; and that, too, from the mouth of their Almighty Author.

It was this devotion to the works of Nature that, in his Georgics, inspired the rural Virgil to write so inimitably ; and who can forbear joining with him in this declaration of his, which has been the rapture of ages ?

> Me vero primum dulces ante omnia Musae,
> Quarum sacra fero ingenti perculsus amore,
> Accipiant : caelique vias et sidera monstrent,
> Defectus solis varios, lunaeque labores :
> Unde tremor terris : qua vi maria alta tumescant
> Obicibus ruptis, rursusque in seipsa residant :
> Quid tantum oceano properent se tingere soles
> Hyberni : vel quae tardis mora noctibus obstet.
> Sin, has ne possim naturae accedere partes,
> Frigidus obstiterit circum praecordia sanguis ;
> Rura mihi et rigui placeant in vallibus amnes,
> Flumina amem silvasque inglorius.

Which may be Englished thus :—

> Me may the Muses, my supreme delight !
> Whose priest I am, smit with immense desire,
> Snatch to their care ; the starry tracts disclose,
> The sun's distress, the labours of the moon :
> Whence the earth quakes : and by what force the deeps
> Heave at the rocks, then on themselves reflow :
> Why winter-suns to plunge in ocean speed :
> And what retards the lazy summer-night.

But, lest I should these mystic-truths attain,
If the cold current freezes round my heart,
The country me, the brooky vales may please
Mid woods and streams unknown.

I cannot put an end to this Preface without taking the freedom to offer my most sincere and grateful acknowledgments to all those gentlemen who have given my first performance so favourable a reception.

It is with the blest pleasure, and a rising ambition, that I reflect on the honour Mr. Hill has done me in recommending my poem to the world after a manner so peculiar to himself—than whom none approves and obliges with a nobler and more unreserving promptitude of soul. His favours are the very smiles of humanity, graceful and easy, flowing from and to the heart. This agreeable train of thought awakens naturally in my mind all the other parts of his great and amiable character, which I know not well how to quit, and yet dare not here pursue.

Every reader who has a heart to be moved must feel the most gentle power of poetry in the lines with which Mira has graced my poem.

It perhaps might be reckoned vanity in me to say how richly I value the approbation of a gentleman of Mr. Malloch's fine and exact taste, so justly dear and valuable to all those that have the happiness of knowing him, and who—to say no more of him—will abundantly make good to the world the early promise his admired piece of *William and Margaret* has given.

I only wish my description of the various appearance of nature in Winter (and, as I purpose, in the other Seasons) may have the good fortune to give the reader some of that true pleasure which they, in their agreeable succession, are always sure to inspire into my heart.

[Following the above Preface came some lines by Aaron Hill, ' To Mr. Thomson, doubtful to what patron he should address his poem, called *Winter ;* ' some more by Mira, ' To Mr. Thomson on his blooming *Winter ;* ' and yet some more by David Malloch, ' To Mr. Thomson, on his publishing the Second Edition of his poem, called *Winter.*' They are of no merit.]

Line 18. Lord Wilmington had been Sir Spencer Compton, Speaker of the House of Commons, when Thomson first inscribed to him in March, 1726.

276. Following the preceding line—

Tipt with a wreath high-curling in the sky
(originally—i.e. in the second ed. of *Winter*, 1726—

That curls its wreaths amid the freezing sky),

here, in the second ed. (1726), was inserted a passage of twelve
lines descriptive of the bear in Russian wilds, viz. :—

> In Russia's wide immeasurable moors,
> Where Winter keeps his unrejoicing court,
> And in his airy hall the loud misrule
> Of driving tempest is for ever heard—
> Seen by the wildered traveller who roams
> Guideless the yew-clad stony wastes, the Bear,
> Rough tenant of these shades ! shaggy with ice
> And dangling snow, stalks through the woods forlorn.
> Slow-paced and sourer as the storms increase,
> He makes his bed beneath the inclement wreath,
> And, scorning the complainings of distress,
> Hardens his heart against assailing want.

See ll. 827–33 *infra* for a condensation of these lines, beginning
' There through the piny forest half-absorpt ', made for the ed.
of 1744. But before the final condensation was made, the passage
of the second ed., given above, had been thus altered and amplified
for the ed. of 1730 :—

> Yet more outrageous is the season still,
> A deeper horror, in Siberian wilds ;
> Where Winter keeps his unrejoicing court,
> And in his airy hall the loud misrule
> Of driving tempest is for ever heard.
> There through the ragged woods absorpt in snow,
> Sole tenant of these shades, the shaggy bear,
> With dangling ice all horrid, stalks forlorn.
> Slow-paced and sourer as the storms increase,
> He makes his bed beneath the drifted snow,
> And, scorning the complainings of distress,
> Hardens his heart against assailing want.
> While, tempted vigorous o'er the marble waste,
> On sleds reclined, the furry Russian sits,
> And, by his reindeer drawn, behind him throws
> A shining kingdom in a winter's day.

359. *The generous band.* The Jail Committee, in the year
1729.—T.

453–529. This passage appeared in the first ed. (1726) as follows:
>   Lycurgus then,
> Severely good ; and him of rugged Rome,
> Numa, who softened her rapacious sons ;
> Cimon, sweet-souled ; and Aristides, just;
> Unconquered Cato, virtuous in extreme ;
> With that attempered hero, mild and firm,
> Who wept the brother while the tyrant bled ;
> Scipio, the humane warrior, gently brave,

Fair learning's friend, who early sought the shade
To dwell with innocence and truth retired ;
And, equal to the best, the Theban, he
Who single raised his country into fame.
Thousands behind, the boast of Greece and Rome,
Whom virtue owns, the tribute of a verse
Demand : but who can count the stars of heaven ?
Who sing their influence on this lower world ?

The text of the second ed. (also 1726) differs only from the above in transferring the line about Cato two lines lower, so as to have the Grecian worthies together: the 'attempered hero' is Timoleon.

Edd. 1730-38 follow the text of the second ed. from ' Lycurgus then ' to ' Scipio the humane warrior, gently brave ', except that they give 'human' instead of 'humane'; and here they proceed:

Who soon the race of spotless glory ran,
And, warm in youth, to the poetic shade
With friendship and philosophy retired ;
And, equal to the best, the Theban twain
Who single raised their country into fame.
Thousands behind, (&c., as in ed. 1726).

By ' the Theban twain ' are meant Pelopidas and Epaminondas.

457. *The firm devoted chief.* Leonidas.—T.

464. *a haughty rival.* Themistocles.—T.

476. *the Theban pair.* Pelopidas and Epaminondas.—T.

507. *The public father.* Marcus Junius Brutus.—T.

513. *Thy willing victim, Carthage.* Regulus.—T.

655. *generous Bevil.* A character in *The Conscious Lovers,* written by Sir Richard Steele.—T.

808. *rich Cathay.* The old name of China.—T.

836. *frosty Caurus.* The north-west wind.—T.

840. *horde on horde.* The wandering Scythian clans.—T.

875. M. de Maupertuis, in his book on the figure of the Earth, after having described the beautiful lake and mountain of Niemi in Lapland, says: ' From this height we had occasion several times to see those vapours rise from the lake which the people of the country call *Haltios,* and which they deem to be the guardian spirits of the mountains. We had been frighted with stories of bears that haunted this place, but saw none. It seemed rather a place of resort for fairies and genii than bears.'—T.

876. The same author observes: ' I was surprised to see upon the banks of this river (the Tenglio) roses of as lively a red as any that are in our gardens.'—T.

893. *beneath another sky.* The other hemisphere.—T.

925. *the Briton's fate.* Sir Hugh Willoughby, sent by Queen Elizabeth to discover the north-east passage.—T.

A HYMN

ON THE SEASONS

[First published in 1730 (121 ll.); final edition in author's lifetime, 1746 (118 ll.).]

THESE, as they change, Almighty Father! these
Are but the varied God. The rolling year
Is full of thee. Forth in the pleasing Spring
Thy beauty walks, thy tenderness and love.
Wide flush the fields; the softening air is balm;
Echo the mountains round; the forest smiles;
And every sense, and every heart, is joy.
Then comes thy glory in the Summer-months,
With light and heat refulgent. Then thy sun
Shoots full perfection through the swelling year : 10
And oft thy voice in dreadful thunder speaks,
And oft, at dawn, deep noon, or falling eve,
By brooks and groves, in hollow-whispering gales.
Thy bounty shines in Autumn unconfined,
And spreads a common feast for all that lives.
In Winter awful thou! with clouds and storms
Around thee thrown, tempest o'er tempest rolled,

6 the forests live 1730–38.   9 refulgent] severe.   Prone
1730–38.   11 dreadful] awful 1730–38.
   14, 15 For these two lines the original text (1730–38) gives—
      A yellow-floating pomp, thy bounty shines
      In Autumn unconfined. Thrown from thy lap,
      Profuse o'er nature falls the lucid shower
      Of beamy fruits, and in a radiant stream
      Into the stores of sterile Winter pours.
16 awful] dreadful 1730–38.

Majestic darkness ! On the whirlwind's wing
Riding sublime, thou bidst the world adore,
And humblest nature with thy northern blast.   20

Mysterious round ! what skill, what force divine,
Deep-felt in these appear ! a simple train,
Yet so delightful mixed, with such kind art,
Such beauty and beneficence combined,
Shade unperceived so softening into shade,
And all so forming an harmonious whole
That, as they still succeed, they ravish still.
But, wandering oft with brute unconscious gaze,
Man marks not thee, marks not the mighty hand
That, ever busy, wheels the silent spheres,   30
Works in the secret deep, shoots steaming thence
The fair profusion that o'erspreads the Spring,
Flings from the sun direct the flaming day,
Feeds every creature, hurls the tempest forth,
And, as on earth this grateful change revolves,
With transport touches all the springs of life.

Nature, attend ! join, every living soul
Beneath the spacious temple of the sky,
In adoration join ; and ardent raise
One general song ! To him, ye vocal gales,   40
Breathe soft, whose spirit in your freshness breathes :
Oh ! talk of him in solitary glooms,

18 Majestic darkness] Horrible blackness 1730-38.   19
adore] be low 1730-38.
    23-6 The original text (1730-38) gives—
        Yet so harmonious mixed, so fitly joined,
        One following one in such enchanting sort,
        Shade unperceived so softening into shade,
        And all so forming such a perfect whole, &c.
    28 wandering] wondering 1730-38.   29 Thee not 1730-38.
40 An universal hymn ! to him, ye gales 1730-38.   41 in your
freshness breathes] teaches you to breathe 1730-38.

Where, o'er the rock, the scarcely-waving pine
Fills the brown shade with a religious awe.
And ye, whose bolder note is heard afar,
Who shake the astonished world, lift high to Heaven
The impetuous song, and say from whom you rage.
His praise, ye brooks, attune, ye trembling rills ;
And let me catch it as I muse along.
Ye headlong torrents, rapid and profound ;   50
Ye softer floods, that lead the humid maze
Along the vale ; and thou, majestic main,
A secret world of wonders in thyself,
Sound his stupendous praise, whose greater voice
Or bids you roar or bids your roarings fall.
Soft roll your incense, herbs, and fruits, and flowers,
In mingled clouds to him, whose sun exalts,
Whose breath perfumes you, and whose pencil paints.
Ye forests, bend ; ye harvests, wave to him—
Breathe your still song into the reaper's heart   60
As home he goes beneath the joyous moon.
Ye that keep watch in heaven, as earth asleep
Unconscious lies, effuse your mildest beams,
Ye constellations ! while your angels strike
Amid the spangled sky the silver lyre.
Great source of day ! best image here below
Of thy Creator, ever pouring wide
From world to world the vital ocean round !
On nature write with every beam his praise.
The thunder rolls : be hushed the prostrate world, 70
While cloud to cloud returns the solemn hymn.

44 shade] void 1730-38.   54 stupendous] tremendous
1730-38.   56 Soft roll] Roll up 1730-38.   57 exalts] elates
1730-38.   58 breath] hand 1730-38.   61 As home he goes
beneath] Homeward rejoicing with 1730-38.   64 angles (*a misprint*) 1730.   67 pouring] darting 1730-38.   71 solemn]
dreadful 1730-38.

Bleat out afresh, ye hills ; ye mossy rocks,
Retain the sound ; the broad responsive low,
Ye valleys, raise ; for the Great Shepherd reigns,
And his unsuffering kingdom yet will come.
Ye woodlands all, awake : a boundless song
Burst from the groves ; and, when the restless day,
Expiring, lays the warbling world asleep,
Sweetest of birds, sweet Philomela ! charm
The listening shades, and teach the night his praise ! 80
Ye, chief, for whom the whole creation smiles,
At once the head, the heart, the tongue of all,
Crown the great hymn ! In swarming cities vast,
Assembled men, to the deep organ join
The long-resounding voice, oft breaking clear
At solemn pauses through the swelling bass ;
And, as each mingling flame increases each,
In one united ardour rise to heaven.
Or, if you rather choose the rural shade,
And find a fane in every sacred grove,   90
There let the shepherd's flute, the virgin's lay,
The prompting seraph, and the poet's lyre
Still sing the God of Seasons as they roll.
For me, when I forget the darling theme,
Whether the blossom blows, the summer-ray
Russets the plain, inspiring autumn gleams,

75 And yet again the golden age returns 1730–38; followed by—
    Wildest of creatures, be not silent here,
    But, hymning horrid, let the desert roar !—
struck out in 1744.
    76 boundless] general 1730–38.   80 teach the night his
praise] through the midnight hour ; followed by—
    Trilling prolong the wildly-luscious note,
    That night as well as day may vouch his praise 1730–38.
    82 the tongue] and mouth 1730–38.   84 Assembled] Con-
course of 1730–38.   87 frame (a *misprint*) 1730.   90 And]
To 1730–38.   91 lay] chant 1730–88.   96 inspiring] delicious
1730–38.

Or winter rises in the blackening east,
Be my tongue mute, may fancy paint no more,
And, dead to joy, forget my heart to beat !   99

Should fate command me to the farthest verge
Of the green earth, to distant barbarous climes,
Rivers unknown to song, where first the sun
Gilds Indian mountains, or his setting beam
Flames on the Atlantic isles, 'tis nought to me ;
Since God is ever present, ever felt,
In the void waste as in the city full,
And where he vital spreads there must be joy.
When even at last the solemn hour shall come,
And wing my mystic flight to future worlds,
I cheerful will obey ; there, with new powers,   110
Will rising wonders sing : I cannot go
Where universal love not smiles around,
Sustaining all yon orbs and all their sons ;
From seeming evil still educing good,
And better thence again, and better still,
In infinite progression. But I lose
Myself in him, in light ineffable !
Come then, expressive Silence, muse his praise.

97 blackening] reddening 1730-38.   98 may fancy
all edd., 1730–46.   101 distant] hostile 1730–38.
107-13 For these seven lines the original text of the Hymn
(1730-38) gives the following three :—
    Rolls the same kindred Seasons round the world,
    In all apparent, wise and good in all ;
    Since he sustains and animates the whole.
114 educes 1730–38.

THE CASTLE OF INDOLENCE:

AN ALLEGORICAL POEM

[First published (probably in May) in 1748 ; first ed. in 4to, and second in 8vo, both in the same year. Thomson died in the following August, about four months after the appearance of this exquisite poem. The text of the second edition, as being the last to receive the author's revision, is given here.]

ADVERTISEMENT

This Poem being writ in the manner of Spenser, the obsolete words, and a simplicity of diction in some of the lines which borders on the ludicrous, were necessary to make the imitation more perfect. And the style of that admirable poet, as well as the measure in which he wrote, are as it were appropriated by custom to all allegorical poems writ in our language—just as in French the style of Marot, who lived under Francis I, has been used in tales and familiar epistles by the politest writers of the age of Louis XIV.—T.

THE CASTLE OF INDOLENCE

CANTO I

The Castle hight of Indolence,
And its false luxury ;
Where for a little time, alas !
We lived right jollily.

I

O MORTAL man, who livest here by toil,
Do not complain of this thy hard estate ;
That like an emmet thou must ever moil
Is a sad sentence of an ancient date :
And, certes, there is for it reason great ;
For, though sometimes it makes thee weep and wail,
And curse thy stars, and early drudge and late,
Withouten that would come an heavier bale,
Loose life, unruly passions, and diseases pale.

II

In lowly dale, fast by a river's side,
With woody hill o'er hill encompassed round,
A most enchanting wizard did abide,
Than whom a fiend more fell is nowhere found.
It was, I ween, a lovely spot of ground ;
And there a season atween June and May,
Half prankt with spring, with summer half im-
    browned,
A listless climate made, where, sooth to say,
No living wight could work, ne carèd even for play.

III

Was nought around but images of rest :
Sleep-soothing groves, and quiet lawns between ;
And flowery beds that slumbrous influence kest,
From poppies breathed; and beds of pleasant green,
Where never yet was creeping creature seen.
Meantime unnumbered glittering streamlets played,
And hurlèd everywhere their waters sheen;
That, as they bickered through the sunny glade,
Though restless still themselves, a lulling murmur
made.

IV

Joined to the prattle of the purling rills,
Were heard the lowing herds along the vale,
And flocks loud-bleating from the distant hills,
And vacant shepherds piping in the dale :
And now and then sweet Philomel would wail,
Or stock-doves plain amid the forest deep,
That drowsy rustled to the sighing gale ;
And still a coil the grashopper did keep :
Yet all these sounds yblent inclinèd all to sleep.

V

Full in the passage of the vale, above,
A sable, silent, solemn forest stood ;
Where nought but shadowy forms were seen to
move,
As Idless fancied in her dreaming mood.
And up the hills, on either side, a wood
Of blackening pines, ay waving to and fro,
Sent forth a sleepy horror through the blood ;
And where this valley winded out, below,
The murmuring main was heard, and scarcely heard,
to flow.

VI

A pleasing land of drowsyhed it was :
Of dreams that wave before the half-shut eye ;
And of gay castles in the clouds that pass,
For ever flushing round a summer sky :
There eke the soft delights, that witchingly
Instil a wanton sweetness through the breast,
And the calm pleasures always hovered nigh ;
But whate'er smacked of noyance, or unrest,
Was far far off expelled from this delicious nest.

VII

The landskip such, inspiring perfect ease ;
Where INDOLENCE (for so the wizard hight)
Close-hid his castle mid embowering trees,
That half shut out the beams of Phoebus bright,
And made a kind of checkered day and night.
Meanwhile, unceasing at the massy gate,
Beneath a spacious palm, the wicked wight
Was placed ; and, to his lute, of cruel fate
And labour harsh complained, lamenting man's estate.

VIII

Thither continual pilgrims crowded still
From all the roads of earth that pass there by :
For, as they chaunced to breathe on neighbouring
    hill,
The freshness of this valley smote their eye,
And drew them ever and anon more nigh,
Till clustering round the enchanter false they hung,
Ymolten with his syren melody ;
While o'er th' enfeebling lute his hand he flung,
And to the trembling chord these tempting verses
    sung :

IX

'Behold! ye pilgrims of this earth, behold!
See all but man with unearned pleasure gay.
See her bright robes the butterfly unfold,
Broke from her wintry tomb in prime of May.
What youthful bride can equal her array?
Who can with her for easy pleasure vie?
From mead to mead with gentle wing to stray,
From flower to flower on balmy gales to fly,
Is all she has to do beneath the radiant sky.

X

'Behold the merry minstrels of the morn,
The swarming songsters of the careless grove,
Ten thousand throats that, from the flowering thorn,
Hymn their good God, and carol sweet of love,
Such grateful kindly raptures them emove!
They neither plough nor sow; ne, fit for flail,
E'er to the barn the nodding sheaves they drove
Yet theirs each harvest dancing in the gale,
Whatever crowns the hill, or smiles along the vale.

XI

'Outcast of Nature, man! the wretched thrall
Of bitter-dropping sweat, of sweltry pain,
Of cares that eat away thy heart with gall,
And of the vices, an inhuman train,
That all proceed from savage thirst of gain:
For when hard-hearted Interest first began
To poison earth, Astraea left the plain;
Guile, Violence, and Murder seized on man,
And, for soft milky streams, with blood the rivers ran.

XII

'Come, ye, who still the cumbrous load of life
Push hard up hill; but, as the farthest steep
You trust to gain, and put an end to strife,
Down thunders back the stone with mighty sweep,
And hurls your labours to the valley deep,
Forever vain : come, and withouten fee
I in oblivion will your sorrows steep,
Your cares, your toils ; will steep you in a sea
Of full delight : O come, ye weary wights, to me !

XIII

'With me, you need not rise at early dawn,
To pass the joyless day in various stounds ;
Or, louting low, on upstart fortune fawn,
And sell fair honour for some paltry pounds ;
Or through the city take your dirty rounds
To cheat, and dun, and lie, and visit pay,
Now flattering base, now giving secret wounds ;
Or prowl in courts of law for human prey,
In venal senate thieve, or rob on broad highway.

XIV

'No cocks, with me, to rustic labour call,
From village on to village sounding clear ;
To tardy swain no shrill-voiced matrons squall ;
No dogs, no babes, no wives to stun your ear ;
No hammers thump ; no horrid blacksmith sear,
Ne noisy tradesman your sweet slumbers start
With sounds that are a misery to hear :
But all is calm as would delight the heart
Of Sybarite of old, all nature, and all art.

XV

'Here nought but candour reigns, indulgent ease,
Good-natured lounging, sauntering up and down :
They who are pleased themselves must always
        please ;
On others' ways they never squint a frown,
Nor heed what haps in hamlet or in town.
Thus, from the source of tender Indolence,
With milky blood the heart is overflown,
Is soothed and sweetened by the social sense ;
For interest, envy, pride, and strife are banished hence.

XVI

' What, what is virtue but repose of mind ?
A pure ethereal calm that knows no storm,
Above the reach of wild ambition's wind,
Above those passions that this world deform,
And torture man, a proud malignant worm !
But here, instead, soft gales of passion play,
And gently stir the heart, thereby to form
A quicker sense of joy ; as breezes stray
Across the enlivened skies, and make them still more
        gay.

XVII

' The best of men have ever loved repose :
They hate to mingle in the filthy fray ;
Where the soul sours, and gradual rancour grows,
Imbittered more from peevish day to day.
Even those whom fame has lent her fairest ray,
The most renowned of worthy wights of yore,
From a base world at last have stolen away :
So Scipio, to the soft Cumaean shore
Retiring, tasted joy he never knew before.

XVIII

' But if a little exercise you chuse,
Some zest for ease, 'tis not forbidden here.
Amid the groves you may indulge the muse,
Or tend the blooms, and deck the vernal year ;
Or softly stealing, with your watery gear,
Along the brooks, the crimson-spotted fry
You may delude : the whilst, amused, you hear
Now the hoarse stream, and now the zephyr's sigh,
Attunèd to the birds, and woodland melody.

XIX

' O grievous folly ! to heap up estate,
Losing the days you see beneath the sun ;
When, sudden, comes blind unrelenting fate,
And gives the untasted portion you have won
With ruthless toil, and many a wretch undone,
To those who mock you gone to Pluto's reign,
There with sad ghosts to pine, and shadows dun :
But sure it is of vanities most vain,
To toil for what you here untoiling may obtain.'

XX

He ceased. But still their trembling ears retained
The deep vibrations of his witching song ;
That, by a kind of magic power, constrained
To enter in, pell-mell, the listening throng.
Heaps poured on heaps, and yet they slipt along
In silent ease : as when, beneath the beam
Of summer moons, the distant woods among,
Or by some flood all silvered with the gleam,
The soft-embodied fays through airy portal stream.

XXI

By the smooth demon so it ordered was,
And here his baneful bounty first began :
Though some there were who would not further pass,
And his alluring baits suspected han.
The wise distrust the too fair-spoken man.
Yet through the gate they cast a wishful eye :
Not to move on, perdie, is all they can ;
For, do their very best, they cannot fly,
But often each way look, and often sorely sigh.

XXII

When this the watchful wicked wizard saw,
With sudden spring he leaped upon them strait ;
And, soon as touched by his unhallowed paw,
They found themselves within the cursèd gate,
Full hard to be repassed, like that of Fate.
Not stronger were of old the giant-crew,
Who sought to pull high Jove from regal state,
Though feeble wretch he seemed, of sallow hue :
Certes, who bides his grasp, will that encounter rue.

XXIII

For whomsoe'er the villain takes in hand,
Their joints unknit, their sinews melt apace ;
As lithe they grow as any willow-wand,
And of their vanished force remains no trace :
So when a maiden fair, of modest grace,
In all her buxom blooming May of charms,
Is seizèd in some losel's hot embrace,
She waxeth very weakly as she warms,
Then sighing yields her up to love's delicious harms.

XXIV

Waked by the crowd, slow from his bench arose
A comely full-spread porter, swoln with sleep :
His calm, broad, thoughtless aspect breathed repose;
And in sweet torpor he was plungèd deep,
Ne could himself from ceaseless yawning keep ;
While o'er his eyes the drowsy liquor ran,
Through which his half-waked soul would faintly
　　peep.
Then, taking his black staff, he called his man,
And roused himself as much as rouse himself he can.

XXV

The lad leaped lightly at his master's call.
He was, to weet, a little roguish page,
Save sleep and play who minded nought at all,
Like most the untaught striplings of his age.
This boy he kept each band to disengage,
Garters and buckles, task for him unfit,
But ill-becoming his grave personage,
And which his portly paunch would not permit.
So this same limber page to all performèd it.

XXVI

Meantime the master-porter wide displayed
Great store of caps, of slippers, and of gowns,
Wherewith he those who entered in arrayed,
Loose as the breeze that plays along the downs,
And waves the summer woods when evening frowns.
O fair undress, best dress ! it checks no vein,
But every flowing limb in pleasure drowns,
And heightens ease with grace. This done, right fain
Sir Porter sat him down, and turned to sleep again.

XXVII

Thus easy robed, they to the fountain sped,
That in the middle of the court up-threw
A stream, high-spouting from its liquid bed,
And falling back again in drizzly dew :
There each deep draughts, as deep he thirsted, drew ;
It was a fountain of Nepenthe rare :
Whence, as Dan Homer sings, huge pleasaunce grew,
And sweet oblivion of vile earthly care,
Fair gladsome waking thoughts, and joyous dreams
  more fair.

XXVIII

This rite performed, all inly pleased and still,
Withouten trump was proclamation made :—
' Ye sons of Indolence, do what you will ;
And wander where you list, through hall or glade :
Be no man's pleasure for another's staid :
Let each as likes him best his hours employ,
And curst be he who minds his neighbour's trade !
Here dwells kind ease, and unreproving joy :
He little merits bliss who others can annoy.'

XXIX

Strait of these endless numbers, swarming round
As thick as idle motes in sunny ray,
Not one eftsoons in view was to be found,
But every man strolled off his own glad way.
Wide o'er this ample court's blank area,
With all the lodges that thereto pertained,
No living creature could be seen to stray ;
While solitude and perfect silence reigned :
So that to think you dreamt you almost was con-
  strained.

XXX

As when a shepherd of the Hebrid Isles,
Placed far amid the melancholy main,
(Whether it be lone fancy him beguiles,
Or that aerial beings sometimes deign
To stand embodied to our senses plain)
Sees on the naked hill, or valley low,
The whilst in ocean Phoebus dips his wain,
A vast assembly moving to and fro ;
Then all at once in air dissolves the wondrous show.

XXXI

Ye gods of quiet, and of sleep profound,
Whose soft dominion o'er this castle sways,
And all the widely-silent places round,
Forgive me, if my trembling pen displays
What never yet was sung in mortal lays.
But how shall I attempt such arduous string ?
I who have spent my nights and nightly days
In this soul-deadening place, loose-loitering—
Ah ! how shall I for this uprear my moulted wing ?

XXXII

Come on, my muse, nor stoop to low despair,
Thou imp of Jove, touched by celestial fire !
Thou yet shalt sing of war, and actions fair,
Which the bold sons of Britain will inspire ;
Of ancient bards thou yet shalt sweep the lyre ;
Thou yet shalt tread in tragic pall the stage,
Paint love's enchanting woes, the hero's ire,
The sage's calm, the patriot's noble rage,
Dashing corruption down through every worthless age.

XXXIII

The doors, that knew no shrill alarming bell,
Ne cursèd knocker plied by villain's hand,
Self-opened into halls, where, who can tell
What elegance and grandeur wide expand
The pride of Turkey and of Persia land ?
Soft quilts on quilts, on carpets carpets spread,
And couches stretched around in seemly band ;
And endless pillows rise to prop the head ;
So that each spacious room was one full-swelling bed.

XXXIV

And everywhere huge covered tables stood,
With wines high-flavoured and rich viands crowned
Whatever sprightly juice or tastful food
On the green bosom of this Earth are found,
And all old Ocean genders in his round—
Some hand unseen these silently displayed,
Even undemanded by a sign or sound ;
You need but wish, and, instantly obeyed,
Fair-ranged the dishes rose, and thick the glasses
    played.

XXXV

Here freedom reigned without the least alloy ;
Nor gossip's tale, nor ancient maiden's gall,
Nor saintly spleen durst murmur at our joy,
And with envenomed tongue our pleasures pall.
For why ? there was but one great rule for all ;
To wit, that each should work his own desire,
And eat, drink, study, sleep, as it may fall,
Or melt the time in love, or wake the lyre,
And carol what, unbid, the Muses might inspire.

XXXVI

The rooms with costly tapestry were hung,
Where was inwoven many a gentle tale,
Such as of old the rural poets sung
Or of Arcadian or Sicilian vale :
Reclining lovers, in the lonely dale,
Poured forth at large the sweetly tortured heart ;
Or, looking tender passion, swelled the gale,
And taught charmed echo to resound their smart ;
While flocks, woods, streams around, repose and peace
    impart.

XXXVII

Those pleased the most, where, by a cunning hand,
Depeinten was the patriarchal age ;
What time Dan Abraham left the Chaldee land,
And pastured on from verdant stage to stage,
Where fields and fountains fresh could best engage.
Toil was not then. Of nothing took they heed,
But with wild beasts the silvan war to wage,
And o'er vast plains their herds and flocks to feed :
Blest sons of nature they ! true golden age indeed !

XXXVIII

Sometimes the pencil, in cool airy halls,
Bade the gay bloom of vernal landskips rise,
Or Autumn's varied shades imbrown the walls :
Now the black tempest strikes the astonished eyes ;
Now down the steep the flashing torrent flies ;
The trembling sun now plays o'er ocean blue,
And now rude mountains frown amid the skies ;
Whate'er Lorrain light-touched with softening hue,
Or savage Rosa dashed, or learnèd Poussin drew.

K

XXXIX

Each sound too here to languishment inclined,
Lulled the weak bosom, and incucèd ease.
Aerial music in the warbling wind,
At distance rising oft, by small degrees,
Nearer and nearer came, till o'er the trees
It hung, and breathed such soul-dissolving airs
As did, alas ! with soft perdition please :
Entangled deep in its enchanting snares,
The listening heart forgot all duties and all cares.

XL

A certain music, never known before,
Here soothed the pensive melancholy mind ;
Full easily obtained. Behoves no more,
But sidelong to the gently-waving wind
To lay the well-tuned instrument reclined ;
From which, with airy flying fingers light,
Beyond each mortal touch the most refined,
The god of winds drew sounds of deep delight :
Whence, with just cause, The Harp of Aeolus it hight.

XLI

Ah me ! what hand can touch the strings so fine ?
Who up the lofty diapasan roll
Such sweet, such sad, such solemn airs divine,
Then let them down again into the soul ?
Now rising love they fanned ; now pleasing dole
They breathed, in tender musings, through the
        heart ;
And now a graver sacred strain they stole,
As when seraphic hands an hymn impart :
Wild warbling Nature all, above the reach of Art !

XLII

Such the gay splendour, the luxurious state,
Of Caliphs old, who on the Tygris' shore,
In mighty Bagdat, populous and great,
Held their bright court, where was of ladies store ;
And verse, love, music still the garland wore :
When sleep was coy, the bard in waiting there
Cheered the lone midnight with the muse's lore ;
Composing music bade his dreams be fair,
And music lent new gladness to the morning air.

XLIII

Near the pavilions where we slept, still ran
Soft-tinkling streams, and dashing waters fell,
And sobbing breezes sighed, and oft began
(So worked the wizard) wintry storms to swell,
As heaven and earth they would together mell :
At doors and windows, threatening, seemed to call
The demons of the tempest, growling fell ;
Yet the least entrance found they none at all ;
Whence sweeter grew our sleep, secure in massy hall.

XLIV

And hither Morpheus sent his kindest dreams,
Raising a world of gayer tinct and grace ;
O'er which were shadowy cast Elysian gleams,
That played in waving lights from place to place,
And shed a roseate smile on nature's face.
Not Titian's pencil e'er could so array,
So fleece with clouds the pure ethereal space ;
Ne could it e'er such melting forms display,
As loose on flowery beds all languishingly lay.

XLV

No, fair illusions ! artful phantoms, no !
My muse will not attempt your fairy-land :
She has no colours that like you can glow ;
To catch your vivid scenes too gross her hand.
But sure it is, was ne'er a subtler band
Than these same guileful angel-seeming sprights,
Who thus in dreams voluptuous, soft, and bland,
Poured all the Arabian heaven upon our nights,
And blessed them oft besides with more refined
    delights.

XLVI

They were in sooth a most enchanting train,
Even feigning virtue ; skilful to unite
With evil good, and strew with pleasure pain.
But, for those fiends whom blood and broils delight,
Who hurl the wretch as if to hell outright
Down, down black gulfs where sullen waters sleep,
Or hold him clambering all the fearful night
On beetling cliffs, or pent in ruins deep—
They, till due time should serve, were bid far hence
    to keep.

XLVII

Ye guardian spirits, to whom man is dear,
From these foul demons shield the midnight gloom !
Angels of fancy and of love, be near,
And o'er the wilds of sleep diffuse a bloom ;
Evoke the sacred shades of Greece and Rome,
And let them virtue with a look impart !
But chief, a while O ! lend us from the tomb
Those long-lost friends for whom in love we smart,
And fill with pious awe and joy-mixt woe the heart !

XLVIII

Or are you sportive ?—bid the morn of youth
Rise to new light, and beam afresh the days
Of innocence, simplicity, and truth,
To cares estranged, and manhood's thorny ways
What transport to retrace our boyish plays,
Our easy bliss, when each thing joy supplied—
The woods, the mountains, and the warbling maze
Of the wild brooks !   But, fondly wandering wide,
My muse, resume the task that yet doth thee abide.

XLIX

One great amusement of our household was—
In a huge crystal magic globe to spy,
Still as you turned it, all things that do pass
Upon this ant-hill earth ;   where constantly
Of idly-busy men the restless fry
Run bustling to and fro with foolish haste
In search of pleasures vain, that from them fly,
Or which, obtained, the caitiffs dare not taste :
When nothing is enjoyed, can there be greater waste ?

L

Of Vanity the Mirror this was called.
Here you a muckworm of the town might see
At his dull desk, amid his legers stalled,
Eat up with carking care and penurie,
Most like to carcase parched on gallow-tree.
' A penny savèd is a penny got '—
Firm to this scoundrel maxim keepeth he,
Ne of its rigour will he bate a jot,
Till it has quenched his fire, and banishèd his pot.

LI

Strait from the filth of this low grub, behold !
Comes fluttering forth a gaudy spendthrift heir,
All glossy gay, enamelled all with gold,
The silly tenant of the summer-air.
In folly lost, of nothing takes he care ;
Pimps, lawyers, stewards, harlots, flatterers vile,
And thieving tradesmen him among them share :
His father's ghost from Limbo-lake the while
Sees this, which more damnation doth upon him pile.

LII

This globe pourtrayed the race of learned men,
Still at their books, and turning o'er the page,
Backwards and forwards : oft they snatch the pen
As if inspired, and in a Thespian rage ;
Then write, and blot, as would your ruth engage.
Why, authors, all this scrawl and scribbling sore ?
To lose the present, gain the future age,
Praisèd to be when you can hear no more,
And much enriched with fame when useless worldly
    store !

LIII

Then would a splendid city rise to view,
With carts, and cars, and coaches roaring all :
Wide-poured abroad, behold the prowling crew ;
See how they dash along from wall to wall !
At every door, hark how they thundering call !
Good Lord ! what can this giddy rout excite ?
Why ? each on each to prey, by guile or gall ;
With flattery these, with slander those to blight,
And make new tiresome parties for the coming night.

LIV

The puzzling sons of party next appeared,
In dark cabals and nightly juntos met ;
And now they whispered close, now shrugging reared
The important shoulder ; then, as if to get
New light, their twinkling eyes were inward set.
No sooner Lucifer recalls affairs,
Than forth they various rush in mighty fret ;
When lo ! pushed up to power, and crowned their
    cares,
In comes another set, and kicketh them down stairs.

LV

But what most showed the vanity of life
Was to behold the nations all on fire,
In cruel broils engaged, and deadly strife :
Most Christian kings, inflamed by black desire,
With honourable ruffians in their hire,
Cause war to rage, and blood around to pour.
Of this sad work when each begins to tire,
They sit them down just where they were before,
Till for new scenes of woe peace shall their force
    restore.

LVI

To number up the thousands dwelling here,
An useless were, and eke an endless task—
From kings, and those who at the helm appear,
To gipsies brown in summer-glades who bask.
Yea, many a man, perdie, I could unmask,
Whose desk and table make a solemn show
With tape-tied trash, and suits of fools, that ask
For place or pension, laid in decent row;
But these I passen by, with nameless numbers moe.

LVII

Of all the gentle tenants of the place,
There was a man of special grave remark :
A certain tender gloom o'erspread his face,
Pensive, not sad ; in thought involved, not dark :
As soote this man could sing as morning-lark,
And teach the noblest morals of the heart ;
But these his talents were yburied stark ;
Of the fine stores he nothing would impart,
Which or boon nature gave or nature-painting art.

LVIII

To noontide shades incontinent he ran
Where purls the brook with sleep-inviting sound ;
Or, when Dan Sol to slope his wheels began,
Amid the broom he basked him on the ground,
Where the wild thyme and camomil are found :
There would he linger till the latest ray
Of light sat quivering on the welkin's bound ;
Then homeward through the twilight shadows stray,
Sauntering and slow. So had he passèd many a day.

LIX

Yet not in thoughtless slumber were they past :
For oft the heavenly fire, that lay concealed
Emongst the sleeping embers, mounted fast,
And all its native light anew revealed.
Oft as he traversed the cerulean field,
And marked the clouds that drove before the wind,
Ten thousand glorious systems would he build,
Ten thousand great ideas filled his mind ;
But with the clouds they fled, and left no trace behind.

LX

With him was sometimes joined in silent walk
(Profoundly silent, for they never spoke)
One shyer still, who quite detested talk :
Oft, stung by spleen, at once away he broke
To groves of pine and broad o'ershadowing oak ;
There, inly thrilled, he wandered all alone,
And on himself his pensive fury wroke,
Ne ever uttered word, save when first shone
The glittering star of eve—' Thank heaven ! the day
    is done.'

LXI

Here lurked a wretch who had not crept abroad
For forty years, ne face of mortal seen—
In chamber brooding like a loathly toad ;
And sure his linen was not very clean.
Through secret loophole, that had practised been
Near to his bed, his dinner vile he took ;
Unkempt, and rough, of squalid face and mien,
Our castle's shame ! whence, from his filthy nook,
We drove the villain out for fitter lair to look.

LXII

One day there chanced into these halls to rove
A joyous youth, who took you at first sight ;
Him the wild wave of pleasure hither drove,
Before the sprightly tempest tossing light :
Certes, he was a most engaging wight,
Of social glee, and wit humane though keen,
Turning the night to day and day to night :
For him the merry bells had rung, I ween,
If, in this nook of quiet, bells had ever been.

LXIII

But not even pleasure to excess is good :
What most elates then sinks the soul as low :
When spring-tide joy pours in with copious flood,
The higher still the exulting billows flow,
The farther back again they flagging go
And leave us grovelling on the dreary shore.
Taught by this son of joy, we found it so;
Who, whilst he staid, kept in a gay uproar
Our maddened Castle all, the abode of sleep no more.

LXIV

As when in prime of June a burnished fly,
Sprung from the meads, o'er which he sweeps along,
Cheered by the breathing bloom and vital sky,
Tunes up amid these airy halls his song,
Soothing at first the gay reposing throng :
And oft he sips their bowl ; or, nearly drowned,
He, thence recovering, drives their beds among,
And scares their tender sleep with trump profound ;
Then out again he flies, to wing his mazy round.

LXV

Another guest there was, of sense refined,
Who felt each worth,—for every worth he had;
Serene yet warm, humane yet firm his mind,
As little touched as any man's with bad:
Him through their inmost walks the Muses lad,
To him the sacred love of Nature lent;
And sometimes would he make our valley glad.
Whenas we found he would not here be pent,
To him the better sort this friendly message sent:—

LXVI

'Come, dwell with us! true son of virtue, come!
But if, alas! we cannot thee persuade
To lie content beneath our peaceful dome,
Ne ever more to quit our quiet glade;
Yet, when at last thy toils, but ill apaid,
Shall dead thy fire, and damp its heavenly spark,
Thou wilt be glad to seek the rural shade,
There to indulge the muse, and nature mark:
We then a lodge for thee will rear in Hagley Park.'

LXVII

Here whilom ligged the Esopus of the age;
But, called by fame, in soul yprickèd deep,
A noble pride restored him to the stage,
And roused him like a giant from his sleep.
Even from his slumbers we advantage reap:
With double force the astonished scene he wakes,
Yet quits not nature's bounds. He knows to keep
Each due decorum: now the heart he shakes,
And now with well-urged sense the enlightened judge-
ment takes.

LXVIII

A bard here dwelt, more fat than bard beseems
Who, void of envy, guile, and lust of gain,
On virtue still, and nature's pleasing themes,
Poured forth his unpremeditated strain,
The world forsaking with a calm disdain:
Here laughed he careless in his easy seat;
Here quaffed, encircled with the joyous train;
Oft moralizing sage; his ditty sweet
He loathèd much to write, ne carèd to repeat.

LXIX

Full oft by holy feet our ground was trod ;
Of clerks good plenty here you mote espy.
A little, round, fat, oily man of God
Was one I chiefly marked among the fry :
He had a roguish twinkle in his eye,
And shone all glittering with ungodly dew,
If a tight damsel chanced to trippen by ;
Which when observed, he shrunk into his mew,
And straight would recollect his piety anew.

LXX

Nor be forgot a tribe who minded nought
(Old inmates of the place) but state affairs :
They looked, perdie, as if they deeply thought ;
And on their brow sat every nation's cares.
The world by them is parcelled out in shares,
When in the Hall of Smoke they congress hold,
And the sage berry sun-burnt Mocha bears
Has cleared their inward eye : then, smoke-enrolled,
Their oracles break forth, mysterious as of old.

LXXI

Here languid Beauty kept her pale-faced court :
Bevies of dainty dames of high degree
From every quarter hither made resort ;
Where, from gross mortal care and business free,
They lay poured out in ease and luxury.
Or, should they a vain show of work assume,
Alas ! and well-a-day ! what can it be ?
To knot, to twist, to range the vernal bloom ;
But far is cast the distaff, spinning-wheel, and loom.

LXXII

Their only labour was to kill the time ;
And labour dire it is, and weary woe.
They sit, they loll, turn o'er some idle rhyme ;
Then, rising sudden, to the glass they go,
Or saunter forth with tottering step and slow :
This soon too rude an exercise they find ;
Strait on the couch their limbs again they throw,
Where, hours on hours, they sighing lie reclined,
And court the vapoury god soft-breathing in the wind.

LXXIII

Now must I mark the villainy we found,
But ah ! too late, as shall eftsoons be shown.
A place here was, deep, dreary, under ground ;
Where still our inmates, when unpleasing grown,
Diseased, and loathsome, privily were thrown.
Far from the light of heaven they languished there,
Unpitied, uttering many a bitter groan ;
For of these wretches taken was no care :
Fierce fiends and hags of hell their only nurses were.

LXXIV

Alas the change ! from scenes of joy and rest
To this dark den, where sickness tossed alway.
Here Lethargy, with deadly sleep opprest,
Stretched on his back a mighty lubbard lay,
Heaving his sides, and snorèd night and day :
To stir him from his traunce it was not eath,
And his half-opened eyne he shut straitway ;
He led, I wot, the softest way to death,
And taught withouten pain and strife to yield the
    breath.

LXXV

Of limbs enormous, but withal unsound,
Soft-swoln, and pale, here lay the Hydropsy :
Unwieldy man ! with belly monstrous round,
For ever fed with watery supply ;
For still he drank, and yet he still was dry.
And moping here did Hypochondria sit,
Mother of Spleen, in robes of various dye,
Who vexèd was full oft with ugly fit ;
And some her frantic deemed, and some her deemed
    a wit.

LXXVI

A lady proud she was, of ancient blood,
Yet oft her fear her pride made crouchen low :
She felt, or fancied in her fluttering mood,
All the diseases which the spittles know,
And sought all physic which the shops bestow,
And still new leaches and new drugs would try,
Her humour ever wavering to and fro ;
For sometimes she would laugh, and sometimes cry,
Then sudden waxèd wroth ; and all she knew not why.

LXXVII

Fast by her side a listless maiden pined,
With aching head and squeamish heart-burnings ;
Pale, bloated, cold, she seemed to hate mankind,
Yet loved in secret all forbidden things.
And here the Tertian shakes his chilling wings :
The sleepless Gout here counts the crowing cocks—
A wolf now gnaws him, now a serpent stings :
Whilst Apoplexy crammed Intemperance knocks
Down to the ground at once, as butcher felleth ox.

CANTO II

I

ESCAPED the castle of the sire of sin,
Ah ! where shall I so sweet a dwelling find ?
For all around without, and all within,
Nothing save what delightful was and kind,
Of goodness savouring and a tender mind,
E'er rose to view. But now another strain,
Of doleful note, alas ! remains behind :
I now must sing of pleasure turned to pain,
And of the false enchanter, Indolence, complain.

II

Is there no patron to protect the Muse,
And fence for her Parnassus' barren soil ?
To every labour its reward accrues,
And they are sure of bread who swink and moil ;
But a fell tribe the Aonian hive despoil,
As ruthless wasps oft rob the painful bee :
Thus, while the laws not guard that noblest toil,
Ne for the Muses other meed decree,
They praisèd are alone, and starve right merrily.

III

I care not, fortune, what you me deny :
You cannot rob me of free nature's grace ;
You cannot shut the windows of the sky,
Through which Aurora shows her brightening face :
You cannot bar my constant feet to trace
The woods and lawns by living stream at eve.
Let health my nerves and finer fibres brace,
And I their toys to the great children leave :
Of fancy, reason, virtue, nought can me bereave.

IV

Come, then, my muse, and raise a bolder song :
Come, lig no more upon the bed of sloth,
Dragging the lazy languid line along,
Fond to begin, but still to finish loth,
Thy half-writ scrolls all eaten by the moth :
Arise, and sing that generous imp of fame
Who, with the sons of softness nobly wroth,
To sweep away this human lumber came,
Or in a chosen few to rouse the slumbering flame.

V

In Fairy-land there lived a knight of old,
Of feature stern, Selvaggio well ycleped,
A rough unpolished man, robust and bold,
But wondrous poor : he neither sowed nor reaped,
Ne stores in summer for cold winter heaped ;
In hunting all his days away he wore ;
Now scorched by June, now in November steeped,
Now pinched by biting January sore,
He still in woods pursued the libbard and the boar.

VI

As he one morning, long before the dawn,
Pricked through the forest to dislodge his prey,
Deep in the winding bosom of a lawn,
With wood wild-fringed, he marked a taper's ray,
That from the beating rain and wintry fray
Did to a lonely cot his steps decoy :
There, up to earn the needments of the day,
He found dame Poverty, nor fair nor coy ;
Her he compressed, and filled her with a lusty boy.

VII

Amid the greenwood shade this boy was bred,
And grow at last a knight of muchel fame,
Of active mind and vigorous lustyhed,
The Knight of Arts and Industry by name.
Earth was his bed, the boughs his roof did frame ;
He knew no beverage but the flowing stream ;
His tasteful well-earned food the silvan game,
Or the brown fruit with which the woodlands teem :
The same to him glad summer or the winter breme.

VIII

So passed his youthly morning, void of care,
Wild as the colts that through the commons run :
For him no tender parents troubled were ;
He of the forest seemed to be the son,
And certes had been utterly undone
But that Minerva pity of him took,
With all the gods that love the rural wonne,
That teach to tame the soil and rule the crook ;
Ne did the sacred Nine disdain a gentle look.

IX

Of fertile genius, him they nurtured well
In every science and in every art
By which mankind the thoughtless brutes excel,
That can or use, or joy, or grace impart,
Disclosing all the powers of head and heart :
Ne were the goodly exercises spared
That brace the nerves or make the limbs alert,
And mix elastic force with firmness hard :
Was never knight on ground mote be with him
     compared.

X

Sometimes, with early morn, he mounted gay
The hunter-steed, exulting o'er the dale,
And drew the roseate breath of orient day :
Sometimes, retiring to the secret vale,
Yclad in steel, and bright with burnished mail,
He strained the bow, or tossed the sounding spear,
Or, darting on the goal, outstript the gale,
Or wheeled the chariot in its mid career,
Or strenuous wrestled hard with many a tough com-
     peer.

XI

At other times he pryed through Nature's store,
Whate'er she in the ethereal round contains,
Whate'er she hides beneath her verdant floor,
The vegetable and the mineral reigns ;
Or else he scanned the globe, those small domains,
Where restless mortals such a turmoil keep,
Its seas, its floods, its mountains, and its plains ;
But more he searched the mind, and roused from
     sleep
Those moral seeds whence we heroic actions reap.

XII

Nor would he scorn to stoop from high pursuits
Of heavenly Truth, and practise what she taught.
Vain is the tree of knowledge without fruits.
Sometimes in hand the spade or plough he caught,
Forth-calling all with which boon earth is fraught ;
Sometimes he plied the strong mechanic tool,
Or reared the fabric from the finest draught ;
And oft he put himself to Neptune's school,
Fighting with winds and waves on the vext ocean
    pool.

XIII

To solace then these rougher toils he tried
To touch the kindling canvas into life ;
With nature his creating pencil vied,—
With nature joyous at the mimic strife :
Or to such shapes as graced Pygmalion's wife
He hewed the marble ; or with varied fire
He roused the trumpet and the martial fife,
Or bade the lute sweet tenderness inspire,
Or verses framed that well might wake Apollo's lyre.

XIV

Accomplished thus he from the woods issúed,
Full of great aims and bent on bold emprise ;
The work which long he in his breast had brewed
Now to perform he ardent did devise,
To-wit, a barbarous world to civilize.
Earth was till then a boundless forest wild—
Nought to be seen but savage wood and skies ;
No cities nourished arts, no culture smiled,
No government, no laws, no gentle manners mild.

XV

A rugged wight, the worst of brutes, was man ;
On his own wretched kind he, ruthless, preyed :
The strongest still the weakest over-ran ;
In every country mighty robbers swayed,
And guile and ruffian force were all their trade.
Life was not life, but rapine, want, and woe ;
Which this brave knight, in noble anger, made
To swear he would the rascal rout o'erthrow,
For, by the Powers Divine, it should no more be so !

XVI

It would exceed the purport of my song
To say how this best sun, from orient climes,
Came beaming life and beauty all along,
Before him chasing indolence and crimes.
Still, as he passed, the nations he sublimes,
And calls forth arts and virtue with his ray :
Then Egypt, Greece, and Rome their golden times
Successive had ; but now in ruins grey
They lie, to slavish sloth and tyranny a prey.

XVII

To crown his toils, Sir Industry then spread
The swelling sail, and made for Britain's coast.
A sylvan life till then the natives led,
In the brown shades and greenwood forest lost,
All careless rambling where it liked them most—
Their wealth the wild-deer bouncing through the
        glade ;
They lodged at large, and lived at Nature's cost ;
Save spear and bow withouten other aid ;
Yet not the Roman steel their naked breast dismayed.

XVIII

He liked the soil, he liked the clement skies,
He liked the verdant hills and flowery plains ;
' Be this my great, my chosen isle ! (he cries)
This—whilst my labours liberty sustains—
This Queen of Ocean all assault disdains.'
Nor liked he less the genius of the land,
To freedom apt and persevering pains,
Mild to obey, and generous to command,
Tempered by forming Heaven with kindest firmest
    hand.

XIX

Here by degrees his master-work arose,
Whatever arts and industry can frame,
Whatever finished agriculture knows,
Fair Queen of Arts ! from heaven itself who came
When Eden flourished in unspotted fame ;
And still with her sweet innocence we find,
And tender peace, and joys without a name,
That, while they rapture, tranquillize the mind ;
Nature and Art at once, delight and use combined.

XX

Then towns he quickened by mechanic arts,
And bade the fervent city glow with toil ;
Bade social commerce raise renownèd marts,
Join land to land, and marry soil to soil,
Unite the poles, and without bloody spoil
Bring home of either Ind the gorgeous stores ;
Or, should despotic rage the world embroil,
Bade tyrants tremble on remotest shores,
While o'er the encircling deep Britannia's thunder
    roars.

XXI

The drooping Muses then he westward called,
From the famed city by Propontis Sea,
What time the Turk the enfeebled Grecian thralled ;
Thence from their cloistered walks he set them free,
And brought them to another Castalie,
Where Isis many a famous noursling breeds,
Or where old Cam soft paces o'er the lea
In pensive mood, and tunes his Doric reeds,
The whilst his flocks at large the lonely shepherd feeds.

XXII

Yet the fine arts were what he finished least.
For why ? They are the quintessence of all,
The growth of labouring time, and slow increast ;
Unless, as seldom chances, it should fall
That mighty patrons the coy sisters call
Up to the sunshine of uncumbered ease,
Where no rude care the mounting thought may
    thrall,
And where they nothing have to do but please :
Ah ! gracious God ! thou knowst they ask no other
    fees.

XXIII

But now, alas ! we live too late in time :
Our patrons now even grudge that little claim,
Except to such as sleek the soothing rhyme ;
And yet, forsooth, they wear Maecenas' name,
Poor sons of puffed-up vanity, not fame.
Unbroken spirits, cheer ! still, still remains
The eternal patron, Liberty ; whose flame,
While she protects, inspires the noblest strains.
The best and sweetest far are toil-created gains.

XXIV

Whenas the knight had framed in Britain-land
A matchless form of glorious government,
In which the sovereign laws alone command,
Laws stablished by the public free consent,
Whose majesty is to the sceptre lent—
When this great plan, with each dependent art,
Was settled firm, and to his heart's content,
Then sought he from the toilsome scene to part,
And let life's vacant eve breathe quiet through the
    heart.

XXV

For this he chose a farm in Deva's vale,
Where his long alleys peeped upon the main.
In this calm seat he drew the healthful gale,
Commixed the chief, the patriot, and the swain,
The happy monarch of his sylvan train !
Here, sided by the guardians of the fold,
He walked his rounds, and cheered his blest domain ;
His days, the days of unstained nature, rolled
Replete with peace and joy, like patriarch's of old.

XXVI

Witness, ye lowing herds, who lent him milk ;
Witness, ye flocks, whose woolly vestments far
Exceed soft India's cotton, or her silk ;
Witness, with Autumn charged, the nodding car
That homeward came beneath sweet evening's star,
Or of September moons the radiance mild.
O hide thy head, abominable War !
Of crimes and ruffian idleness the child !
From heaven this life ysprung, from hell thy glories
    vild !

XXVII

Nor from his deep retirement banished was
The amusing cares of rural industry.
Still, as with grateful change the seasons pass,
New scenes arise, new landskips strike the eye,
And all the enlivened country beautify :
Gay plains extend where marshes slept before ;
O'er recent meads the exulting streamlets fly ;
Dark frowning heaths grow bright with Ceres' store ;
And woods imbrown the steep, or wave along the shore.

XXVIII

As nearer to his farm you made approach,
He polished nature with a finer hand :
Yet on her beauties durst not art encroach ;
'Tis art's alone these beauties to expand.
In graceful dance immingled, o'er the land
Pan, Pales, Flora, and Pomona played :
Even here, sometimes, the rude wild common fand
An happy place ; where, free and unafraid,
Amid the flowering brakes each coyer creature strayed.

XXIX

But in prime vigour what can last for ay ?
That soul-enfeebling wizard, Indolence,
I whilom sung, wrought in his works decay :
Spread far and wide was his curst influence ;
Of public virtue much he dulled the sense,
Even much of private ; eat our spirit out,
And fed our rank luxurious vices : whence
The land was overlaid with many a lout ;
Not, as old fame reports, wise, generous, bold, and stout.

XXX

A rage of pleasure maddened every breast ;
Down to the lowest lees the ferment ran :
To his licentious wish each must be blest,
With joy be fevered,—snatch it as he can.
Thus Vice the standard reared ; her arrier-ban
Corruption called, and loud she gave the word :—
' Mind, mind yourselves ! why should the vulgar
      man,
The lacquey, be more virtuous than his lord ?
Enjoy this span of life ! 'tis all the gods afford.'

XXXI

The tidings reached to where in quiet hall
The good old knight enjoyed well-earned repose :
' Come, come, Sir Knight! thy children on thee call;
Come, save us yet, ere ruin round us close !
The demon Indolence thy toils o'erthrows.'
On this the noble colour stained his cheeks,
Indignant glowing through the whitening snows
Of venerable eld ; his eye full-speaks
His ardent soul, and from his couch at once he breaks.

XXXII

' I will (he cried), so help me God ! destroy
That villain Archimage.'—His page then strait
He to him called—a fiery-footed boy
Benempt Dispatch. ' My steed be at the gate ;
My bard attend ; quick, bring the net of fate.'
This net was twisted by the Sisters Three ;
Which, when once cast o'er hardened wretch, too
      late
Repentance comes : replevy cannot be
From the strong iron grasp of vengeful destiny.

XXXIII

He came, the bard, a little Druid wight,
Of withered aspect ; but his eye was keen,
With sweetness mixed. In russet brown bedight,
As is his sister of the copses green,
He crept along, unpromising of mien.
Gross he who judges so. His soul was fair ;
Bright as the children of yon azure sheen,
True comeliness, which nothing can impair,
Dwells in the mind : all else is vanity and glare.

XXXIV

'Come,' quoth the knight; ' a voice has reached mine
    ear :
The demon Indolence threats overthrow
To all that to mankind is good and dear.
Come, Philomelus, let us instant go
O'erturn his bowers and lay his castle low.
Those men, those wretched men, who *will* be slaves,
Must drink a bitter wrathful cup of woe :
But some there be thy song, as from their graves,
Shall raise. Thrice happy he who without rigour
    saves ! '

XXXV

Issuing forth, the knight bestrode his steed
Of ardent bay, and on whose front a star
Shone blazing bright: sprung from the generous
    breed
That whirl of active Day the rapid car,
He pranced along, disdaining gate or bar,
Meantime, the bard on milk-white palfrey rode ;
An honest sober beast, that did not mar
His meditations, but full softly trode :
And much they moralized as thus yfere they yode.

XXXVI

They talked of virtue, and of human bliss.
What else so fit for man to settle well ?
And still their long researches met in this,
This truth of truths, which nothing can refel :—
' From virtue's fount the purest joys outwell,
Sweet rills of thought that cheer the conscious soul ;
While vice pours forth the troubled streams of hell,
The which, howe'er disguised, at last with dole
Will through the tortured breast their fiery torrent
    roll.'

XXXVII

At length it dawned, that fatal valley gay,
O'er which high wood-crowned hills their summits
    rear.
On the cool height awhile our palmers stay,
And spite even of themselves their senses cheer ;
Then to the wizard's wonne their steps they steer.
Like a green isle it broad beneath them spread,
With gardens round, and wandering currents clear,
And tufted groves to shade the meadow-bed,
Sweet airs and song ; and without hurry all seemed
    glad.

XXXVIII

' As God shall judge me, Knight ! we must forgive
(The half-enraptured Philomelus cried)
The frail good man deluded here to live,
And in these groves his musing fancy hide.
Ah, nought is pure ! It cannot be denied
That virtue still some tincture has of vice,
And vice of virtue. What should then betide,
But that our charity be not too nice ?
Come, let us those we can to real bliss entice.'

XXXIX

' Ay, sicker,' quoth the knight, ' all flesh is frail,
To pleasant sin and joyous dalliance bent ;
But let not brutish vice of this avail,
And think to scape deservèd punishment.
Justice were cruel, weakly to relent ;
From Mercy's self she got her sacred glaive :
Grace be to those who can and will repent ;
But penance long and dreary to the slave,
Who must in floods of fire his gross foul spirit lave.'

XL

Thus, holding high discourse, they came to where
The cursèd carle was at his wonted trade ;
Still tempting heedless men into his snare,
In witching wise, as I before have said.
But when he saw, in goodly gear arrayed,
The grave majestic knight approaching nigh,
And by his side the bard so sage and staid,
His countenance fell ; yet oft his anxious eye
Marked them, like wily fox who roosted cock doth spy.

XLI

Nathless, with feigned respect, he bade give back
The rabble-rout, and welcomed them full kind ;
Struck with the noble twain, they were not slack
His orders to obey, and fall behind.
Then he resumed his song ; and unconfined
Poured all his music, ran through all his strings :
With magic dust their eyne he tries to blind,
And virtue's tender airs o'er weakness flings.
What pity, base his song who so divinely sings !

XLII

Elate in thought, he counted them his own,
They listened so intent with fixed delight :
But they instead, as if transmewed to stone,
Marvelled he could with such sweet art unite
The lights and shades of manners, wrong and right.
Meantime the silly crowd the charm devour,
Wide-pressing to the gate. Swift on the Knight
He darted fierce to drag him to his bower,
Who backening shunned his touch, for well he knew
    its power.

XLIII

As in thronged amphitheatre of old
The wary retiarius trapped his foe,
Even so the Knight, returning on him bold,
At once involved him in the net of woe
Whereof I mention made not long ago.
Enraged at first, he scorned so weak a jail,
And leaped, and flew, and flouncèd to and fro ;
But, when he found that nothing could avail,
He sat him felly down, and gnawed his bitter nail.

XLIV

Alarmed, the inferior demons of the place
Raised rueful shrieks and hideous yells around ;
Black ruptured clouds deformed the welkin's face,
And from beneath was heard a wailing sound,
As of infernal sprights in cavern bound ;
A solemn sadness every creature strook,
And lightnings flashed, and horror rocked the
    ground :
Huge crowds on crowds outpoured, with blemished
    look,
As if on time's last verge this frame of things had
    shook.

XLV

Soon as the short-lived tempest was yspent,
Steamed from the jaws of vext Avernus' hole,
And hushed the hubbub of the rabblement,
Sir Industry the first calm moment stole :
' There must,' he cried, ' amid so vast a shoal,
Be some who are not tainted at the heart,
Not poisoned quite by this same villain's bowl :
Come, then, my bard, thy heavenly fire impart ;
Touch soul with soul, till forth the latent spirit start.'

XLVI

The bard obeyed ; and, taking from his side,
Where it in seemly sort depending hung,
His British harp, its speaking strings he tried,
The which with skilful touch he deftly strung,
Till tinkling in clear symphony they rung.
Then, as he felt the muses come along,
Light o'er the chords his raptured hand he flung,
And played a prelude to his rising song :
The whilst, like midnight mute, ten thousands round
    him throng.

XLVII

Thus, ardent, burst his strain :—' Ye hapless race,
Dire-labouring here to smother reason's ray
That lights our Maker's image in our face,
And gives us wide o'er earth unquestioned sway ;
What is the adored Supreme perfection ? say !
What, but eternal never-resting soul,
Almighty power, and all-directing day,
By whom each atom stirs, the planets roll ;
Who fills, surrounds, informs, and agitates the whole ?

XLVIII

' Come, to the beaming God your hearts unfold !
Draw from its fountain life ! 'Tis thence alone
We can excel. Up from unfeeling mould
To seraphs burning round the Almighty's throne,
Life rising still on life in higher tone
Perfection forms, and with perfection bliss.
In universal nature this clear shown
Not needeth proof : to prove it were, I wis,
To prove the beauteous world excels the brute abyss.

XLIX

' Is not the field, with lively culture green,
A sight more joyous than the dead morass ?
Do not the skies, with active ether clean
And fanned by sprightly zephyrs, far surpass
The foul November fogs and slumbrous mass
With which sad nature veils her drooping face ?
Does not the mountain stream, as clear as glass,
Gay-dancing on, the putrid pool disgrace ?
The same in all holds true, but chief in human race.

L

' It was not by vile loitering in ease
That Greece obtained the brighter palm of art ;
That soft yet ardent Athens learned to please,
To keen the wit, and to sublime the heart —
In all supreme ! complete in every part !
It was not thence majestic Rome arose,
And o'er the nations shook her conquering dart :
For sluggard's brow the laurel never grows ;
Renown is not the child of indolent repose.

LI

' Had unambitious mortals minded nought
But in loose joy their time to wear away,
Had they alone the lap of dalliance sought,
Pleased on her pillow their dull heads to lay,
Rude nature's state had been our state to-day ;
No cities e'er their towery fronts had raised,
No arts had made us opulent and gay,
With brother-brutes the human race had graz'd,
None e'er had soared to fame, none honoured been,
    none praised.

LII

' Great Homer's song had never fired the breast
To thirst of glory and heroic deeds ;
Sweet Maro's muse, sunk in inglorious rest,
Had silent slept amid the Mincian reeds :
The wits of modern time had told their beads,
And monkish legends been their only strains ;
Our Milton's Eden had lain wrapt in weeds,
Our Shakespeare strolled and laughed with War-
    wick swains,
Ne had my master Spenser charmed his Mulla's plains.

LIII

' Dumb, too, had been the sage historic muse,
And perished all the sons of ancient fame ;
Those starry lights of virtue, that diffuse
Through the dark depth of time their vivid flame,
Had all been lost with such as have no name.
Who then had scorned his ease for others' good ?
Who then had toiled, rapacious men to tame ?
Who in the public breach devoted stood,
And for his country's cause been prodigal of blood ?

LIII. 6, other's *second* ed. (1748).

LIV

' But, should to fame your hearts impervious be,
If right I read, you pleasure all require :
Then hear how best may be obtained this fee,
How best enjoyed this nature's wide desire.
Toil, and be glad! let Industry inspire
Into your quickened limbs her buoyant breath !
Who does not act is dead ; absorpt entire
In miry sloth, no pride, no joy he hath :
O leaden-hearted men, to be in love with death !

LV

' Better the toiling swain, oh happier far !
Perhaps the happiest of the sons of men !
Who vigorous plies the plough, the team, or car,
Who houghs the field, or ditches in the glen,
Delves in his garden, or secures his pen :
The tooth of avarice poisons not his peace ;
He tosses not in sloth's abhorrèd den ;
From vanity he has a full release ;
And, rich in nature's wealth, he thinks not of increase.

LVI

' Good Lord ! how keen are his sensations all !
His bread is sweeter than the glutton's cates ;
The wines of France upon the palate pall
Compared with what his simple soul elates,
The native cup whose flavour thirst creates ;
At one deep draught of sleep he takes the night ;
And, for that heart-felt joy which nothing mates,
Of the pure nuptial bed the chaste delight,
The losel is to him a miserable wight.

L

LVII

‘ But what avail the largest gifts of Heaven,
When drooping health and spirits go amiss ?
How tasteless then whatever can be given !
Health is the vital principle of bliss,
And exercise of health.   In proof of this,
Behold the wretch who slugs his life away
Soon swallowed in disease’s sad abyss ;
While he whom toil has braced, or manly play,
Has light as air each limb, each thought as clear as day.

LVIII

‘ O who can speak the vigorous joys of health ?
Unclogged the body, unobscured the mind :
The morning rises gay ; with pleasing stealth
The temperate evening falls serene and kind.
In health the wiser brutes true gladness find.
See how the younglings frisk along the meads
As May comes on and wakes the balmy wind !
Rampant with life, their joy all joy exceeds :
Yet what save high-strung health this dancing
    pleasaunce breeds ?

LIX

‘ But here, instead, is fostered every ill
Which or distempered minds or bodies know.
Come, then, my kindred spirits ! do not spill
Your talents here.   This place is but a show
Whose charms delude you to the den of woe :
Come, follow me ; I will direct you right,
Where pleasure’s roses, void of serpents, grow,
Sincere as sweet.   Come, follow this good knight ;
And you will bless the day that brought him to your
    sight.

LX

' Some he will lead to courts, and some to camps ;
To senates some, and public sage debates,
Where, by the solemn gleam of midnight lamps,
The world is poised, and managed mighty states ;
To high discovery some, that new creates
The face of earth ; some to the thriving mart :
Some to the rural reign, and softer fates ;
To the sweet muses some, who raise the heart :
All glory shall be yours, all nature, and all art.

LXI

' There are, I see, who listen to my lay,
Who wretched sigh for virtue, but despair.
" All may be done (methinks I hear them say),
Even death despised by generous actions fair ;
All : but, for those who to these bowers repair,
Their every power dissolved in luxury,
To quit of torpid sluggishness the lair
And from the powerful arms of sloth get free—
'Tis rising from the dead ! Alas, it cannot be ! "

LXII

' Would you then learn to dissipate the band
Of these huge threatening difficulties dire
That in the weak man's way like lions stand,
His soul appal, and damp his rising fire ?
Resolve ! resolve ! and to be men aspire !
Exert that noblest privilege, alone
Here to mankind indulged ; control desire ;
Let godlike reason from her sovereign throne
Speak the commanding word *I will !* and it is done.

LXIII

' Heavens ! can you, then, thus waste in shameful
wise
Your few important days of trial here ?
Heirs of eternity, yborn to rise
Through endless states of being, still more near
To bliss approaching, and perfection clear—
Can you renounce a fortune so sublime,
Such glorious hopes, your backward steps to steer,
And roll, with vilest brutes, through mud and slime ?
No, no !—your heaven-touched hearts disdain the
sordid crime ! '

LXIV

' Enough ! enough !' they cried. Strait, from the
crowd
The better sort on wings of transport fly—
As, when amid the lifeless summits proud
Of Alpine cliffs, where to the gelid sky
Snows piled on snows in wintry torpor lie,
The rays divine of vernal Phoebus play,
The awakened heaps, in streamlets from on high,
Roused into action, lively leap away,
Glad-warbling through the vales, in their new being
gay.

LXV

Not less the life, the vivid joy serene,
That lighted up these new-created men,
Than that which wings the exulting spirit clean,
When, just delivered from this fleshly den,
It soaring seeks its native skies agen.
How light its essence ! how unclogged its powers,
Beyond the blazon of my mortal pen !
Even so we glad forsook these sinful bowers ;
Even such enraptured life, such energy was ours.

LXVI

But far the greater part, with rage inflamed,
Dire-muttered curses and blasphemed high Jove.
' Ye sons of hate ! (they bitterly exclaimed)
What brought you to this seat of peace and love ?
While with kind nature here amid the grove
We passed the harmless sabbath of our time,
What to disturb it could, fell men ! emove
Your barbarous hearts ? Is happiness a crime ?
Then do the fiends of hell rule in yon Heaven sublime.'

LXVII

' Ye impious wretches, (quoth the Knight in wrath)
Your happiness behold ! ' Then strait a wand
He waved, an anti-magic power that hath
Truth from illusive falsehood to command.
Sudden the landskip sinks on every hand ;
The pure quick streams are marshy puddles found ;
On baleful heaths the groves all blackened stand ;
And, o'er the weedy foul abhorrèd ground,
Snakes, adders, toads, each loathly creature crawls
        around.

LXVIII

And here and there, on trees by lightning scathed,
Unhappy wights who loathèd life yhung ;
Or in fresh gore and recent murder bathed
They weltering lay ; or else, infuriate flung
Into the gloomy flood, while ravens sung
The funeral dirge, they down the torrent rolled :
These, by distempered blood to madness stung,
Had doomed themselves ; whence oft, when night
        controlled
The world, returning hither their sad spirits howled.

LXIX

Meantime a moving scene was open laid.
That lazar-house, I whilom in my lay
Depainten have, its horrors deep-displayed,
And gave unnumbered wretches to the day,
Who tossing there in squalid misery lay.
Soon as of sacred light the unwonted smile
Poured on these living catacombs its ray,
Through the drear caverns stretching many a mile,
The sick up-raised their heads, and dropped their
woes a while.

LXX

' O Heaven ! ' they cried, ' and do we once more see
Yon blessed sun, and this green earth so fair ?
Are we from noisome damps of pest-house free ?
And drink our souls the sweet ethereal air ?
O thou, or knight or God, who holdest there
That fiend, oh keep him in eternal chains !
But what for us, the children of despair,
Brought to the brink of hell, what hope remains ?
Repentance does itself but aggravate our pains.'

LXXI

The gentle knight, who saw their rueful case,
Let fall adown his silver beard some tears.
' Certes,' quoth he, ' it is not even in grace
To undo the past, and eke your broken years :
Nathless, to nobler worlds repentance rears
With humble hope her eye ; to her is given
A power the truly contrite heart that cheers ;
She quells the brand by which the rocks are riven ;
She more than merely softens, she rejoices Heaven.

LXXII

'Then patient bear the sufferings you have earned,
And by these sufferings purify the mind ;
Let wisdom be by past misconduct learned :
Or pious die, with penitence resigned ;
And to a life more happy and refined
Doubt not you shall, new creatures, yet arise.
Till then, you may expect in me to find
One who will wipe your sorrow from your eyes,
One who will soothe your pangs, and wing you to the
          skies.'

LXXIII

They silent heard, and poured their thanks in tears.
' For you (resumed the Knight, with sterner tone)
Whose hard dry hearts the obdurate demon sears—
That villain's gifts will cost you many a groan ;
In dolorous mansion long you must bemoan
His fatal charms, and weep your stains away ;
Till, soft and pure as infant goodness grown,
You feel a perfect change : then, who can say
What grace may yet shine forth in Heaven's eternal
          day ? '

LXXIV

This said, his powerful wand he waved anew :
Instant, a glorious angel-train descends,
The charities, to-wit, of rosy hue :
Sweet love their looks a gentle radiance lends,
And with seraphic flame compassion blends.
At once delighted to their charge they fly :
When lo ! a goodly hospital ascends,
In which they bade each human aid be nigh,
That could the sick-bed smoothe of that unhappy fry.

LXXV

It was a worthy edifying sight,
And gives to human-kind peculiar grace,
To see kind hands attending day and night
With tender ministry from place to place.
Some prop the head ; some from the pallid face
Wipe off the faint cold dews weak nature sheds ;
Some reach the healing draught : the whilst, to
  chase
The fear supreme, around their softened beds,
Some holy man by prayer all opening heaven dispreads.

LXXVI

Attended by a glad acclaiming train
Of those he rescued had from gaping hell,
Then turned the knight ; and, to his hall again
Soft-pacing, sought of Peace the mossy cell.
Yet down his cheeks the gems of pity fell,
To see the helpless wretches that remained,
There left through delves and deserts dire to yell :
Amazed, their looks with pale dismay were stained,
And, spreading wide their hands, they meek repen-
  tance feigned.

LXXVII

But ah ! their scornèd day of grace was past :
For (horrible to tell !) a desert wild
Before them stretched, bare, comfortless, and vast ;
With gibbets, bones, and carcases defiled.
There nor trim field nor lively culture smiled ;
Nor waving shade was seen, nor fountain fair :
But sands abrupt on sands lay loosely piled,
Through which they floundering toiled with painful
  care,
Whilst Phoebus smote them sore, and fired the cloud-
  less air.

LXXVIII

Then, varying to a joyless land of bogs,
The saddened country a gray waste appeared,
Where nought but putrid steams and noisome fogs
For ever hung on drizzly Auster's beard ;
Or else the ground, by piercing Caurus seared,
Was jagged with frost or heaped with glazèd snow :
Through these extremes a ceaseless round they
    steered,
By cruel fiends still hurried to and fro,
Gaunt Beggary, and Scorn, with many hell-hounds
    moe.

LXXIX

The first was with base dunghill rags yclad,
Tainting the gale in which they fluttered light ;
Of morbid hue his features, sunk and sad ;
His hollow eyne shook forth a sickly light ;
And o'er his lank jawbone, in piteous plight,
His black rough beard was matted rank and vile ;
Direful to see ! a heart-appalling sight !
Meantime foul scurf and blotches him defile ;
And dogs, where'er he went, still barkèd all the while.

LXXX

The other was a fell despightful fiend—
Hell holds none worse in baleful bower below ;
By pride, and wit, and rage, and rancour keened ;
Of man, alike if good or bad, the foe :
With nose upturned, he always made a show
As if he smelt some nauseous scent ; his eye
Was cold and keen, like blast from boreal snow ;
And taunts he casten forth most bitterly.
Such were the twain that off drove this ungodly fry.

LXXXI

Even so through Brentford town, a town of mud,
An herd of bristly swine is pricked along ;
The filthy beasts, that never chew the cud,
Still grunt, and squeak, and sing their troublous
      song,
And oft they plunge themselves the mire among ;
But ay the ruthless driver goads them on,
And ay of barking dogs the bitter throng
Makes them renew their unmelodious moan ;
Ne ever find they rest from their unresting fone.

NOTES TO THE CASTLE OF INDOLENCE

' After fourteen or fifteen years *The Castle of Indolence* comes abroad in a fortnight ' : so wrote Thomson in the middle of April, 1748, to William Paterson, his friend and successor in the office of Surveyor-General of the Leeward Islands. The slow and leisurely composition of the poem was therefore begun before Thomson went to live at Richmond, in 1736, and covered the whole of his period of residence there. It was probably published early in May. The first edition was in quarto ; the second, published in the same year, in octavo. The text of the latter is followed in the present edition. Thomson died in August of the same year.

Murdoch, Thomson's first and kindliest biographer, thus describes the origin and growth of *The Castle of Indolence* :—
' It was at first little more than a few detached stanzas in the way of raillery on himself, and on some of his friends, who would reproach him with indolence, while he thought them at least as indolent as himself. But he saw very soon that the subject deserved to be treated more seriously, and in a form fitted to convey one of the most important moral lessons.'

The poem is more exquisite and free in point of style than *The Seasons*, but less poetical and less popular. As Gray hints, it is best enjoyed in detached stanzas. It is for the pocket of poet or artist who loves to linger over its exquisitely presented imagery or sentiment, while *The Seasons* is for the inn parlour, and the general reader who is pleased with broad general effects.

The first canto, which sets forth the pleasures of indolence, is at best an apology for an indolent life ; the second is a warning intended to discourage the indulgence of indolence. There is poetry in the first canto : the second is mostly didactic.

CANTO I. stanza XXX. l. 1.   Those islands on the western coast of Scotland, called the Hebrides.—T.

I. XL. 9.   This is not an imagination of the author, there being in fact such an instrument, called Aeolus's harp, which, when placed against a little rushing or current of air, produces the effect here described.—T.

I. XLII. 7.   The Arabian Caliphs had poets among the officers of their court whose office it was to do what is here mentioned.—T.

I. LIV. 6.   Lucifer—the Morning Star.—T.

I. LVII. 2.   *a man of special grave remark.*   Probably William Paterson ; perhaps Collins.

I. LX. 3.   *One shyer still.*   Supposed to be Dr. Armstrong.

I. LXI. 1.   *Here lurked a wretch.*   Said to have been ' Henry Welby, Esquire, an eccentric solitaire of the period '.

I. LXII. 2.   *A joyous youth.*   John Forbes, son of the Lord President.

I. LXV. 1.   *Another guest.*   George Lyttelton, of Hagley Park.

I. LXVII. 1.   *the Esopus of the age.*   Quin, the actor—temporarily driven from the stage by the success of his young rival, Garrick.

I. LXVIII. 1.   *A bard here dwelt.*   Thomson himself.   ' The following lines of this stanza were writ by a friend of the author '—says Thomson in a footnote.   The friend is supposed to have been Lyttelton.

I. LXIX. 3.   *A little, round, fat, oily man of God.*   The Rev. Patrick Murdoch, at one time tutor to John Forbes ; the ' Soporific doctor ' of the *Miscellaneous Poems*—which see.

I. LXXIV–LXXVII.   Written by Dr. Armstrong.

II. XXI. 2.   *the famed city by Propontis Sea.*   Constantinople.—T.

II. XLIII. 2.   *The wary retiarius.*   A gladiator who made use of a net which he threw over his adversary.—T.

EXPLANATION OF THE OBSOLETE WORDS USED IN THIS POEM

[As given in 2nd ed. 1748.]

Archimage, *the chief, or greatest of magicians or enchanters.*

Atween, *between.*

Bale, *sorrow, trouble, misfortune.*

Benempt, *named.*

Blazon, *painting, displaying.*

Carol, *to sing songs of joy.*

Certes, *certainly.*

Eath, *easy.*

Eftsoons, *immediately, often, afterwards.*

Gear (*or* Geer), *furniture, equipage, dress.*

Glaive, *sword* (Fr.).

Han, *have.*

Hight, *is named, called.*

Idless, *idleness.*

Imp, *child, or offspring ; from the* Saxon *impan, to graft or plant.*

Kest, *for cast.*

Lad, *for led.*

Lea, *a piece of land, or meadow.*

Libbard, *leopard.*

Lig, *to lie.*

Losel, *a loose, idle fellow.*

Louting, *bowing, bending.*

Mell, *mingle.*

Moe, *more.*

Moil, *labour.*

Muchel (*or* Mochel), *much, great.*

Nathless, *nevertheless.*

Ne, *nor.*

Needments, *necessaries.*

Noursling, *a nurse, or what is nursed.*

Noyance, *harm.*

Perdie (Fr. *par Dieu*), *an old oath.*

Prick'd through the forest, *rode through the forest.*

Sear, *dry, burnt up.*

Sheen, *bright, shining.*

Sicker, *sure, surely.*

Soote, *sweet, or sweetly.*

Sooth, *true, or truth.*

Stound, *misfortune, pang.*

Sweltry, *sultry, consuming with heat.*

Swink, *to labour.*

Transmewed, *transformed.*

Unkempt (Lat. *incomptus*), *unadorned.*

Vild, *vile.*

Ween, *to think, be of opinion.*

Weet, *to know ; to weet, to wit.*

Whilom, *ere-while, formerly.*

Wis (*for* Wist), *to know, think, understand.*

Wonne (a Noun), *dwelling.*

N.B.—*The letter* Y *is frequently placed in the beginning of a word, by* Spenser, *to lengthen it a syllable.*

Yborn, *born.*

Yblent (*or* blent), *blended, mingled.*

Yclad, *clad.*

Ycleped, *called, named.*

Yfere, *together.*

Ymolten, *melted.*

Yode (*preter tense of* yede), *went.*

LIBERTY : A POEM

IN FIVE PARTS

[First published 1735 and 1736. The text here followed bears
date 1738.]

TO HIS ROYAL HIGHNESS FREDERICK, PRINCE OF WALES

SIR,

When I reflect upon that ready condescension, that preventing generosity, with which your Royal Highness received the following poem under your protection, I can alone ascribe it to the recommendation and influence of the subject. In you the cause and concerns of Liberty have so zealous a patron, as entitles whatever may have the least tendency to promote them to the distinction of your favour. And who can entertain this delightful reflection without feeling a pleasure far superior to that of the fondest author, and of which all true lovers of their country must participate? To behold the noblest dispositions of the prince and of the patriot united—an overflowing benevolence, generosity, and candour of heart joined to an enlightened zeal for Liberty, an intimate persuasion that on it depends the happiness and glory both of kings and people—to see these shining out in public virtues, as they have hitherto smiled in all the social lights and private accomplishments of life, is a prospect that cannot but inspire a general sentiment of satisfaction and gladness, more easy to be felt than expressed.

If the following attempt to trace Liberty from the first ages down to her excellent establishment in Great Britain can at all merit your approbation, and prove an entertainment to your Royal Highness; if it can in any degree answer the dignity of the subject, and of the name under which I presume to shelter it— I have my best reward, particularly as it affords me an opportunity of declaring that I am, with the greatest zeal and respect,

SIR,
Your Royal Highness's
most obedient
and most devoted servant,
JAMES THOMSON.

THE CONTENTS OF PART I

THE following Poem is thrown into the form of a Poetical Vision. Its scene the ruins of ancient Rome. The Goddess of Liberty, who is supposed to speak through the whole, appears, characterized as British Liberty, *to verse* 44. Gives a view of ancient Italy, and particularly of Republican Rome, in all her magnificence and glory, *to verse* 106. This contrasted by modern Italy, its valleys, mountains, culture, cities, people ; the difference appearing strongest in the capital city, Rome, *to verse* 227. The ruins of the great works of Liberty more magnificent than the borrowed pomp of Oppression ; and from them revived Sculpture, Painting, and Architecture, *to verse* 249. The old Romans apostrophized, with regard to the several melancholy changes in Italy : Horace, Tully, and Virgil, with regard to their Tibur, Tusculum, and Naples, *to verse* 285. That once finest and most ornamented part of Italy, all along the coast of Baiae, how changed, *to verse* 315. This desolation of Italy applied to Britain, *to verse* 338. Address to the Goddess of Liberty, that she would deduce from the first ages, her chief establishments, the description of which constitutes the subject of the following parts of this Poem. She assents, and commands what she says to be sung in Britain ; whose happiness, arising from freedom and a limited monarchy, she marks, *to verse* 378. An immediate Vision attends, and paints her words. Invocation.

LIBERTY

PART I

ANCIENT AND MODERN ITALY COMPARED

[First published early in 1735.]

O MY lamented Talbot! while with thee
The muse gay roved the glad Hesperian round,
And drew the inspiring breath of ancient arts ;
Ah ! little thought she her returning verse
Should sing our darling subject to thy shade.
And does the mystic veil, from mortal beam,
Involve those eyes where every virtue smiled,
And all thy father's candid spirit shone ?
The light of reason, pure, without a cloud ;
Full of the generous heart, the mild regard ;   10
Honour disdaining blemish, cordial faith,
And limpid truth, that looks the very soul.
But to the death of mighty nations turn
My strain ; be there absorbed the private tear.
    Musing, I lay ; warm from the sacred walks,
Where at each step imagination burns :
While scattered wide around, awful, and hoar,
Lies, a vast monument, once glorious Rome,
The tomb of empire ! ruins ! that efface
Whate'er, of finished, modern pomp can boast. 20
    Snatched by these wonders to that world where
        thought
Unfettered ranges, fancy's magic hand
Led me anew o'er all the solemn scene,

Still in the mind's pure eye more solemn dressed :
When straight, methought, the fair majestic power
Of Liberty appeared. Not, as of old,
Extended in her hand the cap, and rod,
Whose slave-enlarging touch gave double life :
But her bright temples bound with British oak,
And naval honours nodded on her brow.   30
Sublime of port : loose o'er her shoulder flowed
Her sea-green robe, with constellations gay.
An island-goddess now ; and her high care
The queen of isles, the mistress of the main.
My heart beat filial transport at the sight ;
And, as she moved to speak, the awakened muse
Listened intense. Awhile she looked around,
With mournful eye the well-known ruins marked,
And then, her sighs repressing, thus began :
    ' Mine are these wonders, all thou seest is mine ; 40
But ah, how changed ! the falling poor remains
Of what exalted once the Ausonian shore.
Look back through time ; and, rising from the gloom,
Mark the dread scene, that paints whate'er I say.
    ' The great republic see ! that glowed, sublime,
With the mixed freedom of a thousand states ;
Raised on the thrones of kings her curule chair,
And by her fasces awed the subject world.
See busy millions quickening all the land,
With cities thronged, and teeming culture high :
For nature then smiled on her free-born sons,   51
And poured the plenty that belongs to men.
Behold, the country cheering, villas rise
In lively prospect by the secret lapse
Of brooks now lost, and streams renowned in song ;
In Umbria's closing vales, or on the brow
Of her brown hills that breathe the scented gale ;
On Baia's viny coast, where peaceful seas,

Fanned by kind zephyrs, ever kiss the shore,
And suns unclouded shine, through purest air ;   60
Or in the spacious neighbourhood of Rome,
Far shining upward to the Sabine hills,
To Anio's roar, and Tibur's olive shade,
To where Preneste lifts her airy brow,
Or downwards spreading to the sunny shore
Where Alba breathes the freshness of the main.
' See distant mountains leave their valleys dry,
And o'er the proud arcade their tribute pour,
To lave imperial Rome. For ages laid,
Deep, massy, firm, diverging every way,   70
With tombs of heroes sacred, see her roads—
By various nations trod and suppliant kings,
With legions flaming or with triumph gay.
' Full in the centre of these wondrous works,
The pride of earth ! Rome in her glory see !
Behold her demigods, in senate met ;
All head to counsel, and all heart to act :
The commonweal inspiring every tongue
With fervent eloquence, unbribed, and bold ;
Ere tame corruption taught the servile herd   80
To rank obedient to a master's voice.
' Her forum see, warm, popular, and loud,
In trembling wonder hushed, when the two sires,
As they the private father greatly quelled,
Stood up the public fathers of the state.
See justice judging there, in human shape.
Hark ! how with freedom's voice it thunders high,
Or in soft murmurs sinks to Tully's tongue.
' Her tribes, her census, see ; her generous troops,
Whose pay was glory, and their best reward   90
Free for their country and for me to die ;
Ere mercenary murder grew a trade.
' Mark, as the purple triumph waves along,

The highest pomp and lowest fall of life.
' Her festive games, the school of heroes, see ;
Her circus, ardent with contending youth ;
Her streets, her temples, palaces, and baths,
Full of fair forms, of beauty's eldest born,
And of a people cast in virtue's mould—
While sculpture lives around, and Asian hills   100
Lend their best stores to heave the pillared dome ;
All that to Roman strength the softer touch
Of Grecian art can join. But language fails
To paint this sun, this centre of mankind ;
Where every virtue, glory, treasure, art,
Attracted strong, in heightened lustre met.
' Need I the contrast mark ? unjoyous view !
A land in all, in government and arts,
In virtue, genius, earth, and heaven, reversed.
Who but these far-famed ruins to behold,   110
Proofs of a people, whose heroic aims
Soared far above the little selfish sphere
Of doubting modern life—who but inflamed
With classic zeal, these consecrated scenes
Of men and deeds to trace, unhappy land !
Would trust thy wilds and cities loose of sway ?
' Are these the vales that once exulting states
In their warm bosom fed ? The mountains these,
On whose high-blooming sides my sons of old
I bred to glory ? These dejected towns,   120
Where, mean and sordid, life can scarce subsist,
The scenes of ancient opulence and pomp ?
' Come ! by whatever sacred name disguised,
Oppression, come ! and in thy works rejoice !
See nature's richest plains to putrid fens
Turned by thy fury. From their cheerful bounds,
See razed the enlivening village, farm, and seat.
First, Rural Toil, by thy rapacious hand

Robbed of his poor reward, resigned the plough ;
And now he dares not turn the noxious glebe.   130
'Tis thine entire.   The lonely swain himself,
Who loves at large along the grassy downs
His flocks to pasture, thy drear champaign flies
Far as the sickening eye can sweep around,
'Tis all one desert, desolate, and grey,
Grazed by the sullen buffalo alone ;
And, where the rank uncultivated growth
Of rotting ages taints the passing gale,
Beneath the baleful blast the city pines,
Or sinks enfeebled, or infected burns.   140
Beneath it mourns the solitary road,
Rolled in rude mazes o'er the abandoned waste ;
While ancient ways, ingulfed, are seen no more.
    ' Such thy dire plains, thou self-destroyer ! foe
To humankind ! Thy mountains, too, profuse
Where savage nature blooms, seem their sad plaint
To raise against thy desolating rod.
There on the breezy brow, where thriving states
And famous cities once to the pleased sun
Far other scenes of rising culture spread,   150
Pale shine thy ragged towns.   Neglected round,
Each harvest pines ; the livid, lean produce
Of heartless labour : while thy hated joys,
Not proper pleasure, lift the lazy hand.
Better to sink in sloth the woes of life,
Than wake their rage with unavailing toil.
Hence drooping art almost to nature leaves
The rude unguided year.   Thin wave the gifts
Of yellow Ceres, thin the radiant blush
Of orchard reddens in the warmest ray.   160
To weedy wildness run, no rural wealth
(Such as dictators fed) the garden pours.

133 champian (misprint for 'champain ') ed. 1738.

Crude the wild olive flows, and foul the vine ;
Nor juice Caecubian nor Falernian more
Streams life and joy, save in the muse's bowl
Unseconded by art, the spinning race
Draw the bright thread in vain, and idly toil.
In vain, forlorn in wilds, the citron blows ;
And flowering plants perfume the desert gale.
Through the vile thorn the tender myrtle twines.
Inglorious droops the laurel, dead to song,   171
And long a stranger to the hero's brow.
 ' Nor half thy triumph this : cast, from brute fields,
Into the haunts of men thy ruthless eye.
There buxom plenty never turns her horn ;
The grace and virtue of exterior life,
No clean convenience reigns ; even sleep itself
Least delicate of powers, reluctant there
Lays on the bed impure his heavy head.
Thy horrid walk ! Dead, empty, unadorned,   180
See streets whose echoes never know the voice
Of cheerful hurry, commerce many-tongued,
And art mechanic at his various task
Fervent employed. Mark the desponding race,
Of occupation void, as void of hope ;
Hope, the glad ray, glanced from Eternal Good,
That life enlivens, and exalts its powers,
With views of fortune—madness all to them !
By thee relentless seized their better joys,
To the soft aid of cordial airs they fly,   190
Breathing a kind oblivion o'er their woes,
And love and music melt their souls away.
From feeble Justice, see how rash Revenge,
Trembling, the balance snatches, and the sword,
Fearful himself, to venal ruffians gives.
See where God's altar, nursing murder, stands
With the red touch of dark assassins stained.

' But chief let Rome, the mighty city ! speak
The full-exerted genius of thy reign.
Behold her rise amid the lifeless waste,   200
Expiring nature all corrupted round ;
While the lone Tiber, through the desert plain,
Winds his waste stores, and sullen sweeps along.
Patched from my fragments, in unsolid pomp,
Mark how the temple glares ; and, artful dressed,
Amusive draws the superstitious train.
Mark how the palace lifts a lying front,
Concealing often, in magnific jail,
Proud want ; a deep unanimated gloom !
And oft adjoining to the drear abode   210
Of misery, whose melancholy walls
Seem its voracious grandeur to reproach.
Within the city bounds the desert see ;
See the rank vine o'er subterranean roofs
Indecent spread ; beneath whose fretted gold
It once exulting flowed. The people mark !
Matchless, while fired by me ; to public good
Inexorably firm, just, generous, brave,
Afraid of nothing but unworthy life,
Elate with glory, an heroic soul   220
Known to the vulgar breast : behold them now
A thin despairing number, all-subdued,
The slaves of slaves, by superstition fooled,
By vice unmanned and a licentious rule,
In guile ingenious, and in murder brave.
Such in one land, beneath the same fair clime,
Thy sons, Oppression, *are* ; and such *were* mine.
    ' Even with thy laboured pomp, for whose vain show
Deluded thousands starve—all age-begrimed,
Torn, robbed, and scattered in unnumbered sacks,
And by the tempest of two thousand years   231
Continual shaken, let my ruins vie—

These roads that yet the Roman hand assert,
Beyond the weak repair of modern toil ;
These fractured arches, that the chiding stream
No more delighted hear ; these rich remains
Of marbles now unknown, where shines imbibed
Each parent ray ; these massy columns, hewed
From Afric's farthest shore ; one granite all,
These obelisks high-towering to the sky,   240
Mysterious marked with dark Egyptian lore ;
These endless wonders that this sacred way
Illumine still, and consecrate to fame ;
These fountains, vases, urns, and statues, charged
With the fine stores of art-completing Greece.
Mine is, besides, thy every later boast—
Thy Buonarotis, thy Palladios mine ;
And mine the fair designs which Raphael's soul,
O'er the live canvas emanating, breathed.
    'What would you say, ye conquerors of earth ! 250
Ye Romans ! could you raise the laurelled head ;
Could you the country see, by seas of blood
And the dread toil of ages won so dear,
Your pride, your triumph, your supreme delight !
For whose defence oft, in the doubtful hour,
You rush with rapture down the gulf of fate,
Of death ambitious ! till by awful deeds,
Virtues, and courage that amaze mankind
The queen of nations rose ; possessed of all
Which nature, art, and glory could bestow—   260
What would you say, deep in the last abyss
Of slavery, vice, and unambitious want,
Thus to behold her sunk ? your crowded plains
Void of their cities ; unadorned your hills ;
Ungraced your lakes ; your ports to ships unknown ;
Your lawless floods and your abandoned streams—
These could you know, these could you love again ?

Thy Tibur, Horace, could it now inspire
Content, poetic ease, and rural joy
Soon bursting into song—while through the groves
Of headlong Anio, dashing to the vale   271
In many a tortured stream, you mused along ?
Yon wild retreat, where superstition dreams,
Could, Tully, you your Tusculum believe ?
And could you deem yon naked hills, that form,
Famed in old song, the ship-forsaken bay,
Your Formian shore ? Once the delight of earth,
Where art and nature, ever smiling, joined
On the gay land to lavish all their stores—
How changed, how vacant, Virgil, wide around,   280
Would now your Naples seem ? disastered less
By black Vesuvius thundering o'er the coast
His midnight earthquakes and his mining fires
Than by despotic rage, that inward gnaws,
A native foe—a foreign, tears without.
First from your flattered Caesars this began :
Till, doomed to tyrants an eternal prey,
Thin peopled spreads at last the syren plain,
That the dire soul of Hannibal disarmed ;
And wrapped in weeds the shore of Venus lies.   290
There Baia sees no more the joyous throng,
Her banks all beaming with the pride of Rome ;
No generous vines now bask along the hills,
Where sport the breezes of the Tyrrhene main ;
With baths and temples mixed, no villas rise,
Nor, art-sustained amid reluctant waves,
Draw the cool murmurs of the breathing deep ;
No spreading ports their sacred arms extend ;
No mighty moles the big intrusive storm,
From the calm station, roll resounding back.   300
An almost total desolation sits,
A dreary stillness, saddening o'er the coast,

Where, when soft suns and tepid winters rose,
Rejoicing crowds inhaled the balm of peace,
Where citied hill to hill reflected blaze,
And where with Ceres Bacchus wont to hold
A genial strife. Her youthful form robust
Even nature yields, by fire and earthquake rent—
Whole stately cities in the dark abrupt
Swallowed at once, or vile in rubbish laid,   310
A nest for serpents ; from the red abyss
New hills explosive thrown ; the Lucrine lake
A reedy pool; and all to Cuma's point
The sea recovering his usurped domain,
And poured triumphant o'er the buried dome.
  ' Hence, Britain, learn—my best established, last,
And, more than Greece or Rome, my steady reign ;
The land where, king and people equal bound
By guardian laws, my fullest blessings flow,
And where my jealous unsubmitting soul,   320
The dread of tyrants ! burns in every breast—
Learn hence, if such the miserable fate
Of an heroic race, the masters once
Of humankind, what, when deprived of me,
How grievous must be thine ? In spite of climes,
Whose sun-enlivened ether wakes the soul
To higher powers ; in spite of happy soils,
That, but by labour's slightest aid impelled,
With treasures teem, to thy cold clime unknown ;
If there desponding fail the common arts   330
And sustenance of life, could life itself,
Far less a thoughtless tyrant's hollow pomp,
Subsist with thee ? Against depressing skies,
Joined to full-spread oppression's cloudy brow,
How could thy spirits hold ? where vigour find
Forced fruits to tear from their unnative soil,
Or, storing every harvest in thy ports,

To plough the dreadful all-producing wave ? '
   Here paused the Goddess. By the pause assured,
In trembling accents thus I moved my prayer :   340
   ' Oh first, and most benevolent of powers !
Come from eternal splendours, here on earth,
Against despotic pride and rage and lust,
To shield mankind ; to raise them to assert
The native rights and honour of their race—
Teach me, thy lowest subject, but in zeal
Yielding to none, the progress of thy reign,
And with a strain from thee enrich the muse.
As thee alone she serves, her patron, thou,
And great inspirer be ! then will she joy,   350
Though narrow life her lot, and private shade :
And, when her venal voice she barters vile
Or to thy open or thy secret foes,
May ne'er those sacred raptures touch her more,
By slavish hearts unfelt ! and may her song
Sink in oblivion with the nameless crew,
Vermin of state ! to thy o'erflowing light
That owe their being, yet betray thy cause.
   Then, condescending kind, the heavenly Power
Returned :—' What here, suggested by the scene,   360
I slight unfold, record and sing at home,
In that blest isle, where (so we spirits move)
With one quick effort of my will I am.
There truth unlicensed walks ; and dares accost
Even kings themselves, the monarchs of the free !
Fixed on my rock, there, an indulgent race
O'er Britons wield the sceptre of their choice ;
And there, to finish what his sires began,
A Prince behold ! for me who burns sincere,
Even with a subject's zeal. He my great work   370
Will parent-like sustain ; and, added, give
The touch the graces and the muses owe.

For Britain's glory swells his panting breast,
And ancient arts he emulous revolves—
His pride to let the smiling heart abroad,
Through clouds of pomp, that but conceal the man ;
To please his pleasure ; bounty his delight ;
And all the soul of Titus dwells in him.'
    Hail, glorious theme ! but how, alas ! shall verse,
From the crude stores of mortal language drawn, 380
How faint and tedious, sing what, piercing deep,
The Goddess flashed at once upon my soul ?
For, clear precision all, the tongue of gods
Is harmony itself ; to every ear
Familiar known, like light to every eye.
Meantime disclosing ages, as she spoke,
In long succession poured their empires forth ;
Scene after scene, the human drama spread ;
And still the embodied picture rose to sight.

    O thou ! to whom the muses owe their flame ;   390
Who bidd'st, beneath the pole, Parnassus rise,
And Hippocrene flow ; with thy bold ease,
The striking force, the lightning of thy thought,
And thy strong phrase, that rolls profound and clear ;
Oh, gracious Goddess ! reinspire my song ;
While I, to nobler than poetic fame
Aspiring, thy commands to Britons bear.

THE CONTENTS OF PART II

LIBERTY traced from the pastoral ages, and the first uniting of neighbouring families into civil government, *to verse* 46. The several establishments of Liberty, in Egypt, Persia, Phoenicia, Palestine, slightly touched upon, down to her great establishment in Greece, *to verse* 85. Geographical description of Greece, *to verse* 107. Sparta and Athens, the two principal states of Greece, described, *to verse* 158. Influence of Liberty over all the Grecian states ; with regard to their government, their politeness, their virtues, their arts, and sciences. The vast superiority it gave them, in point of force and bravery, over the Persians, exemplified by the action of Thermopylae, the battle of Marathon, and the retreat of the Ten Thousand. Its full exertion, and most beautiful effects in Athens, *to verse* 210. Liberty the source of free philosophy. The various schools which took their rise from Socrates, *to verse* 242. Enumeration of fine arts : Eloquence, Poetry, Music, Sculpture, Painting, and Architecture ; the effects of Liberty in Greece, and brought to their utmost perfection there, *to verse* 392. Transition to the modern state of Greece, *to verse* 420. Why Liberty declined, and was at last entirely lost among the Greeks, *to verse* 481. Concluding Reflection.

PART II. GREECE

[First published in 1735.]

THUS spoke the Goddess of the fearless eye,
And at her voice renewed the vision rose :
' First, in the dawn of time, with eastern swains
In woods, and tents, and cottages I lived ;
While on from plain to plain they led their flocks
In search of clearer spring and fresher field.
These, as increasing families disclosed
The tender state, I taught an equal sway.
Few were offences, properties, and laws.
Beneath the rural portal, palm-o'erspread,   10
The father senate met. There justice dealt,
With reason then and equity the same,
Free as the common air her prompt decree ;

Nor yet had stained her sword with subjects' blood.
The simpler arts were all their simple wants
Had urged to light.   But instant, these supplied,
Another set of fonder wants arose,
And other arts with them of finer aim ;
Till, from refining want to want impelled,
The mind by thinking pushed her latent powers,   20
And life began to glow and arts to shine.
   ' At first, on brutes alone the rustic war
Launched the rude spear ; swift, as he glared along,
On the grim lion, or the robber wolf.
For then young sportive life was void of toil,
Demanding little, and with little pleased.
But, when to manhood grown, and endless joys,
Led on by equal toils, the bosom fired—
Lewd lazy rapine broke primeval peace,
And, hid in caves and idle forests drear,   30
From the lone pilgrim and the wandering swain
Seized what he durst not earn.   Then brother's blood
First horrid smoked on the polluted skies.
Awful in justice, then the burning youth,
Led by their tempered sires, on lawless men,
The last worst monsters of the shaggy wood,
Turned the keen arrow, and the sharpened spear.
Then war grew glorious.   Heroes then arose,
Who, scorning coward self, for others lived,
Toiled for their ease, and for their safety bled.   40
West with the living day to Greece I came :
Earth smiled beneath my beam : the muse before
Sonorous flew—that low till then in woods
Had tuned the reed, and sighed the shepherd's pain.
But now, to sing heroic deeds, she swelled
A nobler note, and bade the banquet burn.
   'For Greece my sons of Egypt I forsook—
A boastful race ! that in the vain abyss

Of fabling ages loved to lose their source,
And with their river traced it from the skies.   50
While there my laws alone despotic reigned,
And king, as well as people, proud obeyed.
I taught them science, virtue, wisdom, arts,
By poets, sages, legislators sought ;
The school of polished life, and human kind.
But, when mysterious superstition came,
And, with her civil sister leagued, involved
In studied darkness the desponding mind—
Then tyrant power the righteous scourge unloosed :
For yielded reason speaks the soul a slave.   60
Instead of useful works, like nature's great,
Enormous cruel wonders crushed the land ;
And round a tyrant's tomb, who none deserved,
For one vile carcass perished countless lives.
Then the great dragon couched amid his floods,
Swelled his fierce heart, and cried, "This flood is mine,
'Tis I that bid it flow." But, undeceived,
His frenzy soon the proud blasphemer felt ;
Felt that, without my fertilizing power,
Suns lost their force, and Niles o'erflowed in vain.
Nought could retard me : nor the frugal state   71
Of rising Persia, sober in extreme
Beyond the pitch of man, and thence reversed
Into luxurious waste ; nor yet the ports
Of old Phoenicia, first for letters famed,
That paint the voice, and silent speak to sight,
Of arts prime source, and guardian ! by fair stars
First tempted out into the lonely deep,
To whom I first disclosed mechanic arts
The winds to conquer, to subdue the waves,   80
With all the peaceful power of ruling trade,
Earnest of Britain ; nor by these retained,
Nor by the neighbouring land whose palmy shore

The silver Jordan laves. Before me lay
The promised land of arts, and urged my flight.
 'Hail, nature's utmost boast ! unrivalled Greece !
My fairest reign ! where every power benign
Conspired to blow the flower of human kind,
And lavished all that genius can inspire.
Clear sunny climates, by the breezy main,   90
Ionian or Aegean, tempered kind :
Light, airy soils : a country rich and gay,
Broke into hills with balmy odours crowned,
And, bright with purple harvest, joyous vales :
Mountains and streams where verse spontaneous flowed,
Whence deemed by wondering men the seat of gods,
And still the mountains and the streams of song :
All that boon nature could luxuriant pour
Of high materials, and my restless arts
Frame into finished life. How many states,   100
And clustering towns, and monuments of fame,
And scenes of glorious deeds in little bounds !
From the rough tract of bending mountains, beat
By Adria's here, there by Aegean waves,
To where the deep-adorning Cyclad Isles
In shining prospect rise, and on the shore
Of farthest Crete resounds the Libyan main !
 'O'er all two rival cities reared the brow,
And balanced all. Spread on Eurotas' bank,
Amid a circle of soft-rising hills,   110
The patient Sparta one : the sober, hard,
And man-subduing city, which no shape
Of pain could conquer, nor of pleasure charm.
Lycurgus there built, on the solid base
Of equal life, so well a tempered state,
Where mixed each government in such just poise,
Each power so checking and supporting each,

107 Lybian ed. 1738.

That firm for ages and unmoved it stood,
The fort of Greece! without one giddy hour,
One shock of faction or of party rage.   120
For, drained the springs of wealth, corruption there
Lay withered at the root. Thrice happy land!
Had not neglected art, with weedy vice
Confounded, sunk. But, if Athenian arts
Loved not the soil, yet there the calm abode
Of wisdom, virtue, philosophic ease,
Of manly sense and wit, in frugal phrase
Confined, and pressed into Laconic force.
There too, by rooting thence still treacherous self,
The public and the private grew the same.   130
The children of the nursing public all,
And at its table fed—for that they toiled,
For that they lived entire, and even for that
The tender mother urged her son to die.
    ' Of softer genius, but not less intense
To seize the palm of empire, Athens strove.
Where, with bright marbles big and future pomp,
Hymettus spread, amid the scented sky,
His thymy treasures to the labouring bee,
And to botanic hand the stores of health;   140
Wrapt in a soul-attenuating clime,
Between Ilissus and Cephissus glowed
This hive of science, shedding sweets divine
Of active arts and animated arms.
There, passionate for me, an easy-moved,
A quick, refined, a delicate, humane,
Enlightened people reigned. Oft on the brink
Of ruin, hurried by the charm of speech
Enforcing hasty counsel immature,
Tottered the rash democracy—unpoised,   150
And by the rage devoured that ever tears
A populace unequal, part too rich

And part or fierce with want or abject grown.
Solon at last, their mild restorer, rose,
Allayed the tempest, to the calm of laws
Reduced the settling whole, and, with the weight
Which the two senates to the public lent,
As with an anchor fixed the driving state.
  ' Nor was my forming care to these confined.
For emulation through the whole I poured,   160
Noble contention ! who should most excel
In government well poised, adjusted best
To public weal ; in countries cultured high ;
In ornamented towns, where order reigns,
Free social life, and polished manners fair ;
In exercise, and arms—arms only drawn
For common Greece to quell the Persian pride ;
In moral science and in graceful arts.
Hence, as for glory peacefully they strove,
The prize grew greater, and the prize of all.   170
By contest brightened, hence the radiant youth
Poured every beam, by generous pride inflamed
Felt every ardour burn—their great reward
The verdant wreath which sounding Pisa gave.
  ' Hence flourished Greece ; and hence a race of men,
As gods by conscious future times adored,
In whom each virtue wore a smiling air,
Each science shed o'er life a friendly light,
Each art was nature. Spartan valour hence,
At the famed pass, firm as an isthmus stood ;   180
And the whole eastern ocean, waving far
As eye could dart its vision, nobly checked ;
While in extended battle, at the field
Of Marathon, my keen Athenians drove
Before their ardent band an host of slaves.
  ' Hence through the continent ten thousand Greeks
Urged a retreat, whose glory not the prime

M

Of victories can reach. Deserts in vain
Opposed their course, and hostile lands unknown,
And deep rapacious floods, dire banked with death, 190
And mountains in whose jaws destruction grinned,
Hunger and toil, Armenian snows and storms,
And circling myriads still of barbarous foes.
Greece in their view, and glory yet untouched,
Their steady column pierced the scattering herds
Which a whole empire poured ; and held its way
Triumphant, by the sage-exalted chief
Fired and sustained. Oh light and force of mind,
Almost almighty in severe extremes !
The sea at last from Colchian mountains seen, 200
Kind-hearted transport round their captains threw
The soldiers' fond embrace ; o'erflowed their eyes
With tender floods, and loosed the general voice
To cries resounding loud—" The sea ! the sea ! "
' In Attic bounds hence heroes, sages, wits,
Shone thick as stars, the milky way of Greece !
And, though gay wit and pleasing grace was theirs,
All the soft modes of elegance and ease,
Yet was not courage less, the patient touch
Of toiling art, and disquisition deep. 210
' My spirit pours a vigour through the soul,
The unfettered thought with energy inspires,
Invincible in arts, in the bright field
Of nobler science as in that of arms.
Athenians thus not less intrepid burst
The bonds of tyrant darkness than they spurned
The Persian chains : while through the city, full
Of mirthful quarrel and of witty war,
Incessant struggled taste, refining taste,
And friendly free discussion, calling forth 220
From the fair jewel, truth, its latent ray.
O'er all shone out the great Athenian sage,

And father of philosophy—the sun,
From whose white blaze emerged each various sect
Took various tints, but with diminished beam.
Tutor of Athens! he in every street
Dealt priceless treasure—goodness his delight,
Wisdom his wealth, and glory his reward.
Deep through the human heart with playful art
His simple question stole, as into truth   230
And serious deeds he smiled the laughing race,
Taught moral happy life, whate'er can bless
Or grace mankind; and what he taught he was.
Compounded high, though plain, his doctrine broke
In different schools—the bold poetic phrase
Of figured Plato; Xenophon's pure strain,
Like the clear brook that steals along the vale;
Dissecting truth, the Stagyrite's keen eye;
The exalted Stoic pride; the Cynic sneer;
The slow-consenting Academic doubt;   240
And, joining bliss to virtue, the glad ease
Of Epicurus, seldom understood.
They, ever candid, reason still opposed
To reason; and, since virtue was their aim,
Each by sure practice tried to prove his way
The best. Then stood untouched the solid base
Of Liberty, the liberty of mind;
For systems yet, and soul-enslaving creeds,
Slept with the monsters of succeeding times.   249
From priestly darkness sprung the enlightening arts
Of fire, and sword, and rage, and horrid names.
    ' O Greece! thou sapient nurse of finer arts
Which to bright science blooming fancy bore!
Be this thy praise, that thou, and thou alone,
In these hast led the way, in these excelled,
Crowned with the laurel of assenting time.
    ' In thy full language, speaking mighty things,

Like a clear torrent close, or else diffused
A broad majestic stream, and rolling on
Through all the winding harmony of sound—   260
In it the power of eloquence at large
Breathed the persuasive or pathetic soul,
Stilled by degrees the democratic storm,
Or bade it threatening rise, and tyrants shook
Flushed at the head of their victorious troops.
In it the muse, her fury never quenched
By mean unyielding phrase or jarring sound,
Her unconfined divinity displayed,
And still harmonious formed it to her will—
Or soft depressed it to the shepherd's moan   270
Or raised it swelling to the tongue of gods.
  'Heroic song was thine ; the fountain-bard,
Whence each poetic stream derives its course!
Thine the dread moral scene, thy chief delight !
Where idle fancy durst not mix her voice
When reason spoke august, the fervent heart
Or plained or stormed, and in the impassioned man,
Concealing art with art, the poet sunk.
This potent school of manners, but when left
To loose neglect a land-corrupting plague,   280
Was not unworthy deemed of public care
And boundless cost by thee—whose every son,
Even last mechanic, the true taste possessed
Of what had flavour to the nourished soul.
  'The sweet enforcer of the poet's strain,
Thine was the meaning music of the heart.
Not the vain trill, that, void of passion, runs
In giddy mazes, tickling idle ears ;
But that deep-searching voice, and artful hand,
To which respondent shakes the varied soul.   290
  'Thy fair ideas, thy delightful forms,
By love imagined, and the graces touched,

The boast of well pleased nature ! Sculpture seized,
And bade them ever smile in Parian stone.
Selecting beauty's choice, and that again
Exalting, blending in a perfect whole,
Thy workmen left even nature's self behind.
From those far different whose prolific hand
Peoples a nation, they for years on years,
By the cool touches of judicious toil,   300
Their rapid genius curbing, poured it all
Through the live features of one breathing stone.
There, beaming full, it shone, expressing gods—
Jove's awful brow, Apollo's air divine,
The fierce atrocious frown of sinewed Mars,
Or the sly graces of the Cyprian queen.
Minutely perfect all ! Each dimple sunk,
And every muscle swelled, as nature taught.
In tresses, braided gay, the marble waved ;
Flowed in loose robes, or thin transparent veils ; 310
Sprung into motion ; softened into flesh ;
Was fired to passion, or refined to soul.
   ' Nor less thy pencil with creative touch
Shed mimic life, when all thy brightest dames
Assembled Zeuxis in his Helen mixed ;
And when Apelles, who peculiar knew
To give a grace that more than mortal smiled,
The soul of beauty ! called the queen of love
Fresh from the billows blushing orient charms.
Even such enchantment then thy pencil poured   320
That cruel-thoughted war the impatient torch
Dashed to the ground, and, rather than destroy
The patriot picture, let the city 'scape.
   ' First, elder Sculpture taught her sister art
Correct design ; where great ideas shone,
And in the secret trace expression spoke ;
Taught her the graceful attitude, the turn

And beauteous airs of head ; the native act,
Or bold or easy ; and, cast free behind,
The swelling mantle's well adjusted flow.　　330
Then the bright muse, their eldest sister, came,
And bade her follow where she led the way—
Bade earth, and sea, and air in colours rise,
And copious action on the canvas glow :
Gave her gay fable ; spread invention's store ;
Enlarged her view ; taught composition high,
And just arrangement, circling round one point
That starts to sight, binds and commands the whole.
Caught from the heavenly muse a nobler aim,
And scorning the soft trade of mere delight,　　340
O'er all thy temples, porticos, and schools,
Heroic deeds she traced, and warm displayed
Each moral beauty to the ravished eye.
There, as the imagined presence of the god
Aroused the mind, or vacant hours induced
Calm contemplation, or assembled youth
Burned in ambitious circle round the sage,
The living lesson stole into the heart
With more prevailing force than dwells in words.
These rouse to glory ; while to rural life　　350
The softer canvas oft reposed the soul.
There gaily broke the sun-illumined cloud :
The lessening prospect, and the mountain blue
Vanished in air ; the precipice frowned dire ;
White down the rock the rushing torrent dashed ;
The sun shone trembling o'er the distant main ;
The tempest foamed immense ; the driving storm
Saddened the skies, and, from the doubling gloom,
On the scathed oak the ragged lightning fell ;
In closing shades, and where the current strays, 360
With peace and love and innocence around,
Piped the lone shepherd to his feeding flock ;

Round happy parents smiled their younger selves ;
And friends conversed, by death divided long.
' To public virtue thus the smiling arts,
Unblemished handmaids, served ; the graces they
To dress this fairest Venus. Thus revered,
And placed beyond the reach of sordid care,
The high awarders of immortal fame,
Alone for glory thy great masters strove ;   370
Courted by kings, and by contending states
Assumed the boasted honour of their birth.
' In architecture too thy rank supreme !
That art where most magnificent appears
The little builder man ; by thee refined,
And, smiling high, to full perfection brought.
Such thy sure rules that Goths of every age,
Who scorned their aid, have only loaded earth
With laboured heavy monuments of shame.
Not those gay domes that o'er thy splendid shore 380
Shot, all proportion, up. First, unadorned
And nobly plain, the manly Doric rose ;
The Ionic then, with decent matron grace,
Her airy pillar heaved ; luxuriant, last,
The rich Corinthian spread her wanton wreath.
The whole so measured true, so lessened off
By fine proportion, that the marble pile,
Formed to repel the still or stormy waste
Of rolling ages, light as fabrics looked
That from the magic wand aerial rise.   390
' These were the wonders that illumined Greece,
From end to end '——Here interrupting warm,
' Where are they now ? (I cried) say, goddess, where ?
And what the land, thy darling thus of old ? '
' Sunk ! (she resumed), deep in the kindred gloom
Of superstition and of slavery sunk !
No glory now can touch their hearts, benumbed

By loose dejected sloth and servile fear ;
No science pierce the darkness of their minds ;
No nobler art the quick ambitious soul   400
Of imitation in their breast awake.
Even to supply the needful arts of life
Mechanic toil denies the hopeless hand.
Scarce any trace remaining, vestige grey,
Or nodding column on the desert shore
To point where Corinth or where Athens stood.
A faithless land of violence, and death !
Where commerce parleys dubious on the shore ;
And his wild impulse curious search restrains,
Afraid to trust the inhospitable clime.   410
Neglected nature fails ; in sordid want
Sunk and debased, their beauty beams no more.
The sun himself seems, angry, to regard
Of light unworthy the degenerate race,
And fires them oft with pestilential rays—
While earth, blue poison steaming on the skies,
Indignant shakes them from her troubled sides.
But as from man to man, fate's first decree,
Impartial death the tide of riches rolls,
So states must die and Liberty go round.   420
' Fierce was the stand ere virtue, valour, arts,
And the soul fired by me (that often, stung
With thoughts of better times and old renown,
From hydra-tyrants tried to clear the land)
Lay quite extinct in Greece, their works effaced,
And gross o'er all unfeeling bondage spread.
Sooner I moved my much reluctant flight,
Poised on the doubtful wing, when Greece with Greece,
Embroiled in foul contention, fought no more
For common glory and for common weal,   430
But, false to Freedom, sought to quell the free ;
Broke the firm band of peace and sacred love,

That lent the whole irrefragable force,
And, as around the partial trophy blushed,
Prepared the way for total overthrow.
Then to the Persian power, whose pride they scorned,
When Xerxes poured his millions o'er the land,
Sparta, by turns, and Athens vilely sued ;
Sued to be venal parricides, to spill
Their country's bravest blood, and on themselves
To turn their matchless mercenary arms.   441
Peaceful in Susa, then, sat the great king ;
And by the trick of treaties, the still waste
Of sly corruption and barbaric gold,
Effected what his steel could ne'er perform.
Profuse he gave them the luxurious draught,
Inflaming all the land—unbalanced wide
Their tottering states ; their wild assemblies ruled,
As the winds turn at every blast the seas—
And by their listed orators, whose breath   450
Still with a factious storm infested Greece,
Roused them to civil war, or dashed them down
To sordid peace—peace ! that, when Sparta shook
Astonished Artaxerxes on his throne,
Gave up, fair-spread o'er Asia's sunny shore,
Their kindred cities to perpetual chains.
What could so base, so infamous a thought
In Spartan hearts inspire ? Jealous they saw
Respiring Athens rear again her walls :
And the pale fury fired them once again   460
To crush this rival city to the dust.
For now no more the noble social soul
Of Liberty my families combined ;
But by short views and selfish passions broke,
Dire as when friends are rankled into foes
They mixed severe, and waged eternal war :
Nor felt they furious their exhausted force ;

Nor, with false glory, discord, madness blind,
Saw how the blackening storm from Thracia came.
Long years rolled on, by many a battle stained,   470
The blush and boast of fame ! where courage, art,
And military glory shone supreme :
But let detesting ages from the scene
Of Greece self-mangled turn the sickening eye.
At last, when bleeding from a thousand wounds
She felt her spirits fail, and in the dust
Her latest heroes, Nicias, Conon, lay,
Agesilaus, and the Theban friends—
The Macedonian vulture marked his time,
By the dire scent of Cheronaea lured,   480
And, fierce descending, seized his hapless prey.
   ' Thus tame submitted to the victor's yoke
Greece, once the gay, the turbulent, the bold ;
For every grace, and muse, and science born ;
With arts of war, of government elate ;
To tyrants dreadful, dreadful to the best ;
Whom I myself could scarcely rule : and thus
The Persian fetters, that enthralled the mind,
Were turned to formal and apparent chains.
   ' Unless corruption first deject the pride   490
And guardian vigour of the free-born soul,
All crude attempts of violence are vain ;
For, firm within, and while at heart untouched,
Ne'er yet by force was freedom overcome.
But, soon as Independence stoops the head,
To vice enslaved and vice-created wants,
Then to some foul corrupting hand, whose waste
These heightened wants with fatal bounty feeds—
From man to man the slackening ruin runs,
Till the whole state unnerved in slavery sinks.'   500

THE CONTENTS OF PART III

As this part contains a description of the establishment of Liberty in Rome, it begins with a view of the Grecian Colonies settled in the southern parts of Italy, which with Sicily constituted the Great Greece of the Ancients. With these colonies the Spirit of Liberty and of Republics spreads over Italy, *to verse* 31. Transition to Pythagoras and his philosophy, which he taught through these free states and cities, *to verse* 70. Amidst the many small Republics in Italy, Rome the destined seat of Liberty. Her establishment there dated from the expulsion of the Tarquins. How differing from that in Greece, *to verse* 87. Reference to a view of the Roman Republic given in the first part of this Poem : to mark its rise and fall the peculiar purport of this. During its first ages, the greatest force of Liberty and Virtue exerted, *to verse* 102. The source whence derived the Heroic Virtues of the Romans. Enumeration of these Virtues. Thence their security at home ; their glory, success, and empire abroad, *to verse* 225. Bounds of the Roman empire geographically described, *to verse* 256. The states of Greece restored to Liberty by Titus Quintus Flaminius, the highest instance of public generosity and beneficence, *to verse* 327. The loss of Liberty in Rome, [*to verse* 360]. Its causes, progress, and completion in the death of Brutus, *to verse* 483. Rome under the emperors, *to verse* 511. From Rome the Goddess of Liberty goes among the Northern Nations ; where, by infusing into them her Spirit and general principles, she lays the groundwork of her future establishments ; sends them in vengeance on the Roman Empire, now totally enslaved ; and then, with Arts and Sciences in her train, quits Earth during the dark ages, *to verse* 548. The celestial regions, to which Liberty retired, not proper to be opened to the view of mortals.

PART III. ROME

[First published in the end of 1735.]

HERE melting mixed with air the ideal forms
That painted still whate'er the goddess sung.
Then I, impatient :—' From extinguished Greece,
To what new region streamed the human day ? '
She softly sighing, as when Zephyr leaves,
Resigned to Boreas, the declining year,
Resumed :—' Indignant, these last scenes I fled ;
And long ere then, Leucadia's cloudy cliff
And the Ceraunian hills behind me thrown,
All Latium stood aroused. Ages before,   10
Great mother of republics ! Greece had poured,
Swarm after swarm, her ardent youth around.
On Asia, Afric, Sicily, they stooped,
But chief on fair Hesperia's winding shore ;
Where, from Lacinium to Etrurian vales,
They rolled increasing colonies along,
And lent materials for my Roman reign.
With them my spirit spread ; and numerous states
And cities rose on Grecian models formed,
As its parental policy and arts   20
Each had imbibed. Besides, to each assigned,
A guardian genius o'er the public weal
Kept an unclosing eye ; tried to sustain
Or more sublime the soul infused by me :
And strong the battle rose, with various wave,
Against the tyrant demons of the land.
Thus they their little wars and triumphs knew,
Their flows of fortune and receding times—
But almost all below the proud regard
Of story vowed to Rome, on deeds intent   30
That truth beyond the flight of fable bore.

'Not so the Samian sage ; to him belongs
The brightest witness of recording fame.
For these free states his native isle forsook
And a vain tyrant's transitory smile,
He sought Crotona's pure salubrious air,
And through Great Greece his gentle wisdom taught—
Wisdom that calmed for listening years the mind,
Nor ever heard amid the storm of zeal.
His mental eye first launched into the deeps   40
Of boundless ether, where unnumbered orbs,
Myriads on myriads, through the pathless sky
Unerring roll, and wind their steady way.
There he the full consenting choir beheld ;
There first discerned the secret band of love,
The kind attraction that to central suns
Binds circling earths, and world with world unites.
Instructed thence, he great ideas formed
Of the whole-moving, all-informing God,
The Sun of beings ! beaming unconfined   50
Light, life, and love, and ever active power—
Whom nought can image, and who best approves
The silent worship of the moral heart,
That joys in bounteous Heaven and spreads the joy.
Nor scorned the soaring sage to stoop to life,
And bound his reason to the sphere of man.
He gave the four yet reigning virtues name,
Inspired the study of the finer arts,
That civilize mankind, and laws devised
Where with enlightened justice mercy mixed.   60
He even into his tender system took
Whatever shares the brotherhood of life :
He taught that life's indissoluble flame,
From brute to man, and man to brute again,
For ever shifting, runs the eternal round ;

46 to] no (a misprint) ed. 1738.

Thence tried against the blood-polluted meal,
And limbs yet quivering with some kindred soul,
To turn the human heart.　Delightful truth!
Had he beheld the living chain ascend,
And not a circling form, but rising whole.　　　70
　' Amid these small republics one arose
On yellow Tiber's bank, almighty Rome,
Fated for me.　A nobler spirit warmed
Her sons ; and, roused by tyrants, nobler still
It burned in Brutus, the proud Tarquins chased
With all their crimes, bade radiant eras rise
And the long honours of the consul line.
　' Here from the fairer, not the greater, plan
Of Greece I varied ; whose unmixing states,
By the keen soul of emulation pierced,　　　80
Long waged alone the bloodless war of arts,
And their best empire gained.　But to diffuse
O'er men an empire was my purpose now—
To let my martial majesty abroad ;
Into the vortex of one state to draw
The whole mixed force, and liberty, on earth ;
To conquer tyrants, and set nations free.
　' Already have I given, with flying touch,
A broken view of this my amplest reign.
Now, while its first, last, periods you survey,　　90
Mark how it labouring rose, and rapid fell.
　' When Rome in noon-tide empire grasped the world,
And, soon as her resistless legions shone,
The nations stooped around, though then appeared
Her grandeur most, yet in her dawn of power,
By many a jealous equal people pressed,
Then was the toil, the mighty struggle then.
Then for each Roman I an hero told ;
And every passing sun and Latian scene
Saw patriot virtues then and awful deeds　　　100

That or surpass the faith of modern times
Or, if believed, with sacred horror strike.
  'For then, to prove my most exalted power,
I to the point of full perfection pushed,
To fondness and enthusiastic zeal,
The great, the reigning passion of the free.
That godlike passion ! which, the bounds of self
Divinely bursting, the whole public takes
Into the heart, enlarged, and burning high
With the mixed ardour of unnumbered selves—   110
Of all who safe beneath the voted laws
Of the same parent state fraternal live.
From this kind sun of moral nature flowed
Virtues that shine the light of humankind,
And, rayed through story, warm remotest time.
These virtues too, reflected to their source,
Increased its flame. The social charm went round,
The fair idea, more attractive still
As more by virtue marked ; till Romans, all
One band of friends, unconquerable grew.   120
  'Hence, when their country raised her plaintive voice,
The voice of pleading nature was not heard ;
And in their hearts the fathers throbbed no more—
Stern to themselves, but gentle to the whole.
Hence sweetened pain, the luxury of toil;
Patience, that baffled fortune's utmost rage ;
High-minded hope, which at the lowest ebb,
When Brennus conquered and when Cannae bled,
The bravest impulse felt and scorned despair.
Hence moderation a new conquest gained—   130
As on the vanquished, like descending heaven,
Their dewy mercy dropped, their bounty beamed,
And by the labouring hand were crowns bestowed.
Fruitful of men, hence hard laborious life,
Which no fatigue can quell, no season pierce.

Hence Independence, with his little pleased,
Serene and self-sufficient like a god,
In whom corruption could not lodge one charm;
While he his honest roots to gold preferred ;
While truly rich, and by his Sabine field   140
The man maintained, the Roman's splendour all
Was in the public wealth and glory placed—
Or ready, a rough swain, to guide the plough,
Or else, the purple o'er his shoulder thrown
In long majestic flow, to rule the state
With wisdom's purest eye, or, clad in steel,
To drive the steady battle on the foe.
Hence every passion, even the proudest, stooped
To common good—Camillus, thy revenge ;
Thy glory, Fabius. All submissive hence,   150
Consuls, dictators, still resigned their rule,
The very moment that the laws ordained.
Though conquest o'er them clapped her eagle wings,
Her laurels wreathed, and yoked her snowy steeds
To the triumphal car—soon as expired
The latest hour of sway, taught to submit
(A harder lesson that than to command),
Into the private Roman sunk the Chief.
If Rome was served and glorious, careless they
By whom. Their country's fame they deemed their own,
And, above envy, in a rival's train   161
Sung the loud Iös by themselves deserved.
Hence matchless courage. On Cremera's bank,
Hence fell the Fabii ; hence the Decii died ;
And Curtius plunged into the flaming gulf.
Hence Regulus the wavering fathers firmed
By dreadful counsel never given before,
For Roman honour sued, and his own doom.
Hence he sustained to dare a death prepared
By Punic rage. On earth his manly look   170

Relentless fixed, he from a last embrace,
By chains polluted, put his wife aside,
His little children climbing for a kiss ;
Then dumb through rows of weeping, wondering friends,
A new illustrious exile ! pressed along.
Nor less impatient did he pierce the crowds
Opposing his return, than if, escaped
From long litigious suits, he glad forsook
The noisy town a while and city cloud
To breathe Venafrian or Tarentine air.   180
Need I these high particulars recount ?
The meanest bosom felt a thirst for fame ;
Flight their worst death, and shame their only fear.
Life had no charms, nor any terrors fate,
When Rome and glory called. But, in one view,
Mark the rare boast of these unequalled times.
Ages revolved unsullied by a crime :
Astrea reigned, and scarcely needed laws
To bind a race elated with the pride
Of virtue, and disdaining to descend   190
To meanness, mutual violence, and wrongs.
While war around them raged, in happy Rome
All peaceful smiled, all save the passing clouds
That often hang on Freedom's jealous brow ;
And fair unblemished centuries elapsed
When not a Roman bled but in the field.
Their virtue such that an unbalanced state,
Still between noble and plebeian tossed,
As flowed the wave of fluctuating power,
By that kept firm and with triumphant prow   200
Rode out the storms. Oft though the native feuds
That from the first their constitution shook
(A latent ruin, growing as it grew)
Stood on the threatening point of civil war
Ready to rush—yet could the lenient voice

Of wisdom, soothing the tumultuous soul,
These sons of virtue calm. Their generous hearts,
Unpetrified by self, so naked lay
And sensible to truth that o'er the rage
Of giddy faction, by oppression swelled,   210
Prevailed a simple fable, and at once
To peace recovered the divided state.
But, if their often-cheated hopes refused
The soothing touch, still, in the love of Rome,
The dread dictator found a sure resource.
Was she assaulted ? was her glory stained ?
One common quarrel wide inflamed the whole.
Foes in the forum in the field were friends,
By social danger bound—each fond for each,
And for their dearest country all, to die.   220
  ' Thus up the hill of empire slow they toiled,
Till, the bold summit gained, the thousand states
Of proud Italia blended into one ;
Then o'er the nations they resistless rushed,
And touched the limits of the failing world.
  ' Let fancy's eye the distant lines unite.
See that which borders wild the western main,
Where storms at large resound, and tides immense ;
From Caledonia's dim cerulean coast,
And moist Hibernia, to where Atlas, lodged   230
Amid the restless clouds and leaning heaven,
Hangs o'er the deep that borrows thence its name.
Mark that opposed, where first the springing morn
Her roses sheds, and shakes around her dews—
From the dire deserts by the Caspian laved
To where the Tigris and Euphrates, joined,
Impetuous tear the Babylonian plain,
And blest Arabia aromatic breathes.
See that dividing far the watery north,
Parent of floods ! from the majestic Rhine,   240

Drunk by Batavian meads, to where, seven-mouthed,
In Euxine waves the flashing Danube roars ;
To where the frozen Tanais scarcely stirs
The dead Maeotic pool, or the long Rha
In the black Scythian sea his torrent throws.
Last, that beneath the burning zone behold.
See where it runs from the deep-loaded plains
Of Mauritania to the Libyan sands,
Where Ammon lifts amid the torrid waste
A verdant isle with shade and fountain fresh,   250
And farther to the full Egyptian shore,
To where the Nile from Ethiopian clouds,
His never drained ethereal urn, descends.
In this vast space what various tongues and states !
What bounding rocks and mountains, floods and seas !
What purple tyrants quelled, and nations freed !
' O'er Greece descended chief, with stealth divine,
The Roman bounty in a flood of day :
As at her Isthmian games, a fading pomp !
Her full-assembled youth innumerous swarmed. 260
On a tribunal raised Flaminius sat :
A victor he, from the deep phalanx pierced
Of iron-coated Macedon, and back
The Grecian tyrant to his bounds repelled.
In the high thoughtless gaiety of game,
While sport alone their unambitious hearts
Possessed, the sudden trumpet, sounding hoarse,
Bade silence o'er the bright assembly reign.
Then thus a herald :—" To the states of Greece
The Roman people unconfined restore   270
Their countries, cities, liberties, and laws :
Taxes remit, and garrisons withdraw."
The crowd, astonished half, and half informed,
Stared dubious round ; some questioned, some
      exclaimed

(Like one who dreaming, between hope and fear,
Is lost in anxious joy)—" Be that again,
Be that again proclaimed, distinct and loud."
Loud and distinct it was again proclaimed ;
And, still as midnight in the rural shade
When the gale slumbers, they the words devoured.
A while severe amazement held them mute,   281
Then, bursting broad, the boundless shout to heaven
From many a thousand hearts ecstatic sprung.
On every hand rebellowed to their joy
The swelling sea, the rocks and vocal hills :
Through all her turrets stately Corinth shook ;
And, from the void above of shattered air,
The flitting bird fell breathless to the ground.
What piercing bliss, how keen a sense of fame
Did then, Flaminius, reach thy inmost soul !   290
And with what deep-felt glory didst thou then
Escape the fondness of transported Greece !
Mixed in a tempest of superior joy,
They left the sports ; like Bacchanals they flew,
Each other straining in a strict embrace,
Nor strained a slave ; and loud acclaims till night
Round the Proconsul's tent repeated rung.
Then, crowned with garlands, came the festive hours ;
And music, sparkling wine, and converse warm
Their raptures waked anew. "Ye gods ! " they cried,
" Ye guardian gods of Greece ! and are we free ?   301
Was it not madness deemed the very thought ?
And is it true ?   How did we purchase chains ?
At what a dire expense of kindred blood ?
And are they now dissolved ?   And scarce one drop
For the fair first of blessings have we paid ?
Courage and conduct in the doubtful field
When rages wide the storm of mingling war

283 hearts] Heart ed. 1738.

Are rare indeed ; but how to generous ends
To turn success and conquest, rarer still—   310
That the great gods and Romans only know.
Lives there on earth, almost to Greece unknown,
A people so magnanimous to quit
Their native soil, traverse the stormy deep,
And by their blood and treasure, spent for us,
Redeem our states. our liberties, and laws !
There does ! there does ! Oh Saviour Titus ! Rome ! "
Thus through the happy night they poured their souls,
And in my last reflected beams rejoiced.
As when the shepherd, on the mountain brow,   320
Sits piping to his flocks and gamesome kids ;
Meantime the sun, beneath the green earth sunk,
Slants upward o'er the scene a parting gleam :
Short is the glory that the mountain gilds,
Plays on the glittering flocks and glads the swain ;
To western worlds irrevocable rolled,
Rapid the source of light recalls his ray.'
     Here interposing I :—' Oh, Queen of men !
Beneath whose sceptre in essential rights
Equal they live, though placed for common good 330
Various, or in subjection or command,
And that by common choice—alas ! the scene,
With virtue, freedom, and with glory bright,
Streams into blood and darkens into woe.'
Thus she pursued :—' Near this great era, Rome
Began to feel the swift approach of fate,
That now her vitals gained—still more and more
Her deep divisions kindling into rage
And war, with chains and desolation charged.
From an unequal balance of her sons   340
These fierce contentions sprung : and, as increased
This hated inequality, more fierce
They flamed to tumult. Independence failed—

Here by luxurious wants, by real there ;
And with this virtue every virtue sunk
As, with the sliding rock, the pile sustained.
A last attempt, too late, the Gracchi made
To fix the flying scale and poise the state.
On one side swelled aristocratic Pride,
With Usury, the villain! whose fell gripe   350
Bends by degrees to baseness the free soul,
And Luxury rapacious, cruel, mean,
Mother of vice! While on the other crept
A populace in want, with pleasure fired ;
Fit for proscriptions, for the darkest deeds,
As the proud feeder bade ; inconstant, blind,
Deserting friends at need, and duped by foes ;
Loud and seditious, when a chief inspired
Their headlong fury, but, of him deprived,
Already slaves that licked the scourging hand.   360
  'This firm republic that against the blast
Of opposition rose, that (like an oak,
Nursed on feracious Algidum, whose boughs
Still stronger shoot beneath the rigid axe)
By loss, by slaughter, from the steel itself
Even force and spirit drew, smit with the calm,
The dead serene of prosperous fortune, pined.
Nought now her weighty legions could oppose ;
Her terror, once, on Afric's tawny shore
Now smoked in dust, a stabling now for wolves ;   370
And every dreaded power received the yoke.
Besides, destructive, from the conquered east
In the soft plunder came that worst of plagues,
The pestilence of mind, a fevered thirst
For the false joys which luxury prepares.
Unworthy joys! that wasteful leave behind
No mark of honour in reflecting hour,
No secret ray to glad the conscious soul—

At once involving in one ruin wealth
And wealth-acquiring powers, while stupid self,
Of narrow gust, and hebetating sense   381
Devour the nobler faculties of bliss.
Hence Roman virtue slackened into sloth,
Security relaxed the softening state,
And the broad eye of government lay closed.
No more the laws inviolable reigned,
And public weal no more : but party raged,
And partial power and licence unrestrained
Let discord through the deathful city loose.
First, mild Tiberius, on thy sacred head   390
The fury's vengeance fell ; the first whose blood
Had, since the consuls, stained contending Rome.
Of precedent pernicious ! with thee bled
Three hundred Romans ; with thy brother, next,
Three thousand more—till, into battles turned
Debates of peace, and forced the trembling laws,
The forum and comitia horrid grew,
A scene of bartered power or reeking gore.
When, half-ashamed, corruption's thievish arts
And ruffian force begin to sap the mounds   400
And majesty of laws ; if not in time
Repressed severe, for human aid too strong
The torrent turns, and overbears the whole.
   ' Thus luxury, dissension, a mixed rage
Of boundless pleasure and of boundless wealth,
Want wishing change, and waste-repairing war,
Rapine for ever lost to peaceful toil,
Guilt unatoned, profuse of blood revenge,
Corruption all avowed, and lawless force,
Each heightening each, alternate shook the state.   410
Meantime ambition, at the dazzling head

395 into] in two (a misprint) ed. 1738.
406 Want wishing Change and Waste repairing War ed. 1738.

Of hardy legions, with the laurels heaped
And spoil of nations, in one circling blast
Combined in various storm, and from its base
The broad republic tore. By virtue built
It touched the skies, and spread o'er sheltered earth
An ample roof : by virtue too sustained,
And balanced steady, every tempest sung
Innoxious by, or bade it firmer stand.
But when, with sudden and enormous change,　420
The first of mankind sunk into the last,
As once in virtue, so in vice extreme,
This universal fabric yielded loose,
Before ambition still ; and thundering down,
At last, beneath its ruins crushed a world.
A conquering people to themselves a prey
Must ever fall, when their victorious troops,
In blood and rapine savage grown, can find
No land to sack and pillage but their own.
　' By brutal Marius, and keen Sylla, first　430
Effused the deluge dire of civil blood,
Unceasing woes began, and this, or that,
(Deep-drenching their revenge) nor virtue spared,
Nor sex, nor age, nor quality, nor name ;
Till Rome, into an human shambles turned,
Made deserts lovely.—Oh, to well-earned chains,
Devoted race !—If no true Roman then,
No Scaevola, there was to raise for me
A vengeful hand—was there no father, robbed
Of blooming youth to prop his withered age ?　440
No son, a witness to his hoary sire
In dust and gore defiled ? no friend, forlorn ?
No wretch that doubtful trembled for himself ?
None brave, or wild, to pierce a monster's heart,
Who, heaping horror round, no more deserved
The sacred shelter of the laws he spurned ?

No :—Sad o'er all profound dejection sat ;
And nerveless fear. The slave's asylum theirs—
Or flight, ill-judging that the timid back
Turns weak to slaughter, or partaken guilt.   450
In vain from Sylla's vanity I drew
An unexampled deed. The power resigned,
And all unhoped the commonwealth restored,
Amazed the public, and effaced his crimes.
Through streets yet streaming from his murderous
          hand
Unarmed he strayed, unguarded, unassailed,
And on the bed of peace his ashes laid—
A grace, which I to his demission gave.
But with him died not the despotic soul.
Ambition saw that stooping Rome could bear   460
A master, nor had virtue to be free.
Hence, for succeeding years, my troubled reign
No certain peace, no spreading prospect knew.
Destruction gathered round. Still the black soul
Or of a Catiline or Rullus swelled
With fell designs ; and all the watchful art
Of Cicero demanded, all the force,
All the state-wielding magic of his tongue,
And all the thunder of my Cato's zeal.
With these I lingered ; till the flame anew   470
Burst out in blaze immense, and wrapped the world.
The shameful contest sprung ; to whom mankind
Should yield the neck—to Pompey, who concealed
A rage impatient of an equal name,
Or to the nobler Caesar, on whose brow
O'er daring vice deluding virtue smiled,
And who no less a vain superior scorned.
Both bled, but bled in vain. New traitors rose.
The venal will be bought, the base have lords.
To these vile wars I left ambitious slaves ;   480

And from Philippi's field, from where in dust
The last of Romans, matchless Brutus! lay,
Spread to the north untamed a rapid wing.
  'What though the first smooth Caesars arts caressed,
Merit, and virtue, simulating me?
Severely tender, cruelly humane
The chain to clinch, and make it softer sit
On the new-broken still ferocious state!
From the dark third, succeeding, I beheld
The imperial monsters all—a race on earth   490
Vindictive sent, the scourge of humankind!
Whose blind profusion drained a bankrupt world;
Whose lust to forming nature seems disgrace;
And whose infernal rage bade every drop
Of ancient blood that yet retained my flame,
To that of Paetus, in the peaceful bath
Or Rome's affrighted streets inglorious flow.
But almost just the meanly patient death
That waits a tyrant's unprevented stroke.
Titus indeed gave one short evening gleam;   500
More cordial felt, as in the midst it spread
Of storm and horror. The delight of men!
He who the day when his o'erflowing hand
Had made no happy heart concluded lost;
Trajan and he, with the mild sire and son,
His son of virtue! eased awhile mankind;
And arts revived beneath their gentle beam.
Then was their last effort: what sculpture raised
To Trajan's glory following triumphs stole,
And mixed with Gothic forms (the chisel's shame)
On that triumphal arch the forms of Greece.   511
  'Meantime o'er rocky Thrace and the deep vales
Of gelid Haemus I pursued my flight;
And, piercing farthest Scythia, westward swept
Sarmatia, traversed by a thousand streams,

A sullen land of lakes, and fens immense,
Of rocks, resounding torrents, gloomy heaths,
And cruel deserts black with sounding pine,
Where nature frowns—though sometimes into smiles
She softens, and immediate at the touch   520
Of southern gales throws from the sudden glebe
Luxuriant pasture and a waste of flowers.
But, cold-compressed, when the whole-loaded heaven
Descends in snow, lost in one white abrupt
Lies undistinguished Earth ; and, seized by frost,
Lakes, headlong streams, and floods, and oceans sleep.
Yet there life glows ; the furry millions there
Deep-dig their dens beneath the sheltering snows :
And there a race of men prolific swarms,
To various pain, to little pleasure used,   530
On whom keen-parching beat Riphaean winds,
Hard like their soil, and like their climate fierce,
The nursery of nations !—These I roused,
Drove land on land, on people people poured,
Till from almost perpetual night they broke
As if in search of day, and o'er the banks
Of yielding empire, only slave-sustained,
Resistless raged—in vengeance urged by me.
  ' Long in the barbarous heart the buried seeds
Of freedom lay, for many a wintry age ;   540
And, though my spirit worked, by slow degrees
Nought but its pride and fierceness yet appeared.
Then was the night of time, that parted worlds.
I quitted earth the while. As when the tribes
Aerial, warned of rising winter, ride
Autumnal winds, to warmer climates borne—
So, arts and each good genius in my train,
I cut the closing gloom, and soared to heaven.
  ' In the bright regions there of purest day,
Far other scenes and palaces arise,   550

Adorned profuse with other arts divine.
All beauty here below, to them compared,
Would, like a rose before the midday sun,
Shrink up its blossom—like a bubble break
The passing poor magnificence of kings.
For there the king of nature in full blaze
Calls every splendour forth, and there his court,
Amid ethereal powers and virtues holds—
Angel, archangel, tutelary gods,
Of cities, nations, empires, and of worlds.   560
But sacred be the veil that kindly clouds
A light too keen for mortals—wraps a view
Too softening fair, for those that here in dust
Must cheerful toil out their appointed years.
A sense of higher life would only damp
The schoolboy's task, and spoil his playful hours.
Nor could the child of reason, feeble man,
With vigour through this infant-being drudge,
Did brighter worlds, their unimagined bliss
Disclosing, dazzle and dissolve his mind.'   570

THE CONTENTS OF PART IV

DIFFERENCE betwixt the Ancients and Moderns slightly touched
upon, *to verse* 29. Description of the Dark Ages. The Goddess
of Liberty, who during these is supposed to have left earth,
returns, attended with Arts and Science, *to verse* 99. She
first descends on Italy. Sculpture, Painting, and Architecture
fix at Rome, to revive their several arts by the great models
of antiquity there, which many barbarous invasions had not
been able to destroy. The revival of these arts marked out.
That sometimes arts may flourish for a while under despotic
governments, though never the natural and genuine production
of them, *to verse* 253. Learning begins to dawn. The Muse
and Science attend Liberty, who in her progress towards Great
Britain raises several free states and cities. These enumerated,
to verse 380. Author's exclamation of joy, upon seeing the

British seas and coasts rise in the Vision, which painted whatever the Goddess of Liberty said. She resumes her narration, the Genius of the Deep appears, and addressing Liberty, associates Great Britain into his dominion, *to verse* 450. Liberty received and congratulated by Britannia, and the native Genii or Virtues of the island. These described. Animated by the presence of Liberty, they begin their operations. Their beneficent influence contrasted with the works and delusions of opposing Demons, *to verse* 623. Concludes with an abstract of the English history, marking the several advances of Liberty, down to her complete establishment at the Revolution.

PART IV. BRITAIN

[First published, 1736.]

STRUCK with the rising scene, thus I amazed :—
' Ah, Goddess, what a change ! is Earth the same ?
Of the same kind the ruthless race she feeds ?
And does the same fair sun and ether spread
Round this vile spot their all-enlivening soul ?
Lo ! beauty fails ; lost in unlovely forms
Of little pomp, magnificence no more
Exalts the mind, and bids the public smile—
While to rapacious interest Glory leaves
Mankind, and every grace of life is gone.'   10
   To this the power, whose vital radiance calls
From the brute mass of man an ordered world :
' Wait till the morning shines, and from the depth
Of Gothic darkness springs another day.
True, genius droops ; the tender ancient taste
Of Beauty, then fresh blooming in her prime,
But faintly trembles through the callous soul ;
And Grandeur, or of morals or of life,
Sinks into safe pursuits and creeping cares.
Even cautious virtue seems to stoop her flight,   20
And aged life to deem the generous deeds

Of youth romantic. Yet in cooler thought
Well reasoned, in researches piercing deep
Through nature's works, in profitable arts,
And all that calm experience can disclose,
(Slow guide, but sure) behold the world anew
Exalted rise, with other honours crowned ;
And, where my Spirit wakes the finer powers,
Athenian laurels still afresh shall bloom.
   ' Oblivious ages passed ; while earth, forsook   30
By her best genii, lay to demons foul
And unchained furies an abandoned prey.
Contention led the van ; first small of size,
But soon dilating to the skies she towers :
Then, wide as air, the livid fury spread,
And high her head above the stormy clouds
She blazed in omens, swelled the groaning winds
With wild surmises, battlings, sounds of war—
From land to land the maddening trumpet blew,
And poured her venom through the heart of man. 40
Shook to the pole, the north obeyed her call.
Forth rushed the bloody power of Gothic war,
War against human kind : Rapine, that led
Millions of raging robbers in his train :
Unlistening, barbarous force, to whom the sword
Is reason, honour, law : the foe of arts
By monsters followed, hideous to behold,
That claimed their place. Outrageous mixed with these
Another species of tyrannic rule ;
Unknown before, whose cankerous shackles seized
The envenomed soul ; a wilder Fury, she   51
Even o'er her Elder Sister tyrannized,
Or, if perchance agreed, inflamed her rage.
Dire was her train, and loud : the sable band,
Thundering—" Submit, ye Laity ! ye profane !

Earth is the Lord's, and therefore ours ; let kings
Allow the common claim, and half be theirs ;
If not, behold ! the sacred lightning flies ! "
Scholastic Discord, with an hundred tongues,
For science uttering jangling words obscure,   60
Where frighted reason never yet could dwell.
Of peremptory feature, cleric pride,
Whose reddening cheek no contradiction bears;
And holy slander, his associate firm,
On whom the lying spirit still descends—
Mother of tortures ! persecuting zeal,
High flashing in her hand the ready torch,
Or poniard bathed in unbelieving blood ;
Hell's fiercest fiend ! of saintly brow demure,
Assuming a celestial seraph's name,   70
While she beneath the blasphemous pretence
Of pleasing parent Heaven, the source of love !
Has wrought more horrors, more detested deeds
Than all the rest combined. Led on by her,
And wild of head to work her fell designs,
Came idiot Superstition ; round with ears
Innumerous strowed, ten thousand monkish forms
With legends plied them, and with tenets, meant
To charm or scare the simple into slaves,
And poison reason ; gross, she swallows all,   80
The most absurd believing ever most.
Broad o'er the whole her universal night,
The gloom still doubling, Ignorance diffused.
 ' Nought to be seen, but visionary monks
To councils strolling and embroiling creeds,
Banditti saints disturbing distant lands,
And unknown nations wandering for a home.
All lay reversed—the sacred arts of rule
Turned to flagitious leagues against mankind,
And arts of plunder more and more avowed ;   90

Pure plain devotion to a solemn farce ;
To holy dotage virtue, even to guile,
To murder, and a mockery of oaths ;
Brave ancient freedom to the rage of slaves,
Proud of their state and fighting for their chains ;
Dishonoured courage to the bravo's trade,
To civil broil ; and glory to romance.
Thus human life, unhinged, to ruin reeled,
And giddy reason tottered on her throne.
  ' At last heaven's best inexplicable scheme,   100
Disclosing, bade new brightening eras smile.
The high command gone forth, Arts in my train,
And azure-mantled Science, swift we spread
A sounding pinion. Eager pity, mixed
With indignation, urged our downward flight.
On Latium first we stooped, for doubtful life
That panted, sunk beneath unnumbered woes.
Ah, poor Italia ! what a bitter cup
Of vengeance hast thou drained ! Goths, Vandals,
    Huns,
Lombards, barbarians broke from every land,   110
How many a ruffian form hast thou beheld !
What horrid jargons heard, where rage alone
Was all thy frighted ear could comprehend !
How frequent by the red inhuman hand,
Yet warm with brother's, husband's, father's blood,
Hast thou thy matrons and thy virgins seen
To violation dragged, and mingled death !
What conflagrations, earthquakes, ravage, floods,
Have turned thy cities into stony wilds ;
And succourless and bare the poor remains   120
Of wretches forth to nature's common cast !
Added to these the still continual waste
Of inbred foes that on thy vitals prey,
And, double tyrants, seize the very soul.

Where hadst thou treasures for this rapine all ?
These hungry myriads that thy bowels tore,
Heaped sack on sack, and buried in their rage
Wonders of art ; whence this grey scene, a mine
Of more than gold becomes and orient gems,
Where Egypt, Greece, and Rome united glow.   130
‘ Here Sculpture, Painting, Architecture, bent
From ancient models to restore their arts,
Remained. A little trace we how they rose.
‘ Amid the hoary ruins, Sculpture first,
Deep digging, from the cavern dark and damp,
Their grave for ages, bade her marble race
Spring to new light. Joy sparkled in her eyes,
And old remembrance thrilled in every thought,
As she the pleasing resurrection saw.
In leaning site, respiring from his toils,   140
The well known hero who delivered Greece,
His ample chest all tempested with force,
Unconquerable reared. She saw the head,
Breathing the hero, small, of Grecian size,
Scarce more extensive than the sinewy neck ;
The spreading shoulders, muscular and broad ;
The whole a mass of swelling sinews, touched
Into harmonious shape ; she saw, and joyed.
The yellow hunter, Meleager, raised
His beauteous front, and through the finished whole
Shows what ideas smiled of old in Greece.   151
Of raging aspect rushed impetuous forth
The Gladiator : pitiless his look,
And each keen sinew braced, the storm of war,
Ruffling, o’er all his nervous body frowns.
The dying other from the gloom she drew.
Supported on his shortened arm he leans,
Prone, agonizing ; with incumbent fate
Heavy declines his head ; yet dark beneath

N

The suffering feature sullen vengeance lours,　160
Shame, indignation, unaccomplished rage;
And still the cheated eye expects his fall.
All conquest-flushed from prostrate Python came
The quivered God.　In graceful act he stands,
His arm extended with the slackened bow :
Light flows his easy robe, and fair displays
A manly-softened form.　The bloom of gods
Seems youthful o'er the beardless cheek to wave :
His features yet heroic ardour warms ;
And sweet subsiding to a native smile,　170
Mixed with the joy elating conquest gives,
A scattered frown exalts his matchless air.
On Flora moved ;　her full proportioned limbs
Rise through the mantle fluttering in the breeze.
The queen of love arose, as from the deep
She sprung in all the melting pomp of charms.
Bashful she bends, her well-taught look aside
Turns in enchanting guise, where dubious mix
Vain conscious beauty, a dissembled sense
Of modest shame, and slippery looks of love.　180
The gazer grows enamoured, and the stone,
As if exulting in its conquest, smiles.
So turned each limb, so swelled with softening art,
That the deluded eye the marble doubts.
At last her utmost masterpiece she found
That Maro fired—the miserable sire,
Wrapt with his sons in fate's severest grasp .
The serpents, twisting round, their stringent folds
Inextricable tie.　Such passion here,
Such agonies, such bitterness of pain　190
Seem so to tremble through the tortured stone
That the touched heart engrosses all the view.
Almost unmarked the best proportions pass
That ever Greece beheld ;　and, seen alone,

On the rapt eye the imperious passions seize—
The father's double pangs, both for himself
And sons convulsed ; to heaven his rueful look,
Imploring aid, and half accusing, cast ;
His fell despair with indignation mixed,
As the strong curling monsters from his side   200
His full extended fury cannot tear.
More tender touched, with varied art, his sons
All the soft rage of younger passions show.
In a boy's helpless fate one sinks oppressed ;
While, yet unpierced, the frighted other tries
His foot to steal out of the horrid twine.
  ' She bore no more, but straight from Gothic rust
Her chisel cleared, and dust and fragments drove
Impetuous round. Successive as it went
From son to son, with more enlivening touch,   210
From the brute rock it called the breathing form ;
Till, in a legislator's awful grace
Dressed, Buonaroti bade a Moses rise,
And, looking love immense, a Saviour God.
  ' Of these observant, Painting felt the fire
Burn inward. Then ecstatic she diffused
The canvas, seized the pallet, with quick hand
The colours brewed ; and on the void expanse
Her gay creation poured, her mimic world.
Poor was the manner of her eldest race,   220
Barren, and dry ; just struggling from the taste
That had for ages scared in cloisters dim
The superstitious herd : yet glorious then
Were deemed their works ; where undeveloped lay
The future wonders that enriched mankind,
And a new light and grace o'er Europe cast.
Arts gradual gather streams. Enlarging this,
To each his portion of her various gifts
The Goddess dealt, to none indulging all ;

No, not to Raphael. At kind distance still 230
Perfection stands, like happiness, to tempt
The eternal chase. In elegant design,
Improving nature : in ideas, fair
Or great, extracted from the fine antique ;
In attitude, expression, airs divine—
Her sons of Rome and Florence bore the prize.
To those of Venice she the magic art
Of colours melting into colours gave.
Theirs too it was by one embracing mass
Of light and shade, that settles round the whole,
Or varies tremulous from part to part, 241
O'er all a binding harmony to throw,
To raise the picture, and repose the sight.
The Lombard school, succeeding, mingled both.
' Meantime dread fanes and palaces around
Reared the magnific front. Music again
Her universal language of the heart
Renewed ; and, rising from the plaintive vale,
To the full concert spread, and solemn quire. 249
' Even bigots smiled ; to their protection took
Arts not their own, and from them borrowed pomp—
For in a tyrant's garden these awhile
May bloom, though freedom be their parent soil.
' And, now confessed, with gently-growing gleam
The morning shone, and westward streamed its light.
The muse awoke. Not sooner on the wing
Is the gay bird of dawn. Artless her voice,
Untaught and wild, yet warbled through the woods
Romantic lays. But as her northern course
She, with her tutor Science, in my train, 260
Ardent pursued, her strains more noble grew—
While reason drew the plan, the heart informed
The moral page, and fancy lent it grace.
' Rome and her circling deserts cast behind,

I passed not idle to my great sojourn.
' On Arno's fertile plain, where the rich vine
Luxuriant o'er Etrurian mountains roves,
Safe in the lap reposed of private bliss,
I small republics raised. Thrice happy they !
Had social freedom bound their peace, and arts,
Instead of ruling power, ne'er meant for them,   271
Employed their little cares, and saved their fate.
' Beyond the rugged Apennines, that roll
Far through Italian bounds their wavy tops,
My path too I with public blessings strowed :
Free states and cities, where the Lombard plain,
In spite of culture negligent and gross,
From her deep bosom pours unbidden joys,
And green o'er all the land a garden spreads.
' The barren rocks themselves beneath my foot
Relenting bloomed on the Ligurian shore.   281
Thick-swarming people there, like emmets, seized
Amid surrounding cliffs the scattered spots
Which nature left in her destroying rage,
Made their own fields, nor sighed for other lands.
There, in white prospect from the rocky hill
Gradual descending to the sheltered shore,
By me proud Genoa's marble turrets rose.
And, while my genuine spirit warmed her sons,
Beneath her Dorias, not unworthy, she   290
Vied for the trident of the narrow seas,
Ere Britain yet had opened all the main.
' Nor be the then triumphant state forgot,
Where, pushed from plundered earth, a remnant still,
Inspired by me, through the dark ages kept
Of my old Roman flame some sparks alive—
The seeming god-built city ! which my hand
Deep in the bosom fixed of wondering seas.
Astonished mortals sailed with pleasing awe

Around the sea-girt walls, by Neptune fenced,   300
And down the briny street, where on each hand,
Amazing seen amid unstable waves,
The splendid palace shines, and rising tides,
The green steps marking, murmur at the door.
To this fair queen of Adria's stormy gulf,
The mart of nations ! long obedient seas
Rolled all the treasure of the radiant East.
But now no more. Than one great tyrant worse
(Whose shared oppression lightens, as diffused),
Each subject tearing, many tyrants rose.   310
The least the proudest. Joined in dark cabal,
They, jealous, watchful, silent, and severe,
Cast o'er the whole indissoluble chains :
The softer shackles of luxurious ease
They likewise added, to secure their sway.
Thus Venice fainter shines ; and Commerce thus,
Of toil impatient, flags the drooping sail.
Bursting, besides, his ancient bounds, he took
A larger circle ; found another seat,
Opening a thousand ports, and charmed with toil 320
Whom nothing can dismay far other sons.
  ' The mountains then, clad with eternal snow,
Confessed my power. Deep as the rampart rocks
By nature thrown insuperable round,
I planted there a league of friendly states,
And bade plain freedom their ambition be.
There in the vale, where rural plenty fills
From lakes and meads and furrowed fields her horn,
Chief where the Leman pure emits the Rhone,
Rare to be seen ! unguilty cities rise,   330
Cities of brothers formed—while equal life,
Accorded gracious with revolving power,
Maintains them free ; and, in their happy streets,

323 rampant (a misprint) ed. 1738.

Nor cruel deed nor misery is known.
For valour, faith, and innocence of life
Renowned, a rough laborious people there
Not only give the dreadful Alps to smile,
And press their culture on retiring snows ;
But, to firm order trained and patient war,
They likewise know, beyond the nerve remiss   340
Of mercenary force, how to defend
The tasteful little their hard toil has earned,
And the proud arm of Bourbon to defy.
　' Even, cheered by me, their shaggy mountains
　　　charm
More than or Gallic or Italian plains ;
And sickening fancy oft, when absent long,
Pines to behold their Alpine views again—
The hollow-winding stream : the vale, fair-spread
Amid an amphitheatre of hills,
Whence, vapour-winged, the sudden tempest springs ;
From steep to steep ascending, the gay train   351
Of fogs thick-rolled into romantic shapes ;
The flitting cloud, against the summit dashed ;
And, by the sun illumined, pouring bright
A gemmy shower—hung o'er amazing rocks,
The mountain ash, and solemn sounding pine ;
The snow-fed torrent, in white mazes tossed
Down to the clear ethereal lake below ;
And, high o'ertopping all the broken scene,
The mountain fading into sky, where shines   360
On winter winter shivering, and whose top
Licks from their cloudy magazine the snows.
　' From these descending, as I waved my course
O'er vast Germania, the ferocious nurse
Of hardy men, and hearts affronting death,
I gave some favoured cities there to lift
A nobler brow, and through their swarming streets,

More busy, wealthy, cheerful, and alive,
In each contented face to look my soul.
  'Thence the loud Baltic passing, black with storm,
To wintry Scandinavia's utmost bound—   371
There I the manly race, the parent hive
Of the mixed kingdoms, formed into a state
More regularly free. By keener air
Their genius purged, and tempered hard by frost,
Tempest and toil their nerves, the sons of those
Whose only terror was a bloodless death,
They, wise and dauntless, still sustain my cause.
Yet there I fixed not. Turning to the south,
The whispering zephyrs sighed at my delay.'   380
  Here, with the shifted vision, burst my joy :
' O the dear prospect ! O majestic view !
See Britain's empire ! lo ! the watery vast
Wide-waves, diffusing the cerulean plain.
And now, methinks, like clouds at distance seen,
Emerging white from deeps of ether, dawn
My kindred cliffs ; whence, wafted in the gale,
Ineffable, a secret sweetness breathes.
Goddess, forgive !—My heart, surprised, o'erflows
With filial fondness for the land you bless.'   390
As parents to a child complacent deign
Approvance, the celestial Brightness smiled;
Then thus—' As o'er the wave-resounding deep
To my near reign, the happy isle, I steered
With easy wing—behold ! from surge to surge
Stalked the tremendous Genius of the Deep.
Around him clouds in mingled tempest hung ;
Thick flashing meteors crowned his starry head ;
And ready thunder reddened in his hand,
Or from it streamed compressed the gloomy cloud. 400
Where'er he looked, the trembling waves recoiled.
He needs but strike the conscious flood, and shook

From shore to shore, in agitation dire,
It works his dreadful will.   To me his voice
(Like that hoarse blast that round the cavern howls,
Mixed with the murmurs of the falling main),
Addressed, began—" By fate commissioned, go,
My sister-goddess now, to yon blest isle,
Henceforth the partner of my rough domain.
All my dread walks to Britons open lie.   410
Those that refulgent, or with rosy morn
Or yellow evening, flame ; those that, profuse
Drunk by equator suns, severely shine ;
Or those that, to the poles approaching, rise
In billows rolling into Alps of ice.
Even, yet untouched by daring keel, be theirs
The vast Pacific—that on other worlds,
Their future conquest, rolls resounding tides.
Long I maintained inviolate my reign ;
Nor Alexanders me, nor Caesars braved.   420
Still in the crook of shore the coward sail
Till now low crept ; and peddling commerce plied
Between near joining lands.   For Britons, chief,
It was reserved, with star-directed prow,
To dare the middle deep, and drive assured
To distant nations through the pathless main.
Chief, for their fearless hearts the glory waits,
Long months from land, while the black stormy night
Around them rages, on the groaning mast
With unshook knee to know their giddy way ;   430
To sing, unquelled, amid the lashing wave ;
To laugh at danger.   Theirs the triumph be,
By deep invention's keen pervading eye,
The heart of courage, and the hand of toil,
Each conquered ocean staining with their blood,
Instead of treasure robbed by ruffian war,
Round social earth to circle fair exchange

And bind the nations in a golden chain.
To these I honoured stoop. Rushing to light
A race of men behold ! whose daring deeds   440
Will in renown exalt my nameless plains
O'er those of fabling earth, as hers to mine
In terror yield. Nay, could my savage heart
Such glories check, their unsubmitting soul
Would all my fury brave, my tempest climb,
And might in spite of me my kingdom force."
Here, waiting no reply, the shadowy Power
Eased the dark sky, and to the deeps returned—
While the loud thunder rattling from his hand,
Auspicious, shook opponent Gallia's shore.   450
    ' Of this encounter glad, my way to land
I quick pursued, that from the smiling sea
Received me joyous. Loud acclaims were heard ;
And music, more than mortal, warbling, filled
With pleased astonishment the labouring hind,
Who for a while the unfinished furrow left,
And let the listening steer forget his toil.
Unseen by grosser eye, Britannia breathed,
And her aerial train, these sounds of joy.
For of old time, since first the rushing flood,   460
Urged by almighty power, this favoured isle
Turned flashing from the continent aside,
Indented shore to shore ·responsive still,
Its guardian she—the Goddess, whose staid eye
Beams the dark azure of the doubtful dawn.
Her tresses, like a flood of softened light
Through clouds imbrowned, in waving circles play.
Warm on her cheek sits beauty's brightest rose.
Of high demeanour, stately, shedding grace
With every motion. Full her rising chest ;   470
And new ideas from her finished shape
Charmed Sculpture taking might improve her art.

Such the fair guardian of an isle that boasts,
Profuse as vernal blooms, the fairest dames.
High shining on the promontory's brow,
Awaiting me, she stood with hope inflamed,
By my mixed spirit burning in her sons,
To firm, to polish, and exalt the state.
' The native genii round her radiant smiled.
Courage, of soft deportment, aspect calm,   480
Unboastful, suffering long, and, till provoked,
As mild and harmless as the sporting child ;
But, on just reason, once his fury roused,
No lion springs more eager to his prey—
Blood is a pastime ; and his heart, elate,
Knows no depressing fear. That Virtue known
By the relenting look, whose equal heart
For others feels as for another self—
Of various name, as various objects wake,
Warm into action, the kind sense within :   490
Whether the blameless poor, the nobly maimed,
The lost to reason, the declined in life,
The helpless young that kiss no mother's hand,
And the grey second infancy of age
She gives in public families to live,
A sight to gladden heaven ! whether she stands
Fair-beckoning at the hospitable gate,
And bids the stranger take repose and joy ;
Whether, to solace honest labour, she
Rejoices those that make the land rejoice ;   500
Or whether to philosophy and arts
(At once the basis and the finished pride
Of government and life) she spreads her hand,
Nor knows her gift profuse, nor seems to know,
Doubling her bounty, that she gives at all.
Justice to these her awful presence joined,
The mother of the state ! No low revenge,

No turbid passions in her breast ferment :
Tender, serene, compassionate of vice,
As the last woe that can afflict mankind,   510
She punishment awards ; yet of the good
More piteous still, and of the suffering whole,
Awards it firm. So fair her just decree,
That, in his judging peers, each on himself
Pronounces his own doom. O happy land !
Where reigns alone this justice of the free !
Mid the bright group, Sincerity his front,
Diffusive, reared ; his pure untroubled eye
The fount of truth. The Thoughtful Power, apart,
Now pensive cast on earth his fixed regard,   520
Now, touched celestial, launched it on the sky.
The genius he whence Britain shines supreme,
The land of light and rectitude of mind.
He, too, the fire of fancy feeds intense,
With all the train of passions thence derived—
Not kindling quick, a noisy transient blaze,
But gradual, silent, lasting, and profound.
Near him Retirement, pointing to the shade,
And Independence stood—the generous pair
That simple life, the quiet-whispering grove,   530
And the still raptures of the free-born soul
To cates prefer by virtue bought, not earned,
Proudly prefer them to the servile pomp
And to the heart-embittered joys of slaves.
Or should the latter, to the public scene
Demanded, quit his silvan friend awhile—
Nought can his firmness shake, nothing seduce
His zeal, still active for the commonweal ;
Nor stormy tyrants, nor corruption's tools,
Foul ministers, dark-working by the force   540
Of secret-sapping gold. All their vile arts,
Their shameful honours, their perfidious gifts,

He greatly scorns ; and, if he must betray
His plundered country or his power resign,
A moment's parley were eternal shame :
Illustricus into private life again,
From dirty levees he unstained ascends,
And firm in senates stands the patriot's ground,
Or draws new vigour in the peaceful shade.
Aloof the Bashful Virtue hovered coy,   550
Proving by sweet distrust distrusted worth.
Rough Labour closed the train : and in his hand
Rude, callous, sinew-swelled, and black with toil,
Came manly Indignation. Sour he seems,
And more than seems, by lawless pride assailed ;
Yet kind at heart, and just, and generous ; there
No vengeance lurks, no pale insidious gall ;
Even in the very luxury of rage,
He softening can forgive a gallant foe ;
The nerve, support, and glory of the land !   560
Nor be Religion, rational and free,
Here passed in silence ; whose enraptured eye
Sees heaven with earth connected, human things
Linked to divine : who not from servile fear,
By rites for some weak tyrant incense fit,
The God of love adores, but from a heart
Effusing gladness, into pleasing awe
That now astonished swells, now in a calm
Of fearless confidence that smiles serene ;
That lives devotion, one continual hymn,   570
And then most grateful when heaven's bounty most
Is right enjoyed. This ever cheerful power
O'er the raised circle rayed superior day.
' I joyed to join the virtues, whence my reign
O'er Albion was to rise. Each cheering each,
And, like the circling planets from the sun,
All borrowing beams from me, a heightened zeal

Impatient fired us to commence our toils,
Or pleasures rather. Long the pungent time
Passed not in mutual hails ; but, through the land
Darting our light, we shone the fogs away.   581
    ' The virtues conquer with a single look.
Such grace, such beauty, such victorious light,
Live in their presence, stream in every glance,
That the soul won, enamoured, and refined,
Grows their own image, pure ethereal flame.
Hence the foul demons that oppose our reign
Would still from us deluded mortals wrap ;
Or in gross shades they drown the visual ray,
Or by the fogs of prejudice, where mix   590
Falsehood and truth confounded, foil the sense
With vain refracted images of bliss.
But chief around the court of flattered kings
They roll the dusky rampart, wall o'er wall
Of darkness pile, and with their thickest shade
Secure the throne. No savage Alp, the den
Of wolves and bears and monstrous things obscene,
That vex the swain and waste the country round,
Protected lies beneath a deeper cloud :
Yet there we sometimes send a searching ray.   600
As, at the sacred opening of the morn,
The prowling race retire ; so, pierced severe,
Before our potent blaze these demons fly,
And all their works dissolve—the whispered tale,
That, like the fabling Nile, no fountain knows ;
Fair-faced deceit, whose wily conscious eye
Ne'er looks direct ; the tongue that licks the dust,
But, when it safely dares, as prompt to sting ;
Smooth crocodile destruction, whose fell tears
Ensnare ; the Janus-face of courtly pride—   610
One to superiors heaves submissive eyes,
On hapless worth the other scowls disdain ;

Cheeks that for some weak tenderness, alone,
Some virtuous slip, can wear a blush ; the laugh
Profane, when midnight bowls disclose the heart,
At starving virtue and at virtue's fools ;
Determined to be broke, the plighted faith ;
Nay more, the godless oath, that knows no ties :
Soft-buzzing slander—silky moths, that eat
An honest name : the harpy hand and maw 620
Of avaricious luxury, who makes
The throne his shelter, venal laws his fort,
And, by his service, who betrays his king.

'Now turn your view, and mark from Celtic night
To present grandeur how my Britain rose.
' Bold were those Britons, who, the careless sons
Of nature, roamed the forest-bounds, at once
Their verdant city, high-embowering fane,
And the gay circle of their woodland wars :
For by the Druid taught, that death but shifts
The vital scene, they that prime fear despised ; 631
And, prone to rush on steel, disdained to spare
An ill-saved life that must again return.
Erect from nature's hand, by tyrant force
And still more tyrant custom unsubdued,
Man knows no master save creating heaven,
Or such as choice and common good ordain.
This general sense, with which the nations I
Promiscuous fire, in Britons burned intense,
Of future times prophetic. Witness, Rome, 640
Who saw'st thy Caesar from the naked land,
Whose only fort was British hearts, repelled,
To seek Pharsalian wreaths. Witness the toil,
The blood of ages, bootless to secure
Beneath an empire's yoke a stubborn isle,
Disputed hard and never quite subdued.

The north remained untouched, where those who
　　scorned
To stoop retired ; and, to their keen effort
Yielding at last, recoiled the Roman power.
In vain, unable to sustain the shock,　　　　650
From sea to sea desponding legions raised
The wall immense—and yet, on summer's eve,
While sport his lambkins round, the shepherd's gaze.
Continual o'er it burst the northern storm ;
As often, checked, receded—threatening hoarse
A swift return.　But the devouring flood
No more endured control, when, to support
The last remains of empire, was recalled
The weary Roman, and the Briton lay
Unnerved, exhausted, spiritless, and sunk.　　660
Great proof ! how men enfeeble into slaves.
The sword behind him flashed ; before him roared,
Deaf to his woes, the deep.　Forlorn, around
He rolled his eye—not sparkling ardent flame
As when Caractacus to battle led
Silurian swains, and Boadicea taught
Her raging troops the miseries of slaves.
　' Then (sad relief !) from the bleak coast that hears
The German Ocean roar, deep-blooming, strong,
And yellow-haired, the blue-eyed Saxon came.
He came implored, but came with other aim　671
Than to protect.　For conquest and defence
Suffices the same arm.　With the fierce race
Poured in a fresh invigorating stream,
Blood, where unquelled a mighty spirit glowed.
Rash war and perilous battle their delight ;
And immature, and red with glorious wounds,
Unpeaceful death their choice—deriving thence
A right to feast and drain immortal bowls
In Odin's hall, whose blazing roof resounds　　680

The genial uproar of those shades who fall
In desperate fight or by some brave attempt ;
And, though more polished times the martial creed
Disown, yet still the fearless habit lives.
Nor were the surly gifts of war their all.
Wisdom was likewise theirs, indulgent laws,
The calm gradations of art-nursing peace,
And matchless orders, the deep basis still
On which ascends my British reign. Untamed
To the refining subtleties of slaves, 690
They brought a happy government along ;
Formed by that freedom which, with secret voice,
Impartial nature teaches all her sons,
And which of old through the whole Scythian mass
I strong inspired. Monarchical their state,
But prudently confined, and mingled wise
Of each harmonious power : only, too much,
Imperious war into their rule infused,
Prevailed their general-king and chieftain-thanes.
 ' In many a field, by civil fury stained, 700
Bled the discordant Heptarchy ; and long
(Educing good from ill) the battle groaned
Ere, blood-cemented, Anglo-Saxons saw
Egbert and peace on one united throne.
 ' No sooner dawned the fair disclosing calm
Of brighter days, when lo ! the north anew,
With stormy nations black, on England poured
Woes the severest e'er a people felt.
The Danish raven, lured by annual prey,
Hung o'er the land incessant. Fleet on fleet 710
Of barbarous pirates, unremitting tore
The miserable coast. Before them stalked,
Far seen, the demon of devouring flame ;
Rapine, and murder, all with blood besmeared,
Without or ear or eye or feeling heart :

While close behind them marched the sallow power
Of desolating famine, who delights
In grass-grown cities and in desert fields ;
And purple-spotted pestilence, by whom
Even friendship scared, in sickening horror sinks
Each social sense and tenderness of life.   721
Fixing at last, the sanguinary race
Spread, from the Humber's loud resounding shore
To where the Thames devolves his gentle maze,
And with superior arm the Saxon awed.
But superstition first, and monkish dreams
And monk-directed cloister-seeking kings
Had eat away his vigour, eat away
His edge of courage, and depressed the soul
Of conquering freedom which he once respired.   730
Thus cruel ages passed ; and rare appeared
White-mantled Peace, exulting o'er the vale ;
As when, with Alfred, from the wilds she came
To policed cities and protected plains.
Thus by degrees the Saxon empire sunk,
Then set entire in Hastings' bloody field.
  ' Compendious war ! (on Britain's glory bent,
So fate ordained) in that decisive day,
The haughty Norman seized at once an isle
For which through many a century in vain   740
The Roman, Saxon, Dane had toiled and bled.
Of Gothic nations this the final burst ;
And, mixed the genius of these people all,
Their virtues mixed in one exalted stream,
Here the rich tide of English blood grew full.
  ' Awhile my spirit slept ; the land awhile,
Affrighted, drooped beneath despotic rage.
Instead of Edward's equal gentle laws,
The furious victor's partial will prevailed.
All prostrate lay ; and, in the secret shade,   750

Deep-stung but fearful, Indignation gnashed
His teeth. Of freedom, property, despoiled,
And of their bulwark, arms ; with castles crushed,
With ruffians quartered o'er the bridled land—
The shivering wretches, at the curfew sound,
Dejected shrunk into their sordid beds,
And, through the mournful gloom, of ancient times
Mused sad, or dreamt of better. Even to feed
A tyrant's idle sport the peasant starved :
To the wild herd the pasture of the tame,　　　760
The cheerful hamlet, spiry town was given,
And the brown forest roughened wide around.
　' But this so dead, so vile submission long
Endured not. Gathering force, my gradual flame
Shook off the mountain of tyrannic sway.
Unused to bend, impatient of control,
Tyrants themselves the common tyrant checked.
The church, by kings intractable and fierce,
Denied her portion of the plundered state,
Or, tempted by the timorous and weak,　　　770
To gain new ground first taught their rapine law.
The Barons next a nobler league began,
Both those of English and of Norman race,
In one fraternal nation blended now,
The nation of the free ! Pressed by a band
Of Patriots, ardent as the summer's noon
That looks delighted on, the tyrant see !
Mark ! how with feigned alacrity he bears
His strong reluctance down, his dark revenge,
And gives the charter by which life indeed　　　780
Becomes of price, a glory to be man.
　' Through this, and through succeeding reigns affirmed
These long-contested rights, the wholesome winds
Of opposition hence began to blow;

And often since have lent the country life.
Before their breath corruption's insect-blights,
The darkening clouds of evil counsel, fly ;
Or, should they sounding swell, a putrid court,
A pestilential ministry, they purge,
And ventilated states renew their bloom.   790
  ' Though with the tempered monarchy here mixed
Aristocratic sway, the people still,
Flattered by this or that, as interest leaned,
No full protection knew. For me reserved,
And for my commons, was that glorious turn.
They crowned my first attempt—in senates rose,
The fort of freedom ! Slow till then, alone
Had worked that general liberty, that soul
Which generous nature breathes, and which, when left
By me to bondage was corrupted Rome,   800
I through the northern nations wide diffused.
Hence many a people, fierce with freedom, rushed
From the rude iron regions of the north,
To Libyan deserts swarm protruding swarm,
And poured new spirit through a slavish world.
Yet, o'er these Gothic states, the king and chiefs
Retained the high prerogative of war,
And with enormous property engrossed
The mingled power. But on Britannia's shore
Now present, I to raise my reign began   810
By raising the democracy, the third
And broadest bulwark of the guarded state.
Then was the full the perfect plan disclosed
Of Britain's matchless constitution, mixed
Of mutual checking and supporting powers,
King, lords, and commons ; nor the name of free
Deserving, while the vassal-many drooped :
For, since the moment of the whole they form,
So, as depressed or raised, the balance they

Of public welfare and of glory cast.   820
Mark from this period the continual proof.
' When kings of narrow genius, minion-rid,
Neglecting faithful worth for fawning slaves;
Proudly regardless of their people's plaints,
And poorly passive of insulting foes ;
Double, not prudent, obstinate, not firm,
Their mercy fear, necessity their faith ;
Instead of generous fire, presumptuous, hot,
Rash to resolve, and slothful to perform ;
Tyrants at once and slaves, imperious, mean,   830
To want rapacious joining shameful waste ;
By counsels weak and wicked, easy roused
To paltry schemes of absolute command,
To seek their splendour in their sure disgrace,
And in a broken ruined people wealth—
When such o'ercast the state, no bond of love,
No heart, no soul, no unity, no nerve
Combined the loose disjointed public, lost
To fame abroad, to happiness at home.
' But when an Edward, and a Henry breathed 840
Through the charmed whole one all-exerting soul ;
Drawn sympathetic from his dark retreat,
When wide-attracted merit round them glowed ;
When counsels just, extensive, generous, firm,
Amid the maze of state, determined kept
Some ruling point in view ; when, on the stock
Of public good and glory grafted, spread
Their palms, their laurels—or, if thence they strayed,
Swift to return, and patient of restraint ;
When regal state, pre-eminence of place,   850
They scorned to deem pre-eminence of ease,
To be luxurious drones, that only rob
The busy hive ; as in distinction, power,

840 a Henry] an Henry ed. 1738

Indulgence, honour, and advantage first—
When they too claimed in virtue, danger, toil
Superior rank, with equal hand prepared
To guard the subject and to quell the foe :
When such with me their vital influence shed,
No muttered grievance, hopeless sigh was heard ;
No foul distrust through wary senates ran,   860
Confined their bounty, and their ardour quenched ;
On aid, unquestioned, liberal aid was given ;
Safe in their conduct, by their valour fired,
Fond where they led victoricus armies rushed ;
And Cressy, Poitiers, Agincourt proclaim
What kings supported by almighty love
And people fired with liberty can do.
   ' Be veiled the savage reigns, when kindred rage
The numerous once Plantagenets devoured,
A race to vengeance vowed ! and when, oppressed
By private feuds, almost extinguished lay   871
My quivering flame. But, in the next, behold !
A cautious tyrant lend it oil anew.
   ' Proud, dark, suspicious, brooding o'er his gold,
As how to fix his throne he jealous cast
His crafty views around ; pierced with a ray,
Which on his timid mind I darted full,
He marked the barons of excessive sway,
At pleasure making and unmaking kings ;
And hence, to crush these petty tyrants, planned
A law, that let them, by the silent waste   881
Of luxury, their landed wealth diffuse,
And with that wealth their implicated power.
By soft degrees a mighty change ensued,
Even working to this day. With streams, deduced
From these diminished floods, the country smiled.
As, when impetuous from the snow-heaped Alps,
To vernal suns relenting, pours the Rhine,

While undivided, oft with wasteful sweep
He foams along ; but through Batavian meads,
Branched into fair canals, indulgent flows,   891
Waters a thousand fields, and culture, trade,
Towns, meadows, gliding ships, and villas mixed,
A rich, a wondrous landscape rises round.
' His furious son the soul-enslaving chain,
Which many a doting venerable age
Had link by link strong twisted round the land,
Shook off. No longer could be borne a power,
From heaven pretended, to deceive, to void
Each solemn tie, to plunder without bounds,   900
To curb the generous soul, to fool mankind ;
And, wild at last, to plunge into a sea
Of blood and horror. The returning light,
That first through Wickliff streaked the priestly gloom,
Now burst in open day. Bared to the blaze,
Forth from the haunts of superstition crawled
Her motley sons, fantastic figures all ;
And, wide dispersed, their useless fetid wealth
In graceful labour bloomed, and fruits of peace.
' Trade, joined to these, on every sea displayed
A daring canvas, poured with every tide   911
A golden flood. From other worlds were rolled
The guilty glittering stores, whose fatal charms,
By the plain Indian happily despised,
Yet worked his woe ; and to the blissful groves,
Where nature lived herself among her sons,
And innocence and joy for ever dwelt,
Drew rage unknown to pagan climes before,
The worst the zeal-inflamed barbarian drew.
Be no such horrid commerce, Britain, thine !   920
But want for want with mutual aid supply.
' The commons thus enriched, and powerful grown,
Against the barons weighed. Eliza then,

Amid these doubtful motions steady, gave
The beam to fix. She, like the secret eye
That never closes on a guarded world,
So sought, so marked, so seized the public good
That, self-supported, without one ally,
She awed her inward, quelled her circling foes.
Inspired by me, beneath her sheltering arm,　　930
In spite of raging universal sway
And raging seas repressed, the Belgic states,
My bulwark on the continent, arose.
Matchless in all the spirit of her days!
With confidence unbounded, fearless love
Elate, her fervent people waited gay,
Cheerful demanded the long threatened fleet,
And dashed the pride of Spain around their isle.
Nor ceased the British thunder here to rage :
The deep, reclaimed, obeyed its awful call ;　　940
In fire and smoke Iberian ports involved,
The trembling foe even to the centre shook
Of their new conquered world, and, skulking, stole
By veering winds their Indian treasure home.
Meantime, peace, plenty, justice, science, arts,
With softer laurels crowned her happy reign.
　‘ As yet uncircumscribed the regal power,
And wild and vague prerogative remained—
A wide voracious gulf, where swallowed oft
The helpless subject lay. This to reduce　　950
To the just limit was my great effort.
　‘ By means that evil seem to narrow man
Superior beings work their mystic will :
From storm and trouble thus a settled calm,
At last, effulgent, o’er Britannia smiled.
　‘ The gathering tempest, heaven - commissioned,
　　came,
Came in the prince, who, drunk with flattery, dreamt

His vain pacific counsels ruled the world ;
Though scorned abroad, bewildered in a maze
Of fruitless treaties ; while at home enslaved,   960
And by a worthless crew insatiate drained,
He lost his people's confidence and love :
Irreparable loss ! whence crowns become
An anxious burden. Years inglorious passed :
Triumphant Spain the vengeful draught enjoyed—
Abandoned Frederick pined, and Raleigh bled.
But nothing that to these internal broils,
That rancour, he began ; while lawless sway
He, with his slavish doctors, tried to rear
On metaphysic, on enchanted ground,   970
And all the mazy quibbles of the schools :
As if for one, and sometimes for the worst,
Heaven had mankind in vengeance only made.
Vain the pretence ! not so the dire effect,
The fierce, the foolish discord thence derived,
That tears the country still, by party rage
And ministerial clamour kept alive.
In action weak, and for the wordy war
Best fitted, faint this prince pursued his claim—
Content to teach the subject herd, how great,   980
How sacred he ! how despicable they !
    ' But his unyielding son these doctrines drank
With all a bigot's rage (who never damps
By reasoning his fire); and what they taught,
Warm and tenacious, into practice pushed.
Senates, in vain, their kind restraint applied :
The more they struggled to support the laws,
His justice-dreading ministers the more
Drove him beyond their bounds. Tired with the check
Of faithful love, and with the flattery pleased   990
Of false designing guilt, the fountain he
Of public wisdom and of justice shut.

Wide mourned the land. Straight to the voted aid
Free, cordial, large, of never-failing source,
The illegal imposition followed harsh,
With execration given, or ruthless squeezed
From an insulted people by a band
Of the worst ruffians, those of tyrant power.
Oppression walked at large, and poured abroad
Her unrelenting train—informers, spies,   1000
Bloodhounds, that sturdy freedom to the grave
Pursue ; projectors of aggrieving schemes,
Commerce to load for unprotected seas,
To sell the starving many to the few,
And drain a thousand ways the exhausted land.
Even from that place whence healing peace should
        flow,
And gospel truth, inhuman bigots shed
Their poison round ; and on the venal bench,
Instead of justice, party held the scale,
And violence the sword. Afflicted years,   1010
Too patient, felt at last their vengeance full.
 ' Mid the low murmurs of submissive fear
And mingled rage my Hampden raised his voice,
And to the laws appealed ; the laws no more
In judgement sat, behoved some other ear.
When instant from the keen resentive north,
By long oppression by religion roused,
The guardian army came. Beneath its wing
Was called, though meant to furnish hostile aid,
The more than Roman senate. There a flame   1020
Broke out that cleared, consumed, renewed the land.
In deep emotion hurled, nor Greece nor Rome
Indignant bursting from a tyrant's chain,
While, full of me, each agitated soul
Strung every nerve and flamed in every eye,
Had e'er beheld such light and heat combined !

Such heads and hearts ! such dreadful zeal, led on
By calm majestic wisdom, taught its course
What nuisance to devour ; such wisdcm fired
With unabating zeal, and aimed sincere   1030
To clear the weedy state, restore the laws,
And for the future to secure their sway.
  ' This then the purpose of my mildest sons.
But man is blind. A nation once inflamed
(Chief, should the breath of factious fury blow,
With the wild rage of mad enthusiast swelled)
Not easy cools again. From breast to breast,
From eye to eye, the kindling passions mix
In heightened blaze ; and, ever wise and just,
High heaven to gracious ends directs the storm. 1040
Thus in one conflagration Britain wrapt,
And by confusion's lawless sons despoiled,
King, lords, and commons, thundering to the ground,
Successive, rushed—Lo ! from their ashes rose,
Gay-beaming radiant youth, the phoenix State.
  ' The grievous yoke of vassalage, the yoke
Of private life, lay by those flames dissolved ;
And, from the wasteful, the luxurious king,
Was purchased that which taught the young to bend.
Stronger restored, the commons taxed the whole, 1050
And built on that eternal rock their power.
The crown, of its hereditary wealth
Despoiled, on senates more dependent grew,
And they more frequent, more assured. Yet lived,
And in full vigour spread, that bitter root,
The passive doctrines—by their patrons first
Opposed ferocious, when they touch themselves.
  ' This wild delusive cant ; the rash cabal
Of hungry courtiers, ravenous for prey ;
The bigot, restless in a double chain   1060
To bind anew the land ; the constant need

Of finding faithless means, of shifting forms,
And flattering senates to supply his waste ;
These tore some moments from the careless prince,
And in his breast awaked the kindred plan.
By dangerous softness long he mined his way—
By subtle arts, dissimulation deep,
By sharing what corruption showered profuse,
By breathing wide the gay licentious plague,
And pleasing manners, fitted to deceive.   1070
   ' At last subsided the delirious joy,
On whose high billow, from the saintly reign,
The nation drove too far. A pensioned king,
Against his country bribed by Gallic gold ;
The port pernicious sold, the Scylla since
And fell Charybdis of the British seas ;
Freedom attacked abroad, with surer blow
To cut it off at home ; the saviour-league
Of Europe broke ; the progress even advanced
Of universal sway which to reduce   1080
Such seas of blood and treasure Britain cost ;
The millions, by a generous people given,
Or squandered vile, or to corrupt, disgrace,
And awe the land with forces not their own
Employed ; the darling church herself betrayed—
All these, broad glaring, oped the general eye,
And waked my spirit, the resisting soul.
   ' Mild was, at first, and half ashamed the check
Of senates, shook from the fantastic dream
Of absolute submission, tenets vile !   1090
Which slaves would blush to own, and which, reduced
To practise, always honest nature shock.
Not even the mask removed, and the fierce front
Of tyranny disclosed ; nor trampled laws ;
Nor seized each badge of freedom through the land ;
Nor Sidney bleeding for the unpublished page ;

Nor on the bench avowed corruption placed,
And murderous rage itself, in Jefferies' form ;
Nor endless acts of arbitrary power,
Cruel, and false, could raise the public arm.   1100
Distrustful, scattered, of combining chiefs
Devoid, and dreading blind rapacious war,
The patient public turns not till impelled
To the near verge of ruin. Hence I roused
The bigot king, and hurried fated on
His measures immature. But chief his zeal,
Out-flaming Rome herself, portentous scared
The troubled nation : Mary's horrid days
To fancy bleeding rose, and the dire glare
Of Smithfield lightened in its eyes anew.   1110
Yet silence reigned. Each on another scowled
Rueful amazement, pressing down his rage—
As, mustering vengeance, the deep thunder frowns,
Awfully still, waiting the high command
To spring. Straight from his country, Europe, saved
To save Britannia, lo ! my darling son,
Than hero more ! the patriot of mankind !
Immortal Nassau came. I hushed the deep
By demons roused, and bade the listed winds,
Still shifting as behoved, with various breath   1120
Waft the deliverer to the longing shore.
See, wide alive, the foaming channel bright
With swelling sails and all the pride of war !
Delightful view when justice draws the sword !
And mark, diffusing ardent soul around
And sweet contempt of death, my streaming flag !
Even adverse navies blessed the binding gale,
Kept down the glad acclaim, and silent joyed.
Arrived, the pomp and not the waste of arms
His progress marked. The faint opposing host   1130
For once, in yielding their best victory found,

And by desertion proved exalted faith :
While his the bloodless conquest of the heart,
Shouts without groan, and triumph without war.
 ' Then dawned the period destined to confine
The surge of wild prerogative, to raise
A mound restraining its imperious rage,
And bid the raving deep no farther flow.
Nor were, without that fence, the swallowed state
Better than Belgian plains without their dykes,
Sustaining weighty seas. This, often saved   1141
By more than human hand, the public saw,
And seized the white-winged moment. Pleased to
     yield
Destructive power, a wise heroic prince
Even lent his aid. Thrice happy ! did they know
Their happiness, Britannia's bounded kings.
What though not theirs the boast in dungeon glooms
To plunge bold freedom ; or to cheerless wilds
To drive him from the cordial face of friend ;
Or fierce to strike him at the midnight hour   1150
By mandate blind—not justice, that delights
To dare the keenest eye of open day ?
What though no glory to control the laws
And make injurious will their only rule
They deem it ? What though, tools of wanton power,
Pestiferous armies swarm not at their call ?
What though they give not a relentless crew
Of civil furies, proud oppression's fangs !
To tear at pleasure the dejected land,
With starving labour pampering idle waste ?   1160
To clothe the naked, feed the hungry, wipe
The guiltless tear from lone affliction's eye,
To raise hid merit, set the alluring light
Of virtue high to view, to nourish arts,
Direct the thunder of an injured state,

Make a whole glorious people sing for joy,
Bless humankind, and through the downward depth
Of future times to spread that better sun
Which lights up British soul—for deeds like these,
The dazzling fair career unbounded lies ;   1170
While (still superior bliss !) the dark abrupt
Is kindly barred, the precipice of ill.
O luxury divine ! O poor to this,
Ye giddy glories of despotic thrones !
By this, by this indeed, is imaged heaven,
By boundless good without the power of ill.
    ' And now behold ! exalted as the cope
That swells immense o'er many-peopled earth,
And like it free, my fabric stands complete,
The palace of the laws. To the four heavens   1180
Four gates impartial thrown, unceasing crowds,
With kings themselves the hearty peasant mixed,
Pour urgent in. And though to different ranks
Responsive place belongs, yet equal spreads
The sheltering roof o'er all ; while plenty flows,
And glad contentment echoes round the whole.
Ye floods, descend ! Ye winds, confirming, blow !
Nor outward tempest, nor corrosive time,
Nought but the felon undermining hand
Of dark corruption, can its frame dissolve,   1190
And lay the toil of ages in the dust.'

THE CONTENTS OF PART V

THE author addresses the Goddess of Liberty, marking the happiness and grandeur of Great Britain, as arising from her influence, *to verse* 87. She resumes her discourse, and points out the chief Virtues which are necessary to maintain her establishment there, *to verse* 373. Recommends, as its last ornament and finishing, Sciences, Fine Arts, and Public works ; the encouragement of these urged from the example of France, though under a despotic government, *to verse* 548. The whole concludes with a prospect of future times, given by the Goddess of Liberty : this described by the author as it passes in vision before him.

PART V. THE PROSPECT

[Published, 1736.]

HERE interposing, as the Goddess paused ;—
' O blest Britannia ! in thy presence blest,
Thou guardian of mankind ! whence spring alone
All human grandeur, happiness, and fame ;
For toil, by thee protected, feels no pain,
The poor man's lot with milk and honey flows,
And, gilded with thy rays, even death looks gay.
Let other lands the potent blessings boast
Of more exalting suns. Let Asia's woods,
Untended, yield the vegetable fleece :   10
And let the little insect-artist form,
On higher life intent, its silken tomb.
Let wondering rocks, in radiant birth, disclose
The various tinctured children of the sun.
From the prone beam let more delicious fruits
A flavour drink that in one piercing taste
Bids each combine. Let Gallic vineyards burst
With floods of joy ; with mild balsamic juice

The Tuscan olive. Let Arabia breathe
Her spicy gales, her vital gums distil.   20
Turbid with gold, let southern rivers flow,
And orient floods draw soft, o'er pearls, their maze.
Let Afric vaunt her treasures ; let Peru
Deep in her bowels her own ruin breed,
The yellow traitor that her bliss betrayed—
Unequalled bliss !—and to unequalled rage !
Yet nor the gorgeous east, nor golden south,
Nor, in full prime, that new discovered world
Where flames the falling day, in wealth and praise
Shall with Britannia vie while, Goddess, she   30
Derives her praise from thee, her matchless charms.
Her hearty fruits the hand of freedom own ;
And warm with culture, her thick clustering fields,
Prolific teem. Eternal verdure crowns
Her meads ; her gardens smile eternal spring.
She gives the hunter-horse, unquelled by toil,
Ardent to rush into the rapid chase ;
She, whitening o'er her downs, diffusive pours
Unnumbered flocks ; she weaves the fleecy robe,
That wraps the nations ; she to lusty droves   40
The richest pasture spreads ; and, hers, deep-wave
Autumnal seas of pleasing plenty round.
These her delights—and by no baneful herb,
No darting tiger, no grim lion's glare,
No fierce-descending wolf, no serpent rolled
In spires immense progressive o'er the land
Disturbed. Enlivening these, add cities full
Of wealth, of trade, of cheerful toiling crowds ;
Add thriving towns ; add villages and farms,
Innumerous sowed along the lively vale,   50
Where bold unrivalled peasants happy dwell ;
Add ancient seats, with venerable oaks
Embosomed high, while kindred floods below

o

Wind through the mead ; and those of modern hand
More pompous add, that splendid shine afar.
Need I her limpid lakes, her rivers name,
Where swarm the finny race ? Thee, chief, O Thames !
On whose each tide, glad with returning sails,
Flows in the mingled harvest of mankind ?
And thee, thou Severn, whose prodigious swell   60
And waves resounding imitate the main ?
Why need I name her deep capacious ports,
That point around the world ? and why her seas ?
All ocean is her own, and every land
To whom her ruling thunder ocean bears.
She too the mineral feeds—the obedient lead ;
The warlike iron, nor the peaceful less,
Forming of life art-civilized the bond ;
And that the Tyrian merchant sought of old,
Not dreaming then of Britain's brighter fame.   70
She rears to freedom an undaunted race :
Compatriot zealous, hospitable, kind,
Hers the warm Cambrian ; hers the lofty Scot,
To hardship tamed, active in arts and arms,
Fired with a restless, an impatient flame,
That leads him raptured where ambition calls ;
And English merit hers—where meet combined
Whate'er high fancy, sound judicious thought,
An ample generous heart, undrooping soul,
And firm tenacious valour can bestow.   80
Great nurse of fruits, of flocks, of commerce, she !
Great nurse of men ! by thee, O Goddess, taught,
Her old renown I trace, disclose her source
Of wealth, of grandeur, and to Britons sing
A strain the muses never touched before.
  ' But how shall this thy mighty kingdom stand ?
On what unyielding base ? how finished shine ? '
  At this her eye, collecting all its fire,

Beamed more than human ; and her awful voice
Majestic thus she raised : ' To Britons bear   90
This closing strain, and with intenser note
Loud let it sound in their awakened ear :—
  ' On virtue can alone my kingdom stand,
On public virtue, every virtue joined.
For, lost this social cement of mankind,
The greatest empires by scarce-felt degrees
Will moulder soft away, till, tottering loose,
They prone at last to total ruin rush.
Unblessed by virtue, government a league
Becomes, a circling junto of the great,   100
To rob by law ; religion mild, a yoke
To tame the stooping soul, a trick of state
To mask their rapine, and to share the prey.
What are without it senates, save a face
Of consultation deep and reason free,
While the determined voice and heart are sold ?
What boasted freedom, save a sounding name ?
And what election, but a market vile
Of slaves self-bartered ?   Virtue ! without thee,
There is no ruling eye, no nerve, in states ;   110
War has no vigour, and no safety peace :
Even justice warps to party, laws oppress,
Wide through the land their weak protection fails,
First broke the balance, and then scorned the sword.
Thus nations sink, society dissolves ;
Rapine and guile and violence break loose,
Everting life, and turning love to gall ;
Man hates the face of man, and Indian woods
And Libya's hissing sands to him are tame.
  ' By those three virtues be the frame sustained   120
Of British freedom—independent life ;
Integrity in office ; and, o'er all
Supreme, a passion for the commonweal.

' Hail ! independence, hail ! heaven's next best gift
To that of life and an immortal soul !
The life of life ! that to the banquet high
And sober meal gives taste ; to the bowed roof
Fair-dreamed repose, and to the cottage charms.
Of public freedom, hail, thou secret source !
Whose streams, from every quarter confluent, form 130
My better Nile, that nurses human life.
By rills from thee deduced, irriguous, fed,
The private field looks gay, with nature's wealth
Abundant flows, and blooms with each delight
That nature craves. Its happy master there,
The only freeman, walks his pleasing round—
Sweet-featured peace attending ; fearless truth ;
Firm resolution ; goodness, blessing all
That can rejoice ; contentment, surest friend ;
And, still fresh stores from nature's book derived,
Philosophy, companion ever new.   141
These cheer his rural, and sustain or fire,
When into action called, his busy hours.
Meantime true-judging moderate desires,
Economy and taste, combined, direct
His clear affairs, and from debauching fiends
Secure his little kingdom. Nor can those
Whom fortune heaps, without these virtues, reach
That truce with pain, that animated ease,
That self-enjoyment springing from within,   150
That independence, active or retired,
Which make the soundest bliss of man below :
But, lost beneath the rubbish of their means,
And drained by wants to nature all unknown,
A wandering, tasteless, gaily wretched train,
Though rich, are beggars, and though noble, slaves.
    ' Lo ! damned to wealth, at what a gross expense
They purchase disappointment, pain, and shame.

Instead of hearty hospitable cheer,
See how the hall with brutal riot flows ;   160
While, in the foaming flood fermenting steeped,
The country maddens into party rage.
Mark those disgraceful piles of wood and stone ;
Those parks and gardens, where, his haunts betrimmed,
And nature by presumptuous art oppressed,
The woodland genius mourns. See the full board
That steams disgust, and bowls that give no joy !
No truth invited there to feed the mind,
Nor wit the wine-rejoicing reason quaffs.
Hark how the dome with insolence resounds!   170
With those retained by vanity to scare
Repose and friends. To tyrant fashion, mark
The costly worship paid, to the broad gaze
Of fools ! From still delusive day to day,
Led an eternal round of lying hope,
See, self-abandoned, how they roam adrift
Dashed o'er the town, a miserable wreck !
Then to adore some warbling eunuch turned,
With Midas' ears they crowd ; or to the buzz
Of masquerade unblushing ; or, to show   180
Their scorn of nature, at the tragic scene
They mirthful sit, or prove the comic true.
But, chief, behold around the rattling board,
The civil robbers ranged ! and even the fair,
The tender fair, each sweetness laid aside,
As fierce for plunder as all-licensed troops
In some sacked city. Thus dissolved their wealth,
Without one generous luxury dissolved,
Or quartered on it many a needless want,
At the thronged levee bends the venal tribe ;   190
With fair but faithless smiles each varnished o'er,
Each smooth as those that mutually deceive,
And for their falsehood each despising each ;

Till, shook their patron by the wintry winds,
Wide flies the withered shower, and leaves him bare.
O far superior Afric's sable sons
By merchant pilfered to these willing slaves !
And rich as unsqueezed favourite to them
Is he who can his virtue boast alone !
  ' Britons ! be firm ; nor let corruption sly   200
Twine round your heart indissoluble chains.
The steel of Brutus burst the grosser bonds
By Caesar cast o'er Rome ; but still remained
The soft enchanting fetters of the mind,
And other Caesars rose. Determined, hold
Your independence ; for, that once destroyed,
Unfounded, freedom is a morning dream
That flits aerial from the spreading eye.
  ' Forbid it, Heaven ! that ever I need urge
Integrity in office on my sons ;   210
Inculcate common honour—not to rob ;
And whom ? the gracious, the confiding hand,
That lavishly rewards ; the toiling poor,
Whose cup with many a bitter drop is mixed,
The guardian public, every face they see,
And every friend,—nay, in effect themselves.
As in familiar life the villain's fate
Admits no cure ; so, when a desperate age
At this arrives, I the devoted race
Indignant spurn, and hopeless soar away.   220
  ' But, ah, too little known to modern times !
Be not the noblest passion passed unsung,
That ray peculiar, from unbounded love
Effused, which kindles the heroic soul—
Devotion to the public. Glorious flame !
Celestial ardour ! in what unknown worlds,
Profusely scattered through the blue immense,
Hast thou been blessing myriads, since in Rome,

Old virtuous Rome, so many deathless names
From thee their lustre drew ? since, taught by thee,
Their poverty put splendour to the blush,   231
Pain grew luxurious, and even death delight ?
O wilt thou ne'er, in thy long period, look,
With blaze direct, on this my last retreat ?
  ' 'Tis not enough, from self right-understood
Reflected, that thy rays inflame the heart :
Though virtue not disdains appeals to self,
Dreads not the trial ; all her joys are true,
Nor is there any real joy save hers.
Far less the tepid, the declaiming race,   240
Foes to corruption, to its wages friends,
Or those whom private passions, for a while,
Beneath my standard list, can they suffice
To raise and fix the glory of my reign !
  ' An active flood of universal love
Must swell the breast. First, in effusion wide,
The restless spirit roves creation round,
And seizes every being ; stronger then
It tends to life, whate'er the kindred search
Of bliss allies ; then, more collected still,   250
It urges human kind ; a passion grown,
At last the central parent public calls
Its utmost effort forth, awakes each sense,
The comely, grand, and tender. Without this,
This awful pant, shook from sublimer powers
Than those of self, this heaven-infused delight,
This moral gravitation, rushing prone
To press the public good, my system soon,
Traverse, to several selfish centres drawn,
Will reel to ruin—while for ever shut   260
Stand the bright portals of desponding fame.
  ' From sordid self shoot up no shining deeds,
None of those ancient lights that gladden earth,

Give grace to being, and arouse the brave
To just ambition, virtue's quickening fire!
Life tedious grows, an idly bustling round,
Filled up with actions animal and mean,
A dull gazette! The impatient reader scorns
The poor historic page; till kindly comes
Oblivion, and redeems a people's shame.   270
Not so the times when, emulation-stung,
Greece shone in genius, science, and in arts,
And Rome in virtues dreadful to be told!
To live was glory then! and charmed mankind,
Through the deep periods of devolving time,
Those, raptured, copy; these, astonished, read.
  'True, a corrupted state, with every vice
And every meanness foul, this passion damps.
Who can unshocked behold the cruel eye?
The pale inveigling smile? the ruffian front?   280
The wretch abandoned to relentless self,
Equally vile if miser or profuse?
Powers not of God, assiduous to corrupt?
The fell deputed tyrant, who devours
The poor and weak, at distance from redress?
Delirious faction bellowing loud my name?
The false fair-seeming patriot's hollow boast?
A race resolved on bondage, fierce for chains,
My sacred rights a merchandise alone
Esteeming, and to work their feeder's will   290
By deeds, a horror to mankind, prepared,
As were the dregs of Romulus of old?
Who these indeed can undetesting see?—
But who unpitying? to the generous eye
Distress is virtue; and, though self-betrayed,
A people struggling with their fate must rouse
The hero's throb. Nor can a land at once
Be lost to virtue quite. How glorious then!

Fit luxury for gods ! to save the good,
Protect the feeble, dash bold vice aside,   300
Depress the wicked, and restore the frail.
Posterity, besides—the young are pure,
And sons may tinge their father's cheek with shame.
  ' Should then the times arrive(which Heaven avert!)
That Britons bend unnerved, not by the force
Of arms, more generous and more manly, quelled,
But by corruption's soul-dejecting arts,
Arts impudent and gross ! by their own gold,
In part bestowed to bribe them to give all ;
With party raging, or immersed in sloth,   310
Should they Britannia's well fought laurels yield
To slily conquering Gaul, even from her brow
Let her own naval oak be basely torn
By such as tremble at the stiffening gale,
And nerveless sink while others sing rejoiced;
Or (darker prospect ! scarce one gleam behind
Disclosing) should the broad corruptive plague
Breathe from the city to the farthest hut
That sits serene within the forest shade,
The fevered people fire, inflame their wants   320
And their luxurious thirst, so gathering rage
That, were a buyer found, they stand prepared
To sell their birthright for a cooling draught;
Should shameless pens for plain corruption plead,
The hired assassins of the commonweal !
Deemed the declaiming rant of Greece and Rome ;
Should public virtue grow the public scoff,
Till private, failing, staggers through the land—
Till round the city loose mechanic want,
Dire-prowling nightly, makes the cheerful haunts
Of men more hideous than Numidian wilds,   331
Nor from its fury sleeps the vale in peace,
And murders, horrors, perjuries abound—

Nay, till to lowest deeds the highest stoop,
The rich, like starving wretches, thirst for gold,
And those on whom the vernal showers of heaven
All-bounteous fall and that prime lot bestow,
A power to live to nature and themselves,
In sick attendance wear their anxious days
With fortune joyless, and with honours mean: 340
Meantime, perhaps, profusion flows around,
The waste of war without the works of peace,
No mark of millions in the gulf absorbed
Of uncreating vice, none but the rage
Of roused corruption still demanding more:
That very portion which (by faithful skill
Employed) might make the smiling public rear
Her ornamented head, drilled through the hands
Of mercenary tools, serves but to nurse
A locust band within, and in the bud   350
Leaves starved each work of dignity and use:
    ' I paint the worst; but should these times arrive,
If any nobler passion yet remain,
Let all my sons all parties fling aside,
Despise their nonsense, and together join ;
Let worth and virtue scorning low despair,
Exerted full, from every quarter shine
Commixed in heightened blaze. Light flashed to light,
Moral or intellectual, more intense
By giving glows—as, on pure winter's eve,   360
Gradual the stars effulge ; fainter, at first,
They straggling rise, but, when the radiant host,
In thick profusion poured, shine out immense,
Each casting vivid influence on each,
From pole to pole a glittering deluge plays
And worlds above rejoice and men below.
    ' But why to Britons this superfluous strain ?—

360 pure] poor (a misprint) ed. 1738.

Good nature, honest truth even somewhat blunt,
Of crooked baseness an indignant scorn,
A zeal unyielding in their country's cause,   370
And ready bounty, wont to dwell with them :
Nor only wont—wide o'er the land diffused,
In many a blest retirement still they dwell.
' To softer prospect turn we now the view,
To laurelled science, arts, and public works,
That lend my finished fabric comely pride,
Grandeur and grace. Of sullen genius he !
Cursed by the muses ! by the graces loathed !
Who deems beneath the public's high regard
These last enlivening touches of my reign.   380
However puffed with power and gorged with wealth
A nation be ; let trade enormous rise,
Let East and South their mingled treasure pour
Till, swelled impetuous, the corrupting flood
Burst o'er the city and devour the land—
Yet, these neglected, these recording arts,
Wealth rots, a nuisance ; and, oblivious sunk,
That nation must another Carthage lie.
If not by them, on monumental brass,
On sculptured marble, on the deathless page   390
Impressed, renown had left no trace behind :
In vain, to future times, the sage had thought,
The legislator planned, the hero found
A beauteous death, the patriot toiled in vain.
The awarders they of fame's immortal wreath !
They rouse ambition, they the mind exalt,
Give great ideas, lovely forms infuse,
Delight the general eye, and, dressed by them,
The moral Venus glows with double charms.
' Science, my close associate, still attends   400
Where'er I go. Sometimes, in simple guise,
She walks the furrow with the consul-swain.

Whispering unlettered wisdom to the heart
Direct ; or sometimes, in the pompous robe
Of fancy dressed, she charms Athenian wits,
And a whole sapient city round her burns.
Then o'er her brow Minerva's terrors nod :
With Xenophon, sometimes, in dire extremes
She breathes deliberate soul, and makes retreat
Unequalled glory : with the Theban sage,   410
Epaminondas, first and best of men !
Sometimes she bids the deep-embattled host,
Above the vulgar reach resistless formed,
March to sure conquest—never gained before !
Nor on the treacherous seas of giddy state
Unskilful she : when the triumphant tide
Of high-swoln empire wears one boundless smile,
And the gale tempts to new pursuits of fame,
Sometimes, with Scipio, she collects her sail,
And seeks the blissful shore of rural ease   420
Where, but the Aonian maids, no sirens sing ;
Or, should the deep-brewed tempest muttering rise,
While rocks and shoals perfidious lurk around,
With Tully she her wide-reviving light
To senates holds, a Catiline confounds,
And saves awhile from Caesar sinking Rome.
Such the kind power whose piercing eye dissolves
Each mental fetter and sets reason free ;
For me inspiring an enlightened zeal,
The more tenacious as the more convinced   430
How happy freemen, and how wretched slaves.
To Britons not unknown, to Britons full
The Goddess spreads her stores, the secret soul
That quickens trade, the breath unseen that wafts
To them the treasures of a balanced world.
But finer arts (save what the muse has sung
In daring flight, above all modern wing)

Neglected droop the head ; and public works,
Broke by corruption into private gain,
Not ornament, disgrace—not serve, destroy.   440
  ' Shall Britons, by their own joint wisdom ruled
Beneath one royal head, whose vital power
Connects, enlivens, and exerts the whole ;
In finer arts, and public works, shall they
To Gallia yield ? yield to a land that bends,
Depressed and broke, beneath the will of one ?
Of one who, should the unkingly thirst of gold,
Or tyrant passions, or ambition prompt,
Calls locust-armies o'er the blasted land,
Drains from its thirsty bounds the springs of wealth
His own insatiate reservoir to fill,   451
To the lone desert patriot-merit frowns,
Or into dungeons arts, when they, their chains
Indignant bursting, for their nobler works
All other licence scorn but truth's and mine.
Oh shame to think ! shall Britons, in the field
Unconquered still, the better laurel lose ?
Even in that monarch's reign who vainly dreamt,
By giddy power betrayed and flattered pride,
To grasp unbounded sway ; while, swarming round,
His armies dared all Europe to the field ;   461
To hostile hands while treasure flowed profuse,
And, that great source of treasure, subjects' blood,
Inhuman squandered, sickened every land ;
From Britain, chief, while my superior sons,
In vengeance rushing, dashed his idle hopes,
And bade his agonizing heart be low :
Even then, as in the golden calm of peace,
What public works, at home, what arts arose !
What various science shone ! what genius glowed !
  ' 'Tis not for me to paint, diffusive shot   471
O'er fair extents of land, the shining road ;

The flood-compelling arch ; the long canal,
Through mountains piercing and uniting seas ;
The dome resounding sweet with infant joy,
From famine saved, or cruel-handed shame ;
And that where valour counts his noble scars ;
The land where social pleasure loves to dwell,
Of the fierce demon, Gothic duel, freed ;
The robber from his farthest forest chased ;   480
The turbid city cleared and by degrees
Into sure peace, the best police, refined,
Magnificence, and grace, and decent joy.
Let Gallic bards record how honoured arts
And science, by despotic bounty blessed,
At distance flourished from my parent-eye ;
Restoring ancient taste how Boileau rose ;
How the big Roman soul shook in Corneille
The trembling stage ; in elegant Racine
How the more powerful though more humble voice
Of nature-painting Greece resistless breathed   491
The whole awakened heart ; how Molière's scene,
Chastised and regular, with well judged wit,
Not scattered wild, and native humour graced,
Was life itself ; to public honours raised,
How learning in warm seminaries spread,
And, more for glory than the small reward,
How emulation strove ; how their pure tongue
Almost obtained what was denied their arms ;
From Rome, awhile, how painting, courted long,   500
With Poussin came—ancient design, that lifts
A fairer front and looks another soul ;
How the kind art, that, of unvalued price,
The famed and only picture easy gives,
Refined her touch, and through the shadowed piece
All the live spirit of the painter poured ;
Coyest of arts, how sculpture northward deigned

A look, and bade ner Girardon arise ;
How lavish grandeur blazed, the barren waste
Astonished saw the sudden palace swell,   510
And fountains spout amid its arid shades ;
For leagues, bright vistas opening to the view,
How forests in majestic gardens smiled ;
How menial arts, by their gay sisters taught,
Wove the deep flower, the blooming foliage trained
In joyous figures o'er the silky lawn,
The palace cheered, illumed the storied wall,
And with the pencil vied the glowing loom.
  ' These laurels, Louis, by the droppings raised
Of thy profusion, its dishonour shade,   520
And green through future times shall bind thy brow ;
While the vain honours of perfidious war
Wither, abhorred or in oblivion lost.
With what prevailing vigour had they shot,
And stole a deeper root, by the full tide
Of war-sunk millions fed ?   Superior still,
How had they branched luxuriant to the skies
In Britain planted, by the potent juice
Of freedom swelled ?   Forced is the bloom of arts,
A false uncertain spring, when bounty gives,   530
Weak without me, a transitory gleam.
Fair shine the slippery days, enticing skies
Of favour smile, and courtly breezes blow ;
Till arts, betrayed, trust to the flattering air
Their tender blossom : then malignant rise
The blights of envy, of those insect clouds,
That, blasting merit, often cover courts.
Nay, should, perchance, some kind Maecenas aid
The doubtful beamings of his prince's soul,
His wavering ardour fix, and unconfined   540
Diffuse his warm beneficence around ;
Yet death, at last, and wintry tyrants come,

Each sprig of genius killing at the root.
But, when with me imperial bounty joins,
Wide o'er the public blows eternal spring ;
While mingled autumn every harvest pours
Of every land, whate'er invention, art,
Creating toil, and nature can produce.'

Here ceased the Goddess ; and her ardent wings,
Dipped in the colours of the heavenly bow,   550
Stood waving radiance round, for sudden flight
Prepared, when thus impatient burst my prayer :
　' O forming light of life ! O better sun !
Sun of mankind ! by whom the cloudy north,
Sublimed, not envies Languedocian skies
That, unstained ether all, diffusive smile—
When shall we call these ancient laurels ours ?
And when thy work complete?' Straight with her hand,
Celestial red, she touched my darkened eyes.
As at the touch of day the shades dissolve,   560
So quick, methought, the misty circle cleared
That dims the dawn of being here below ;
The future shone disclosed, and, in long view,
Bright rising eras instant rushed to light.
　' They come ! great Goddess ! I the times behold !
The times our fathers in the bloody field
Have earned so dear, and, not with less renown,
In the warm struggles of the senate-fight.
The times I see whose glory to supply,
For toiling ages, commerce round the world   570
Has winged unnumbered sails and from each land
Materials heaped that, well employed, with Rome
Might vie our grandeur, and with Greece our art!
　' Lo ! princes I behold ! contriving still,
And still conducting firm some brave design ;
Kings ! that the narrow joyless circle scorn,

Burst the blockade of false designing men,
Of treacherous smiles, of adulation fell,
And of the blinding clouds around them thrown :
Their court rejoicing millions ; worth, alone,   580
And virtue dear to them ; their best delight,
In just proportion, to give general joy ;
Their jealous care thy kingdom to maintain ;
The public glory theirs ; unsparing love
Their endless treasure, and their deeds their praise
With thee they work. Nought can resist your force :
Life feels it quickening in her dark retreats :
Strong spread the blooms of genius, science, art ;
His bashful bounds disclosing merit breaks ;
And, big with fruits of glory, virtue blows   590
Expansive o'er the land. Another race
Of generous youth, of patriot sires, I see !
Not those vain insects fluttering in the blaze
Of court, and ball, and play—those venal souls,
Corruption's veteran unrelenting bands,
That, to their vices slaves, can ne'er be free.
    ' I see the fountains purged ! whence life derives
A clear or turbid flow ; see the young mind
Not fed impure by chance, by flattery fooled,
Or by scholastic jargon bloated proud,   600
But filled and nourished by the light of truth.
Then, beamed through fancy the refining ray,
And, pouring on the heart, the passions feel
At once informing light and moving flame ;
Till moral, public, graceful action crowns
The whole. Behold ! the fair contention glows
In all that mind or body can adorn
And form to life. Instead of barren heads,
Barbarian pedants, wrangling sons of pride,
And truth-perplexing metaphysic wits,   610
Men, patriots, chiefs, and citizens are formed.

' Lo ! justice, like the liberal light of heaven,
Unpurchased shines on all ; and from her beam,
Appalling guilt, retire the savage crew
That prowl amid the darkness they themselves
Have thrown around the laws. Oppression grieves :
See how her legal furies bite the lip
While Yorks and Talbots their deep snares detect,
And seize swift justice through the clouds they
  raise.
' See ! social labour lifts his guarded head, 620
And men not yield to government in vain.
From the sure land is rooted ruffian force,
And the lewd nurse of villains, idle waste ;
Lo ! razed their haunts, down dashed their maddening
  bowl,
A nation's poison, peauteous order reigns !
Manly submission, unimposing toil,
Trade without guile, civility that marks
From the foul herd of brutal slaves thy sons,
And fearless peace. Or, should affronting war
To slow but dreadful vengeance rouse the just, 630
Unfailing fields of freemen I behold
That know with their own proper arm to guard
Their own blest isle against a leaguing world.
Despairing Gaul her boiling youth restrains,
Dissolved her dream of universal sway :
The winds and seas are Britain's wide domain,
And not a sail but by permission spreads.
' Lo ! swarming southward on rejoicing suns
Gay colonies extend—the calm retreat
Of undeserved distress, the better home 640
Of those whom bigots chase from foreign lands ;
Not built on rapine, servitude, and woe,
And in their turn some petty tyrant's prey,
But, bound by social freedom, firm they rise ;

Such as, of late, an Oglethorpe has formed,
And, crowding round, the charmed Savannah sees.
' Horrid with want and misery, no more
Our streets the tender passenger afflict.
Nor shivering age, nor sickness without friend
Or home or bed to bear his burning load,   650
Nor agonizing infant, that ne'er earned
Its guiltless pangs, I see ! The stores profuse
Which British bounty has to these assigned
No more the sacrilegious riot swell
Of cannibal devourers ! right applied,
No starving wretch the land of freedom stains—
If poor, employment finds ; if old, demands,
If sick, if maimed, his miserable due ;
And will, if young, repay the fondest care.
Sweet sets the sun of stormy life ; and sweet   660
The morning shines, in mercy's dews arrayed.
Lo ! how they rise ! these families of heaven !
That, chief, (but why, ye bigots ! why so late ?)
Where blooms and warbles glad a rising age ;
What smiles of praise ! And, while their song ascends,
The listening seraph lays his lute aside.
' Hark ! the gay muses raise a nobler strain,
With active nature, warm impassioned truth,
Engaging fable, lucid order, notes
Of various string, and heart-felt image filled.   670
Behold ! I see the dread delightful school
Of tempered passions and of polished life
Restored : behold ! the well dissembled scene
Calls from embellished eyes the lovely tear,
Or lights up mirth in modest cheeks again.
Lo ! vanished monster-land. Lo ! driven away
Those that Apollo's sacred walks profane—
Their wild creation scattered, where a world
Unknown to nature, Chaos more confused,

O'er the brute scene its ouran-outangs pours ;
Detested forms ! that, on the mind impressed, 681
Corrupt, confound, and barbarize an age.
   ' Behold ! all thine again the sister-arts,
Thy graces they, knit in harmonious dance.
Nursed by the treasure from a nation drained
Their works to purchase, they to nobler rouse
Their untamed genius, their unfettered thought;
Of pompous tyrants and of dreaming monks
The gaudy tools and prisoners no more.
   ' Lo! numerous domes a Burlington confess— 690
For kings and senates fit ; the palace see !
The temple breathing a religious awe ;
Even framed with elegance the plain retreat,
The private dwelling. Certain in his aim,
Taste, never idly working, saves expense.
   ' See ! sylvan scenes, where art alone pretends
To dress her mistress and disclose her charms—
Such as a Pope in miniature has shown,
A Bathurst o'er the widening forest spreads,
And such as form a Richmond, Chiswick, Stowe.
   ' August around what public works I see ! 701
Lo! stately streets, lo! squares that court the breeze;
In spite of those to whom pertains the care
Ingulfing more than founded Roman ways,
Lo! rayed from cities o'er the brightened land,
Connecting sea to sea, the solid road.
Lo ! the proud arch (no vile exactor's stand)
With easy sweep bestrides the chasing flood.
See ! long canals, and deepened rivers join
Each part with each, and with the circling main
The whole enlivened isle. Lo ! ports expand, 711
Free as the winds and waves, their sheltering arms.
Lo ! streaming comfort o'er the troubled deep,
On every pointed coast the lighthouse towers ;

And, by the broad imperious mole repelled,
Hark ! how the baffled storm indignant roars.'

As thick to view these varied wonders rose,
Shook all my soul with transport, unassured
The Vision broke ; and on my waking eye
Rushed the still ruins of dejected Rome.   720

NOTES TO LIBERTY

The poem was the result of Thomson's tour on the Continent,
taken, in 1730-31, in company with young Charles Talbot. It
may have been suggested by Addison's *Letter from Italy*. Thomson intended it to be, and even regarded it as, his greatest work.
But it was unpopular from the first, and it has remained unread
since Johnson gave up the attempt. That critic had hardly begun
to read it when he laid it aside, because he did not think Liberty
to be in need of either praise or defence ; and for that reason he
hazarded neither commendation nor censure. He noticed, however, that the public laid it on a high shelf to ' harbour spiders
and to gather dust '. Yet the fact remains that *Liberty*, though
on the whole tedious, contains learning, eloquence, imagination,
and rises at times to altitudes of true poetic vision, more especially
in the fourth and fifth parts. Thomson would doubtless have
done better if he had kept to his original plan of presenting ' a
poetical landscape of various countries, mixed with moral obser-
vations on their government '—much as Goldsmith afterwards
did in *The Traveller*. Nature was his theme rather than the history of civilization.

Liberty was published in separate parts in 1735 and 1736. Of
Part I, 3,000 copies were printed ; of Parts II and III, 2,000 ; and
of Parts IV and V, only 1,000—a gradual reduction which shows
the comparative and unexpected failure of the work with the
reading public.

PART I, line 1 *O my lamented Talbot.* Charles Richard Talbot,
only son of the Solicitor-General. On the recommendation of
Dr. Rundle, Thomson had been selected as young Talbot's travelling tutor on the Continent, in 1730-31. They visited Italy
together. In September, 1733, young Talbot died, and Thomson
here laments his early death. He was a few years afterwards

to lament the death of the father, Lord Chancellor Talbot, in ' Memorial Verses ', which are placed among the *Miscellaneous Poems*.

I. 83 *the two sires*. L. J. Brutus and Virginius.—T.

I. 242 Via Sacra.—T.

I. 247, 248 M. Angelo Buonaroti, Palladio, and Raphael D'Urbino—the three great modern masters in sculpture, architecture, and painting.—T.

I. 273 *Yon wild retreat*. Tusculum is reckoned to have stood at a place now called Grotta Ferrata, a convent of monks.—T.

I. 276 *the ship-forsaken bay*. The Bay of Mola (anciently Formiae) into which Homer brings Ulysses and his companions. Near Formiae Cicero had a villa.—T.

I. 288 Campagna Felice, adjoining to Capua.—T.

I. 290 The coast of Baiae, which was formerly adorned with the works mentioned in the following lines ; and where, amidst many magnificent ruins, those of a temple erected to Venus are still to be seen.—T.

I. 303 All along this coast the ancient Romans had their winter retreats ; and several populous cities stood.—T.

PART II, line 57 Civil Tyranny.—T.

II. 63 The Pyramids.—T.

II. 65 The Tyrants of Egypt.—T.

II. 138 A mountain near Athens.—T.

II. 142 Two rivers between which Athens was situated.—T.

II. 157 The Areopagus, or Supreme Court of Judicature, which Solon reformed and improved : and the council of Four Hundred, by him instituted. In this council all affairs of state were deliberated, before they came to be voted in the assembly of the people.—T.

II. 174 Pisa, or Olympia, the city where the Olympic games were celebrated.—T.

II. 180 The Straits of Thermopylae.—T.

II. 197 Xenophon.—T.

II. 222 Socrates.—T.

II. 272 Homer.—T.

II. 323 When Demetrius besieged Rhodes, and could have reduced the city by setting fire to that quarter of it where stood the house of the celebrated Protogenes, he chose rather to raise the siege than hazard the burning of a famous picture called Jasylus, the masterpiece of that painter.—T.

II. 442 So the Kings of Persia were called by the Greeks.—T.

II. 453 The peace made by Antalcidas, the Lacedemonian admiral, with the Persians ; by which the Lacedemonians abandoned all the Greeks established in the lesser Asia, to the dominion of the King of Persia.—T.

II. 459 Athens had been dismantled by the Lacedemonians, at the end of the first Peloponnesian war, and was at this time restored by Conon to its former splendour.—T.

II. 470 The Peloponnesian war.—T.

II. 478 Pelopidas and Epaminondas.—T.

II. 480 The battle of Cheronaea, in which Philip of Macedon utterly defeated the Greeks.—T.

PART III, line 7 The last struggles of liberty in Greece.—T.

III. 15 Lacinium, a promontory in Calabria.—T.

III. 32 Pythagoras.—T.

III. 34 Samos, over which then reigned the tyrant Polycrates. —T.

III. 37 The southern parts of Italy and Sicily, so called because of the Grecian colonies there settled.—T.

III. 38 His scholars were enjoined silence for five years.—T.

III. 57 The four cardinal virtues.—T.

III. 244 Rha, the ancient name of the Volga.—T.

III. 245 The Caspian Sea.—T.

III. 264 The King of Macedonia.—T.

III. 286 The Isthmian games were celebrated at Corinth.—T.

III. 369 Carthage.—T.

III. 390 Tib. Gracchus.—T.

III. 465 Publius Servilius Rullus, tribune of the people, proposed an Agrarian Law, in appearance very advantageous for the people, but destructive of their liberty : and which was defeated by the eloquence of Cicero in his speech against Rullus. —T.

III. 489 *the dark third.* Tiberius.—T.

III. 496 Thrasea Paetus, put to death by Nero. Tacitus introduces the account he gives of his death, thus :—' After having inhumanly slaughtered so many illustrious men, he (Nero) burned at last with a desire of cutting off virtue itself in the person of Thrasea,' &c.—T.

III. 505 Antoninus Pius, and his adopted son Marcus Aurelius, afterwards called Antoninus Philosophus.—T.

III. 511 Constantine's arch, to build which that of Trajan was destroyed, sculpture having been then almost entirely lost.—T.

III. 515 The ancient Sarmatia contained a vast tract of country running all along the north of Europe and Asia.—T.

III. 527, 528 See *Winter,* 809 *seqq.*

PART IV, line 49 Church Power, or Ecclesiastical Tyranny.—T.

IV. 52 *her elder sister.* Civil Tyranny.—T.

IV. 86 *Banditti saints.* Crusaders.

IV. 91 The corruptions of the Church of Rome.—T.

IV. 94 *the rage of slaves.* Vassalage, whence the attachment of clans to their chief.—T.

IV. 96 *the bravo's trade.* Duelling.—T.

IV. 123 *inbred foes.* The Hierarchy.—T.

IV. 141 The Hercules of Farnese.—T. The passage which describes the Greek statues is, says Mr. G. C. Macaulay (*English Men of Letters—James Thomson*), ' perhaps the first of the kind in English poetry.'

IV. 153 The Fighting Gladiator.—T.

IV. 156 The Dying Gladiator.—T. The description that follows is not unworthy to be read even after Byron's.

IV. 164 The Apollo of Belvidere.—T.

IV. 175 The Venus of Medici.—T.

IV. 185 The group of Laocoon and his two sons destroyed by two serpents. See Aeneid II, ver. 199-227.—T.

IV. 213, 214 Esteemed the two finest pieces of modern sculpture. It is reported of Michael Angelo Buonaroti, the most celebrated master in modern sculpture, that he wrought with a kind of inspiration or enthusiastical fury, which produced the effect here mentioned.—T.

IV. 244 *The Lombard school.* The school of the Caracci.—T.

IV. 266 The river Arno runs through Florence.—T.

IV. 269 The republics of Florence, Pisa, Lucca, and Sienna. They formerly have had very cruel wars together, but are now all peaceably subject to the Great Duke of Tuscany, except it be Lucca, which still maintains the form of a republic.—T.

IV. 282 The Genoese Territory is reckoned very populous, but the towns and villages for the most part lie hid among the Apennine rocks and mountains.—T.

IV. 284 According to Dr. Burnet's system of the Deluge.—T.

IV. 293 Venice was the most flourishing city in Europe, with regard to trade, before the passage to the East Indies by the Cape of Good Hope and America was discovered.—T.

IV. 294 Those who fled to some marshes in the Adriatic gulf, from the desolation spread over Italy by an irruption of the Huns, first founded there this famous city, about the beginning of the fifth century.—T.

IV. 319 *A larger circle.* The main ocean. *another seat.* Great Britain.—T.

IV. 325 The Swiss Cantons.—T.

IV. 329 Geneva, situated on the Lacus Lemanus, a small state, but noble example of the blessings of civil and religious liberty. It is remarkable that since the founding of this Republic not one citizen has been so much as suspected to have been guilty of corruption or public rapine. A virtue this ! meriting the attention of every Briton.—T.

IV. 347 It is reported of the Swiss that, after having been long absent from their native country, they are seized with such a violent desire of seeing it again as affects them with a kind of languishing indisposition, called ' the Swiss sickness '.—T.

IV. 366 The Hanse Towns.—T.

IV. 372 *the manly race.* The Swedes.—T.

IV. 377 Here Thomson, in a footnote, refers the reader to a passage from Sir William Temple's *Essay on Heroic Virtue*, with which he illustrates lines 678–84 *infra.*

IV. 624 Great Britain was peopled by the Celtae or Gauls.—T.

IV. 630 The Druids among the ancient Gauls and Britons had the care and direction of all religious matters.—T.

IV. 645 The Roman Empire.—T.

IV. 647 Caledonia, inhabited by the Scots and Picts ; whither a great many Britons, who would not submit to the Romans, retired.—T.

IV. 652 The wall of Severus, built upon Adrian's rampart, which ran for eighty miles quite across the country, from the mouth of the Tyne to Solway Frith.—T.

IV. 654 Irruptions of the Scots and Picts.—T.

IV. 658 The Roman empire being miserably torn by the northern nations, Britain was for ever abandoned by the Romans in the year 426 or 427.—T.

IV. 662 The Britons applying to Aetius, the Roman general, for assistance, thus expressed their miserable condition :—' We know not which way to turn us. The Barbarians drive us to sea, and the sea forces us back to the Barbarians ; between which we have only the choice of two deaths, either to be swallowed up by the waves, or butchered by the sword.'—T.

IV. 665 King of the Silures, famous for his great exploits, and accounted the best general Great Britain had ever produced. The Silures were esteemed the bravest and most powerful of all the Britons : they inhabited Herefordshire, Radnorshire, Brecknockshire, Monmouthshire, and Glamorganshire.—T.

IV. 666 Queen of the Iceni : her story is well known.—T.

IV. 678 It is certain, that an opinion was fixed and general among them (the Goths) that death was but the entrance into another life; that all men who lived lazy and unactive lives, and died natural deaths, by sickness or by age, went into vast caves under ground, all dark and miry, full of noisome creatures usual to such places, and there for ever grovelled in endless stench and misery. On the contrary, all who gave themselves to warlike actions and enterprises, to the conquest of their neighbours and the slaughter of their enemies, and died in battle, or of violent deaths upon bold adventures or resolutions, went immediately to the vast hall or palace of Odin, their god of war, who eternally kept open house for all such guests, where they were entertained at infinite tables, in perpetual feasts and mirth, carousing in bowls made of the skulls of their enemies they had slain ; according to the number of whom, every one in these mansions of pleasure was the most honoured and best entertained.—*Sir William Temple's Essay on Heroic Virtue.*—T.

IV. 701 The seven kingdoms of the Anglo-Saxons, considered as being united into one common government, under a general in chief or monarch, and by the means of an assembly general, or wittenagemot.—T.

IV. 704 Egbert, King of Wessex, who, after having reduced all the other kingdoms of the Heptarchy under his dominion, was the first king of England.—T.

IV. 709 A famous Danish standard was called Reafan, or Raven. The Danes imagined that, before a battle, the Raven wrought upon this standard clapped its wings or hung down its head, in token of victory or defeat.—T.

IV. 733 Alfred the Great, renowned in war, and no less famous in peace for his many excellent institutions, particularly that of juries.—T.

IV. 736 The battle of Hastings, in which Harold II, the last of the Saxon kings, was slain, and William the Conqueror made himself master of England.—T.

IV. 748 Edward the Confessor, who reduced the West Saxon, Mercian, and Danish laws into one body ; which from that time became common to all England, under the name of ' The Laws of Edward '.—T.

IV. 755 The Curfew-Bell (from the French Couvrefeu) which was rung every night at eight of the clock, to warn the English to put out their fires and candles, under the penalty of a severe fine.—T.

IV. 762 The New Forest in Hampshire ; to make which, the country for above thirty miles in compass was laid waste.—T.

IV. 775 On June 5, 1215, King John, met by the Barons on Runnemede, signed the Great Charter of Liberties, or Magna Charta.—T.

IV. 784 The league formed by the Barons, during the reign of John, in the year 1213, was the first confederacy made in England in defence of the nation's interest against the King.—T.

IV. 796 The commons are generally thought to have been first represented in parliament towards the end of Henry III's reign. To a parliament called in the year 1264, each county was ordered to send four knights, as representatives of their respective shires: and to a parliament called in the year following, each county was ordered to send, as their representatives, two knights, and each city and borough as many citizens and burgesses. Till then, history makes no mention of them ; whence a very strong argument may be drawn, to fix the original of the House of Commons to that era.—T.

IV. 840 Edward III, and Henry V.—T.

IV. 865 Three famous battles, gained by the English over the French.—T.

IV. 867 During the civil wars, betwixt the families of York and Lancaster.—T.

IV. 872 Henry VII.—T.

IV. 879 The famous Earl of Warwick, during the reigns of Henry VI and Edward IV was called the ' King Maker '.—T.

IV. 881 Permitting the Barons to alienate their lands.—T.

IV. 895 Henry VIII. Of papal dominion.—T.

IV. 904 John Wickliff, doctor of divinity, who, towards the close of the fourteenth century, published doctrines very contrary to those of the church of Rome, and particularly denying the papal authority. His followers grew very numerous, and were called Lollards.—T.

IV. 906 Suppression of monasteries.—T.

IV. 912 *other worlds*. The Spanish West Indies.—T.

IV. 931 The dominion of the house of Austria.—T.

IV. 937 The Spanish Armada. Rapin says that after proper measures had been taken the enemy was expected with uncommon alacrity.—T.

IV. 957 *the prince*. James I.

IV. 966 *Abandoned Frederick*. Elector Palatine, who had been chosen king of Bohemia, but was stripped of all his dominions and dignities by the Emperor Ferdinand, whilst James I, his father-in-law, being amused from time to time, endeavoured to mediate a peace.—T.

IV. 970 The monstrous and till then unheard-of doctrines of divine indefeasible hereditary right, passive obedience, &c.—T.

IV. 975 The parties of Whig and Tory.—T.

IV. 982 Charles I.—T.

IV. 991 *the fountain* [*of public wisdom and of justice*]. Parliament.—T.

IV. 1003 Ship-money.—T.

IV. 1004 Monopolies.—T.

IV. 1008 *Their poison.* The raging High-Church sermons of those times, inspiring at once a spirit of slavish submission to the Court and of bitter persecution against those whom they call Church and State Puritans.—T.

IV. 1045 *the phoenix State.* At the Restoration.—T.

IV. 1048 *the luxurious king.* Charles II.—T.

IV. 1049 *that which taught the young to bend.* Court of Wards. —T.

IV. 1075 Dunkirk.—T.

IV. 1077 The war in conjunction with France against the Dutch. —T.

IV. 1078 *the Saviour-League.* The Triple Alliance.—T.

IV. 1080 *universal sway.* Under Lewis XIV.—T.

IV. 1084 A standing army, raised without the consent of Parliament.—T.

IV. 1095 *each badge of freedom.* The Charters of Corporations. —T.

IV. 1105 *The bigot king.* James II.—T.

IV. 1118 The Prince of Orange, in his passage to England, though his fleet had been at first dispersed by a storm, was afterwards extremely favoured by several changes of wind.—T.

IV. 1122 Rapin, in his *History of England.*—The third of November the fleet entered the Channel, and lay by between Calais and Dover, to stay for the ships that were behind. Here the Prince called a council of war. It is easy to imagine what a glorious show the fleet made. Five or six hundred ships in so narrow a channel, and both the English and French shores covered with numberless spectators, are no common sight. For my part, who was then on board the fleet, I own it struck me extremely.—T.

IV. 1126 *my streaming flag.* The Prince placed himself in the main body, carrying a flag with English colours, and their highnesses' arms surrounded with this motto, ' The Protestant Religion and the Liberties of England ; ' and underneath the motto of the house of Nassau, ' Je maintiendrai,' I will maintain—*Rapin.*—T.

IV. 1127 The English fleet.—T.

IV. 1130 The king's army.—T.

IV. 1143 *Pleased to yield.* By the Bill of Rights and the Act of Succession.—T.

IV. 1144 William III.—T.

PART V, line 69 *that the Tyrian merchant sought of old.* Tin. —T.

V. 285 *The poor and weak.* Lord Molesworth, in his account of Denmark, says, ' It is observed, that in limited monarchies and commonwealths, a neighbourhood to the seat of the government is advantageous to the subjects ; whilst the distant provinces are less thriving, and more liable to oppression.'—T.

V. 409 The famous Retreat of the Ten Thousand was chiefly conducted by Xenophon.—T.

V. 411 Epaminondas, after having beat the Lacedemonians and their allies, in the battle of Leuctra, made an incursion at the head of a powerful army into Laconia. It was now six hundred years since the Dorians had possessed this country, and in all that time the face of an enemy had not been seen within their territories.—*Plutarch* in *Agesilaus.*—T.

V. 458 Louis XIV.—T.

V. 473 *the long canal.* The canal of Languedoc.—T.

V. 475, 477 The Hospitals for Foundlings and Invalids.—T.

V. 496 *warm seminaries.* The Academies of Sciences, the *Belles Lettres,* and Painting.—T.

V. 503 *the kind art of unvalued price.* Engraving.—T.

V. 518 *the glowing loom.* The tapestry of the Gobelins.—T. The Gobelins were originally a family of dyers, who (in the sixteenth century) added to their business as dyers the manufacture of tapestry, with which their name has ever since been associated.

V. 645 The reference is to the colonization of the State of Georgia.

V. 662 A Hospital for Foundlings.—T.

V. 680 *ouran-outangs.* Creatures which, of all brutes, most resemble man. See Dr. Tyson's Treatise on this animal.—T.

V. 690 Richard Boyle, Earl of Burlington, architect of Chiswick House, Burlington House, &c.

V. 698 At Twickenham.

V. 699 Okely Woods, near Cirencester.—T.

LYRICAL PIECES

RULE, BRITANNIA!

[This famous ode, which appeared in the last scene (Act II, Sc. v) of *Alfred: A Masque*, a dramatic piece in which Mallet collaborated with Thomson, was published in 1740. It has sometimes been attributed to Mallet. The evidence is in favour of Thomson's authorship.]

WHEN Britain first, at Heaven's command,
  Arose from out the azure main,
This was the charter of the land,
  And guardian angels sung this strain—
    ' Rule, Britannia, rule the waves;
    Britons never will be slaves.'

The nations, not so blest as thee,
  Must in their turns to tyrants fall ;
While thou shalt flourish great and free,
  The dread and envy of them all.   10
    ' Rule,' &c.

Still more majestic shalt thou rise,
  More dreadful from each foreign stroke :
As the loud blast that tears the skies
  Serves but to root thy native oak.
    ' Rule,' &c.

Thee haughty tyrants ne'er shall tame ;
  All their attempts to bend thee down
Will but arouse thy generous flame,
  But work their woe and thy renown.   20
    ' Rule,' &c.

To thee belongs the rural reign ;
 Thy cities shall with commerce shine ;
All thine shall be the subject main,
 And every shore it circles thine.
 ' Rule,' &c.

The Muses, still with freedom found,
 Shall to thy happy coast repair :
Blest isle ! with matchless beauty crowned,
 And manly hearts to guard the fair.   30
 ' Rule, Britannia, rule the waves ;
 Britons never will be slaves.'

ODE

TELL me, thou soul of her I love,
 Ah ! tell me, whither art thou fled ?
To what delightful world above,
 Appointed for the happy dead ?

Or dost thou free at pleasure roam,
 And sometimes share thy lover's woe
Where, void of thee, his cheerless home
 Can now, alas ! no comfort know ?

Oh ! if thou hoverest round my walk,
 While, under every well-known tree,   10
I to thy fancied shadow talk,
 And every tear is full of thee—

Should then the weary eye of grief
 Beside some sympathetic stream
In slumber find a short relief,
 Oh, visit thou my soothing dream !
 [Cp. Burns's *To Mary in Heaven.*]

COME, GENTLE GOD

[Published in *The Gentleman's Magazine*, February, 1736.]

COME, gentle god of soft desire,
    Come and possess my happy breast ;
Not fury-like in flames and fire,
    Or frantic folly's wildness drest.

But come in friendship's angel-guise ;
    Yet dearer thou than friendship art,
More tender spirit in thy eyes,
    More sweet emotions at the heart.

O, come with goodness in thy train,
    With peace and pleasure void of storm ;   10
And, wouldst thou me for ever gain,
    Put on Amanda's winning form.

[For Amanda, see note on line 483 of *Spring.*]

SONG

ONE day the god of fond desire,
    On mischief bent, to Damon said,
' Why not disclose your tender fire ?
    Not own it to the lovely maid ? '

The shepherd marked his treacherous art,
    And, softly sighing, thus replied :
' 'Tis true, you have subdued my heart,
    But shall not triumph o'er my pride.

' The slave in private only bears
    Your bondage, who his love conceals ;   10
But, when his passion he declares,
    You drag him at your chariot-wheels.'

SONG

HARD is the fate of him who loves
Yet dares not tell his trembling pain
But to the sympathetic groves,
But to the lonely listening plain.

Oh ! when she blesses next your shade,
Oh ! when her footsteps next are seen
In flowery tracts along the mead,
In fresher mazes o'er the green,

Ye gentle spirits of the vale,
To whom the tears of love are dear,   10
From dying lilies waft a gale
And sigh my sorrows in her ear.

Oh ! tell her what she cannot blame,
Though fear my tongue must ever bind ;
Oh ! tell her that my virtuous flame
Is as her spotless soul refined.

Not her own guardian angel eyes
With chaster tenderness his care ;
Not purer her own wishes rise,
Not holier her own sighs in prayer.   20

But, if at first her virgin fear
Should start at love's suspected name,
With that of friendship soothe her ear—
True love and friendship are the same.

TO AMANDA

COME, dear Amanda, quit the town,
And to the rural hamlets fly ;
Behold ! the wintry storms are gone,
A gentle radiance glads the sky ;

P

The birds awake, the flowers appear,
  Earth spreads a verdant couch for thee;
'Tis joy and music all we hear,
  'Tis love and beauty all we see.

Come, let us mark the gradual spring,
  How peeps the bud, the blossom blows;   10
Till Philomel begins to sing,
  And perfect May to swell the rose.

Even so thy rising charms improve,
  As life's warm season grows more bright;
And, opening to the sighs of love,
  Thy beauties glow with full delight.

TO AMANDA

UNLESS with my Amanda blest,
  In vain I twine the woodbine bower;
Unless to deck her sweeter breast,
  In vain I rear the breathing flower.

Awakened by the genial year,
  In vain the birds around me sing;
In vain the freshening fields appear:
  Without my love there is no Spring,

TO MYRA

O THOU whose tender serious eyes
  Expressive speak the mind I love—
The gentle azure of the skies,
  The pensive shadows of the grove—

O mix their beauteous beams with mine,
  And let us interchange our hearts ;
Let all their sweetness on me shine,
  Poured through my soul be all their darts.

Ah, 'tis too much ! I cannot bear
  At once so soft, so keen a ray :   10
In pity then, my lovely fair,
  O turn those killing eyes away !

But what avails it to conceal
  One charm where nought but charms I see ?
Their lustre then again reveal,
  And let me, Myra, die of thee !

[Myra is Amanda. The poem was enclosed in a letter to
Mrs. Robertson (Amanda's sister), in 1742, and was first printed
in the Earl of Buchan's Essay.]

TO FORTUNE

For ever, Fortune, wilt thou prove
An unrelenting foe to love,
And, when we meet a mutual heart,
Come in between and bid us part ;

Bid us sigh on from day to day,
And wish, and wish the soul away ;
Till youth and genial years are flown,
And all the life of life is gone ?

But busy, busy still art thou,
To bind the loveless joyless vow,   10
The heart from pleasure to delude,
And join the gentle to the rude.

For once, O Fortune ! hear my prayer,
And I absolve thy future care—
All other blessings I resign ;
Make but the dear Amanda mine !

THE BASHFUL LOVER

[From a MS. believed to be in Thomson's handwriting.]

SWEET tyrant Love, but hear me now !
And cure while young this pleasing smart ;
Or rather, aid my trembling vow,
And teach me to reveal my heart.

Tell her whose goodness is my bane,
Whose looks have smiled my peace away,
Oh ! whisper now she gives me pain,
Whilst undesigning, frank, and gay.

'Tis not for common charms I sigh,
For what the vulgar beauty call ;   10
'Tis not a cheek, a lip, an eye ;
But 'tis the soul that lights them all.

For that I drop the tender tear,
For that I make this artless moan,
Oh, sigh it, Love ! into her ear,
And make the bashful lover known.

TO THE NIGHTINGALE

O NIGHTINGALE, best poet of the grove,
That plaintive strain can ne'er belong to thee,
Blest in the full possession of thy love :
O lend that strain, sweet nightingale, to me !

'Tis mine, alas ! to mourn my wretched fate :
  I love a maid who all my bosom charms,
Yet lose my days without this lovely mate ;
  Inhuman fortune keeps her from my arms.

You, happy birds ! by nature's simple laws
  Lead your soft lives, sustained by nature's fare ;
You dwell wherever roving fancy draws,   11
  And love and song is all your pleasing care :

But we, vain slaves of interest and of pride,
  Dare not be blest lest envious tongues should
      blame :
And hence in vain I languish for my bride—
  O mourn with me, sweet bird, my hapless flame.

HYMN ON SOLITUDE

[Drafted in 1725 ; published in Ralph's *Miscellany*, 1729.]

HAIL, mildly pleasing Solitude,
Companion of the wise and good ;
But from whose holy piercing eye
The herd of fools and villains fly.
Oh ! how I love with thee to walk,
And listen to thy whispered talk,
Which innocence and truth imparts,
And melts the most obdúrate hearts.

A thousand shapes you wear with ease,
And still in every shape you please.   10
Now wrapt in some mysterious dream,
A lone philosopher you seem ;
Now quick from hill to vale you fly,
And now you sweep the vaulted sky ;
A shepherd next, you haunt the plain,
And warble forth your oaten strain ;

A lover now, with all the grace
Of that sweet passion in your face ;
Then, calmed to friendship, you assume
The gentle looking Harford's bloom,   20
As, with her Musidora, she
(Her Musidora fond of thee)
Amid the long-withdrawing vale
Awakes the rivalled nightingale.

Thine is the balmy breath of morn,
Just as the dew-bent rose is born ;
And, while meridian fervours beat,
Thine is the woodland dumb retreat ;
But chief, when evening scenes decay
And the faint landskip swims away,   30
Thine is the doubtful soft decline,
And that best hour of musing thine.

Descending angels bless thy train,
The virtues of the sage, and swain—
Plain Innocence in white arrayed
Before thee lifts her fearless head ;
Religion's beams around thee shine
And cheer thy glooms with light divine ;
About thee sports sweet Liberty ;
And wrapt Urania sings to thee.   40

Oh, let me pierce thy secret cell,
And in thy deep recesses dwell !
Perhaps from Norwood's oak-clad hill,
When meditation has her fill,
I just may cast my careless eyes
Where London's spiry turrets rise,
Think of its crimes, its cares, its pain.
Then shield me in the woods again.

A NUPTIAL SONG

[Intended to have been inserted in the fourth act of *Sophonisba,*
Thomson's first play, acted at Drury Lane, February 28, 1730.]

COME, gentle Venus ! and assuage
A warring world, a bleeding age,
For nature lives beneath thy ray :
The wintry tempests haste away,
A lucid calm invests the sea,
Thy native deep is full of thee ;
And flowering earth, where'er you fly,
Is all o'er spring, all sun the sky;
A genial spirit warms the breeze ;
Unseen, among the blooming trees, 10
The feathered lovers tune their throat,
The desert growls a softened note,
Glad o'er the meads the cattle bound,
And love and harmony go round.

But chief into the human heart
You strike the dear delicious dart ;
You teach us pleasing pangs to know,
To languish in luxurious woe,
To feel the generous passions rise,
Grow good by gazing, mild by sighs ; 20
Each happy moment to improve,
And fill the perfect year with love.

Come, thou delight of heaven and earth !
To whom all creatures owe their birth ;
Oh, come ! red-smiling, tender, come !
And yet prevent our final doom.
For long the furious god of war
Has crushed us with his iron car,
Has raged along our ruined plains,
Has cursed them with his cruel stains, 30

Has sunk our youth in endless sleep,
And made the widowed virgin weep.
Now let him feel thy wonted charms,
Oh, take him to thy twining arms !
And, while thy bosom heaves on his,
While deep he prints the humid kiss,
Ah, then ! his stormy heart control,
And sigh thyself into his soul.
  Thy son too, Cupid, we implore
To leave the green Idalian shore.   40
Be he, sweet god ! our only foe :
Long let him draw the twanging bow,
Transfix us with his golden darts,
Pour all his quiver on our hearts,
With gentler anguish make us sigh,
And teach us sweeter deaths to die.

AN ODE ON AEOLUS'S HARP

[First printed in 1748, in *Dodsley's Collection of Poems*, vol. iv, p. 129.]

ETHEREAL race, inhabitants of air,
  Who hymn your God amid the secret grove,
Ye unseen beings, to my harp repair,
  And raise majestic strains, or melt in love.

Those tender notes, how kindly they upbraid !
  With what soft woe they thrill the lover's heart !
Sure from the hand of some unhappy maid
  Who died of love these sweet complainings part.

But hark ! that strain was of a graver tone,
  On the deep strings his hand some hermit throws ;
Or he, the sacred Bard, who sat alone   11
  In the drear waste and wept his people's woes.

Such was the song which Zion's children sung
  When by Euphrates' stream they made their plaint ;
And to such sadly solemn notes are strung
  Angelic harps to soothe a dying saint.

Methinks I hear the full celestial choir
  Through Heaven's high dome their awful anthem
    raise ;
Now chanting clear, and now they all conspire
  To swell the lofty hymn from praise to praise. 20

Let me, ye wandering spirits of the wind,
  Who, as wild fancy prompts you, touch the string,
Smit with your theme, be in your chorus joined,
  For till you cease my muse forgets to sing.

[The ' sacred bard ' of the third stanza is Jeremiah—as Thomson
himself notes.]

MEMORIAL VERSES

ON THE DEATH OF HIS MOTHER

[Written in 1725.]

YE fabled muses, I your aid disclaim,
Your airy raptures, and your fancied flame :
True genuine woe my throbbing breast inspires,
Love prompts my lays, and filial duty fires ;
The soul springs instant at the warm design.
And the heart dictates every flowing line.

See ! where the kindest, best of mothers lies,
And death has shut her ever weeping eyes ;
Has lodged at last in peace her weary breast,
And lulled her many piercing cares to rest.   10
No more the orphan train around her stands,
While her full heart upbraids her needy hands !
No more the widow's lonely fate she feels,
The shock severe that modest wants conceals,
The oppressor's scourge, the scorn of wealthy pride,
And poverty's unnumbered ills beside.
For see ! attended by the angelic throng,
Through yonder worlds of light she glides along,
And claims the well-earned raptures of the sky.
Yet fond concern recalls the mother's eye :   20
She seeks the helpless orphans left behind—
So hardly left ! so bitterly resigned !
Still, still is she my soul's divinest theme,
The waking vision, and the wailing dream :

Amid the ruddy sun's enlivening blaze
O'er my dark eyes her dewy image plays,
And in the dread dominion of the night
Shines out again the sadly pleasing sight.
Triumphant virtue all around her darts,
And more than volumes every look imparts—   30
Looks soft, yet awful ; melting, yet serene ;
Where both the mother and the saint are seen.
But ah ! that night, that torturing night remains—
May darkness dye it with its deepest stains,
May joy on it forsake her rosy bowers,
And screaming sorrow blast its baleful hours !
When on the margin of the briny flood,
Chilled with a sad presaging damp I stood,
Took the last look, ne'er to behold her more,
And mixed our murmurs with the wavy roar,   40
Heard the last words fall from her pious tongue,
Then wild into the bulging vessel flung—
Which soon, too soon, conveyed me from her
    sight,
Dearer than life, and liberty, and light !
Why was I then, ye powers, reserved for this,
Nor sunk that moment in the vast abyss ?
Devoured at once by the relentless wave,
And whelmed for ever in a watery grave ?
Down, ye wild wishes of unruly woe !
I see her with immortal beauty glow ;   50
The early wrinkle, care-contracted, gone,
Her tears all wiped, and all her sorrows flown ;
The exalting voice of Heaven I hear her breathe,
To soothe her soul in agonies of death.
I see her through the mansions blest above,
And now she meets her dear expecting love.
Heart-cheering sight ! but yet, alas ! o'erspread
By the damp gloom of grief's uncheerful shade.

Come, then, of reason the reflecting hour,
And let me trust the kind o'erruling power   60
Who from the night commands the shining day,
The poor man's portion, and the orphan's stay.

[The death of his mother took place in May, 1725. In the previous February he had sailed from Leith for London. His mother, then a widow, was at that time resident in Edinburgh. Thomson never published these memorial lines. They first appeared in 1792.]

   53-4. The meaning here is vague: he probably means, by repeating consolatory texts of Scripture.

TO THE MEMORY OF SIR ISAAC NEWTON

[Written in 1727.]

SHALL the great soul of Newton quit this earth
To mingle with his stars, and every Muse,
Astonished into silence, shun the weight
Of honours due to his illustrious name ?
But what can man ? Even now the sons of light,
In strains high warbled to seraphic lyre,
Hail his arrival on the coast of bliss.
Yet am not I deterred, though high the theme,
And sung to harps of angels, for with you,
Ethereal flames ! ambitious, I aspire   10
In Nature's general symphony to join.
   And what new wonders can ye show your guest !
Who, while on this dim spot where mortals toil
Clouded in dust, from motion's simple laws
Could trace the secret hand of Providence,
Wide-working through this universal frame.
   Have ye not listened while he bound the suns
And planets to their spheres ! the unequal task
Of humankind till then. Oft had they rolled
O'er erring man the year, and oft disgraced   20

The pride of schools, before their course was known
Full in its causes and effects to him,
All-piercing sage ! who sat not down and dreamed
Romantic schemes, defended by the din
Of specious words, and tyranny of names ;
But, bidding his amazing mind attend,
And with heroic patience years on years
Deep-searching, saw at last the system dawn,
And shine, of all his race, on him alone.
    What were his raptures then ! how pure ! how
      strong !   30
And what the triumphs of old Greece and Rome,
By his diminished, but the pride of boys
In some small fray victorious ! when instead
Of shattered parcels of this earth usurped
By violence unmanly, and sore deeds
Of cruelty and blood, Nature herself
Stood all subdued by him, and open laid
Her every latent glory to his view.
    All intellectual eye, our solar round
First gazing through, he, by the blended power 40
Of gravitation and projection, saw
The whole in silent harmony revolve.
From unassisted vision hid, the moons
To cheer remoter planets numerous formed,
By him in all their mingled tracts were seen.
He also fixed our wandering Queen of Night,
Whether she wanes into a scanty orb,
Or, waxing broad, with her pale shadowy light,
In a soft deluge overflows the sky.
Her every motion clear-discerning, he   50
Adjusted to the mutual main and taught
Why now the mighty mass of waters swells
Resistless, heaving on the broken rocks,
And the full river turning—till again

The tide revertive, unattracted, leaves
A yellow waste of idle sands behind.
   Then, breaking hence, he took his ardent flight
Through the blue infinite ; and every star,
Which the clear concave of a winter's night
Pours on the eye, or astronomic tube,   60
Far stretching, snatches from the dark abyss,
Or such as further in successive skies
To fancy shine alone, at his approach
Blazed into suns, the living centre each
Of an harmonious system—all combined,
And ruled unerring by that single power
Which draws the stone projected to the ground.
   O unprofuse magnificence divine !
O wisdom truly perfect ! thus to call
From a few causes such a scheme of things,   70
Effects so various, beautiful, and great,
An universe complete ! And O beloved
Of Heaven ! whose well purged penetrating eye
The mystic veil transpiercing, inly scanned
The rising, moving, wide-established frame.
   He, first of men, with awful wing pursued
The comet through the long elliptic curve,
As round innumerous worlds he wound his way,
Till, to the forehead of our evening sky
Returned, the blazing wonder glares anew,   80
And o'er the trembling nations shakes dismay.
   The heavens are all his own, from the wide
      rule
Of whirling vortices and circling spheres
To their first great simplicity restored.
The schools astonished stood ; but found it vain
To combat still with demonstration strong,
And, unawakened, dream beneath the blaze
Of truth. At once their pleasing visions fled,

With the gay shadows of the morning mixed,
When Newton rose, our philosophic sun !   90
  The aerial flow of sound was known to him,
From whence it first in wavy circles breaks,
Till the touched organ takes the message in.
Nor could the darting beam of speed immense
Escape his swift pursuit and measuring eye.
Even Light itself, which every thing displays,
Shone undiscovered, till his brighter mind
Untwisted all the shining robe of day ;
And, from the whitening undistinguished blaze,
Collecting every ray into his kind,   100
To the charmed eye educed the gorgeous train
Of parent colours. First the flaming red
Sprung vivid forth ; the tawny orange next ;
And next delicious yellow ; by whose side
Fell the kind beams of all-refreshing green.
Then the pure blue, that swells autumnal skies,
Ethereal played ; and then, of sadder hue,
Emerged the deepened indigo, as when
The heavy-skirted evening droops with frost ;
While the last gleamings of refracted light   110
Died in the fainting violet away.
These, when the clouds distil the rosy shower,
Shine out distinct adown the watery bow ;
While o'er our heads the dewy vision bends
Delightful, melting on the fields beneath.
Myriads of mingling dyes from these result,
And myriads still remain—infinite source
Of beauty, ever flushing, ever new.
  Did ever poet image aught so fair,
Dreaming in whispering groves by the hoarse
      brook ?
Or prophet, to whose rapture heaven descends ? 121
Even now the setting sun and shifting clouds,

Seen, Greenwich, from thy lovely heights, declare
How just, how beauteous the refractive law.
The noiseless tide of time, all bearing down
To vast eternity's unbounded sea,
Where the green islands of the happy shine,
He stemmed alone ; and, to the source (involved
Deep in primeval gloom) ascending, raised
His lights at equal distances, to guide   130
Historian wildered on his darksome way.
    But who can number up his labours ? who
His high discoveries sing ? When but a few
Of the deep-studying race can stretch their minds
To what he knew—in fancy's lighter thought
How shall the muse then grasp the mighty theme ?
    What wonder thence that his devotion swelled
Responsive to his knowledge ? For could he
Whose piercing mental eye diffusive saw
The finished university of things   140
In all its order, magnitude, and parts
Forbear incessant to adore that Power
Who fills, sustains, and actuates the whole ?
    Say, ye who best can tell, ye happy few,
Who saw him in the softest lights of life,
All unwithheld, indulging to his friends
The vast unborrowed treasures of his mind,
Oh, speak the wondrous man ! how mild, how calm,
How greatly humble, how divinely good,
How firmly stablished on eternal truth ;   150
Fervent in doing well, with every nerve
Still pressing on, forgetful of the past,
And panting for perfection ; far above
Those little cares and visionary joys
That so perplex the fond impassioned heart
Of ever cheated, ever trusting man.
This, Conduitt, from thy rural hours we hope,

As through the pleasing shade where nature pours
Her every sweet in studious ease you walk,
The social passions smiling at thy heart   160
That glows with all the recollected sage.
And you, ye hopeless gloomy-minded tribe,
You who, unconscious of those nobler flights
That reach impatient at immortal life,
Against the prime endearing privilege
Of being dare contend,—say, can a soul
Of such extensive, deep, tremendous powers,
Enlarging still, be but a finer breath
Of spirits dancing through their tubes awhile,
And then for ever lost in vacant air ?   170
But hark ! methinks I hear a warning voice,
Solemn as when some awful change is come,
Sound through the world—' 'Tis done !—the measure's
   full ;
And I resign my charge.'—Ye mouldering stones
That build the towering pyramid, the proud
Triumphal arch, the monument effaced
By ruthless ruin, and whate'er supports
The worshipped name of hoar antiquity—
Down to the dust ! What grandeur can ye boast
While Newton lifts his column to the skies,   180
Beyond the waste of time. Let no weak drop
Be shed for him. The virgin in her bloom
Cut off, the joyous youth, and darling child—
These are the tombs that claim the tender tear
And elegiac song. But Newton calls
For other notes of gratulation high,
That now he wanders through those endless worlds
He here so well descried, and wondering talks,
And hymns their Author with his glad compeers.
O Britain's boast ! whether with angels thou   190
Sittest in dread discourse, or fellow-blessed,

Who joy to see the honour of their kind ;
Or whether, mounted on cherubic wing,
Thy swift career is with the whirling orbs,
Comparing things with things, in rapture lost,
And grateful adoration for that light
So plenteous rayed into thy mind below
From Light Himself ; oh, look with pity down
On humankind, a frail erroneous race !
Exalt the spirit of a downward world !   200
O'er thy dejected country chief preside,
And be her Genius called ! her studies raise,
Correct her manners, and inspire her youth ;
For, though depraved and sunk, she brought thee
        forth,
And glories in thy name ! she points thee out
To all her sons, and bids them eye thy star :
While, in expectance of the second life
When time shall be no more, thy sacred dust
Sleeps with her kings, and dignifies the scene.

[Newton died March 20, 1727. These lines to his memory
were first published, in folio, in the following June, with a dedication to Sir Robert Walpole, then Prime Minister.

    At line 157 the reference is to an expected (but never written)
Life of Newton, by Mr. Conduitt, who had married Newton's
niece.]

ON THE DEATH OF MR. WILLIAM AIKMAN, THE PAINTER

[Probably written on the Continent in 1731.]

OH, could I draw, my friend, thy genuine mind
Just as the living forms by thee designed,
Of Raphael's figures none should fairer shine,
Nor Titian's colours longer last than mine.

A mind in wisdom old, in lenience young,
From fervent truth where every virtue sprung ;
Where all was real, modest, plain, sincere ;
Worth above show, and goodness unsevere :
Viewed round and round, as lucid diamonds throw
Still as you turn them a revolving glow,　　　　10
So did his mind reflect with secret ray
In various virtues heaven's internal day ;
Whether in high discourse it soared sublime
And sprung impatient o'er the bounds of time,
Or, wandering nature through with raptured eye,
Adored the hand that turned yon azure sky :
Whether to social life he bent his thought,
And the right poise of mingling passions sought,
Gay converse blest ; or in the thoughtful grove
Bid the heart open every source of love :　　　　20
New varying lights still set before your eyes
The just, the good, the social, or the wise.
For such a death who can, who would refuse
The friend a tear, a verse the mournful muse ?

Yet pay we just acknowledgement to heaven,
Though snatched so soon, that Aikman e'er was given.
A friend, when dead, is but removed from sight,
Hid in the lustre of eternal light :
Oft with the mind he wonted converse keeps

In the lone walk, or when the body sleeps   30
Lets in a wandering ray, and all elate
Wings and attracts her to another state ;
And, when the parting storms of life are o'er,
May yet rejoin him in a happier shore.

As those we love decay, we die in part,
String after string is severed from the heart ;
Till loosened life, at last but breathing clay,
Without one pang is glad to fall away.
Unhappy he who latest feels the blow,
Whose eyes have wept o'er every friend laid low, 40
Dragged lingering on from partial death to death,
Till, dying, all he can resign is breath.

[Only the last eight lines were printed in Thomson's *Poems on
Several Occasions*, published by A. Millar (price sixpence) in 1750.
The whole piece was first printed in 1792 from a MS. in the possession of the Earl of Buchan.—William Aikman, only son of
the Sheriff of Forfarshire, is best known as the painter of Gay's
portrait, but he also painted the portrait of Thomson (age *circa* 26)
now in the Scottish Gallery, Edinburgh.   He died in 1731.]
5–24. I leave the punctuation here as I find it, though it shows
a construction by no means clear.

TO THE MEMORY OF THE
RIGHT HONOURABLE THE LORD TALBOT

LATE CHANCELLOR OF GREAT BRITAIN

[First printed in June, 1737, with a dedication to the Rt. Hon.
the Lord Talbot.]

WHILE with the public, you, my Lord, lament
A friend and father lost ; permit the muse,
The muse assigned of old a double theme,
To praise dead worth and humble living pride,
Whose generous task begins where interest ends ;
Permit her on a Talbot's tomb to lay
This cordial verse sincere, by truth inspired,

Which means not to bestow but borrow fame.
Yes, she may sing his matchless virtues now—
Unhappy that she may ! But where begin ?   10
How from the diamond single out each ray,
That, though they tremble with ten thousand hues,
Effuse one poignant undivided light ?

Let the low-minded of these narrow days
No more presume to deem the lofty tale
Of ancient times, in pity to their own,
Romance. In Talbot we united saw
The piercing eye, the quick enlightened soul,
The graceful ease, the flowing tongue of Greece,
Joined to the virtues and the force of Rome.   20
Eternal Wisdom, that all-quickening sun
Whence every life in just proportion draws
Directing light and actuating flame,
Ne'er with a larger portion of its beams
Awakened mortal clay. Hence steady, calm,
Diffusive, deep, and clear his reason saw
With instantaneous view the truth of things ;
Chief what to human life and human bliss
Pertains, that kindest science, fit for man :
And hence, responsive to his knowledge, glowed   30
His ardent virtue. Ignorance and vice
In consort foul agree, each heightening each ;
While virtue draws from knowledge nobler fire,
Is knowledge of true pleasure, proved by deeds.
What grand, what comely, and what tender sense,
What talent, and what virtue was not his ?
All that can render man or great or good,
Give useful worth, or amiable grace ?
Nor could he brook in studious shade to lie
In soft retirement indolently pleased   40
With selfish peace. The Syren of the wise

(Who steals the Aonian song, and in the shape
Of Virtue woos them from a worthless world)
Though deep he felt her charms, could never melt
His strenuous spirit, recollected, calm
As silent night, yet active as the day.
The more the bold, the bustling, and the bad
Usurp the reins of power, the more behoves,
Becomes it virtue with indignant zeal
To check their conjuration. Shall low views   50
Of sneaking interest or luxurious vice,
The villain's passions, quicken more to toil,
And dart a livelier vigour through the soul,
Than those that, mingled with our truest good,
With present honour and immortal fame,
Involve the good of all ? An empty form,
Vain is the virtue that amid the shade
Lamenting lies, with future schemes amused,
While wickedness and folly, kindred powers,
Confound the world. A Talbot's, different far,   60
Sprung into action—action, that disdained
To lose in living death one pulse of life,
That might be saved ; disdained, for coward ease
And her insipid pleasures, to resign
The prize of glory, the keen sweets of toil,
And those high joys that teach the truly great
To live for others, and for others die.
    Early, behold ! he breaks benign on life.
Not breathing more beneficence, the spring
Leads in her swelling train the gentle airs :   70
While gay behind her smiles the kindling waste
Of ruffian storms and Winter's lawless rage.
In him Astrea, to this dim abode
Of ever-wandering men, returned again—
To bless them his delight, to bring them back
From thorny error, from unjoyous wrong,

Into the paths of kind primeval faith,
Of happiness and justice. All his parts,
His virtues all collected sought the good
Of humankind. For that he fervent felt   8c
The throb of patriots, when they model states :
Anxious for that, nor needful sleep could hold
His still-awakened soul ; nor friends had charms
To steal with pleasing guile an healing hour ;
Toil knew no languor, no attraction joy.
The common father such of erring men !
A froward race ! incessant in pursuit
Of flying good or of fallacious bliss ;
Still as they thwart and mingle in the chace,
Now fraud, now force, now cruelty and crimes, 90
Attempting all to seize a brother's prize ;
He sits superior to the little fray,
Detects the legal snares of mazy guile,
With the proud mighty bids the feeble cope,
And into social life the villain daunts.
Be named, victorious ravagers, no more !
Vanish, ye human comets ! shrink your blaze !
Ye that your glory to your terrors owe,
As, o'er the gazing desolated earth,
You scatter famine, pestilence, and war ;   100
Vanish ! before this vernal sun of fame,
Effulgent sweetness ! beaming life and joy.
    How the heart listened while he pleading spoke !
While on the enlightened mind, with winning art,
His gentle reason so persuasive stole
That the charmed hearer thought it was his own.
Ah ! when, ye studious of the laws, again
Shall such enchanting lessons bless your ear ?
When shall again the darkest truths, perplexed,
Be set in ample day ? Again the harsh   110
And arduous open into smiling ease ?

The solid mix with elegant delight ?
To him the purest eloquence indulged
Eternal treasure, light and heat combined,
At once to pour conviction on the soul,
And mould with lawful flame the impassioned heart.
That dangerous gift, which to the strictly just
And good alone belongs, lay safe with him
Reposed. He sacred to his country's cause,
To trampled want and worth, to suffering right, 120
To the lone widow's and her orphan's woes,
Reserved the mighty charm With equal brow,
Despising then the smiles or frowns of power,
He all that noblest eloquence effused
Which wakes the tender or exalting tear,
When generous passions, taught by reason, speak.
Then spoke the man, and over barren art
Prevailed abundant nature. Freedom then
His client was, humanity and truth.
    Placed on the seat of justice, there he reigned
In a superior sphere of cloudless day,   131
A pure intelligence. No tumult there,
No dark emotion, no intemperate heat,
No passion e'er disturbed the clear serene
That round him spread. A zeal for right alone,
The love of justice, like the steady sun
Unbating ardour lent ; and now and then,
Against the sons of violence, of pride,
And bold deceit his indignation gleamed.
As intuition quick, he snatched the truth,   140
Yet with progressive patience, step by step,
Self-diffident, or to the slower kind,
He through the maze of falsehood traced it on,
Till, at the last evolved, it full appeared,
And e'en the loser owned the just decree.
    But, when in senates he, to freedom firm,

Enlightened freedom, planned salubrious laws,
His various learning, his wide knowledge then
His insight deep into Britannia's weal,
Spontaneous seemed from simple sense to flow,　150
And the plain patriot smoothed the brow of law.
No specious swell, no frothy pomp of words
Fell on the cheated ear ; no studied maze
Of declamation to perplex the right
He darkening threw around : safe in itself,
In its own force, almighty Reason spoke ;
While on the great, the ruling point, at once
He streamed decisive day, and showed it vain
To lengthen farther out the clear debate.
Conviction breathes conviction ; to the heart,　160
Poured ardent forth in eloquence unbid,
The heart attends : for, let the venal try
Their every hardening stupefying art,
Truth must prevail, zeal will enkindle zeal,
And Nature, skilful touched, is honest still.
　Behold him in the councils of his prince.
What faithful light he lends ! How rare in courts
Such wisdom ! such abilities ! and, joined
To virtue so determined, public zeal,
And honour of such adamantine proof　170
As even corruption, hopeless and o'erawed,
Durst not have tempted ! Yet of manners mild,
And winning every heart, he knew to please,
Nobly to please ; while equally he scorned
Or adulation to receive or give.
Happy the state where wakes a ruling eye
Of such inspection keen and general care
Beneath a guard so vigilant, so pure,
All-trusted, all-revered, and all-beloved,
Toil may resign his careless head to rest,　180
And ever-jealous freedom sleep in peace.

Ah ! lost untimely ! lost in downward days !
And many a patriot counsel with him lost !
Counsels, that might have humbled Britain's foe,
Her native foe, from eldest time by fate
Appointed, as did once a Talbot's arms.
Let learning, arts, let universal worth
Lament a patron lost, a friend and judge—
Unlike the sons of vanity, that, veiled
Beneath the patron's prostituted name,   190
Dare sacrifice a worthy man to pride,
And flush confusion o'er an honest cheek.
Obliged when he obliged, it seemed a debt
Which he to merit, to the public, paid,
That can alone by virtue stationed high
Recover fame ; to his own heart a debt,
And to the great all-bounteous Source of good !
The gracious flood that cheers the lettered world
Is not the noisy gift of summer's noon,
Whose sudden current from the naked root   200
Washes the little soil which yet remained,
And only more dejects the blushing flowers :
No, 'tis the soft-descending dews at eve,
The silent treasures of the vernal year
Indulging deep their stores the still night long—
Till with returning morn the freshened world
Is fragrance all, all beauty, joy, and song.
Still let me view him in the pleasing light
Of private life, where pomp forgets to glare,
And where the plain unguarded soul is seen.   210
Not only there most amiable, best,
But with that truest greatness he appeared,
Which thinks not of appearing ; kindly veiled
In the soft graces of the friendly scene,
Inspiring social confidence and ease.
As free the converse of the wise and good,

As joyous, disentangling every power,
And breathing mixed improvement with delight,
As when amid the various-blossomed spring,
Or gentle beaming autumn's pensive shade,   220
The philosophic mind with nature talks.
Say ye, his sons, his dear remains, with whom
The father laid superfluous state aside,
Yet swelled your filial duty thence the more,
With friendship swelled it, with esteem, with love,
Beyond the ties of blood, oh ! speak the joy,
The pure serene, the cheerful wisdom mild,
The virtuous spirit, which his vacant hours
In semblance of amusement through the breast
Infused. And thou, O Rundle ! lend thy strain, 230
Thou darling friend ! thou brother of his soul !
In whom the head and heart their stores unite—
Whatever fancy paints, invention pours,
Judgement digests, the well-tuned bosom feels,
Truth natural, moral, or divine has taught,
The virtues dictate, or the Muses sing.
Lend me the plaint, which, to the lonely main,
With memory conversing, you will pour,
As on the pebbled shore you pensive stray
Where Derry's mountains a bleak crescent form, 240
And mid their ample round receive the waves
That from the frozen pole, resounding, rush
Impetuous. Though from native sunshine driven,
Driven from your friends, the sunshine of the soul,
By slanderous zeal and politics infirm,
Jealous of worth ; yet will you bless your lot,
Yet will you triumph in your glorious fate,
Whence Talbot's friendship glows to future times,
Intrepid, warm ; of kindred tempers born ;
Nursed by experience into slow esteem,   250
Calm confidence unbounded love not blind,

And the sweet light from mingled minds disclosed,
From mingled chymic oils as bursts the fire.
I too remember well that mental bowl
Which round his table flowed. The serious there
Mixed with the sportive, with the learned the plain ;
Mirth softened wisdom, candour tempered mirth,
And wit its honey lent without the sting.
Not simple nature's unaffected sons,
The blameless Indians, round their forest cheer, 260
In sunny lawn or shady covert set,
Hold more unspotted converse ; nor, of old,
Rome's awful consuls, her dictator-swains,
As on the product of their Sabine farms
They fared, with stricter virtue fed the soul :
Nor yet in Athens, at an Attic meal,
Where Socrates presided, fairer truth,
More elegant humanity, more grace,
Wit more refined, or deeper science reigned.

But far beyond the little vulgar bounds   270
Of family, of friends, of country kind,
By just degrees and with proportioned flame
Extended his benevolence : a friend
To humankind, to parent nature's works.
Of free access, and of engaging grace,
Such as a brother to a brother owes,
He kept an open judging ear for all,
And spread an open countenance where smiled
The fair effulgence of an open heart ;
While on the rich, the poor, the high, the low   280
With equal ray his ready goodness shone :
For *nothing human foreign was to him.*

Thus to a dread inheritance, my Lord,
And hard to be supported, you succeed :
But, kept by virtue, as by virtue gained,

It will through latest time enrich your race,
When grosser wealth shall moulder into dust,
And with their authors in oblivion sunk
Vain titles lie, the servile badges oft
Of mean submission, not the meed of worth   290
True genuine honour its large patent holds
Of all mankind, through every land and age,
Of universal reason's various sons,
And even of God himself, sole perfect Judge!
Who sees with other eyes than flattering men.
Meantime these noblest honours of the mind
On rigid terms descend : the high-placed heir,
Scanned by the public eye, that with keen gaze
Malignant seeks out faults, cannot through life
Amid the nameless insects of a court,   300
If such to life belong, unheeded steal :
He must be glorious, or he must be base.
This truth to you, who merit well to bear
A name to Britons dear, the officious muse
May safely sing, and sing without reserve.
   Vain were the plaint, and ignorant the tear
That should a Talbot mourn. Ourselves, indeed,
Our sinking country, humankind enslaved,
We may lament. But let us, grateful, joy
That ere such virtues gave our days to shine,   310
Above the dark abyss of modern time,
That we such virtues knew, such virtues felt,
And feel them still, teaching our views to rise
Through ever-brightening scenes of future worlds.
Be dumb, ye worst of zealots ! ye that, prone
To thoughtless dust, renounce that generous hope,
Whence every joy below its spirit draws,
And every pain its balm : a Talbot's light,
A Talbot's virtues claim another source
Than the blind maze of undesigning blood ;   320

Nor, when that vital fountain plays no more,
Can they be quenched amid the gelid stream.

Methinks I see his mounting spirit, freed
From tangling earth, regain the realms of day,
Its native country ; whence to bless mankind
Eternal goodness on this darksome spot
Had rayed it down a while. Behold ! approved
By the tremendous Judge of heaven and earth,
And to the Almighty Father's presence joined,
Whose smile creative beams superior life,   330
He takes his rank in glory and in bliss
Amid the human worthies. Glad around
Crowd his compatriot shades, and point him out
With noble pride Britannia's blameless boast.
Ah ! who is he that with a fonder eye
Meets thine enraptured ?—'Tis the best of sons !
The best of friends ! Too soon is realized
That hope which once forbad thy tears to flow !
Meanwhile the kindred souls of every land
(Howe'er divided in the fretful days   340
Of prejudice and error), mingled now,
In one selected never-jarring state,
Where God himself their only monarch reigns,
Partake the joy ; yet, such the sense that still
Remains of earthly woes, for us below
And for our loss they drop a pitying tear.
But cease, presumptuous muse, nor vainly strive
To quit this cloudy sphere that binds thee down :
'Tis not for mortal hand to trace these scenes—
Scenes, that our gross ideas grovelling cast   350
Behind, and strike our boldest language dumb.

Forgive, immortal shade ! if aught from earth,
From dust low-warbled, to those groves can rise

Where flows unbidden harmony, forgive
This fond superfluous verse. With deep-felt voice,
On every heart impressed, thy deeds themselves
Attest thy praise. Thy praise the widow's sighs
And orphan's tears embalm. The good, the bad,
The sons of justice and the sons of strife,
All that or freedom or that interest prize,   360
A deep-divided nation's parties all
Conspire to swell thy spotless praise to heaven.
They catch it there ; and to seraphic lyre
Celestial voices thy arrival hail.
How vain this tribute then ! this lowly lay !
Yet nothing vain which gratitude inspires.
The muse, besides, her duty thus approves
To virtue, to her country, to mankind,
To forming nature, that in glorious charge,
As to her priestess, has it given to hymn   370
Whatever good and excellent she forms.

[The Lord Chancellor died in February, 1737. The text of
the memorial poem given above is that of 1738, as it appears in
Thomson's WORKS, 8vo, vol. ii, pp. 217–38, following *Liberty* :
the date on the title-page of vol. i is given 1744. Talbot, when
Thomson first knew him, was Solicitor-General ; he became Lord
Chancellor in 1733. It was in the end of 1730 that Thomson was
appointed tutor and travelling companion to young Charles Talbot,
eldest and name-son of the Solicitor-General. Young Talbot died
before his father's elevation to the Chancellorship.—Line 230 :
Dr. Rundle, Bishop of Derry.]

EPITAPH ON MISS ELIZABETH STANLEY,

IN HOLYROOD CHURCH, SOUTHAMPTON

HERE, Stanley, rest! escaped this mortal strife,
Above the joys, beyond the woes of life,
Fierce pangs no more thy lively beauties stain,
And sternly try thee with a year of pain ;
No more sweet patience, feigning oft relief,
Lights thy sick eye to cheat a parent's grief :
With tender art to save her anxious groan,
No more thy bosom presses down its own :
Now well-earned peace is thine, and bliss sincere :
Ours be the lenient, not unpleasing tear !   10
   O born to bloom, then sink beneath the storm ;
To show us virtue in her fairest form ;
To show us artless reason's moral reign,
What boastful science arrogates in vain ;
The obedient passions knowing each their part ;
Calm light the head, and harmony the heart !
   Yes, we must follow soon, will glad obey ;
When a few suns have rolled their cares away,
Tired with vain life, will close the willing eye :
'Tis the great birthright of mankind to die.   20
Blest be the bark that wafts us to the shore
Where death-divided friends shall part no more :
To join thee there, here with thy dust repose,
Is all the hope thy hapless mother knows.

[' A young lady well known to the author, who died at the age
of eighteen, in the year 1738.—T.' See note on lines 564 seqq. of
Summer.]

A POEM TO THE MEMORY OF MR. CONGREVE

ADVERTISEMENT

THE author of the following poem, not having had the happiness of a personal acquaintance with Mr. Congreve, is sensible that he has drawn his private character very imperfectly. This all his friends will readily discover : and, therefore, if any one of them had thought fit to do justice to those amiable qualifications, which made him the love and admiration of all that knew him, these verses had never seen the light.

[Assigned to Thomson, on unsatisfactory evidence, by H. F. Cary. First published in 1729, anonymously. Congreve died in January, 1729.]

OFT has the muse, with mean attempt, employed
Her heaven-born voice to flatter prosperous guilt
Or trivial greatness—often stooped her song
To soothe ambition in his frantic rage,
The dire destroyer! while a bleeding world
Wept o'er his crimes. Of this pernicious skill
Unknowing, I these voluntary lays
To genuine worth devote—to worth by all
Confessed and, mourned—to Congreve now no more.
    First of the fairer kind! by heaven adorned 10
With every nobler praise, whose smile can lift
The muse unknown to fame, indulgent now
Permit her strain, ennobled by a name,
To all the better few, and chief to thee,
Bright Marlborough, ever sacred, ever dear.
    Lamented shade! in him the comic muse,
Parent of gay instruction, lost her loved,
Her last remaining hope ; and pensive now
Resigns to folly and his mimic rout
Her throne usurped—presage of darker times, 20
And deeper woes to come! with taste declined

Fallen virtue droops ; and o'er the ill-omened age,
Unseen, unfeared, impend the thousand ills
That wait on ignorance : no Congreve now
To scourge our crimes, or laugh to scorn our fools,
A new and nameless herd. Nature was his,
Bold, sprightly, various ; and superior art,
Curious to choose each better grace, unseen
Of vulgar eyes ; with delicacy free,
Though laboured happy, and though strong refined.
Judgement, severely cool, o'erlooked his toil,   31
And patient finished all ; each fair design
With freedom regular, correctly great,
A master's skilful daring. Closely wrought
His meaning fable, with deep art perplexed,
With striking ease unravelled ; no thin plot
Seen through at once and scorned ; or ill-concealed
By borrowed aids of mimicry and farce.
His characters strong-featured, equal, just,
From finer nature drawn ; and all the mind   40
Through all her mazes traced ; each darker vice,
And darling folly, under each disguise,
By either sex assumed, of studied ease,
False friendship, loose severity, vain wit,
Dull briskness, shallow depth, or coward rage.
Of the whole muse possessed, his piercing eye
Discerned each richer vein of genuine mirth,
Humour or wit ; where differing, where agreed ;
How counterfeited, or by folly's grin
Or affectation's air ; and what their force   50
To please, to move, to shake the ravished scene
With laughter unreproved. To him the soul,
In all her higher workings, too, was known ;
What passions' tumult there ; whence their prompt
     spring,
Their sudden flood of rage, and gradual fall ;

Infinite motion ! source supreme of bliss
Or woe to man ; our heaven or hell below !
  Such was his public name ; nor less allowed
His private worth ; by nature made for praise.
A pleasing form ; a soul sincere and clear,   60
Where all the human graces mixed their charms,
Pure candour, easy goodness, open truth,
Spontaneous all : where strength and beauty joined,
With wit indulgent ; humble in the height
Of envied honours ; and, but rarely found,
The unjealous friend of every rival worth.
Adorned for social life, each talent his
To win each heart ; the charm of happy ease,
Free mirth, gay earning, ever smiling wit,
To all endeared, a pleasure without pain ;   70
What Halifax approved, and Marlborough mourns.
  Not so the illiberal mind, where knowledge dwells
Uncouth and harsh, with her attendant, pride,
Impatient of attention, prone to blame,
Disdaining to be pleased ; condemning all,
By all condemned ; for social joys unfit,
In solitude self-cursed, the child of spleen.
Obliged, ungrateful ; unobliged, a foe,
Poor, vicious, old ; such fierce-eyed Asper was.
Now meaner Cenus, trivial with design,   80
Courts poor applause by levity of face,
And scorn of serious thought ; to mischief prompt,
Though impotent to wound ; profuse of wealth
Yet friendless and unloved ; vain, fluttering, false,
A vacant head, and an ungenerous heart.
  But slighting these ignoble names, the muse
Pursues her favourite son, and sees him now,
From this dim spot enlarged, triumphant soar
Beyond the walk of time to better worlds,
Where all is new, all wondrous, and all blest !   90

What art thou, death ! by mankind poorly feared,
Yet period of their ills. On thy near shore,
Trembling they stand, and see through dreaded mists
The eternal port, irresolute to leave
This various misery, these air-fed dreams
Which men call life and fame. Mistaken minds !
'Tis reason's prime aspiring, greatly just ;
'Tis happiness supreme, to venture forth
In quest of nobler worlds ; to try the deeps
Of dark futurity, with Heaven our guide,   100
The unerring hand that led us safe through time ;
That planted in the soul this powerful hope,
This infinite ambition of new life
And endless joys, still rising, ever new.
    These Congreve tastes, safe on the ethereal coast,
Joined to the numberless immortal quire
Of spirits blest. High-seated among these,
He sees the public fathers of mankind,
The greatly good, those universal minds
Who drew the sword, or planned the holy scheme,
For liberty and right, to check the rage   111
Of blood-stained tyranny and save a world.
Such, high-born Marlborough, be thy sire divine
With wonder named ; fair freedom's champion he,
By Heaven approved, a conqueror without guilt,
And such, on earth his friend, and joined on high
By deathless love, Godolphin's patriot worth,
Just to his country's fame, yet of her wealth
With honour frugal ; above interest great.
Hail men immortal ! social virtues hail !   120
First heirs of praise !—But I, with weak essay,
Wrong the superior theme ; while heavenly quires,
In strains high-warbled to celestial-harps,
Resound your names ; and Congreve's added voice
In Heaven exalts what he admired below.

With these he mixes, now no more to swerve
From reason's purest law ; no more to please,
Borne by the torrent down, a sensual age.
Pardon, loved shade, that I with friendly blame
Slight note thy error ; not to wrong thy worth 130
Or shade thy memory (far from my soul
Be that base aim !), but haply to deter
From flattering the gross vulgar future pens
Powerful like thine in every grace, and skilled
To win the listening soul with virtuous charms.
If manly thought and wit refined may hope
To please an age in aimless folly sunk,
And sliding swift into the depth of vice !
Consuming pleasure leads the gay and young
Through their vain round, and venal faith the old,
Or avarice mean of soul ; instructive arts 141
Pursued no more ; the general taste extinct,
Or all debased ; even sacred liberty
The great man's jest, and Britain's welfare named,
By her degenerate sons, the poet's dream,
Or fancy's air-built vision, gaily vain.
Such the lost age ; yet still the muse can find,
Superior and apart, a sacred band,
Heroic virtues, who ne'er bowed the knee
To sordid interest ; who dare greatly claim 150
The privilege of men, unfearing truth,
And freedom, heaven's first gift ; the ennobling bliss
That renders life of price, and cheaply saved
At life's expense ; our sum of happiness.
On these the drooping muses fix their eyes ;
From these expect their ancient fame restored.
Nor will the hope be vain ; the public weal
With theirs fast linked ; a generous truth concealed
From narrow-thoughted power, and known alone
To souls of highest rank. With these, the fair 160

Be joined in just applause ; the brighter few,
Who, raised above gay folly, and the whirl
Of fond amusements, emulate thy praise,
Illustrious Marlborough! pleased, like thee, to shine
Propitious on the muse ; whose charms inspire
Her noblest raptures, and whose goodness crowns.

[The piece is forced and rhetorical throughout, the composition
stiff, the judgement often erroneous or insincere, and the flattery
fulsome. Mallet may have written it—never Thomson. The
verses were dedicated to ' Her Grace, Henrietta, Duchess of
Marlborough,' eldest surviving daughter of the great Duke.
J. Millan was the publisher.—At line 71, the reference is to Charles
Montagu, Earl of Halifax.—Lines 79, 80: Asper and Cenus have
not been identified.—Line 117: the Duchess of Marlborough had
married the son of Godolphin, the great statesman.]

EPISTLES

TO DODINGTON

THE HAPPY MAN

[Printed in Ralph's *Miscellany* in 1729. It was to Dodington
Thomson dedicated *Summer*.]

HE's not the happy man to whom is given
A plenteous fortune by indulgent Heaven ;
Whose gilded roofs on shining columns rise,
And painted walls enchant the gazer's eyes ;
Whose table flows with hospitable cheer,
And all the various bounty of the year ;
Whose valleys smile, whose gardens breathe the
    Spring,
Whose curvèd mountains bleat, and forests sing ;
For whom the cooling shade in Summer twines,
While his full cellars give their generous wines ; 10
From whose wide fields unbounded Autumn pours
A golden tide into his swelling stores :
Whose Winter laughs ; for whom the liberal gales
Stretch the big sheet, and toiling commerce sails ;
Whom yielding crowds attend, and pleasure serves,
While youth, and health, and vigour string his nerves;
Even not all these, in one rich lot combined,
Can make the happy man, without the mind ;
Where judgement sits clear-sighted, and surveys
The chain of reason with unerring gaze ; 20
Where fancy lives, and to the brightening eyes
Bids fairer scenes and bolder figures rise ;

Where social love exerts her soft command
And lays the passions with a tender hand,
Whence every virtue flows, in rival strife,
And all the moral harmony of life.

Nor canst thou, Dodington, this truth decline,
Thine is the fortune, and the mind is thine.

[The opening lines of this short piece remind one of the opening
lines of Horace's 18th Ode, Lib. II—
' Non ebur neque aureum
Mea renidet in domo lacunar,' &c.]

TO HIS ROYAL HIGHNESS THE PRINCE OF WALES

[On the birth of the Princess Augusta, July 31, 1737.]

WHILE secret-leaguing nations frown around,
    Ready to pour the long-expected storm—
While she who wont the restless Gaul to bound,
    Britannia, drooping, grows an empty form—
While on our vitals selfish parties prey
And deep corruption eats our soul away—

Yet in the goddess of the main appears
    A gleam of joy, gay-flushing every grace,
As she the cordial voice of millions hears,
    Rejoicing zealous o'er thy rising race.   10
Straight her rekindling eyes resume their fire,
The virtues smile, the muses tune the lyre.

But more enchanting than the muse's song,
    United Britons thy dear offspring hail :
The city triumphs through her glowing throng,
    The shepherd tells his transport to the dale ;
The sons of roughest toil forget their pain,
And the glad sailor cheers the midnight main.

Can aught from fair Augusta's gentle blood,
    And thine, thou friend of liberty ! be born—   20
Can aught save what is lovely, generous, good—
    What will at once defend us and adorn ?
From thence prophetic joy new Edwards eyes;
New Henries, Annas, and Elizas rise.

May fate my fond devoted days extend
    To sing the promised glories of thy reign !
What though, by years depressed, my muse might
        bend ?
    My heart will teach her still a nobler strain :
How with recovered Britain will she soar,
When France insults, and Spain shall rob no more. 30

[These lines (which have been attributed to Thomson) appeared
in *The Gentleman's Magazine* in September, 1737.]

TO THE REV. PATRICK MURDOCH

THUS safely low, my friend, thou canst not fall :
Here reigns a deep tranquillity o'er all ;
No noise, no care, no vanity, no strife ;
Men, woods, and fields, all breathe untroubled life.
Then keep each passion down, however dear ;
Trust me, the tender are the most severe.
Guard, while 'tis thine, thy philosophic ease,
And ask no joy but that of virtuous peace ;
That bids defiance to the storms of fate :
High bliss is only for a higher state !   10

[These lines were probably written shortly after Murdoch's
appointment as Rector of Stradishall, Suffolk, in 1738. See Note
to *The Incomparable Soporific Doctor*, p. 467.]

LINES SENT TO
GEORGE LYTTELTON, ESQ.

SOON AFTER THE DEATH OF HIS WIFE:

WRITTEN IN A COPY OF 'THE SEASONS'.

Go, little book, and find our friend,
  Who nature and the muses loves.
Whose cares the public virtues blend
  With all the softness of the groves.

A fitter time thou canst not choose
  His fostering friendship to repay ;
Go then, and try, my rural muse,
  To steal his widowed hours away.

[See Note to line 906 of *Spring*.]

TO MRS. MENDEZ' BIRTHDAY

Who was born on Valentine's Day.

THINE is the gentle day of love
  When youths and virgins try their fate ;
When, deep retiring to the grove,
  Each feathered songster weds his mate.

With tempered beams the skies are bright,
  Earth decks in smiles her pleasing face ;
Such is the day that gave thee light,
  And speaks as such thy every grace.

TO THE INCOMPARABLE SOPORIFIC DOCTOR

[The Rev. Dr. Patrick Murdoch, Thomson's old and intimate friend and countryman—afterwards his kindly biographer. He was presented to the living of Stradishall in Suffolk in 1737-8 by Admiral Vernon, of Great Thurlow, to whose son he had been tutor. In 1760 he became vicar of Great Thurlow, where he wrote his memoir of the poet. See Note to Stanza LXIX, Canto I, of *The Castle of Indolence*.]

SWEET, sleeky Doctor ! dear pacific soul !
Lay at the beef, and suck the vital bowl !
Still let the involving smoke around thee fly,
And broad-looked dullness settle in thine eye.
Ah ! soft in down those dainty limbs repose,
And in the very lap of slumber doze ;
But chiefly on the lazy day of grace,
Call forth the lambent glories of thy face ;
If aught the thoughts of dinner can prevail—
And sure the Sunday's dinner cannot fail.   10
To the thin church in sleepy pomp proceed,
And lean on the lethargic book thy head.
Those eyes wipe often with the hallowed lawn,
Profoundly nod, immeasurably yawn.
Slow let the prayers by thy meek lips be sung,
Nor let thy thoughts be distanced by thy tongue
If e'er the lingerers are within a call,
Or if on prayers thou deign'st to think at all.
Yet—only yet—the swimming head we bend ;
But when serene, the pulpit you ascend,   20
Through every joint a gentle horror creeps,
And round you the consenting audience sleeps.
So when an ass with sluggish front appears,
The horses start, and prick their quivering ears ;
But soon as e'er the sage is heard to bray,
The fields all thunder, and they bound away.

TO SERAPHINA

THE wanton's charms, however bright,
Are like the false illusive light
Whose flattering unauspicious blaze
To precipices oft betrays.

But that sweet ray your beauties dart,
Which clears the mind and cleans the heart,
Is like the sacred queen of night
Who pours a lovely gentle light
Wide o'er the dark—by wanderers blest,
Conducting them to peace and rest.   10

A vicious love depraves the mind ;
'Tis anguish, guilt, and folly joined ;
But Seraphina's eyes dispense
A mild and gracious influence,
Such as in visions angels shed
Around the heaven-illumined head.

To love thee, Seraphina, sure
Is to be tender, happy, pure ;
'Tis from low passions to escape,
And woo bright virtue's fairest shape ;   20
'Tis ecstasy with wisdom joined,
And heaven infused into the mind.

TO AMANDA

IN IMITATION OF TIBULLUS

Huc ades, et tenerae morbos expelle puellae,
Huc ades, intonsa Phoebe superbe coma, &c.
Tibulli Lib. IV, Car. iv.

COME, healing god ! Apollo, come and aid,
Moved by the tears of love, my tender maid !
No more let sickness dim those radiant eyes
Which never know to cheat or to disguise.
If e'er my verse has pleased thy listening ear,
O now be friendly, now propitious hear !
Bring every virtuous herb, each root and flower
Of cooling juice and salutary power.
Light is the task : to touch a hand so fair,
Divine physician, will repay thy care.   10
    My tears are fled ; the god my suit approves ;
He can't be wretched who sincerely loves.
Protecting Heaven, with more than common care,
Smiles on his hopes and guards him from despair.
    Raise from the pillow, raise thy languid head ;
Come forth, my love, and quit thy sickly bed !
Come forth, my love ! for thee the balmy Spring
Breathes every sweet ; for thee the zephyrs bring
Their healing gales ; for thee the graces lead
The smiling hours, and paint the flowery mead. 20
As nature, drooping long beneath the reign
Of dreary winter, now revives again,
Calls all her beauties out, and charms us more
From what we suffered in their loss before ;
So from thy tedious illness shalt thou rise
More sweetly fair ; and in those languid eyes
And faded cheeks returning health shall place
A fresher bloom and more attractive grace.

Then shall my bounding heart forget its woe,
And think it never more a pain can know ;   30
Then shall my muse thy charms more gaily sing,
And hail thee as the nightingale the spring.

TO AMANDA

AH ! urged too late, from beauty's bondage free,
Why did I trust my liberty with thee ?
And thou, why didst thou with inhuman art,
If not resolved to take, seduce my heart ?
Yes, yes ! you said—for lovers' eyes speak true ;
You must have seen how fast my passion grew :
And, when your glances chanced on me to shine,
How my fond soul ecstatic sprung to thine !
　But mark me, fair one ! what I now declare
Thy deep attention claims and serious care :   10
It is no common passion fires my breast—
I must be wretched, or I must be blest !
My woes all other remedy deny—
Or pitying give me hope, or bid me die !

[These lines were first printed in Lord Buchan's *Essay on
Thomson*.]

TO AMANDA,

WITH A COPY OF 'THE SEASONS'

ACCEPT, loved Nymph, this tribute due
To tender friendship, love, and you ;
But with it take what breathed the whole,
O take to thine the poet's soul.
If fancy here her power displays,
And if a heart exalts these lays,
You fairest in that fancy shine,
And all that heart is fondly thine.

MISCELLANEOUS POEMS

BRITANNIA:

A POEM

[Written in 1727, published in January, 1729.]

——Et tantas audetis tollere moles ?
Quos ego—sed motos praestat componere fluctus.
Post mihi non simili poena commissa luetis.
Maturate fugam, regique haec dicite vestro :
Non illi imperium pelagi, saevumque tridentem,
Sed mihi sorte datum.   VIRGIL, *Aeneid*, i. 134.

As on the sea-beat shore Britannia sat,
Of her degenerate sons the faded fame
Deep in her anxious heart revolving sad—
Bare was her throbbing bosom to the gale,
That, hoarse and hollow, from the bleak surge blew ;
Loose flowed her tresses ; rent her azure robe.
Hung o'er the deep from her majestic brow
She tore the laurel, and she tore the bay.
Nor ceased the copious grief to bathe her cheek ;
Nor ceased her sobs to murmur to the main.   10
Peace discontented, nigh departing, stretched
Her dove-like wings ; and War, though greatly roused,
Yet mourns his fettered hands ; while thus the queen
Of nations spoke ; and what she said the muse
Recorded faithful in unbidden verse :—
    ' Even not yon sail, that from the sky-mixed wave
Dawns on the sight, and wafts the royal youth,
A freight of future glory, to my shore ;
Even not the flattering view of golden days,

And rising periods yet of bright renown,   20
Beneath the Parents, and their endless line
Through late revolving time, can soothe my rage ;
While, unchastised, the insulting Spaniard dares
Infest the trading flood, full of vain war
Despise my navies, and my merchants seize ;
As, trusting to false peace, they fearless roam
The world of waters wild ; made, by the toil,
And liberal blood of glorious ages, mine :
Nor bursts my sleeping thunder on their head.
Whence this unwonted patience ? this weak doubt ?
This tame beseeching of rejected peace ?   31
This meek forbearance ? this unnative fear,
To generous Britons never known before ?
And sailed my fleets for this—on Indian tides
To float, inactive, with the veering winds ?
The mockery of war ! while hot disease
And sloth distempered swept off burning crowds,
For action ardent ; and amid the deep,
Inglorious, sunk them in a watery grave.
There now they lie beneath the rolling flood,   40
Far from their friends, and country, unavenged ;
And back the drooping warship comes again,
Dispirited and thin ; her sons ashamed
Thus idly to review their native shore ;
With not one glory sparkling in their eye,
One triumph on their tongue. A passenger,
The violated merchant comes along—
That far sought wealth, for which the noxious gale
He drew, and sweat beneath equator suns—
By lawless force detained, a force that soon   50
Would melt away, and every spoil resign,
Were once the British lion heard to roar.
Whence is it that the proud Iberian thus
In their own well asserted element

Dares rouse to wrath the masters of the main ?
Who told him that the big incumbent war
Would not, ere this, have rolled his trembling ports
In smoky ruin ? and his guilty stores,
Won by the ravage of a butchered world,
Yet unatoned, sunk in the swallowing deep,   60
Or led the glittering prize into the Thames ?
  ' There was a time (oh, let my languid sons
Resume their spirit at the rousing thought !)
When all the pride of Spain, in one dread fleet,
Swelled o'er the labouring surge like a whole heaven
Of clouds wide-rolled before the boundless breeze.
Gaily the splendid armament along
Exultant ploughed, reflecting a red gleam,
As sunk the sun, o'er all the flaming vast ;
Tall, gorgeous, and elate ; drunk with the dream 70
Of easy conquest ; while their bloated war,
Stretched out from sky to sky, the gathered force
Of ages held in its capacious womb.
But soon, regardless of the cumbrous pomp,
My dauntless Britons came, a gloomy few,
With tempests black, the goodly scene deformed,
And laid their glory waste. The bolts of fate
Resistless thundered through their yielding sides ;
Fierce o'er their beauty blazed the lurid flame ;
And seized in horrid grasp, or shattered wide   80
Amid the mighty waters, deep they sunk.
Then too from every promontory chill,
Rank fen, and cavern where the wild wave works,
I swept confederate winds, and swelled a storm.
Round the glad isle, snatched by the vengeful blast,
The scattered remnants drove ; on the blind shelve,
And pointed rock that marks the indented shore,
Relentless dashed, where loud the northern main
Howls through the fractured Caledonian isles.

'Such were the dawnings of my liquid reign ;
But since, how vast it grew, how absolute,   91
Even in those troubled times when dreadful Blake
Awed angry nations with the British name,
Let every humbled state, let Europe say,
Sustained and balanced by my naval arm.
Ah, what must those immortal spirits think
Of your poor shifts ?   Those, for their country's good,
Who faced the blackest danger, knew no fear,
No mean submission, but commanded peace—
Ah, how with indignation must they burn !   100
(If aught but joy can touch ethereal breasts)
With shame ! with grief ! to see their feeble sons
Shrink from that empire o'er the conquered seas
For which their wisdom planned, their councils
      glowed,
And their veins bled through many a toiling age.
   'Oh, first of human blessings, and supreme !
Fair Peace ! how lovely, how delightful thou !
By whose wide tie the kindred sons of men
Like brothers live, in amity combined
And unsuspicious faith ; while honest toil   110
Gives every joy, and to those joys a right,
Which idle, barbarous rapine but usurps.
Pure is thy reign ; when, unaccursed by blood,
Nought, save the sweetness of indulgent showers,
Trickling distils into the vernant glebe ;
Instead of mangled carcasses, sad-seen,
When the blithe sheaves lie scattered o'er the field ;
When only shining shares, the crooked knife,
And hooks imprint the vegetable wound ;
When the land blushes with the rose alone,   120
The falling fruitage and the bleeding vine.
Oh, Peace ! thou source and soul of social life,
Beneath whose calm inspiring influence,

Science his views enlarges, Art refines,
And swelling Commerce opens all her ports,
Blest be the man divine who gives us thee!
Who bids the trumpet hush his horrid clang,
Nor blow the giddy nations into rage;
Who sheathes the murderous blade; the deadly gun
Into the well piled armoury returns;   130
And every vigour from the work of death
To grateful industry converting, makes
The country flourish, and the city smile.
Unviolated, him the virgin sings;
And him the smiling mother to her train.
Of him the shepherd in the peaceful dale
Chants; and, the treasures of his labour sure,
The husbandman of him, as at the plough
Or team he toils. With him the sailor soothes,
Beneath the trembling moon, the midnight wave;
And the full city, warm from street to street,   141
And shop to shop responsive, rings of him.
Nor joys one land alone: his praise extends
Far as the sun rolls the diffusive day,
Far as the breeze can bear the gifts of peace,
Till all the happy nations catch the song.
    'What would not, Peace! the patriot bear for
        thee?
What painful patience? what incessant care?
What mixed anxiety? what sleepless toil?
Even from the rash protected what reproach?   150
For he thy value knows; thy friendship he
To human nature: but the better thou,
The richer of delight, sometimes the more
Inevitable war; when ruffian force
Awakes the fury of an injured state.
Then the good easy man, whom reason rules,
Who, while unhurt, knew nor offence nor harm,

Roused by bold insult, and injurious rage,
With sharp and sudden check the astonished sons
Of violence confounds ; firm as his cause,   160
His bolder heart ; in awful justice clad ;
His eyes effulging a peculiar fire :
And, as he charges through the prostrate war,
His keen arm teaches faithless men, no more
To dare the sacred vengeance of the just.
  ' And what, my thoughtless sons, should fire you
    more
Than when your well-earned empire of the deep
The least beginning injury receives ?
What better cause can call your lightning forth ?
Your thunder wake ? your dearest life demand ? 170
What better cause, than when your country sees
The sly destruction at her vitals aimed ?
For oh ! it much imports you, 'tis your all,
To keep your trade entire, entire the force
And honour of your fleets—o'er that to watch,
Even with a hand severe and jealous eye.
In intercourse be gentle, generous, just,
By wisdom polished, and of manners fair ;
But on the sea be terrible, untamed,
Unconquerable still : let none escape   180
Who shall but aim to touch your glory there.
Is there the man into the lion's den
Who dares intrude, to snatch his young away ?
And is a Briton seized ? and seized beneath
The slumbering terrors of a British fleet ?
Then ardent rise ! Oh, great in vengeance, rise !
O'erturn the proud, teach rapine to restore :
And, as you ride sublimely round the world,
Make every vessel stoop, make every state
At once their welfare and their duty know.   190
This is your glory, this your wisdom ; this

The native power for which you were designed
By fate, when fate designed the firmest state
That e'er was seated on the subject sea ;
A state, alone, where Liberty should live,
In these late times, this evening of mankind,
When Athens, Rome, and Carthage are no more,
The world almost in slavish sloth dissolved.
For this, these rocks around your coast were thrown ;
For this, your oaks, peculiar hardened, shoot   200
Strong into sturdy growth : for this, your hearts
Swell with a sullen courage, growing still
As danger grows ; and strength, and toil for this
Are liberal poured o'er all the fervent land.
Then cherish this, this unexpensive power,
Undangerous to the public, ever prompt,
By lavish nature thrust into your hand :
And, unencumbered with the bulk immense
Of conquest, whence huge empires rose, and fell
Self-crushed, extend your reign from shore to shore,
Where'er the wind your high behests can blow; 211
And fix it deep on this eternal base.
For, should the sliding fabric once give way,
Soon slackened quite, and past recovery broke,
It gathers ruin as it rolls along,
Steep rushing down to that devouring gulf
Where many a mighty empire buried lies.
And should the big redundant flood of trade,
In which ten thousand thousand labours join
Their several currents, till the boundless tide   220
Rolls in a radiant deluge o'er the land ;
Should this bright stream, the least inflected, point
Its course another way, o'er other lands
The various treasure would resistless pour,
Ne'er to be won again ; its ancient tract
Left a vile channel, desolate, and dead,

With all around a miserable waste.
Not Egypt, were her better heaven, the Nile,
Turned in the pride of flow ; when o'er his rocks,
And roaring cataracts, beyond the reach   230
Of dizzy vision piled, in one wide flash
An Ethiopian deluge foams amain
(Whence wondering fable traced him from the sky) ;
Even not that prime of earth, where harvests
       crowd
On untilled harvests, all the teeming year,
If of the fat o'erflowing culture robbed,
Were then a more uncomfortable wild,
Sterile, and void ; than of her trade deprived,
Britons, your boasted-isle : her princes sunk ;
Her high built honour mouldered to the dust ;   240
Unnerved her force ; her spirit vanished quite ;
With rapid wing her riches fled away ;
Her unfrequented ports alone the sign
Of what she was ; her merchants scattered wide ;
Her hollow shops shut up ; and in her streets,
Her fields, woods, markets, villages, and roads
The cheerful voice of labour heard no more.
   ' Oh, let not then waste luxury impair
That manly soul of toil which strings your nerves,
And your own proper happiness creates !   250
Oh, let not the soft penetrating plague
Creep on the freeborn mind ! and working there,
With the sharp tooth of many a new-formed want,
Endless, and idle all, eat out the heart
Of liberty ; the high conception blast ;
The noble sentiment, the impatient scorn
Of base subjection, and the swelling wish
For general good, erasing from the mind :
While nought save narrow selfishness succeeds,
And low design, the sneaking passions all   260

Let loose, and reigning in the rankled breast.
Induced at last, by scarce perceived degrees,
Sapping the very frame of government
And life, a total dissolution comes ;
Sloth, ignorance, dejection, flattery, fear,
Oppression raging o'er the waste he makes ;
The human being almost quite extinct ;
And the whole state in broad corruption sinks.
Oh, shun that gulf : that gaping ruin shun !
And countless ages roll it far away   270
From you, ye heaven-beloved ! May liberty,
The light of life ! the sun of humankind !
Whence heroes, bards, and patriots borrow flame,
Even where the keen depressive north descends,
Still spread, exalt, and actuate your powers !
While slavish southern climates beam in vain.
And may a public spirit from the throne,
Where every virtue sits, go copious forth,
Live o'er the land ! the finer arts inspire ;
Make thoughtful Science raise his pensive head, 280
Blow the fresh bay, bid Industry rejoice,
And the rough sons of lowest labour smile:
As when, profuse of Spring, the loosened west
Lifts up the pining year, and balmy breathes
Youth, life, and love, and beauty o'er the world.
  ' But haste we from these melancholy shores,
Nor to deaf winds, and waves, our fruitless plaint
Pour weak ; the country claims our active aid ;
That let us roam ; and where we find a spark
Of public virtue, blow it into flame.   290
Lo ! now, my sons, the sons of freedom ! meet
In awful senate ; thither let us fly ;
Burn in the patriot's thought, flow from his tongue
In fearless truth ; myself transformed preside,
And shed the spirit of Britannia round.'

This said, her fleeting form and airy train
Sunk in the gale ; and nought but ragged rocks
Rushed on the broken eye, and nought was heard
But the rough cadence of the dashing wave.

[The text of *Britannia* given above is that of the last ed. (1744)
published in Thomson's lifetime—*Works*, 8vo, vol. i, p. 309.]

A PARAPHRASE

OF THE LATTER PART OF THE SIXTH CHAPTER OF ST. MATTHEW

[Contributed in 1729 to Ralph's *Miscellany*.]

WHEN my breast labours with oppressive care,
And o'er my cheek descends the falling tear ;
While all my warring passions are at strife,
Oh, let me listen to the words of Life !
Raptures deep-felt his doctrine did impart,
And thus he raised from earth the drooping heart :—

' Think not, when all your scanty stores afford
Is spread at once upon the sparing board—
Think not, when worn the homely robe appears,
While on the roof the howling tempest bears—   10
What farther shall this feeble life sustain,
And what shall clothe these shivering limbs again.
Say, does not life its nourishment exceed ?
And the fair body its investing weed ?
Behold ! and look away your low despair—
See the light tenants of the barren air :
To them nor stores nor granaries belong,
Nought but the woodland and the pleasing song ;
Yet your kind heavenly Father bends his eye
On the least wing that flits along the sky.   20

To him they sing when Spring renews the plain,
To him they cry in Winter's pinching reign ;
Nor is their music, nor their plaint in vain
He hears the gay and the distressful call,
And with unsparing bounty fills them all.
  Observe the rising lily's snowy grace ;
Observe the various vegetable race ;
They neither toil nor spin, but careless grow ;
Yet see how warm they blush ! how bright they
    glow !
What regal vestments can with them compare ? 30
What king so shining, and what queen so fair ?
  If ceaseless thus the fowls of heaven he feeds,
If o'er the fields such lucid robes he spreads ;
Will he not care for you, ye faithless, say ?
Is he unwise ? or are ye less than they ? '

ON THE REPORT OF A WOODEN BRIDGE

TO BE BUILT AT WESTMINSTER

[Attributed to Thomson.]

By Rufus' hall, where Thames polluted flows,
Provoked, the Genius of the river rose,
And thus exclaimed : ' Have I, ye British swains,
Have I for ages laved your fertile plains ?
Given herds, and flocks, and villages increase,
And fed a richer than the golden fleece ?
Have I, ye merchants, with each swelling tide,
Poured Afric's treasure in, and India's pride ?
Lent you the fruit of every nation's toil ?
Made every climate yours, and every soil ?   10

Yet, pilfered from the poor, by gaming base,
Yet must a wooden bridge my waves disgrace ?
Tell not to foreign streams the shameful tale,
And be it published in no Gallic vale.'
He said ; and, plunging to his crystal dome,
White o'er his head the circling waters foam.

[These lines appeared in *The Gentleman's Magazine,* 1737.]

JUVENILIA

THE WORKS AND WONDERS OF ALMIGHTY POWER

A FRAGMENT

Now I surveyed my native faculties,
And traced my actions to their teeming source.
Now I explored the universal frame;
Gazed nature through, and with interior light
Conversed with angels and unbodied saints,
That tread the courts of the Eternal King!
Gladly would I declare, in lofty strains,
The power of Godhead to the sons of men.
But thought is lost in its immensity;
Imagination wastes its strength in vain; 10
And fancy tires, and turns within itself,
Struck with the amazing depths of Deity!
 Ah! my loved God! in vain a tender youth
Unskilled in arts of deep philosophy,
Attempts to search the bulky mass of matter;
To trace the rules of motion; and pursue
The phantom Time, too subtile for his grasp!
Yet may I, from thy most apparent works,
Form some idea of their wondrous Author,
And celebrate thy praise with rapturous mind! 20
 How can I gaze upon yon sparkling vault,
And view the planets rolling in their spheres,
Yet be an atheist? Can I see those stars,
And think of others far beyond my ken,

Yet want conviction of creating power ?
What but a Being of immense perfection
Could, through unbounded spaces, thus dispose
Such numerous bodies, all presumptive worlds ?
The undesigning hand of giddy chance
Could never fill, with globes so vast, so bright,   30
That lofty concave !
Where shall I trace the sources of the light ?
What seats assign the element of fire,
That, unconfined, through all the systems breaks ?
Here could I lie, in holy contemplation rapt,
And pass with pleasure an eternal age !
But 'tis too much for my weak mind to know.
Teach me with humble reverence to adore
The mysteries I must not comprehend !

A PARAPHRASE OF PSALM CIV

To praise thy Author, Soul, do not forget ;
Canst thou, in gratitude, deny the debt ?
Lord, thou art great, how great we cannot know ;
Honour and majesty do round thee flow.
The purest rays of primogenial light
Compose thy robes, and make them dazzling bright ;
The heavens and all the wide-spread orbs on high
Thou like a curtain stretched of curious dye ;
On the devouring flood thy chambers are
Establishèd ; a lofty cloud's thy car,   10
Which quick through the ethereal road doth fly
On swift-winged winds that shake the troubled sky.
Of spiritual substance angels thou didst frame,
Active and bright, piercing and quick as flame.
Thou hast firmly founded this unwieldy earth ;
Stand fast for aye, thou saidst, at nature's birth.

The swelling flood thou o'er the earth mad'st creep,
And coveredst it with the vast hoary deep :
Then hills and vales did no distinction know,
But levelled nature lay oppressed below.   20
With speed they, at thy awful thunder's roar,
Shrinkèd within the limits of their shore.
Through secret tracts they up the mountains creep,
And rocky caverns fruitful moisture weep,
Which sweetly through the verdant vales doth
    glide,
Till 'tis devourèd by the greedy tide.
The feeble sands thou hast made the ocean's mounds ;
Its foaming waves shall ne'er repass these bounds,
Again to triumph over the dry grounds.
Between the hills, grazed by the bleating kind,   30
Soft warbling rills their mazy way do find—
By him appointed fully to supply,
When the hot dogstar fires the realms on high,
The raging thirst of every sickening beast,
Of the wild ass that roams the dreary waste.
The feathered nation, by their smiling sides,
In lowly brambles or in trees abides ;
By nature taught, on them they rear their nests,
That with inimitable art are dressed.
They for the shade and safety of the wood   40
With natural music cheer the neighbourhood.
He doth the clouds with genial moisture fill,
Which on the [shr]ivelled ground they bounteously
    distil,
And nature's lap with various blessings crowd :
The giver, God ! all creatures cry aloud.
With freshest green he clothes the fragrant mead,
Whereon the grazing herds wanton and feed.
With vital juice he makes the plants abound,
And herbs securely spring above the ground,

That man may be sustained beneath the toil   50
Of manuring the ill-producing soil,—
Which with a plenteous harvest does at last
Cancel the memory of labours past,
Yields him the product of the generous vine,
And balmy oil that makes his face to shine,
Fills all his granaries with a loaden crop,
Against the barren winter his great prop.
The trees of God with kindly sap do swell,
Even cedars tall in Lebanon that dwell,
Upon whose lofty tops the birds erect   60
Their nests, as careful nature does direct.
The long necked storks unto the fir-trees fly,
And with their crackling cries disturb the sky.
To unfrequented hills wild goats resort,
And on bleak rocks the nimble conies sport.
The changing moon he clad with silver light,
To check the black dominion of the night :
High through the skies in silent state she rides,
And by her rounds the fleeting time divides.
The circling sun doth in due time decline,   70
And unto shades the murmuring world resign.
Dark night thou mak'st succeed the cheerful day,
Which forest beasts from their lone caves survey :
They rouse themselves, creep out, and search their
      prey.
Young hungry lions from their dens come out,
And, mad on blood, stalk fearfully about ;
They break night's silence with their hideous roar,
And from kind heaven their nightly prey implore.
Just as the lark begins to stretch her wing,   79
And, flickering on her nest, makes short essays to sing,
And the sweet dawn, with a faint glimmering light,
Unveils the face of nature to the sight,
To their dark dens they take their hasty flight.

Not so the husbandman,—for with the sun
He does his pleasant course of labours run :
Home with content in the cool e'en returns,
And his sweet toils until the morn adjourns.
How many are thy wondrous works, O Lord !
They of thy wisdom solid proofs afford :
Out of thy boundless goodness thou didst fill,   90
With riches and delights, both vale and hill :
Even the broad ocean, wherein do abide
Monsters that flounce upon the boiling tide,
And swarms of lesser beasts and fish beside.
'Tis there that daring ships before the wind
Do scud amain, and make the port assigned :
'Tis there that Leviathan sports and plays,
And spouts his water in the face of day ;
For food with gaping mouth they wait on thee,
If thou withhold'st, they pine, they faint, they die.
Thou bountifully opest thy liberal hand,   101
And scatterest plenty both on sea and land.
Thy vital Spirit makes all things live below,
The face of nature with new beauties glow.
God's awful glory ne'er will have an end,
To vast eternity it will extend.
When he surveys his works, at the wide sight
He doth rejoice, and take divine delight.
His looks the earth into its centre shakes ;
A touch of his to smoke the mountains makes.   110
I'll to God's honour consecrate my lays,
And when I cease to be I'll cease to praise.
Upon the Lord, a sublime lofty theme,
My meditations sweet, my joys supreme.
Let daring sinners feel thy vengeful rod,
May they no more be known by their abode.
My soul and all my powers, O bless the Lord,
And the whole race of men with one accord.

A COMPLAINT ON THE MISERIES OF LIFE

I LOATHE, O Lord, this life below,
    And all its fading fleeting joys ;
'Tis a short space that's filled with woe,
    Which all our bliss by far outweighs.
When will the everlasting morn
With dawning light the skies adorn ?

Fitly this life's compared to night,
    When gloomy darkness shades the sky ;
Just like the morn's our glimmering light
    Reflected from the Deity.   10
When will celestial morn dispel
These dark surrounding shades of hell ?

I'm sick of this vexatious state,
    Where cares invade my peaceful hours ;
Strike the last blow, O courteous fate,
    I'll smiling fall like mowèd flowers ;
I'll gladly spurn this clogging clay,
And, sweetly singing, soar away.

What's money but refinèd dust ?
    What's honour but an empty name ?   20
And what is soft enticing lust
    But a consuming idle flame ?
Yea, what is all beneath the sky
But emptiness and vanity ?

With thousand ills our life's oppressed ;
    There's nothing here worth living for !
In the lone grave I long to rest,
    And be harassèd here no more :
Where joy's fantastic, grief's sincere,
And where there's nought for which I care.   30

Thy word, O Lord, shall be my guide;
  Heaven, where thou dwellest is my goal;
Through corrupt life grant I may glide
  With an untainted upward soul.
Then may this life, this dreary night
Dispellèd be by morning light.

HYMN ON THE POWER OF GOD

HAIL! Power Divine, whose sole command
  From the dark empty space
Made the broad sea and solid land
  Smile with a heavenly grace;

Made the high mountain and firm rock,
  Where bleating cattle stray;
And the strong, stately, spreading oak,
  That intercepts the day.

The rolling planets thou mad'st move,
  By thy effective will;   10
And the revolving globes above
  Their destined course fulfil.

His mighty power, ye thunders, praise,
  As through the heavens you roll;
And his great name, ye lightnings, blaze
  Unto the distant pole.

Ye seas, in your eternal roar
  His sacred praise proclaim;
While the inactive sluggish shore
  Re-echoes to the same.   20

R

Ye howling winds, howl out his praise,
　　And make the forests bow ;
While through the air, the earth, and seas
　　His solemn praise ye blow.

O you, ye high harmonious spheres,
　　Your powerful mover sing ;
To him, your circling course that steers,
　　Your tuneful praises bring.

Ungrateful mortals, catch the sound,
　　And in your numerous lays　　　　　　30
To all the listening world around
　　The God of nature praise.

A PASTORAL BETWIXT DAVID, THIRSIS, AND THE ANGEL GABRIEL,
UPON THE BIRTH OF OUR SAVIOUR

DAVID

WHAT means yon apparition in the sky,
Thirsis, that dazzles every shepherd's eye ?
I slumbering was when from yon glorious cloud
Came gliding music heavenly, sweet, and loud,
With sacred raptures which my bosom fires,
And with celestial joy my soul inspires ;
It soothes the native horrors of the night,
And gladdens nature more than dawning light.

THIRSIS

But hold ! see hither through the yielding air
An angel comes : for mighty news prepare.　　　10

ANGEL GABRIEL

Rejoice, ye swains, anticipate the morn
With songs of praise ; for lo ! a Saviour's born.

With joyful haste to Bethlehem repair,
And you will find the almighty Infant there ;
Wrapped in a swaddling band you'll find your King,
And in a manger laid : to him your praises bring.

CHORUS OF ANGELS
To God who in the highest dwells
Immortal glory be ;
Let peace be in the humble cells
Of Adam's progeny. 20

DAVID
No more the year shall wintry horrors bring ;
Fixed in the indulgence of eternal spring,
Immortal green shall clothe the hills and vales,
And odorous sweets shall load the balmy gales ;
The silver brooks shall in soft murmurs tell
The joy that shall their oozy channels swell.
Feed on, my flocks, and crop the tender grass;
Let blooming joy appear on every face,
For lo ! this blessed, this propitious morn,
The Saviour of lost mankind is born. 30

THIRSIS
Thou fairest morn that ever sprang from night,
Or decked the opening skies with rosy light,
Well mayst thou shine with a distinguished ray,
Since here Emmanuel condescends to stay,
Our fears, our guilt, our darkness to dispel,
And save us from the horrid jaws of hell;
Who from his throne descended, matchless love !
To guide poor mortals to blest seats above.
But come ! without delay let us be gone;
Shepherd, let's go, and humbly kiss the Son. 40

A PASTORAL BETWEEN THIRSIS AND CORYDON

UPON THE DEATH OF DAMON

(By Damon is meant Mr. W. Riddell.)

[Cf. Allan Ramsay's Pastoral, ' Sandy and Richie '.]

Thir. Say, tell me true, what is the doleful cause
That Corydon is not the man he was ?
Your cheerful presence used to lighten cares,
And from the plains to banish gloomy fears.
Whene'er unto the circling swains you sung,
Our ravished souls upon the music hung ;
The gazing, listening flocks forgot their meat,
While vocal grottoes did your lays repeat :
But now your gravity our mirth rebukes,
And in your downcast and desponding looks   10
Appears some fatal and impending woe ;
I fear to ask, and yet desire to know.
    Cor. The doleful news, how shall I, Thirsis, tell !
In blooming youth the hapless Damon fell :
He 's dead, he 's dead ! and with him all my joy ;
The mournful thought does all gay forms destroy :
This is the cause of my unusual grief,
Which sullenly admits of no relief.
    Thir. Begone all mirth ! begone all sports and
        play !
To a deluge of grief and tears give way.   20
Damon the just, the generous, and the young,
Must Damon's worth and merit be unsung ?
No, Corydon ! the wondrous youth you knew,
How, as in years, so he in virtue grew ;
Embalm his fame in never dying verse,
As a just tribute to his doleful hearse.

Cor. Assist me, mighty grief ; my breast inspire
With generous heats and with thy wildest fire,
While in a solemn and a mournful strain
Of Damon gone for ever I complain.   30
Ye muses, weep; your mirth and songs forbear,
And for him sigh and shed a friendly tear ;
He was your favourite, and by your aid
In charming verse his witty thoughts arrayed ;
He had of knowledge, learning, wit a store;
To it denied he still pressed after more.
He was a pious and a virtuous soul,
And still pressed forward to the heavenly goal ;
He was a faithful, true, and constant friend,
Faithful, and true, and constant to the end.   40
Ye flowers, hang down and droop your [heavy] heads,
No more around your grateful odour spreads;
Ye leafy trees, your blooming honours shed,
Damon for ever from your shade is fled ;
Fled to the mansions of eternal light,
Where endless wonders strike his happy sight.
Ye birds, be mute, as through the trees you fly,
Mute as the grave wherein my friend does lie.
Ye winds, breathe sighs as through the air you rove,
And in sad pomp the trembling branches move.   50
Ye gliding brooks, O weep your channels dry,
My flowing tears them fully shall supply ;
You in soft murmurs may your grief express,
And yours, you swains, in mournful songs confess
I to some dark and gloomy shade will fly,
Dark as the grave wherein my friend does lie ;
And for his death to lonely rocks complain
In mournful accents and a dying strain,
While pining echo answers me again.

OF A COUNTRY LIFE

I HATE the clamours of the smoky towns,
But much admire the bliss of rural clowns ;
Where some remains of innocence appear,
Where no rude noise insults the listening ear ;
Nought but soft zephyrs whispering through the trees,
Or the still humming of the painful bees ;
The gentle murmurs of a purling rill,
Or the unwearied chirping of the drill ;
The charming harmony of warbling birds,
Or hollow lowings of the grazing herds ;   10
The murmuring stockdoves' melancholy coo,
When they their lovèd mates lament or woo ;
The pleasing bleatings of the tender lambs,
Or the indistinct mumbling of their dams ;
The musical discord of chiding hounds,
Whereto the echoing hill or rock resounds ;
The rural mournful songs of lovesick swains,
Whereby they soothe their raging amorous pains ;
The whistling music of the lagging plough,   19
Which does the strength of drooping beasts renew.
  And as the country rings with pleasant sounds,
So with delightful prospects it abounds :
Through every season of the sliding year,
Unto the ravished sight new scenes appear.
  In the sweet Spring the sun's prolific ray
Does painted flowers to the mild air display ;
Then opening buds, then tender herbs are seen,
And the bare fields are all arrayed in green.
  In ripening Summer, the full laden vales
Gives prospect of employment for the flails ;   30
Each breath of wind the bearded groves makes bend,
Which seems the fatal sickle to portend.

In Autumn, that repays the labourer's pains,
Reapers sweep down the honours of the plains.
Anon black Winter, from the frozen north,
Its treasuries of snow and hail pours forth ;
Then stormy winds blow through the hazy sky;
In desolation nature seems to lie ;
The unstained snow from the full clouds descends,
Whose sparkling lustre open eyes offends.   40
In maiden white the glittering fields do shine ;
Then bleating flocks for want of food repine,
With withered eyes they see all snow around,
And with their fore feet paw, and scrape the ground :
They cheerfully do crop the insipid grass,
The shepherds sighing, cry, Alas ! alas !
Then pinching want the wildest beast does tame ;
Then huntsmen on the snow do trace their game ;
Keen frost then turns the liquid lakes to glass,
Arrests the dancing rivulets as they pass.   50
How sweet and innocent are country sports,
And, as men's tempers, various are their sorts.
You, on the banks of soft meandering Tweed,
May in your toils ensnare the watery breed,
And nicely lead the artificial flee,
Which, when the nimble, watchful trout does see,
He at the bearded hook will briskly spring ;
Then in that instant twitch your hairy string,
And, when he 's hooked, you, with a constant
          hand,
May draw him struggling to the fatal land.   60
Then at fit seasons you may clothe your hook
With a sweet bait, dressed by a faithless cook
The greedy pike darts to't with eager haste,
And, being struck, in vain he flies at last ;
He rages, storms, and flounces through the stream,
But all, alas ! his life can not redeem.

At other times you may pursue the chase,
And hunt the nimble hare from place to place.
See, when the dog is just upon the grip,
Out at a side she'll make a handsome skip,   70
And ere he can divert his furious course,
She, far before him, scours with all her force :
She'll shift, and many times run the same ground ;
At last, outwearied by the stronger hound,
She falls a sacrifice unto his hate,
And with sad piteous screams laments her fate.
See how the hawk doth take his towering flight,
And in his course outflies our very sight,
Beats down the fluttering fowl with all his might.
See how the wary gunner casts about,   80
Watching the fittest posture when to shoot :
Quick as the fatal lightning blasts the oak,
He gives the springing fowl a sudden stroke ;
He pours upon't a shower of mortal lead,
And ere the noise is heard the fowl is dead.
Sometimes he spreads his hidden subtile snare,
Of which the entangled fowl was not aware ;
Through pathless wastes he doth pursue his sport,
Where nought but moor-fowl and wild beasts
     resort.
When the noon sun directly darts his beams   90
Upon your giddy heads, with fiery gleams,
Then you may bathe yourself in cooling streams ;
Or to the sweet adjoining grove retire,
Where trees with interwoven boughs conspire
To form a grateful shade ;—there rural swains
Do tune their oaten reeds to rural strains ;
The silent birds sit listening on the sprays,
And in soft charming notes do imitate their lays.
There you may stretch yourself upon the grass,
And, lulled with music, to kind slumbers pass : 100

No meagre cares your fancy will distract,
And on that scene no tragic fears will act ;
Save the dear image of a charming she,
Nought will the object of your vision be.
  Away the vicious pleasures of the town !
Let empty partial fortune on me frown ;
But grant, ye powers, that it may be my lot
To live in peace from noisy towns remote.

[In these verses appears for the first time, scarcely recognizable,
the future author of *The Seasons*. They were contributed to *The
Edinburgh Miscellany*, a magazine published by ' the Athenian
Society ', in 1720.]

UPON HAPPINESS

WARNED by the summer sun's meridian ray,
As underneath a spreading oak I lay,
Contemplating the mighty load of woe
In search of bliss that mortals undergo,
Who, while they think they happiness enjoy,
Embrace a curse wrapt in delusive joy,
I reasoned thus—Since the Creator, God,
Who in eternal love has his abode,
Hath blended with the essence of the soul
An appetite, as fixèd as the pole,   10
That's always eager in pursuit of bliss,
And always veering till it point to this,
There is some object adequate to fill
This boundless wish of our extended will.
Now, while my thought round nature's circle runs
(A bolder journey than the furious sun's)
This chief and satiating good to find,
The attracting centre of the human mind,
My ears they deafened, to my swimming eyes
His magic wand the drowsy god applies,   20

  19 they deafened = became deaf.

Bound all my senses in a silken sleep,
While mimic fancy did her vigils keep ;
Yet still methinks some condescending power
Ranged the ideas in my mind that hour.
Methought I wandering was, with thousands more,
Beneath a high prodigious hill before,
Above the clouds whose towering summit rose,
With utmost labour only gained by those
Who grovelling prejudices threw away,
And with incessant straining climbed their way ; 30
Where all who stood, their failing breath to gain,
With headlong ruin tumbled down amain.
This mountain is through every nation famed,
And, as I learnèd, Contemplation named.
O happy me ! when I had reached its top
Unto my sight a boundless scene did ope.
First, sadly I surveyed with downward eye,
Of restless men below, the busy fry,
Who hunted trifles in an endless maze,
Like foolish boys on sunny summer days   40
Pursuing butterflies with all their might,
Who can't their troubles in the chase requite.
The painted insect he who most admires
Grieves most when it in his rude hand expires ;
Or, should it live, with endless fears is tossed
Lest it take wing and be for ever lost.
Some men I saw their utmost art employ
How to attain a false deceitful joy,
Which from afar conspicuously did blaze,
And at a distance fixed their ravished gaze,   50
But nigh at hand it mocked their fond embrace ;
When lo ! again it flashèd in their eyes,
But still, as they drew near, the fond illusion dies.
Just so I've seen a water-dog pursue
An unflown duck within his greedy view :

When he has, panting, at his prey arrived,
The coxcomb fooling—suddenly it dived ;
He, gripping, is almost with water choked,
And grief, that all his towering hopes are mocked.
Then it emerges, he renews his toil,   60
And o'er and o'er again he gets the foil.
Yea, all the joys beneath the conscious sun,
And softer ones that his inspection shun,
Much of their pleasures in fruition fade ;
Enjoyment o'er them throws a sullen shade.
The reason is, we promise vaster things
And sweeter joys than from their nature springs :
When they are lost, weep the apparent bliss,
And not what really in fruition is ;
So that our griefs are greater than our joys,   70
And real pain springs from fantastic toys.
   Though all terrene delights of men below
Are almost nothing but a glaring show ;
Yet, if there always were a virgin joy,
When t'other fades, to soothe the wanton boy,
He somewhat might excuse his heedless course,
Some show of reason for the same enforce :
But frugal nature wisely does deny
To mankind such profuse variety ;
Has only what is needful to us given,   80
To feed and cheer us in the way to Heaven ;
And more would but the traveller delay,
Impede and clog him in his upward way.
   I from the mount all mortal pleasures saw
Themselves within a narrow compass draw ;
The libertine a nauseous circle run,
And dully acted what he'd often done.
Just so when Luna darts her silver ray,
And pours on silent earth a paler day ;
From Stygian caves the flitting fairies scud,   90

And on the margent of some limpid flood,
Which by reflected moonlight darts a glance,
In midnight circles range themselves and dance.
  To-morrow, cries he, will us entertain :
Pray what's to-morrow but to-day again ?
Deluded youth, no more the chase pursue ;
So oft deceived, no more the toil renew.
But in a constant and a fixed design
Of acting well there is a lasting mine
Of solid satisfaction, purest joy,   100
For virtue's pleasures never, never cloy :
Then hither come, climb up the steep ascent,
Your painful labour you will ne'er repent,
From Heaven itself here you're but one remove,
Here's the praeludium of the joys above,
Here you'll behold the awful Godhead shine,
And all perfections in the same combine ;
You'll see that God, who, by his powerful call,
From empty nothing drew this spacious all,
Made beauteous order the rude mass control.   110
And every part subservient to the whole ;
Here you'll behold upon the fatal tree
The God of nature bleed, expire, and die,
For such as 'gainst his holy laws rebel,
And such as bid defiance to his hell.
Through the dark gulf, here you may clearly pry
'Twixt narrow time and vast eternity ;
Behold the Godhead, just as well as good,
And vengeance poured on tramplers on his blood ;
But all the tears wiped from his people's eyes ; 120
And, for their entrance, cleave the parting skies.
Then sure you will with holy ardours burn,
And to seraphic heats your passion turn ;
Then in your eyes all mortal fair will fade,
And leave of mortal beauties but the shade :

Yourself to him you'll solemnly devote,
To him without whose providence you're not;
You'll of his service relish the delight,
And to his praises all your powers excite ;
You'll celebrate his name in heavenly sound,   130
Which well-pleased skies in echoes will rebound :
This is the greatest happiness that can
Possessèd be in this short life by man.
　　But darkly here the Godhead we survey,
Confined and crampèd in this cage of clay.
What cruel band is this to earth that ties
Our souls from soaring to their native skies
Upon the bright eternal face to gaze,
And there drink in the beatific rays—
There to behold the good one and the fair,   140
A ray from whom all mortal beauties are ?
In beauteous nature all the harmony
Is but the echo of the Deity,
Of all perfection who the centre is,
And boundless ocean of untainted bliss ;
For ever open to the ravished view,
And full enjoyment of the radiant crew
Who live in raptures of eternal joy,
Whose flaming love their tuneful harps employ
In solemn hymns Jehovah's praise to sing,   150
And make all heaven with hallelujahs ring.
　　These realms of light no further I'll explore,
And in these heights I will no longer soar :
Not like our grosser atmosphere beneath,
The ether here 's too thin for me to breathe.
The region is unsufferable bright,
And flashes on me with too strong a light.
Then from the mountain, lo ! I now descend
And to my vision put a hasty end.

　　　[Contributed to *The Edinburgh Miscellany*, 1720.]

VERSES ON RECEIVING A FLOWER
FROM A LADY

MADAM, the flower that I received from you,
Ere I came home, had lost its lovely hue :
As flowers deprivèd of the genial day,
Its sprightly bloom did wither and decay :
Dear, fading flower, I know full well, said I,
The reason that you shed your sweets and die ;
You want the influence of her enlivening eye.
Your case is mine : absence, that plague of love !
With heavy pace makes every minute move :
It of my being is an empty blank,   10
And hinders me myself with men to rank ;
Your cheering presence quickens me again,
And new-sprung life exults in every vein.

[First appeared in 1720 in *The Edinburgh Miscellany*, signed ' *T.*']

ON BEAUTY

BEAUTY deserves the homage of the muse :
Shall mine, rebellious, the dear theme refuse ?
No ; while my breast respires the vital air,
Wholly I am devoted to the fair.
Beauty I'll sing in my sublimest lays,
I burn to give her just, immortal praise.
The heavenly maid with transport I'll pursue
To her abode, and all her graces view.
    This happy place with all delights abounds,
And plenty broods upon the fertile grounds.   10
Here verdant grass their waving . . .
And hills and vales in sweet confusion lie ;

The nibbling flock stray o'er the rising hills,
And all around with bleating music fills ;
High on their fronts tall blooming forests nod,
Of sylvan deities the blest abode ;
The feathered minstrels hop from spray to spray,
And chant their gladsome carols all the day,
Till dusky night, advancing in her car,
Makes with declining light successful war. 20
Then Philomel her mournful lay repeats,
And through her throat breathes melancholy sweets.
Still higher yet wild rugged rocks arise,
That all ascent to human foot denies,
And strike beholders with a dread surprise.
This paradise these towering hills surround,
That thither is one only passage found.
Increasing brooks roll down the mountain's side,
And as they pass the opposing pebbles chide.
.   .   .   .

But vernal showers refresh the blooming year. 30
Their only season is eternal spring,
Which hovers o'er them with a downy wing ;
Blossoms and fruits at once the trees adorn
With glowing blushes, like the rosy morn.
    The way that to this stately palace goes
Of myrtle trees lies 'twixt two even rows,
Which, towering high, with outstretched arms dis-
        played,
Over our heads a living arch have made.
    To sing, my muse, the bold attempt begin,
Of awful beauties you behold within : 40
The Goddess sat upon a throne of gold,
Embossed with figures charming to behold ;
Here new-made Eve stood in her early bloom,
Not yet obscurèd with sin's sullen gloom ;
Her naked beauties do the soul confound,

From every part is given a fatal wound ;
There other beauties of a meaner fame
Oblige the sight, whom here I shall not name.
In her right hand she did a sceptre sway
O'er all mankind, ambitious to obey :   50
Her lovely forehead and her killing eye,
Her blushing cheeks of a vermilion dye,
Her lip's soft pulp, her heaving snowy breast,
Her well-turned arm, her handsome slender waist,
And all below veiled from the curious eye—
Oh ! heavenly maid ! makes all beholders cry.
  Her dress was plain, not pompous as a bride,
Which would her sweeter native beauties hide.
One thing I mind, a spreading hoop she wore,
Than which no thing adorns a lady more.   60
With equal rage could I its beauties sing,
I'd with the hoop make all Parnassus ring.
Around her shoulders, dangling on her throne,
A bright Tartana carelessly was thrown,
Which has already won immortal praise,
Most sweetly sung in Allan Ramsay's lays ;
The wanton Cupids did around her play,
And smiling loves upon her bosom stray ;
With purple wings they round about her flew,
And her sweet lips tinged with ambrosial dew.   70
  Her air was easy, graceful was her mien,
Her presence banished the ungrateful spleen ;
In short, her divine influence refined
Our corrupt hearts, and polishèd mankind.
  Of lovely nymphs she had a smiling train,
Fairer than those e'er graced Arcadia's plain.
The British ladies next to her took place,
Who chiefly did the fair assembly grace.
What blooming virgins can Britannia boast,
Their praises would all eloquence exhaust.   80

With ladies there my ravished eyes did meet
That oft I've seen grace fair Edina's street,
With their broad hoops cut through the willing air,
Pleased to give place unto the lovely fair :
　Sure this is like those blissful seats above ;
[For] here is peace, transporting joy, and love.
　Should I be doomed by cruel angry fate
In some lone isle my lingering end to wait,
Yet happy I ! still happy should I be !
While blest with virtue and a charming she ;　　90
With full content I'd fortune's pride despise,
And die still gazing on her lovely eyes.
　May all the blessings mortals need below,
May all the blessings heaven can bestow,
May every thing that's pleasant, good, or rare,
Be the eternal portion of the fair.

A PASTORAL ENTERTAINMENT

WHILE in heroic numbers some relate
The amazing turns of wise eternal fate,
Exploits of heroes in the dusty field,
That to their name immortal honour yield ;
Grant me, ye powers, fast by the limpid spring
The harmless revels of the plain to sing.
At a rich feast, kept each revolving year,
Their fleecy care when joyful shepherds shear,
A wreath of flowers culled from the neighbouring
　　lands
Is all the prize my humble muse demands.　　10
　Now blithesome shepherds, by the early dawn,
Their new-shorn flocks drive to the dewy lawn ;
While, in a bleating language, each salutes
The welcome morning and their fellow brutes :

Then all preparèd for the rural feast,
And in their finest Sunday habits drest ;
The crystal brook supplied the mirror's place,
[Wherein] they bathed and viewed their cleanly face,
[Then swains] and nymphs resorted to the fields
[Adorned with all the] pomp the country yields. 20
　　The place appointed was a spacious vale,
Fanned always by a cooling western gale,
Which in soft breezes through the meadows stray,
And steals the ripened fragrances away ;
With native incense all the air perfumes,
Renewing with its genial breath the blooms.
Here every shepherd might his flocks survey,
Securely roam and take his harmless play ;
And here were flowers each shepherdess to grace,
On her fair bosom courting but a place.　　　　30
　　Now in this vale, beneath a grateful shade,
By twining boughs of spreading beeches made,
On seats of homely turf themselves they placed,
And cheerfully enjoyed their rural feast,
Consisting of the product of the fields,
And all the luxury the country yields.
　·　　·　　·　　·　　·　　·　　·　　·　　·

No maddening liquors spoiled their harmless mirth ;
But an untainted spring their thirst allayed,
Which in meanders through the valley strayed.
Thrice happy swains ! who spend your golden days 40
In country pastime, and, when night displays
Her sable shade, to peaceful huts retire ;
Can any man a sweeter bliss desire ?
In ancient times so passed the smiling hour,
When our first parents lived in Eden's bower,
Ere care and trouble were pronounced ou[r doom,]
Or sin had blasted the creation's blo[om].

AN ELEGY UPON JAMES THERBURN

IN CHATTO

[Cp. Allan Ramsay's *Elegy on Maggie Johnston* or on *Lucky Wood.*]

Now, Chatto, you're a dreary place—
Pale sorrow broods on ilka face
Therburn has run his . . race,
     *   *   *   *
And now, and now, ah me, alace !
         The carle lies dead.

Having his paternoster said,
He took a dram and went to bed ;
He fell asleep, and death was glad
         That he did catch him ;   10
For Therburn was e'en ill-bested,
         That none did watch him.

For had the carle but been aware,
That meagre death, who none does spare,
T'attempt sic things should ever dare,
         As stop his pipe ;
He might have come to flee or skare
         The greedy gipe.

Now had he but a gill or twae
Death wou'd nae got the victory sae,   20
Nor put poor Therburn o'er the brae,
         Into the grave ;
   .   .   .   .
       .   .   .   .

The fumbling fellow, some folks say,
Should be jobbed on baith night and day ;

She had without'en better play
        Remained still
Barren for ever and for aye,
        Do what he will.   30

Therefore they say he got some help
In getting of the little whelp ;
But passing that, it makes me yelp,
        But what remead ?
Death lent him sic a cursed skelp,
        That now he's dead.

Therburn, for evermore farewell,
And be thy grave baith dry and deep ;
And rest thy carcass soft and well,
        Free from   .   .   40
    .   .   .   . no night .
        Disturb   .   .

[It is scarcely possible that this is Thomson's.]

ON THE HOOP

THE hoop, the darling justly of the fair,
Of every generous swain deserves the care.
It is unmanly to desert the weak,
'Twould urge a stone, if possible to speak ;
To hear stanch hypocrites bawl out, and cry,
' This hoop's a whorish garb, fie ! ladies, fie ! '
O cruel and audacious men, to blast
The fame of ladies, more than vestals chaste ;
Should you go search the globe throughout,
You will find none so pious and devout ;   10
So modest, chaste, so handsome, and so fair,
As our dear Caledonian ladies are.

When awful beauty puts on all her charms,
Nought gives our sex such terrible alarms,
As when the hoop and tartan both combine
To make a virgin like a goddess shine.
Let quakers cut their clothes unto the quick,
And with severities themselves afflict;
But may the hoop adorn Edina's street,
Till the south pole shall with the northern meet! 20

AN ELEGY ON PARTING

It was a sad, ay, 'twas a sad farewell,
I still afresh the pangs of parting feel.
Against my breast my heart impatient beat,
And in deep sighs bemoaned its cruel fate
Thus with the object of my love to part,
My life! my joy! 'twould rend a rocky heart.
    Where'er I turn myself, where'er I go,
I meet the image of my lovely foe;
With witching charms the phantom still appears,
And with her wanton smiles insults my tears;   10
Still haunts the places where we used to walk,
And where with raptures oft I heard her talk:
Those scenes I now with deepest sorrow view,
And sighing bid to all delight adieu.
    While I my head upon this turf recline,
Officious sun, in vain on me you shine;
In vain unto the smiling fields I hie;
In vain the flowery meads salute my eye;
In vain the cheerful birds and shepherds sing,
And with their carols make the valleys ring;   20
Yea, all the pleasure that the country yield
Can't me from sorrow for her absence shield:

With divine pleasure books which one inspire,
Yea, books themselves I do not now admire.
But hark ! methinks some pitying power I hear,
This welcome message whisper in my ear :
' Forget thy groundless griefs, dejected swain—
You and the nymph you love shall meet again ;
No more your muse shall sing such mournful lays,
But bounteous heaven and your kind mistress praise.'

THE MONTH OF MAY

AMONG the changing months May stands confest
The sweetest, and in fairest colours drest ;
Soft as the breeze that fans the smiling field,
Sweet as the breath that opening roses yield,
Fair as the colour lavish nature paints
On virgin flowers free from unodorous taints.
To rural scenes thou tempt'st the busy crowd,
Who in each grove thy praises sing aloud.
The blooming belles and shallow beaux, strange sight !
Turn nymphs and swains, and in their sports delight.

MORNING IN THE COUNTRY

WHEN from the opening chambers of the east
The morning springs, in thousand liveries drest,
The early larks their morning tribute pay,
And in shrill notes salute the blooming day.
Refreshèd fields with pearly dew do shine,
And tender blades therewith their tops incline.
Their painted leaves the unblown flowers expand,
And with their odorous breath perfume the land.
The crowing cock and clattering hen awakes
Dull sleepy clowns, who know the morning breaks.

The herd his plaid around his shoulders throws,   11
Grasps his dear crook, calls on his dog, and goes;
Around the fold he walks with careful pace,
And fallen clods sets in their wonted place ;
Then opes the door, unfolds his fleecy care,
And gladly sees them crop their morning fare !
Down upon easy moss his limbs he lays,
And sings some charming shepherdess's praise.

LISY'S PARTING WITH HER CAT

THE dreadful hour with leaden pace approached,
Lashed fiercely on by unrelenting fate,
When Lisy and her bosom Cat must part :
For now, to school and pensive needle doomed,
She's banished from her childhood's undashed joy,
And all the pleasing intercourse she kept
With her gray comrade, which has often soothed
Her tender moments, while the world around
Glowed with ambition, business, and vice,
Or lay dissolved in sleep's delicious arms ;   10
And from their dewy orbs the conscious stars
Shed on their friendship influence benign.
    But see where mournful Puss, advancing, stood
With outstretched tail, casts looks of anxious woe
On melting Lisy, in whose eye the tear
Stood tremulous, and thus would fain have said,
If nature had not tied her struggling tongue :
' Unkind, O ! who shall now with fattening milk,
With flesh, with bread, and fish beloved, and meat,
Regale my taste ? and at the cheerful fire,   20
Ah, who shall bask me in their downy lap ?
Who shall invite me to the bed, and throw
The bedclothes o'er me in the winter night,

When Eurus roars ?　Beneath whose soothing hand
Soft shall I purr ?　But now, when Lisy 's gone,
What is the dull officious world to me ?
I loathe the thoughts of life : '　Thus plained the
　　Cat,
While Lisy felt, by sympathetic touch,
These anxious thoughts that in her mind revolved,
And casting on her a desponding look,　　　　　30
She snatched her in her arms with eager grief,
And mewing, thus began :—' O Cat beloved !
Thou dear companion of my tender years !
Joy of my youth ! that oft hast licked my hands
With velvet tongue ne'er stained by mouse's blood.
Oh, gentle Cat ! how shall I part with thee ?
How dead and heavy will the moments pass
When you are not in my delighted eye,
With Cubi playing, or your flying tail.
How harshly will the softest muslin feel,　　　40
And all the silk of schools, while I no more
Have your sleek skin to soothe my softened sense ?
How shall I eat while you are not beside
To share the bit ?　How shall I ever sleep
While I no more your lulling murmurs hear ?
Yet we must part—so rigid fate decrees—
But never shall your loved idea dear
Part from my soul, and when I first can mark
The embroidered figure on the snowy lawn,
Your image shall my needle keen employ.　　　50
Hark ! now I'm called away !　O direful sound !
I come—I come, but first I charge you all—
You—you—and you, particularly you,
O, Mary, Mary, feed her with the best,
Repose her nightly in the warmest couch,
And be a Lisy to her ! '—Having said,
She set her down, and with her head across,

Rushed to the evil which she could not shun,
While a sad mew went knelling to her heart !

[A copy of these boyish verses was written out by Thomson for
Lord George Graham. Lisy was the poet's favourite sister
Elizabeth.]

LINES ON MARLEFIELD

(The seat of Sir William Bennet, of Grubbat, Bart.)

WHAT is the task that to the muse belongs ?
What but to deck in her harmonious songs
The beauteous works of nature and of art,
Rural retreats that cheer the heavy heart ?
Then Marlefield begin, my muse, and sing ;
With Marlefield the hills and vales shall ring.
O ! what delight and pleasure 'tis to rove
Through all the walks and alleys of this grove,
Where spreading trees a checkered scene display,
Partly admitting and excluding day ;   10
Where cheerful green and odorous sweets conspire
The drooping soul with pleasure to inspire ;
Where little birds employ their narrow throats
To sing its praises in unlaboured notes.
To it adjoined a rising fabric stands,
Which with its state our silent awe commands.
Its endless beauties mock the poet's pen ;
So to the garden I'll return again.
Pomona makes the trees with fruit abound.
And blushing Flora paints the enamelled ground. 20
Here lavish nature does her stores disclose,
Flowers of all hue, their queen the bashful rose;
With their sweet breath the ambient air's perfumed,
Nor is thereby their fragrant stores consumed:
O'er the fair landscape sportive zephyrs scud,
And by kind force display the infant bud.

The vegetable kind here rear their head,
By kindly showers and heaven's indulgence fed :
Of fabled nymphs such were the sacred haunts,
But real nymphs this charming dwelling vaunts. 30
Now to the greenhouse let's awhile retire,
To shun the heat of Sol's infectious fire :
Immortal authors grace this cool retreat,
Of ancient times and of a modern date.
Here would my praises and my fancy dwell ;
But it, alas, description does excel.
O may this sweet, this beautiful abode
Remain the charge of the eternal God.

A POETICAL EPISTLE TO SIR WILLIAM BENNET

[Written in 1714, *aet.* 14.]

MY trembling muse your honour does address.
That it's a bold attempt most humbly I confess.
If you'll encourage her young fagging flight,
She'll upwards soar and mount Parnassus' height.
If little things with great may be compared,
In Rome it so with the divine Virgil fared ;
The tuneful bard Augustus did inspire
Made his great genius flash poetic fire ;
But, if upon my flight your honour frowns,
The muse folds up her wings, and, dying, justice owns.

INDEX OF FIRST LINES

PRINTED IN GREAT BRITAIN
AT THE UNIVERSITY PRESS, OXFORD
BY VIVIAN RIDLER
PRINTER TO THE UNIVERSITY